# "TURNING THE WORLD UPSIDE DOWN" APPROPRIATING CULTURE: HOW TO LISTEN TO AMERICAN MUSIC, 1900-1960

## VOLUME 2

By Allen Lowe

Copyright 2020/2021
All Rights Reserved

ISBN: 978-0-9899950-6-1

Constant Sorrow Press

# TABLE OF CONTENTS

Chapter 16 A Little Dreck  4
Chapter 17 The Soul Of White Folks  25
Chapter 18 The Minstrel wound  45
Chapter 19 Religious Connotation  68
Chapter 20 Hillbillies with 401k's: That Low Class Twang  93
Chapter 21 Old Music of the Future: Separate and White, The Hard Country  121
Chapter 22 A Trap Set for Squares: Gospel in Drag  149
Chapter 23 Where Folk Dreams Live and Die: Surviving in Their Heads  176
Chapter 24 Black Bleeds Through  204
Chapter 25 A White Spy In the house of love: An Overdose of Reality  231
Chapter 26 Born Again Blues  256
Chapter 27 Church in the Back Seat: If I could Sing Better I Would  285
Chapter 28 Dark Nights of the White Soul  311
Chapter 29 The Song is Him  336
Chapter 30 This is the End (of Part 2)  364
Index  389

# Intro to Part II

It's January 25 2021 and I am just two weeks out of the hospital; it feels like my head's been slammed a few times against a wall. Without knowing the full prognosis I will note that I have had a bit more of the throat cancer that hit me in the Fall of 2019, but which this time required a ten-hour surgery. So be it; it is a fitting end to an insane year of American politics and personal cultural conflict; about two weeks before the surgery, an academic "friend" on Facebook charged me with having a Nazi-like attitude because I referred to black blood in the same sense that W.E.B. Du Bois did; I was under the influence of the following passage from D Bois, in the August 1897 Atlantic: "The history of the American Negro is the history of this strife, — this longing to attain self-conscious manhood, to merge his double self into a better and truer self. In this merging he wishes neither of the older selves to be lost. He does not wish to Africanize America, for America has too much to teach the world and Africa; he does not wish to bleach his Negro blood in a flood of white Americanism, for he believes—foolishly, perhaps, but fervently—that Negro blood has yet a message for the world. He simply wishes to make it possible for a man to be both a Negro and an American without being cursed and spit upon by his fellows, without losing the opportunity of self-development."

Blood is…what, metaphorical here? Well, if I'm a Nazi so is Du Bois. But of course the charge was stupider than stupid, an incoherent attempt by an academic who was just being jealous and asinine. The passage of mine that he was referring is buried in this book. If you find it offensive, let me know. If you find it. But let it be noted that I, a 20th century Jew, have never before been charged with Nazi tendencies. So we have broken some even newer ground in 2020.

Once again, this is dedicated to my wife Helen, to whom all love flows -

-Allen Lowe

# Chapter 16 A Little Dreck

Into each life a little dreck must fall. This is particularly true with popular music. The problem sometimes is in trying to separate the dreck from the stuff that works, that is edifying, even as a form of musical slumming. Is it something that satisfies certain and not always easily identifiable cultural urges in us? Is it the equivalent of B movies which match the escapist needs of the viewer with material that is the occasional stuff of odd and imprecisely remembered dreams? Is there is still some kind of guiding intelligence to it, but one which doesn't necessary translate into intellectual satisfaction (and which raises other questions relative to popular culture)? [1]

I ask all of this as I listen to **Reaching for the Moon**, recorded under the leadership of **Roy Smeck** in **1931**. I have mentioned Smeck before; he was a virtuoso of the Lower Depths, we might say, a performer whose virtuosity was in the service of some supposedly lesser musical forms. Dubbed The Wizard of the Strings (there is a documentary about him of the same title), he was equally adept on guitar, banjo, and ukulele. What I find most appealing about his work is his joyful yet proletarian facility, his anti-elitist comprehension of the material at hand. He was a master of the set piece, well-executed and always performed with a gentleman's phrasing.

I don't know who the singer is on this, but the rolled r's and the bogusly solemn phrasing give it an old-fashioned corniness of the kind evoked by crooning tenors in old films. It is emotion objectified by cheap but effectively-placed symbols. Smeck, on slack-key guitar, has perfect technique. It's as though he is giving the singer something to shoot for, a way to convert corn into the hard stuff of reality; unfortunately the singer does not take him up on it. For this study this recording is something of an anomaly, a

---

[1] This relates to an old peeve of mine, which is the (attempted) elevation, by assorted intellectuals and academics, of certain aspects of pop culture - graphic comic books, bad movies, Kurt Vonnegut and more - into an intellectual sphere which I do not believe they deserve. As Stanley Kauffman wrote years ago, the thing of interest isn't necessarily the pop dream but the way in which the pop dream is developed as a means of delving into other-worldly aspects of experience and consciousness. This is not so easily achieved, and our graphic comic book culture has tended to settle for image as a substitute for intellectual dimension.

mainstream snapshot of the under side of the American pop dream.

The best evidence we have tells us that the singer **Hezekiah Jenkins** was a black man. I can locate only two recordings of his, *The Panic Is On* (about The Depression and the sinking economic ship of state) and the more politically ecumenical **Shout You Cats (1/6/31)**. This is in the Songster vein which we mined so regularly in the first volume of this study. The tune itself shows signs of minstrel life, of vaudeville time and of course Tin Pan Alley attitude and even some progressive musical aptitude - listen at .33 to a typical gesture of those years (though mostly with jazz), the very modern-sounding chromatic chord change (a flat 6 chord) that makes the song sound a little bit "jazzy" without really being jazz. Subjectively it is in the realm of Good Time music, with a little bit of humor dropped in; in the words of the song, a cop is smacked around by one of the dancers present and, instead of smacking him back the cop tells the guy who hit him that "it's ok" and proceeds to join in with a chorus of "shout you cats."

Yes, this is a fantasy (yes, think George Floyd et al), but the mood is so light and bright here that Jenkins, a fine singer who really swings in every sense of the word, carries it off. Musically this presents itself as a form of street-corner jazz, cheerfully syncopated. It is one more of those seriously non-serious songs that Songsters of the African American faith continued to do so well. It has genuine entertainment value and, in a way that *Reaching for the Moon* (see above) fails to do, gives us a guiltless way to enjoy ourselves.

We spoke about **Buster Carter** earlier (see Vol. 15). His duet recordings with **Preston Carter** are early warning signs of Bluegrass, a country form that has been described most famously if somewhat annoyingly as "folk music in overdrive."[2] **Roll in My Sweet Baby's Arms (1931)** is one of the form's standards, distinguishable from later (and actual) Bluegrass in early recordings like this by its less balanced vocal harmonies, its hillbilly

---

[2] By Alan Lomax in a 1959 article in Esquire. I say "annoyingly" because the quasi-musical terminology of the phrase has, to me, the same "finger nails on the blackboard" shrill inaccuracy as the use of the term "timing" has as a descriptor of musical time; see my discussion about this in Volume 1 of this study.

articulation, and the way in which the solo instruments lean heavily on simple and only slightly variable figures. Bluegrass in its prime was a music of instrumental soloist and gospel-quartet harmony; in 1931 it's still a distant image of New Country.

Country music still had a long way to go to reach "maturity," if, that is, by maturity you mean the flattening out of the music's sound, the homogenization of its aesthetic values, and the complete financial conglomeration of its recording wing. Strangely enough the signs were all there by 1931, though often hidden in plain sight. But like some alien force infiltrating our civilization these changed were starting to take human form; Buster Carter's music was sharp and clean and yet still built on the hillbilly model. Like with a lot of these players there was still a bit of the wild man in his musical persona. The more respectable outside world was starting to peek through in terms of technique and subject matter, in the move away from some of country's deeper black role models and sources. The old white sound - the stiffer sonic posturing of older dance music -was - just maybe - starting to poke its foot, once more, in the professional door. Maybe this was just the way the music had to change, and maybe it was a response to the codification of this new and awkward profession, that of *country musician* (soon to be even further transformed by Nashville homogenization). Or maybe it was none of the above, but just a natural evolution of personal styles.

Whatever the cause, some kind of bright sunlight was beginning to poke through the clouds of historical ambiguity. Hence the professional persistence of black/white musicians like **Evans and McClain,** or **The Two Poor Boys** (see also Vol. 15), still racially ambiguous after all these years. Yes, as I said earlier, they were presumptively black, but there is something in everything they do, every odd gesture and turn of phrase (both musical and vocal) that begs for some kind of cultural explanation. They recorded **Take a Look At That Baby** on 5/20/31. For two black hillbillies this is a trip down Tin Pan Alley lane toward the land of jazz. It is jive-talking pop music with a country-tilt, possibly even a foretelling of Western Swing. The recording, even with restoration, is beat to hell, but the spirit is more than willing, even if the musical flesh is of uncertain hue. The mandolin break at about 2:03, a classic old-time musical intervention, and the scatter-scat syllabification, place this performance at the corner of vaudeville and hokum, an intersection full of country music and musicians of all colors.

Of less certain intersection is **W.M. Smith**'s **10/1/32** piano recording of **Sally Gooden**. Country piano (pre-Western Swing, that is) is poorly documented on record,[3] but suffice to say that Smith's straightforward, two-chord romp is similar in intent and execution to a number of instrumental hillbilly pieces of the time which, as I have mentioned, use repetition - of phrase and rhythm - as a basic technique. When I hear pieces like this I hear the sound and rhythm of employment - of musicians accompanying old-time dances and dancers; the simplest way to do this is to stretch out the same phrases, especially if they are user-friendly in that old-time-rhythm way. The melody of *Sally Gooden* is all pentatonics, and its three-chord design insures that no musician playing it will get lost in the changes. And though the piano might seem a less useable instrument in this context - these were the days before portable keyboards - its orchestral qualities were well suited for country performance. The tune itself was considered to be part of the first "commercially released" country recording, by Eck Robertson (see Vol. 3) in 1922; this, of course, is based on certain musical and commercial assumptions with which I occasionally beg to differ, but in official terms it is correct. [4]

But country is as country does. There is a story told by Stanley Dance in his book on the pianist Earl Hines[5] (see Vol. 10) in which Hines and a group of musicians in a jazz band, on tour, happen to hear a song playing on a juke box in which the pianist is clearly Hines. Earl denies it all, as the group on the recording is primitive and, to their ears, amateurish; "I would never," he tells the band, (and I apologize because I don't have access to the book, and I am paraphrasing) "play with a bunch of country guys like that."

The group he was denying happened to be that of the fiddler Clifford Hayes, with whom Hines had indeed recorded a

---

[3] About the only real source extant, that I know of, on the country piano tradition is a fascinating LP released years ago, and now available on the Smithsonian/Folkways web site, called Virginia Traditions: Blue Ridge Piano Styles (https://folkways.si.edu/virginia-traditions-blue-ridge-piano-styles/american-popular-folk-old-time/music/album/smithsonian)

[4] I am talking here, of course, about some of the early commercial and minstrel type recordings discussed in the first volume of this book which I believe reflect the earliest images of country music. For reference see various volumes/chapters therein.

[5] The book, by Stanley Dance, is *The World of Earl Hines*.

few years earlier (they are, sans Hines, the band accompanying Jimmie Rodgers on *My Good Gal's Gone,* see Vol. 15). Most significant is Hines' denigration in the Dance book of the jukebox band as "country," surely in response to the derision of his fellow band members. This goes a long way toward confirming my sense of country music as being broadly reflective, as I have said, of music with a "passive sophistication," though it is a sophistication often buried beneath layers of seeming primitivism and modest technique, and nearly always, in its early days, lacking in some essential polish. The point is that *country* reflects the designation of a much different kind of experience and means of expression than that of some supposedly more complex forms of music. Whether this is actually true or not is debatable; the more pertinent point is that this is the way people heard and described such things back then. Hindsight is nice, but contemporary accounts are better.

And so it is with the (black) singer **Ben Ferguson**'s version of **Try and Treat Her Right**, from 6/16/31, also made with Clifford Haye's band. The chord sequence is straight-out *Muskrat Ramble,* and the opening is straight-on country, of fiddle and guitar, down to the sounds and intervals played by fiddler/leader Hayes. The clarinet solo is relatively in-tune for its type and time, with some nice figures; he clearly has a few technical tricks up his sleeve (check out 1:10 and forward). Most impressive is the guitar solo by the unsung guitar hero Cal Smith. At 1:26 he begins a very nimble chorus that actually swings, further confusing things in stylistic terms; but then, solo country guitar, in its earliest manifestations, was almost identical to that of early jazz.

And on the blues side of country there was **The Gone Dead Train** recorded by **King Solomon Hill** in **1932**. Hill, if we may call him that, is another cypher in the book of American life, though one whose biographical outlines have been battled over by certain blues historians. Hence, as Wikipedia notes:

> The identification of Hill as Joe Holmes was made by the prominent blues scholar Gayle Dean Wardlow and strongly contested by another prominent blues scholar, David Evans. Wardlow eventually found four informants who had known Joe Holmes and identified his voice on the records of King Solomon Hill. One informant lived in a section of Sibley, Louisiana, known as Yellow Pine, within which is a community formerly known as King Solomon Hill, centered on a hill on which stood King Solomon Hill Baptist Church. A retired postal worker confirmed that King Solomon Hill would have been a valid postal address in 1932. The community is now known as Salt Works. No informant remembers Holmes

using the name King Solomon Hill, so Wardlow concluded that Paramount Records chose to use his address as his recording name.

Case closed? Damned if I know; I try to keep my distance in these kinds of disputes. Wardlow is a conscientious guy; Evans is a solid scholar. I would award it to Wardlow in a decision, though I, unlike most other blues observers, don't think Wardlow's evidence is air tight (the more convincing of it is not the postal location but his use of human voice recognition).

All of which provides nearly fatal distraction from the real evidence at hand, the actual performance (Hill recorded only 6 sides, for the unsinkable Paramount Records). The vocal, high-lonesome personified, is majestic in that rising and sinking blues way, in its tidal flow and confident desperation. But the most distinctive thing about this is the piercing, uncanny vocal/instrumental interaction. This is the kind of one-man band I wrote about earlier in some musings on black, one-man orchestration as it is often built into solo performances; it is not call and *then* response, it is call/response all at once, interactive, separate yet together. The independence of each line – of the voice, of the guitar – is paradoxical, as each requires the other to make sense of it and yet each seems isolated, to issue from some mysterious place.

Now that we're here and thinking about the blues it may be a good time to insert a quote which, in this regard, has been disturbing me for some time, showing as it does, I believe, the wrong-headed, liberal silliness which regularly substitutes for true discussion of black music. Writing about the blues and Wardlow's book *Chasin' that Devil Music,* in the Texas Observer (2/19/99) the writer Mark Smith observes (or, really, thinks he is observing) that the music on the accompanying compact disc

"…is like a message in a bottle from a distant time. It is at first strange beyond words – music of a gone world. Charlie Patton's rough howl is almost unintelligible, not entirely because of the poor recording quality, but also because of the abject pain of his expression. Patton sings from a depth of suffering and hardship that is nearly unimaginable to modern listeners."

I find this not only a bit obtuse but arguably racist, in its adoption of certain assumptions and stereotypes. I smell a noble savage in the way Smith draws, in his article, more from received and perceived sociological wisdom than from the sound of the music and the recordings themselves. Even the roughest and least audible of the blues as I have heard it, by Patton and others, is anything BUT beyond words. If it were beyond words we wouldn't have so many damn words coming from the mouths of the singers themselves, so much brilliant abstraction leading from what I hear as the invasion of the conscious by the subconscious. In literature we often speak of subtext, of that which lurks just below the surface of meaning; in the blues I think we need to locate the *uber-text*, that aspect of hyper-reality which exists above (and beyond) the surface of performance. It is in the uber-text of the blues that we hear certain essential life forces as they affirm the working-lives of defiantly suffering men and women, finding voice in delirious texts and irregular beats of musical performance. The result is a celebration of life as it defeats, for at least the length of the performance, suffering, with a simmering, subconscious power that boils over into music and vocalized speech, not beyond words, but *in* words (and yes, in music). As for unimaginable "suffering and hardship," well I would say that 1) the performances themselves make it eminently imaginable, but more important, 2) these performances are ecstatic *alternatives* to the pain of daily life and sub-Southern existence. To draw from them only portraits of pain is to miss, as with Patton, a huge dimension of defiant ecstasy, as released in expression. And it is all entirely intelligible, and beyond pain; these are not, as Duke Ellington might have said, tone parallels to suffering but instead tonal exorcisms, of relief derived from a kind of (successful) aversion therapy: let me repeat over and over the things that I dread and hate and they will soon feel, instead of pain, like abstract objects of inexplicable desire.

    The gospel train was almost literally that, a *train*, on songs like **Clank A Lanka Sleep on Mother** by **The Famous Bluejay Singers of Birmingham (1/32)**. What was the physical model, if there was one, for the locomotive-phrasing on performances like this? In the literature we are told that the Gospel Train represents escape from slavery, both figuratively and literally (thinking the Underground Railroad). In musical terms the voice becomes another instrument in performances like this, and a rhythm instrument at that. Musically we can practically see those train wheels speeding up like in an old newsreel.
    In the early 1930s the hard-gospel movement was still unformed, though what we find, as is usual with music in its early stages, are pockets of radical musical departure from traditional

norms. Hard gospel was the next stage after the still-popular jubilee style. In jubilee vocal performances the voices were very much as one, the harmonic and textural variations internal, like shifting vibrations. The harmonies were rich and relatively pure, though from the beginning it was not unusual to hear formal - or, really, emotional - departures from the set form of vocal-quartet voicing, the occasional lead taking leave from the arrangement in a calculated yet liberating way. This was the path to hard gospel, and as the movement progressed that lead freed itself in even formalized performance. *Clank A Lanka Sleep on Mother* has a steady and intensive buildup, and that singer emerges like those bodies in the uncompleted figure studies by Michelangelo at the Academia museum in Florence, half sculpted, almost pleading for bodily liberation.

**Hallelujah Side** by the **Tindley Quaker City Gospel Singers (3/8/32)** holds a lot in reserve. This is a carefully modulated ensemble, not especially emotional but also not in the least bit cold. These men are well disciplined in a very refined way, full of feeling and not self-conscious about showing a little bit of old-fashioned courtesy to their audience. In performances like this it feels like the group is taking the audience by the hand and showing them the way with old-world courtesy; is this a Southern, gentlemanly thing or some other form of deference? As they do so the two roles - performer and audience - still remain separate and inviolable.

And wonder of wonders, what is that we hear at about .035 from the Tindleys? Yes, those sagging, minstrel harmonies that sound as proto-vaudeville, a minstrelized croon a la black groups like Johnson, Nelson and Porkchop (see Vol. 10); add some low-hanging voices blended together (with a bit less precision but with similar musical side effects) and you have what the academics like to call a continuum, though this is probably not the kind they usually have in mind. Musically-speaking this was neither quite the future nor really the past; because as confusing as it sometimes is, in black music those are often exactly the same.

The persistence of location - even as American music has spread, through radically effecting technologies like radio and recordings, in ways that have tended to eliminate regional isolation - is nowhere more apparent than on **Hi Henry Brown**'s **Preacher Blues**, recorded in **1932**. This performance practically cries out *St.*

*Louis* (when I listened back to it in preparation for this entry I had forgotten what this song or singer was, but knew immediately where the singer was from). And so it goes - because Henry Brown did live in St. Louis

I think…..

But here is the rub - yes, the performer on this track is described as being from St. Louis - he has been included on several collections of blues from that city - and he is often called Hi Henry Brown. But there is also a Henry Brown/bluesman from St. Louis who is recognized as a great barrelhouse pianist (and who lived until 1981, and recorded into the 1960s). A little research shows that Hi Henry Brown was, indeed, a different person; according to the great Stefan Wirz, whose web site *American Music* ought to receive government subsidy (any government will do), Hi Henry Brown was:

"b. about 1884, reportedly in Pace, Bolivar County, Mississippi d. after 1932, presumably in St. Louis, Missouri."

So, mystery solved, and to my added relief he was also a resident of St. Louis, likely part of the 20th century's great black-urban migration from South to North (ever notice that it's never the other way around?).

But to get back to the performance: we have talked of several other St. Louis men - Henry Spaulding (see Vol. 11) and Charley Jordan (see Vol. 13) - and Hi Henry Brown is a perfect stylistic fit with our assumptions about the St. Louis sound. Like those others he has a very bearable lightness of being, which is not to be confused in any way with shallowness. This was a profoundly deep pool of talent. I even hear a stylistic connection to some white ideas about the blues, in the cloudy sonics of the performance. Though Brown has that Delta vocal guttural sound, the guitar part is a wondrously floating object, the vamp played out on the instrument's upper frets. The octave separation of vocal and accompaniment is also effective, the final dominant 7th chord like a gentle but firm farewell.

Every day I am thankful for the internet. Sure, it is full of insane ravings, but it has allowed me to write (particularly during the pandemic) from the comfort of my own couch. Without it I would have no idea that the country singer **Louisiana Lou** was really Eva Conn (her married named), born in - well, it's anybody's guess, but possibly Louisiana, though we do know that she ended up singing for a radio station in Jackson, Mississippi before moving west to Iowa, where she became a local country music hero as both singer and humorist and where she recorded **Go 'long Mule** on **12/4/33**. By this time she was well known as a songwriter and performer in her new Midwestern home, though apparently relocating far away from her (apparent) roots was bad for her historical image - meaning that she seems to have been lost in the commercial shuffle (she made few recordings because the majors didn't have much Midwestern coverage) even as she achieved local celebrity.

*Go Long Mule* is a solid piece of new country. Louisiana Lou has the perfect twang for the new age; it doesn't blur her speech or cover over the words of the song and she is perfectly intelligible on a song that has deep commercial/minstrel roots. As you might have guessed I hear this performance as echoing and predicting the changes that the profession of country will undergo in the next 20 years or so. It is neatly presented; musically-speaking it has its shirttails tucked in, and no loose lyric or musical ends. The accompaniment, uncredited, has a studio sheen; there appear to be two guitars on this, and the simple, classic country lines played by the lead is efficient and professional, more an emulation than an original statement, giving *Go 'Long Mule* a cordial, glossy, country finish. This is radio-hillbilly on its way out, presented for after-dinner distraction; or old-time music sounding a little tired and, just maybe, running out of ideas.

Or was it? Not everywhere. If you looked hard enough, old time music was still there for the taking (or the listening). Medicine shows and other entertainments had their own ideas of revivalism, with singers like **Ben Curry (Laffing Rag, 1/32)**, who we can only guess might have made some kind of career - or, really, living - out of it all. *Laffing Rag* is a remnant, or a variation, of the *Laughing Song* (which was an early hit by the black performer George W. Johnson).[6] Curry is a mystery, another anonymous black performer whose voice and instrumental sound (there is banjo and harmonica on this) are audaciously and even aggressively antiquarian. Unlike, say, some latter-day revivalists who seem stylized in a way calculated to foster certain kinds of cultural association, Curry is a singing monologist, telling a somewhat

---

[6] For a fascinating accounting of Washington's life see Tim Brooks' book *Lost Sounds: Blacks and the Birth of the Recording Industry, 1890-1919*.

incoherent but funny story (at one point his girl rejects him but when he goes out and comes back with a twenty dollar bill she exclaims "baby where you been so long?"). The whole song, as with George Washington Johnson's original, is in the reciting of a series of curious human episodes.

The old songs still lived, but there was something to be said for performers with more "contemporary" ideas, like **Big Bill Broonzy** (see Vol. 14, 27), whose **Long Tall Mama (3/30/32)** is almost startlingly distinct from *Laffing Rag* in its world view. *Long Tall Mama* is big and bouncy, with a hokum-like humor that becomes, in the telling, almost beside the point. But what *is* the point? I would say the point is Broonzy's wonderful, clear diction, his pre-urban soul, and his light and swinging guitar playing, picked with precision and a careless momentum that masks the seriousness of his intentions. This kind of playing has its own diction, like that of a private country language. Listen to the short phrase that begins at about 2:05 and which he re-does right at the end; it's an interlude, an abstraction of a typical blues cadence. Like some of Lonnie Johnson's work it is country blues with a jazz-like urgency to its rhythm, a prevue of the way in which the blues will, before very long, break out of old boxes and jump into some new ones.

There's an old theory of film criticism called *auteur*, from the French word for *author*, which posits that the director of a movie is the ultimate arbiter of the film's quality. The lighting, the blocking of actors, the rhythm of editing, pacing of dialog, the overall visual texture - all, under this theory, are of prime importance and all emerge from the director's creative vision. The result has been a formalist nightmare, in my opinion, in which mediocre films have been praised simply for the way they look and sound and feel; the script or outline (I hesitate to stay *story line* because I am not advocating for old-style narratives; I also love the films of Antonioni) are ignored as mere inconveniences. The *process* becomes *the thing* in a lot of criticism written from this point of view, even as narrative, seen as being of lessor importance, loses itself in ill logic and dull modernist cliche. Some bad worked is swamped by trendy ideas of modernist disconnection (because, I would say, disconnection still required a connective logic). Even *lack of motivation* requires a reason for being, and even irrational actions need to have some form of convincing existential exposition. Narrative is not necessarily a lead anchor; it can be a technique which which to manipulate transitional states of reality.

My point is that mastery of one technical aspect of an art form does not necessarily translate into art; otherwise commercial art (and commercials) would be the highest form of representation, and speed of musical execution would usurp nuance of expression as the ultimate value in music.

Why am I talking about this all of a sudden? Because the way in which we value vernacular musicians is directly related to not just their prowess strictly as singers or musicians, but to what they actually create and/or sing. Any auteur theory of music which we might hold to is subject to our objective evaluation of both the singer *and* the song. Elvis without *That's All Right Momma*, back in 1954, would have been a curiosity more than a musical phenomenon. Though I will grant that sometimes there is an exception that isn't really an exception - a great artist who performs in the services of supposedly lesser material, but who converts that material into something that might objectively be considered art. We experience this frequently in jazz, though the brilliance of a particular Louis Armstrong or Billie Holiday performance might call into question our judgement of whether a song thought of as a poor composition was really a lesser work. When Armstrong or Holiday supposedly convert such things into diamonds of performance, are they rescuing the second rate or are they showing us what was first-rate about what we only *thought* was second rate? I don't have a final answer to that, but I raise the whole subject and ask all of these questions because vernacular song is a procession of compositional oddities. It has great songs that remain great, good songs that remain good, great and good songs that suffer by interpretation, and questionable songs that become basically the equivalent of whomever performs them and becomes, yes, their auteur.

Take the song **Just Because,** by **The Lone Star Cowboys** from **8/1/33**. The Lone Star Cowboys were a Western Swing-type orchestra, and they were described by a company which later reissued their records as a "hot string band." "Hot strings" are really the essence, in my opinion, of early Western Swing, which is basically old-time country music with a bit more improvisational edge, moving beyond country's ragtime obsession and into the realm of early jazz. This format was home for some very sophisticated players, who were improvisors or, at the least, great technicians, and who tried to be jazz musicians while retaining, in their own way, an air of country prerogative. In most of these performances the song was very much the thing, though, in a way newly characteristic of early vernacular music, the performance was also the thing, and even some very shallow material was fleshed out in musically substantive ways.

*Just Because* is very clearly a transitional tune, from the old-time vernacular to the new-time Swing. The composition itself has a Tin-Pan Alley-like arc to it, and was covered over the years by many different types of singers and groups. The introductory mandolin and old-time vocal harmonies look back in time (though Western Swing bands, to their credit and with charm, maintained this vocal informality, in a way that Bluegrass, seemingly built on full-voiced gospel harmony, did not), and the guitar part, expansively improvised, looks forward. And listen to the very sophisticated way in which this same guitar outlines and paraphrases the rhythm, and the sudden ascending pentatonic riff at about 1:13. This is a new type of country of the country. [7]

The day before this same group recorded **Deep Elm Blues (8/4/33)**. The subject of the song is one we have touched on before (see Vol. 7, Willard Robison), about a section of Dallas which was legendary for its sinful commerce. Like a lot of country music this has more pep than swing; in this case, with this particular band, that kind of pep helps to situate it in a lane between old time music and new-time Bluegrass. Bluegrass, which in certain ways is a radical alteration of old time music, represented something of a tightening up of that old time instrumentation, with a more formal layering of vocals. The Lone Star Cowboys were nothing if not adaptable in ways which led, musically speaking, to and from not just bluegrass but also Western Swing. Unlike, say, Evans and McClain, these were the same musicians from song to song (stylistically and sonically) with a similar if diverging musical purpose.

On the other hand, or maybe the same, the **Delmore Brothers (Big River Blues, 8/1/33)** (and this is one of their earliest recordings) have a way of re-enforcing tradition while showing signs of dissatisfaction with it. Harmony-wise they have a looseness that sounds very old-school, in the way in which their voices remain separate and clearly discernible, even as they complement each other harmonically. Those voices, individually and in sum, are very much derivative of informal group and family singing, and there is little gospel fervor to their sound; on the other

---

[7] I am thinking here of Nick Dawidoff's fine book, *In the Country of the Country: A Journey to the Roots of American Music*.

hand there is nothing cold or formal about it either. They are another of those common early country duos, increasingly popular into the modern era of of the music, and a sign of the music's own internal struggle with folk-vernacular sources as acted upon by professional and post-minstrel craft. The dynamic tension produced by differing professional and avocational impulses was nothing new for country (hence the tense but creative dynamic of early-folk-versus-minstrel-versus-ragtime-versus-professional songwriting etiquette), though the way in which it was starting to happen was. With *Big River Blues*, as with the song *Just Because*, the music was now mainstreaming itself, filtering out the blues through a uni-racial lens of Southern tradition, and in some ways, consciously or not, lightening (or whitening) itself for the mass-cult requirements just ahead.

**Miss Handy Hanks**, recorded by **Archie Lewis (3/30/33)** is all and none of the above. This is a minstrel-sounding yet black song sung by a black man, uncredited in any official account as to composer or origin. It has nothing of the blues, yet is no less soulful in its presentation and world view than anything the Delta has given us. Why do I hear it as black? It has that determinedly hallucinatory quality we find throughout the literature of the African American non-blues (well, we do find it in the blues, but in a different way), free-associating with an aptitude for free-floating, sincere optimism (and I may be in a minority here but I hear no signification in this, no extra-musical meaning); in other words, all looks good from the song's point of view, there's crowds of happy, local people gorging themselves on food and drink, the singer is promenading around town with a lady, and, while meals are being served, there is plenty of quaint nostalgia:

Way down South among the fields of cotton
Way down South among the clover and the bees
Way down South among the fields of cotton
I'll take you back, way down home

And most particularly, and possibly most jarring relative to our contemporary values, there is absolutely no irony in a song as sung by a black man about black people just living their lives in peace and quiet, without stereotypical strife or drunken razor fights, unconcerned with whiteness on any level; this is just, in this particular (song) world, the way it was. And there is something more than a little bit liberating about this, its creation of an alternative world of African American peace and freedom. These were just regular people doing regular things, exerting a humanity that was often, sometimes violently, denied them.

*Miss Handy Hanks* might sound to us as the song equivalent of those Hollywood movies of the Depression era which, in order to distract economically-stunted audiences, regularly presented rich (white) people with no discernible means of support, living in mansions with servants and big, winding staircases. That's a possibility here, but it's also possible that it's a subtle gesture of 'fuck you' in the direction of white America for its inability to conceive of black life of the day as anything but grist for white entertainment and derision. Pieces like this, staples of the Songster repertoire, just *were*, and they existed without the need for social utility or explanation. So let 'em alone, ye liberal sociologists.

From time to time in this study I refer to the idea of "swing" like it's a common term, or something, definition-wise, which we all agree on. Well, forget it, because, especially in the jazz world from which I often hide, there is little consensus. One man or woman's swing is another's endless vamping, or a sop to the white revivalist folks, or just aimless (free) jazz noodling. I have a very liberal idea of what swing is, and can hear it in everything from some of the earliest country recordings (like *Ham Beats All Meat*, Vol. 8) to the lysergic drag of some of Albert Ayler's most hallucinatory cries of rhythm and jazz. Particularly in the old days it is wherever it is, sometimes with white folks and sometimes with black folks, but usually arriving from the direction of black folks. *Post-Diasporan rhythms* are what made America great, despite what those orange hats claim, and the beat is in the rhythm and the rhythm is in the beat - and the point is that in American music, even in the most abstract of free-jazz drumming, even when the time is merely suggested, there is a line-of-time that beats by and for post-Africans, in my humble opinion. And swing, in all of these cases, is reducible to certain inalienable, personal yet universal values. In other words, if it makes you move some part of your body, it probably swings.

I am inspired to these ruminations by the recording of **Tampa Strut**, made by a black group, **The Georgia Browns**, on **1/19/33**. This is one of those essential black performances, rhythmically sustainable in ways sometimes approached, but never really equalled, by early white (country) performers. For one thing, the way in which *Tampa Strut* regularly shifts rhythmic direction is uncanny and difficult to describe in words. The song is simply (sic) a harmonica/guitar duo, and it sounds like the most sublime kind of spontaneous orchestration. In a typically African American musical way these are two voices, independent yet co-dependent, each mapped out in musically parallel yet emotionally intersecting ways. The guitar runs a maze of mini-variations, strummed as chords, chord fragments, and then picked along and around the bass; the harmonica player is limited to maybe 5 different notes, varied in texture and arranged according to shifting musical mood. He constantly phrases and then re-phrases those notes, bunches them together as a kind of blues-dissonance, and then re-joins the guitar for a conclusion which is really more pause than ending.

To my ears it is this constant shifting of line which gives performances like this their African-ness, though in making this association I am also drawing upon the work of Robert Farris Thompson. In his book *Flash of the Spirit* he cites an African belief that evil travels in straight lines, and relates this to the way in which, in African expression, "perfect symmetry" is generally avoided. Hence we have, in so much African-American performance, the shifting and even intrusive angularity which gives so much of it its character, its rhythmic, sonic, and even visual signature; and hence, I would add, *Tampa Strut*.

Of late I have become ensconced in some arguments, on Facebook, over whether music is inherently political. I will cite my very specific argument, which is anti-political yet really isn't (and may be hopelessly nuanced) in the next page or so, but one of the things which immediately puts me off of certain kind of politico-cultural dogmatism is hearing performances like that, by a *black* group of, the song **Hambone Am Sweet** (the **Four Southern Singers, 2/23/33**). My fear, as I listen to performances like this, is that the more we try to put cultural artifacts into political boxes of any kind, the less *true* diversity we will recognize and celebrate. A picture of the Four Southern Singers that I saw some years back showed them dressed in what we can only call degrading, racially-retro garb, as though they, as slaves from the antebellum era, had been outfitted as a minstrel fantasy of slave life and then re-activated in the modern era.

Yes, this was a weird and minstrel-ized publicity photo, condemned by the passing of time to be eternally politically incorrect (and for good reason). But to me these were four young, black, professionals, trying to make a living in a world that was not of their own creation; as with the black-faced, black minstrels of yore this was a classic "if you can't beat 'em" situation. From our judgmental perch in the 21st century it is easy to either condemn The Four Southern Singers *or* proffer them political immunity by converting them into ready symbols of American racial oppression. Certainly, any over-arching political interpretation of our cultural history would require we do, at the least, one of those things.

But from my (yes, white) perspective I feel them differently, that it is not my business, as essentialy a 20th century White American living in the 21st, to politicize their decision to pose as they did for such a photo - though as I say that I immediately hear the screams and cries of Americans everywhere (but particularly those on the Left) that my perspective is hopelessly marred by the privileges conferred upon me by race and class. And yes, I answer, it certainly is, and I also know what is coming next - a further oppositional claim that the very act of de-politicizing such a picture and promotional object (which was from the 1930s) is a political act in and of itself, an expression of white (racist) power. Which yes, it might be. But my political mind focuses, instead, on the extreme and unfair anonymity suffered by long-dead black performers, on their day-to-day struggles, on the nastiness and dangers of the system with which they had to make their professional peace; and I think, and I say, let us allow them their true freedom, let us liberate them from these struggles and threats, let us make them less captive of the political system by focusing on their *music*, on the way in which *Hambone Am Sweet,* a kind of odd, post-plantation, Minstrel relic, harmonized with care and post-Diasporan attention to internal, drummed vocalisms, is still a work of African American art. Let us try and find the actual life (lives) which inspired the sound and rhythm of this, divorce them from the white imposition of Minstrel facial recognition, remove them from the shuffling, eyes-averted subjugated life which surrounded it, and look at *Hambone Am Sweet,* if we possibly can, as the work of human beings instead of social symbols.

For something completely different, consider the **Happy Hayseeds' Ladies Quadrille,** from **3/4/30**. We go from the the deep American vernacular, the underbelly of half-truth - is *Hambone Am Sweet* an embarrassing step backwards, of social recidivism; or is it just a perversely nostalgic look at a time when everyone (white) at least believed that everyone knew their place? - to the *Ladies Quadrille,* which evokes old English dance of the 18th and 19th century (which has its own weirdnesses). This is old-world precision from musicians and for audiences who took delight in the obvious sense-memory of pleasant evenings of "civilized" entertainment and recreation. If one (*Hambone*) is political, is the other also? Does this performance by the Happy Hayseeds (a group named with clear ironic intent) avoid the political by simply playing the music with an educated precision, by avoiding any implied editorializing about those not-so-good-old-days? Or is it futile to consider slave-era music as representing anything but a collaborationist cultural attitude?

Well, first of all, they probably *are* trying to evoke that sort of memory association by sound, even possibly with innocent intent, and this performance is as racially specific in the *white* way as anything you will hear in early country music. And yet, you can't place *all* the sins of white folks onto the shoulders of those who don't make obvious restitution - or can you? And are we, in all of this, placing too much burden on the Happy Hayseeds, who probably hoped that by recording this they could preserve the music they loved in a place - the South - for which past, present, and future were, at least for some, equally attractive?

Your move.

What is it about the opening vocal phrase of **Na Pua O Hawaii** by the **George Ku Trio (1932)** (at .022) that gets to me? The musical entrance is like a Hawaiian cloud of joy; the song is sung as though it is, spiritually speaking, in another octave. This sound had its sonic effects on everything from blues players (who either emulated or just happened to be working toward tonal variations similar to Hawaiian music's slack-keyed floaters, and whose falsetto eruptions had a similar affinity) and early (white) country musicians, who had their own falsetto/yodel ambitions and who also admired the blues-adaptable sound of these wayward strings. For further information on what this recording does and means in its own context, let us consult the late historian, slack key performer, and pedophile, Bob Brozman:[8]

"…the George Ku Trio, from 1932. These obscure musicians made 10 sides at this session, featuring the exquisite tone and light touch of steel-player Charles Opununi. Using a National resonator guitar, he achieves the liquid, sweet tone

---

[8] Sad but true, and it all came out after Brozman's death: https://www.santacruz.com/news/the_dark_side_of_genius.html

only obtained by a select few players, such as Sol Hoopii and Jim & Bob, the Genial Hawaiians. NA PUA O HAWAII is a traditional type hula, with fine falsetto vocals, yet the intention of the steel player seems to be to make it swing."

Does it all, when it comes to black "street music," always come back and around to the jug band? The sound of the jug band grabbed me from the first time I heard it, probably on some old Yazoo Records collection. There is something irresistibly and charmingly archaic about the sound of these groups, of the old and now-dead worlds which they seem to evoke so casually. The reality is that the more contemporary musicians, with revivalist ambition, work at trying to summon forth, in musical terms, these long-gone places, the more apparent the futility of the intellectual (or maybe cultural) gesture becomes. These are wonderful and irreducible oddities of sound and time,

Take **Cold Iron Bed** by **Jack Kelly and his South Memphis Jug Band (8/1/33)**. From the first few seconds we have the sense that we are in for a different kind of ride; the percussive, repeating guitar figure, the sub-tone jug, and the ripening fiddle (which sounds like the musical equivalent of a sun rise) all signal that this is more of the same, musically speaking, though of *what* we cannot exactly say; the charm of it all is in how familiar it sounds even in its strangeness. Cue in the jarringly mellow guitar chords at .014, add the crunchy, distant vocal, and you have the jug band in essence: something old and something new, not jazz, not blues, and not simply a rough rendition of pop music. And take into account the unusual intervals played by the fiddler, particularly at the strange (for the time and place) harmonic convergence at 1:14. Is that a major seventh, or is just the third of the fifth chord? It has the *effect* of a major seventh, giving the performance an 'open' and airy sound, avoiding as it does the common blue intervals of the day, the hammered and bent notes that give so much other music a familiar, black sound. The only other pop musician of the day that I can think of who might have played such an interval, bending harmonic boundaries like this in a "pop" way, was Louis Armstrong. And that tempo - call it a walk, a stroll, a drag - think of it in any way you want; only black musicians, even in 1933, as racial worlds collided, could do it like this.

And racial worlds collide, where I live (the USA), with increasing intensity as I write these words. Of late the rhetorical excesses of racial conflict have more than occasionally taken a loaded turn. It is, as always, but a little bit more-so now, hard to publicly defend whiteness in any way, shape, or formal action, and when I, from time to time, stick my (white) neck out I occasionally get clobbered for it. Last year I defended, on Facebook, an old film clip of a white minstrel performer dancing (in front of a black audience). There were catcalls about "that fool" who was, on evidence of this performance, hopelessly deluded in believing that the steps he was performing were as authentic as his blackened face (and I apologize as I have lost the link for the film clip and cannot remember the dancer's name). But I recognized this performer's strange, slithering leg-steps as depicted by W.T. Lhamon in his book on the relationship of 18th and 19th century street performers and blackface minstrelsy, *Raising Cain*. Llhamon described steps very much like these as deriving from early black street choreography. I mentioned this at the time, defending the performance, and it all ended up as a lesson on "how not to become popular on Facebook."

And so it was recently on another musical discussion, with a significantly different orientation and yet with similar external, racial irritants. Someone (white) wrote approvingly of the black pianist **Lil Hardin Armstrong**'s playing, as though she were a convincing blues performer. I begged to differ, but was then further discouraged by some disparaging remarks made in the same thread about the the white pianist **Frank Melrose**. (And just to drop it in here, Lil was a fine singer and an early practicer of scat in the modern sense; check our her version of **Say it Isn't So**, from **9/22/32**). The point being made was that Lil was black and so was, in a built-in way, a blues person; Melrose was white and so was an outsider to the blues. Well, more white critical strangeness; the proof is in the music.

Frank Melrose, a barrelhouse disciple of Jelly Roll Morton, had none of Morton's finesse and little of his deep jazz skill. But Melrose had a lot of blues feeling, a solid technique, and a keyboard touch, as I pointed out in that Facebook discussion, that was about as authentically funky as anyone else in those days. I convinced no one, but I chalked it up to racially-charged silliness; Lil was a trained pianist, but trained in the wrong way (probably classical). She was not a good jazz or blues player and anyone who tries to claim otherwise is interpreting things through a racial blind. Melrose, on the other hand, had a deep blues and barrelhouse soul, defying, particularly for those days, the cultural disadvantage of being white. Check out **Market Street Stomp (4/9/30)**. This is blues through a Morton-esque lens, tinged with a lyricism that immediately places it apart from our more schematic ideas of what constitutes blues and boogie - and which was one of Jelly Roll's great innovations. Morton took the memory of Funky Butt Hall and Buddy Bolden and injected a Creole jazz sensibility, and he had sense enough to scatter the funkier memories of that music throughout. So does Melrose in, yes, a less inspired, but still real, way. At 1:05 he reduces the melodic ranginess of the piece to a boogie woogie line, before effortlessly (at 1:28) and elegantly returning to a ragtime/cum Morton melodic mood. Facebook and America be damned, this is wonderful and timeless piano playing, a real thing at a time when we need some real things.

But no more real than **Swing Low Sweet Chariot**, recorded by **Jules Bledsoe** in **1931**. We speak of black traditions, but the phrase is, as far as I can see, redundant. Black music is its own tradition present and past, two parts which, when summed, usually equal the future. Bledsoe was an African American singer, a baritone who by 1924 was touring under the sponsorship of Sol Hurok, a white entrepreneur of the classical music stage. Bledsoe was the first African American singer to gain "regular employment on Broadway," Wikipedia tells us, and appeared as Joe in Showboat even before Paul Robeson did, singing the song *Old Man River* on stage. *Swing Low Sweet Chariot* may be one of those songs, like *Amazing Grace,* that you (assuming you are just like me) never want to hear again. This song is the victim of 10,000 church renditions, funerals, and memorial services. Bledsoe's performance defies the aesthetic odds; I felt like I was hearing the song for the first time. He is, in my opinion, a much greater singer than Robeson, or even Roland Hayes (see Vo. 20). Bledsoe's voice, in an idiom which stretched the limits of stylistic patience - so patent were its cliches of enunciation and phrasing - was supple in the most soulful way. He sang what he meant, and he meant what he sang.

# Chapter 17: The Soul of White Folks

The Lomaxes, father John and son Alan, were prescient enough to know that it was time to head South before the indigenous music of that region was lost to technological changes, not the least of which was the recording machines which they were depending upon to preserve it. There are many things I like about the Lomaxes, though I have to admit it took me some time to get interested in the work that they did. For some time I thought that the music they saved and preserved was not necessarily, as a body of work, any more interesting than that which was preserved and distributed by commercial record companies. I avoided their work, though I finally realized that this was to my disadvantage. It was not that they were trying to displace what the majors were recording, but that they knew there were important and vital, untapped, and rapidly fading, musical forces in the South, both black and white. There wasn't necessarily money to be made from recording this music, but that was also the point. We are not a country that prioritizes preservation of our own cultural resources, and the Lomaxes were on to something. So they got in their cars, loaded in some extremely heavy recording equipment, and headed for points South and Southwest.

They found a lot of fascinating music that would likely have been lost to time had they not made it a point to record it. One of their better ideas was to head to Southern prisons, on the (reasonable) assumption that (black) inmates were less likely than people on the outside to have had their own musical preferences effected by the intrusive world of certain technologies (radio and recordings). In doing this they found singers like Iron Head Baker, whose recording moniker was **Iron Head Baker and Others**, the others being his fellow prisoners from Central State Prison Farm in Sugar Land, Texas. **Go Down Old Hannah**, which they recorded in **1933**, sounds to me like a typical old-style solo piece, though in this case "solo" means lead and followers. It is slow and deliberative, with some of the clear musical prehistory of the blues; it sounds less emotional than some other pre-blues we have listened to, more meditative and thoughtful - there is a lined-out patience here in the execution of these long, slow verses; the way in which the lead vocal seems to rise over the heads of his accompanying singers brings to mind the kind of unison-based religious singing which so affected white religious sects like the Old Regular Baptists.

This singing style has an open-ended quality tailored, I would guess, for the way in which the work of Southern black Americans was never-ending, whether performed by civilians or on prison work farms (and the distance between the two, especially in those days, was not great; another thing the South gave us was, in effect, the vast criminalization of blackness in all forms and in all places). There is no greater patience required than that of laborers working a form of virtual slavery, whether publicly or privately sponsored, and songs like *Go Down Old Hannah* are like the public utterings of people who cannot really say, in white company, what they think about those conditions.

Another Lomax "discovery" was Huddie Ledbetter, better known as Leadbelly (say that three times fast). I won't go through all the complex of events that led to Leadbelly's release (he was in prison when the Lomaxes met him) or the strangeness and (financial) controversy over his post-prison sponsorship by Alan and John Lomax, his late-in-life fame and schizophrenic celebrity/criminal aura. For that I will refer you to the book written by Charles Wolfe and Kip Lornell, *The Life and Legend of Leadbelly*. Leadbelly was a master singer and Songster, somewhat of a symbol of all that was American in American vernacular song. In my early years I shied away from his music because he seemed too perfect a white liberal public symbol of blackness; in terms of image he seemed drawn to scale as the *American Singer*, a post-Delta sketch of sin and redemption, and my natural inclination to avoid the obvious put me off. But I was very wrong.

An example of why and how I was wrong: **Western Cowboy**, which **Leadbelly** recorded in **July of 1933**. There is, I would suggest, an element of set piece in this, as though Leadbelly is on exhibit, and I say this knowing that I know too much about his life for my evaluation of the performance to be objective. Still, he gets past this very quickly, and the song reminds us that there were black cowboys out on that range and that they shared this life of toil and exploitation with white cowboys. "Kai kai yippee yippee yay," he tells us, with effect, but also wants us to know that he is not just a cowboy but a "poor Western cowboy." And in the midst of it all he points that he is not just a "poor Western cowboy," but also "a long way from home," and so, I would add, a black rounder extension of the more traditionally alienated poor boy, who was also black, alienated, and, like all African Americans, a very, very long way from home.

Leadbelly's brilliance lay in much more than his incredibly varied repertoire. His guitar playing was an independent rhythmic entity, a classically parallel second voice of the kind we hear regularly in recorded black music. As with many of his peers it does it little justice to call it an accompaniment. It is on something of a separate plane, as a kind of old-time, human click track, synchronized in CP time. And never mind that he *was* on exhibit, and increasingly so, in the early, liberal universe of musical preservationists. As with some other black men in the professional world of those days the Lomaxes were his white men (think Louis Armstrong and Joe Glaser, Duke Ellington and Irving Mills), as a kind of professional and social protectorate. Though in the end I would say that, with the Lomaxes, Leadbelly was more their shield than the other way around; thus was it ever with whites trying, in their own strange way, to do good.

The Lomaxes' collecting trips led to an incredible chain reaction of recorded 'heritage' pieces, though the truth was that these recordings were like time capsules that weren't really time capsules but just heretofore hidden (from some people) cultural mirror images reflecting the fluidity of black *and* white culture. Alan Lomax in particular had teams of avocational anthropologists under his sponsorship and that of the Library of Congress, and they seemed, in their travels, to have set off waves of impromptu cultural memory, much of it hidden in plain sight. If the subjects of many of these informal field sessions lacked cultural self consciousness, it is unlikely that they were unaware of what was going on in the world of radio, recordings and traveling entertainments. But there must have been something about the sudden appearance of these strangers in their midst, pulling recording contraptions out of the back of their cars, that set musicians off in ways they would not have been set off in more formal settings. The results ranged from an inflamed amateurism to inspired brilliance, all of the kind that leaves you wondering what the Lomaxes et al missed out there.

What they didn't miss were a number of black hillbilly musicians whose playing is a revelation, amazingly inventive and energetic, like **Blind Pete and Partner**, who recorded **Cackling Hen** on **9/27/34**. This group came from Mississippi. The peak of white hillbilly recording season had long since passed, but these two black men, on fiddle and guitar, play like they are in the middle of a fiddle contest. It is difficult to diagram performances like this historically; it is not out of the realm of possibility that players like this were so deeply a part of a racially shared musical tradition that they were as influenced *by* white musicians as white musicians were influenced by them. But I think that's an ass-backwards way to look at it, if you will excuse the expression. Such a view implies equal intent and influence, which may be true in terms of song choice, but the overwhelming signs, the instrumental timbres, the range of rhythmic motion, the sheer drive-from-the-depths (as opposed to the proto-white manner which led to bluegrass's peppy, tip-toeing accelerations) makes this sound black to the bone.

Listen to this closely; it is like a shredding of that white hillbilly tradition. We have many examples of this piece, or variations on it, in this collection, but this one explodes in our faces like no other. Listen to, at .20, the first falsetto-like stabbings of voice in counterpoint to the guitarist' precise scale manipulations, which both set the musical scene and react to it; the phrasing between .26 and .30, cannily out of tune, a discordant interlude which is basically a summary of (or variation on) the main phrase. And then a falsetto variation occurs at about .34, followed by some bow-stops and pizzicato plucking. The contrast is jarring and dynamic. This is dance music directly from the devil's lair, and the guitar's sudden intervention at 1:26 is like something of a pressure valve, pulling attention away from the fiddle's increasingly desperate, pulsing phrasing. The guitarist does this again at about 1:46, and we suddenly realize that all of this activity and variation are on a single chord, as it all starts to fade with various musical flourishes.

Who were these guys? In the absence of a black hillbilly Who's Who, suffice to say that they were two incredible musicians who recorded this music in a world in which they were anonymous and almost without legal/human status. 'Nuff said.

Or maybe not so anonymous. That black hillbilly lineage is only re-enforced by performances like **Ted's Stomp** by the black group **Louie Bluie and Ted Bogan (3/25/34)**, who are, basically, the Tennessee Chocolate Drops. See Volume 14 for an extensive discussion of this group, who continue with this performance to defy certain kinds of musical gravity. *Ted's Stomp* is really a race between fiddle and guitar, a two-voiced orchestra with textural variation after textural variation. The fiddle throws in a pizzicato section, and the guitar plays some of the most accurate bass lines you will hear in early country music. This is not soloing but a brilliantly-executed counterpoint, of the kind we are starting, in these years, to hear more frequently in country and pre-Bluegrass.

The mobility of these lines is another pointer in the direction of Bluegrass style by a black group, though we won't find this cited in Bluegrass histories, or country music histories, for that matter (or blues histories, from what I have seen, but that may be a different issue). Still it is significant, another sign that that grass was not always blue....

Black Country continues to march forward (or is it backwards?) with more field-research by Lomax and friends, in a recording of **Little Liza Jane** by **Wilson Stavin' Chain Jones & Group** (6/34). This is an absolutely fascinating performance, and argues either for black origins of *Little Liza Jane* or for the continued irrelevance of making such distinctions. Meaning: some white critics are fond of presenting American music as a black/white binary, generally emphasizing the African American side, but using aspects of repertoire as a way to "balance" things on the white side. But even if *Little Liza Jane* was bleached white at its origins (which is far from certain), a performance like this shows how dominant the genetic strain of black music, in all of its aspects (sound, rhythm, language), remained; even if the song was 2 parts white and 2 parts black at its source, in performance it became about 10 parts black. So it goes with a lot of music of the twentieth century.

There is evidence that *Liza Jane* may have dated back to the minstrel stage, since that was a common stage name for female characters in minstrel shows. If I had to take a guess I would suggest that somehow this was an appropriation of black sources, and if this is a guess it is based on the incredible linguistic forward motion of Stavin' Chain's version here (a *stavin' chain*, according to various sources, was used to hold Southern Prisoners together). There is a playful vitality and free-association here that distinguishes it from white Country performance, and yet there is nothing here that would make it anything other than *Country*. This was recorded in Louisiana, and from what I can hear Jones, to further confuse source and result, drops in some French phrases.

Musical influence ran in all directions in those days, and as dominant (and domineering) as black music feels, we ignore white folks at our own peril, as with Cajun music. Much as I often seem to end up arguing otherwise, the blues was a real game changer in vernacular music. It swept over folk sources like a tsunami of feeling, though it is hard, as always in vernacular music, to separate cause and effect. Was the blue impulse in Cajun song simply a response, in sonic terms, to everything around them or did the blues resonate because it was already so much a part of Cajun sound and source? Whatever else was happening, **Le Blues Du Petite Chien** by **Breaux Freres** (or the Breaux Brothers) **(10/9/34)**, recorded in the field by Alan Lomax, shows, along with *Little Liza Jane*, above, not only the brilliance in the "ordinary" that Lomax was looking for, but also that there was a method to Lomax's method. He was exploring the odd and old pathways of American music, to borrow a cliche, but he was also making important critical judgements about authenticity and quality. The depth of feeling in this *Little Dog Blues* and the eccentric way in which the blues harmony is stated directly at some points, implied at others (in a kind of Cajun pedal point), along with the high-beam, other-world intensity of the vocal, makes this the blues, outsourced.

**Harold and Hazel (Wait for Me, 1933)** were a (white) Country duo of a different kind. They were remarkable, vocally and instrumentally, though sadly I am unable to find any documentation of their lives, musical or otherwise, though an entry on Youtube does describe them as regulars on the Renfro Valley Barn Dance, a country radio show which started in Cincinnati in 1937.

We might first take a little time to discuss what an amazing musical city Cincinnati was, a hot bed of both black and white music (it was an early stop on the Underground Railroad), particularly as documented with fascinating detail by Lafcadio Hearn, a Greek immigrant/journalist who entered a common-law marriage with a black woman in that city. Hearn's accounts from the late 1800s of after-hours *black* music in the entertainment underground are some of the most graphic and culturally detailed that we have from that essential era. Black culture at this point is starting to wrestle with the constraints of the poly-minstrel era - meaning that the minstrel form, for all of its variety, was becoming too-heavy a coat of stylistic obligation, and was starting to be discarded in favor of less white-friendly sounds. The entertainments Hearn describes were essentially black and usually black-only, and they are full of the kind of unselfconscious, socially (for African Americans) escapist expression that served, for these laborers, as a racial pressure valve.

On the white side we know that the Midwest was also something of a haven for Country music.9 For me the duo of Hazel and Harold is a revelation. They are a sign of things to come in that music, of style and repertoire (ballads and blues). Hazel has a beautiful balladeer voice, rangy but down-home. Her phrasing and sense of pace is the very model of white Country soul, and it remains so original because it is its own independent tradition. *Wait for Me* has pre-echoes of great country singers like Margaret Lewis (*Reconsider Me, 1962*), whose long, flowing lines were tied together with a tight, flexible vibrato of the kind that Hazel uses so effortlessly. I don't know what happened to Hazel and Harold in later years, but they set a clear musical path; this is only 1933, and few if any singers were phrasing and posing musically in this way. And Harold, it should be mentioned, was a terrific guitarist. Find their version of *Blue Yodel (T For Texas)* (on Youtube) and hear his very advanced guitar playing, showing some of the most modern country chops of the time. 10

(White) Country music, like a lot of black music, had its own wrestling matches with tradition, especially since, by the middle 1930s, the pressures of commercial homogenization were starting to be felt with greater intensity all over the industry. Where cultural success goes money usually follows, and where money follows, conformity reigns - well, maybe not always, but most of the time. One look of New Country was in the dressing up of old-time song with new-time interpretation, sometimes in old-time formats, with Southern vocal twangs you could hang a coat on or blatant, even coarse, banjo strumming. This banjo sound was like the clucking of a chicken; add a male/female duo like **Lulu Belle and Scotty** (**Sugar Babe, 1935**) and you have the vocal equivalent of comedy. They always seem on the verge of breaking out into giggles of one kind or another. Is there an implied sarcasm to Lulu Belle's heavy Southern vocal tics? Yes, in the same way that the comedienne Minnie Pearl's stage persona made only gentle fun of the locals: always in a respectful way. White Southern performers of this genre based a lot of their humor on the hick prototype, in that Yankee-Doodle way. Still, the contrast between old and new,

---

[9] An excellent article on this largely under-documented regional side of the music: https://muse.jhu.edu/article/542876/pdf

[10] T for Texas: https://www.youtube.com/watch?v=BOYRvOKBQpY

city slick vs country cousin, was especially telling as the music stood poised to break out into mass popularity.

From time to time we come across a performer for whom we tend to check all the boxes; is it country or black vernacular music, minstrel song or vaudeville, Songster or pop, or even some kind of pre-jazz, played post-jazz? Well, all of the above; or so it goes with the guitarist/singer **Louis Lasky (How You Want Your Rollin' Done, 4/2/35)**.

Once again, as we say so often here, there is next to nothing available that tells us anything about this singer's life. We know he recorded on second guitar with Big Bill Broonzy, and internet scuttlebutt is that he was an influence on Broonzy (and not the other way around). Given that he appears to be an older performer, this is probably true. *How You Want Your Rollin' Done* is a blues, though it has an odd shape to it, like the head of a bluesman grafted onto the body of a Songster. Meaning, it is clearly blues-like, even country blues-like, in intent and even execution; but it has a different world view. I tend to think *minstrelsy* and *vaudeville* when I hear songs like this, signifying an audience participation that isn't, an imaginary call-and-response.

Rhythmically this is very sophisticated; the accompaniment is based on guitar lines repeated with little melodic variation. Its rhythmic feints, small changes in emphasis, little rhythmic bluffs, and then very emotionally-charged, sudden and idiomatic blues interjections, all make this into something very different from the old-time country blues. The way in which he varies the "meaning" of similar phrases by subtly altering their beginning and ending and by varying them rhythmically is very jazz-like, a method of variation that, just maybe, points to a place of jazz's origin.

From time to time in this study I have wavered in my definition of country music, aside from my idea of the music as one of "passive sophistication." Enough musical styles overlap to make that definition somewhat problematic, but certain things, black and white, leap out at me as fitting that designation precisely. I have described certain black religious recordings as evoking this feeling precisely, of passive sophistication, yes, but also a sense of originating and existing 'out there,' away from the more formal stages of urban life - and I continue to feel this way about incredible recordings like that of **I Feel Like Dyin' in this Army** as done by **Austin Coleman, Joe Washington, & Group (7/34)**. Another of the field recordings made by Lomax's troops, *I Feel Like Dyin' in this Army*, and a few others of the same, Ring-Shout type, are about as close as we will ever get to the primary sources of American vernacular music. So much of America's musical reality is in this recording - in it's transient emotions and rhythmic dynamics (that *hard 4* I am so fond of citing, with the occasional hand claps on the 2 and 4 offbeats, the odd rhythmic tug-of-war of the kind which we hear later on in some blues and in a lot of rock and roll, in which garden-variety syncopation is restrained by the heavier need to feel the *beat*, the down beat, at almost any cost). It is as though everything we hear in early and mid-century American music fed off of this form, musically and emotionally. This is Africa in America, Africa in action here, the proof that the Old world was more than just implied in the New.

The same ritual intensity is heard, of course, in this same group's **My Soul is a Witness**, recorded in the same year **(1934)**. Note in this the way in which the drum rhythm sounds like that of the classic rat-a-tat-tat, dotted eight and sixteenth, triplet-implying swing of the jazz ensemble's ride cymbal. I have never seen this cited before, and unless it is some kind of odd coincidence, it is an amazing equivalent to jazz practice that says more in its repetitive swing than a dozen contextualizations. **J'Ai Fair Tout Le Tour Du Pays** by **Jimmy Peters and the Ring Dance Singers (6/34)**, all French growl, with the drum beat in deep background, is more than a footnote to what we have been listening to, very much of the same kind of religious emotionalism. This is not garden-variety intensity but something that seems to originate in life itself. The strange but canny interaction of voices is another example of the double-voiced practice that I have cited before, which, in black music, becomes as much response and call as the other way around.

Throughout the history of American music we hear a lot of mimesis, as both copy and influence. In jazz we have Sonny Stitt and Paul Quinichette, in relation to Charlie Parker (Stitt) and Lester Young (Quinichette).[11] The difficulty sometimes is in distinguishing

---

[11] For those of you who are uncertain, Stitt was a saxophonist who artfully interpreted Charlie Parker through intense borrowing of one kind or another; Quinichette was a tenor saxophonist who eerily occupied a strange zone of Lester-Young-like being. He always sounds to me on those old records like Lester's ghost, prematurely and somewhat weakly achieving earthly, bodily form.

between the two - copy and influence - and then making dispassionate critical judgements based on that knowledge. Which also raises the question of whether or not, if you listened to a musician of whose pervasive influences you were unaware, and you judged that musician without knowledge of these influences, that would give your evaluation less validity.

Probably, maybe, but I am not exactly sure. Sound is sound; or is it? Like those art forgeries that sit in people's living rooms or on museum walls and make everyone happy, sometimes the appearance of reality is as good as reality itself. Or is it? If I turn in a novel that is, word-for-word, a reprint of *Catch 22*, have I have done my job? No, because there is no interpretive distance between reading something and then re-typing it. A creative forgery, on the other hand, seems to require, at certain levels, interpretive energy, even if that energy is expended in the service of a copy-cat effort. Same thing with jazz style, at least to some extent. A note is not a note unless it has sound and rhythm and resonance.

Case in point: **Larry Hensley**'s version of Blind Lemon Jefferson's **Matchbox Blues (1/25/34)**. Everybody (well, some people) knows this tune through versions by Carl Perkins (see Vol 28) and then, of course, the Beatles. Hensley's is certainly one of the best white "interpretations" I have heard of Lemon, though he does not have a lot of competition (there is also Clarence Green's *Johnson City Blues*, see Vol. 9, which is rougher and not a Jefferson tune, just a Jefferson-like performance, and so a bit different by comparison). Hensley is really a fine performer, and his version of this tune is actually very smooth in the manner of Lemon; even his vocal has a Lemon-esque quality, something of a relief from all the other white country bluesers who were still doing Jimmie Rodgers impersonations. Hensley's guitar playing is steady and his time is precise, just like Lemon's, though as with all such shadows there does appear to be something absent; maybe it's a matter of personal conviction, though there is nothing insincere about this. The lines, the luminous, dense chording, all add up to something very good, just on the other side of "real."

The ghost of Lemon also hovers over **Homer Callahan**'s **My Good Gal Has Thrown Me Down (8/17/34)**. Homer's guitar playing is a little more personal though not as effective as Hensley's. Whereas Hensley really and truly offers variation on certain classic blues vocal/instrumental intersections in terms of mood and continuity, Callahan's guitar playing, in keeping with the general tone of his work, is hit and miss and a bit random. This can work in blues terms, but unfortunately his playing has none of the static conviction of the heavy Southern bluesters, for whom such randomness, as instrumental/vocal counterpoint, was really a form of emotional organization. But I like Homer, whom we will also hear in Volume 18 with his brother (as, yes, the Callahan Brothers). He has a connection to the blues that Hensley lacks, a matter of not necessarily roughness (though that helps) but in the way he (and his brother) seem to be striving to present their own version of blues reality, elusive as it might be. The little pauses in this recording - like Lemon's in manner if not in effect - sound like sincere poses, as though he is trying to take a stand for the Southern White Blues.

**Stuart Hamblen** (**Sunshine Alley, 2/25/35**), a Texan, is considered one of the first singing radio cowboys. His father was a methodist preacher and he himself, after falling off the celebrity wagon, retreated from show business into the religion business (Religions Incorporated, anyone?). By the time he converted in 1963 at a Billie Graham rally (which Graham considered a great turning point for his crusade, as Hamblen was a huge radio celebrity and attracted many other potential converts) Hamblen had had a number of hits and appeared in films with the likes of Gene Autry and Roy Rogers. He was also a drunk, and saved by his conversion. In the meantime he had become a huge star, befriended by the likes of John Wayne, and had his songs done by some major mainstream singers. *Sunshine Alley* is a nice, early predictor of country's future, a mainstream ballad sung with gentle yet manly conviction; this may have been the first arena for the sensitive American male, a musical Burning Man for Country music's school of the natural ballad (soon to be co-opted and wrung - or sung - dry by Nashville). Was this a predictor of the whole Sensitive Man movement?

And I like it, and you might, too, if you can bury your prejudices about country sentimentality. The accompaniment is restrained and appropriate. He dreams of a place where all his troubles fade away, like Sunshine Alley, which is "brighter....because mammy's there; all is sunshine because my mammy's there." Take it as you will, but I am not quite sure what to make of that particular insert. It might have been a matter of commercial memory, reminding his radio listeners that, to coin a phrase, you could take the country out of Minstrelsy, but you couldn't, at least yet, take the Minstrelsy out of country.

One very bad thing in the age of downloads and streaming and reports of the death of the compact disc is that reissue programs seem to be reacting accordingly. The struggle to gather old material, restore it carefully, and then issue it in hard copy - on CDs - is resulting in less and less financial reward, and streaming services who gather older material when it is convenient - like Spotify, for one - tend to do so with little care or concern for source and sound. In other words, if they can find it floating around the cyber world, they can grab it and re-float it onto their services. And everybody knows that old music sounds old, scratchy and noisy and distorted; right? Well, if you are reading this you probably know better, that the golden age of compact reissue was a time in which sound restoration and source became, for a brief time, highest priority. Now, with some notable exception, it does not seems to pay off. Add to this the rise of cheap restoration software (including the heinous de-hiss that is now stalking the digital domain) and you have little mass reissue and instead small corners of collectors, too many of whom cannot discern, apparently, between something de-noised with care and clarity, and something simply de-noised. The result is a series of internet-posted performances that sound like they were drowned in the sink, gurglingly de-hissed and then abandoned like a young woman in a 19th century novel.

I mention all of this by way of the black Cajun singer and accordionist **Amede Ardoin**. Ardoin, who died in 1942 under somewhat indeterminate circumstances (more on that soon) and was the subject of a 2-CD reissue in 2011. Though his work had been reissued earlier, that 2011 compact disc seems to have caught the imagination of journalists, not all of whom are music specialists. His story is a complicated one, as we might expect of a black man playing music in the South in the early part of this century with both black and white musicians. Most hook-able was the story of his decline and death; he was most commonly described as having been the victim of a white beating that left him disabled and eventually led to his loss of capacity (he died in an asylum). What we do not know is if the story of the hate crime that supposedly destroyed his life is true or if, like the myth of Bessie Smith's supposed death because of rejection by a white hospital. The Smith story is false (she died at the side of a road after a car accident) and Ardoin is also said to have been hit by a car and/or suffered from venereal disease; at this stage of the game we will likely never know for sure. But it helped for the sake of sales of the reissue that his life and death had a tragic arc of one kind or another; I hope people also realized that he was a wonderful singer with a weeping, frost-bitten voice. He always sounded a bit lost, as though struggling with the geography of his own difficult life.

Ardoin teamed up for a series of recordings with the great Cajun fiddler **Dennis McGee** (see Vol. 12), with whom he recorded **Sunset** in **1934**. *Sunset* is filled with a pumping accordion whose bellows seems to provide the rhythm of the performance. Truthfully, I cannot find McGee on this record (if he is there he is not audible), but Ardoin, whose time is like a Cajun steamroller, finds the emotional sweet spot in the sound of his own desperation. *Sunset*, as I have seen it translated, seems to be about a singer confused by his own confusion - should he go after the girl he loves or should he return home to his parents? The song has an aimless quality which captures the circumstances perfectly. Vocally and rhythmically it is liked a controlled demolition that never sees ignition.[12]

All of which seems typical of a lot of black recordings of the first third or so of the 20 century. Emotions are on the edge but personal circumstances are shielded by practical considerations - because in the Jim Crow USA (North *and* South) all aspects of life are segregated. Even (or, really, especially) the psyche is part of that separate life; we know that black people rarely confide in white people about what is really on their minds, and for good reason. So is there any reason to believe that things are any different in the earliest records made by black musicians, many of whom seem to be shedding their own emotions as they go? And if so, does it matter that, as has been pointed out in so much of the literature, few black songs of the era are political in the usual, didactic, sense?

There certainly is a bluntness to early black, blues and post-blues, song, which ought to demand our (or, really, white) attention for the way in which it all, in the aggregate, comprises what may be the most accurate and detailed narrative we have of early 20th century black life. Sure, few African Americans of the

---

[12] This blog has some excellent discussion of Ardoin and other Cajun recordings: http://earlycajunmusic.blogspot.com/2017/01/sunset-amede-ardoin-dennis-mcgee.html

time, (particularly but not only in the South) were going to go on record in such a way that registered as political or even social (if there was a difference) protest, but singer after singer stepped up to that recording microphone and registered various kinds of complaint about and testimony on *life*, not as it looked from the outside, but as it really *was*, from the inside looking out. Love and sex, in this sense, become turbulent parallels - not metaphors, because this stuff was all too real on all levels of existence - to daily terror and uncertainty, to fear and expectation that the worst was always about to happen. When this is the prevailing mood in song, there is no need for political diagrams.

Take **Field Mouse Stomp** by **Minnie Wallace and her Night Hawks (1935)**. This is a diatribe, an unrelenting attack on a failed lover, delivered with rhythmic kinks and built on intense vocal and instrumental interactions. You are no good, she says, you are ugly and undependable, and nobody likes you. *Field Mouse Stomp* not a fable but a real thing, and as she sings it it becomes not just that real thing but also a narrative parallel to everything wrong that happens in (black) life - though even more important is that the essence of this message is communicated not just through lyric but in the instrumental, tonal and rhythmic counterpoint to Minnie's voice. All is mixed up in it, but in an organized way; there is a method and vision to this existential fusion of sound and thought. Frustration may be the focus of the song, but its point and purpose is immersion in life of one kind and another, highlighting, to paraphrase Beckett, the frustrated knowledge that *this* life will *always* be just one damn thing after another.

One of the nicest things about American vernacular music is that there appears to be, in its artistic hierarchy, room for just about everyone, no matter how strange the sound and approach. In more recent years the label of "outsider music" has become something of a designation for music that cannot be categorized easily, like "strange" music or any number of other sub-categories. If we go back in time we can find a number of performers who, especially in the early days of American recording, were outsiders, oddballs of sound. Take **Cliff Edwards** (or Ukulele Ike). We have spoken of him before and of his apprenticeship with another obvious outsider, the African American Ukulele player Bob Williams (see Vol. 4). Both men are hard to type, especially as regards the recordings they made in the early days of the profession. The comedic aspects of their work suggest minstrelsy and then, more particularly, vaudeville, though the rhythmic side, the sense of improvised eccentricity, suggests jazz by-way-of vaudeville. By **10/19/34**, when Edwards made a version of W.C. Handy's **St. Louis Blues**, he had appeared in 33 films, and so was more than just another weirdo. He was a star, and this recording reflects, not any diminution of his talents, but a more self-conscious sense of (commercial) production; hence the choral background. Still, Edwards seems to be rebelling here against any suggestion of domestication. The little asides in this, the spoken-word prompts, are not sarcastic or satirical ("don't let me ever hear you crackin' your knuckles against my door"). They are more reminders that Edwards was not just a singer but a recording *personality* and, more significantly, an ironist, always watching you watch him perform.

Just as far outside the norm - well, maybe more so - was **Peetie Wheatstraw and His Blue Blowers'** oddball, eccentric, and just plain thrilling, *unter-jazz* version of **Throw Me in the Alley (8/24/34)**. The first time I heard this recording I was puzzled yet amazed. I had not (and have not to this day) heard anything remotely like this on any other record. Is it jazz? Well, Hense Grundy, the trombonist, has a way with a phrase - he never plays more than about 3 or 4 different notes but seems to repeat them in more and more expressive ways; the fiddler is heavy on blues angles, and the pianist is nimble and light-afoot, and never really reveals what he can (or cannot) do. What *is* this music? Is it typical of some kind of early scene, of oddly limited yet ambitious jazz or would-be jazz musicians? Did anyone play like this in any venue of the day? Was this an offshoot of jug band music? Did these guys crossover, genre-wise? Peetie Wheetstraw himself, maligned by the occasional blues critic, was a prolific pianist/guitarist who made a lot of records in his day, even through the Depression, when the industry sagged. He was, apparently, extremely popular. Billed at times as "The Devil's Son-in-Law," his vocals were rough and untamed, an interesting bridge between the old-time country blues and the new-styled city ones. The new commercial blues was more of an off-the-cuff thing than the old, abandoning the detailed poetry of the older form in favor of glib paraphrase, fragmentations of the black/blues language, and well-worn but always topical takes on love, lust, and life. Certainly *Throw Me in the Alley* (the "alley" was the location of the most down-and-dirty realizations of life in all of its funky forms) is the most crazed kind of folk/professional fusion imaginable, a kind of new-city jazz from the days when folk memory could be of something that happened just a few years - or days - before.

Somewhere else in this study I wrote about the flipping of the influence script - about those times in which the influencers (and please, I am not talking about this is the 'contemporary,' three million followers on youtube/instagram/men's-room-wall sense) became the influenced. It doesn't take a lot of historical observation or knowledge to recognize this. I once wrote of American music as not so much a great melting pot as a great molting pot - in which musicians of all races, backgrounds, etc. sometimes shed their own skins in the search for creative ideas, audiences, and then money (where applicable). So it is with early Hawaiian performers, as an early world-music influence on discerning country musicians of both races and then a commercial force on the domestic front.

As with the **1935** Hawaiian version of **Stack-O-Lee Blues** by the western (far western) band of **King, Queen, and Jack**. If blues players early on recognized how well the slack-keyed twang of the steel guitar attached itself to the bent-tonalities of the blues, so did Hawaiian musicians realize that this tonality added another layer of expression (and commercial possibility) to their own music. Stack-O-Lee - or Stagolee, or whatever version of the title you prefer - is a well worn character of black folk mythology, who embodies the uprise of African American manhood against white hegemony and Supremacy. I will leave it to the academic folk out there to elaborate - just google the title and you will find entry-after-entry of both amateur theory and academic obfuscation on this commanding figure in black folklore. I will stick to the musical aspects of the song here, which are an effective pop-blues fusion. There are two soloists on this recording and the form is not strictly blues - as a matter of fact the chord changes in general not only remind me of Jimmie Rodgers *Waiting for a Train*, but the augmented chord dropped into the second bar gives this a pop-tune/Tin Pan Alley feel. Still, the blues-like tonal crevices are lovingly filled - listen at 1:00 for a falsetto-like interpolation that is, by itself and in contrast with what came before, a perfect emotional resolution.

In early pop-jazz those crevices are filled, when done so appropriately, without stylistic strain. As with **Hoagy Carmichael**, a pop-song composer at a time when that title did not necessarily mean separatist enforcement of musical boundaries. Of course he was a jazz lover who shadowed Bix Beiderbecke and his cohorts from gig-to-gig, and who incorporated many of Bix's ideas and phraseology into his own compositional ideas (but without fear of plagiarism; Carmichael was too original for that). **Moon Country**, recorded under Hoagy's leadership on **3/9/34**, is a perfect example of not only what the best jazz and popular music can and should be, but also an ingenious realization of white jazz, if you will pardon a qualification which is not actually meant to be a qualification. It was out of this lineage - from Bix and friends to the Swing era - that white jazz forged its own path, with an originality of purpose and execution that has suffered, to a great extent, critical neglect in the ensuing years. This was an original racial line-of-thought, and no less interesting or worthy - historically or aesthetically - for its tint (taint?) of White.

Certainly Dick Sudhalter, in his book *Lost Chords*, tried valiantly to resurrect this school of players, and his musical analysis was sharp and accurate. Unfortunately the whole enterprise was marred by his racially-skewed idea that jazz was a co-equal creation of black and white musicians, and by, in his defense of white players, his occasional and completely unnecessary aesthetic slurring of black musicians. Much of my own motivation in doing my own jazz history, *That Devilin' Tune*, was to devise a third way of writing jazz history, by a kind of aesthetic integration and by creating a racially proportionate picture of jazz.

But to get back to *Moon Country*, written by Carmichael with lyrics by Johnny Mercer: this is a perfectly calibrated performance, with Carmichael's smart vocal and gentle but passionate, real-jazz accompaniment. And there are some very interesting oddities here - Jimmy Dorsey's sub-tone clarinet, Red Norvo's strangely resonant and inventive xylophone solo, and, best of all, Tommy Dorsey's brilliant trumpet solo. This was an instrument Tommy soon abandoned entirely for trombone, but his playing, here and elsewhere, showed how real a *jazz* musician he was, in the years before he became a pop star of the Swing Era persuasion. His sounds comes under the Sign of the Bix, but it is instantly obvious that it's not Bix. Dorsey's quirky phrasing and rhythmic eccentricity - he is free of bar-line slavery and even seems to defy his rhythm section with half-bent notes and a constant stream of should-I-or-shouldn't-I ideas - wins out. His solo is the thing you want to turn to when you are in search of the Soul of White Folks.

The Jubilee imprint in black vocal quartet singing is smooth and soothing, but never let it be said that it represents any kind of aesthetic or emotional compromise. In the big picture of quartet singing critical and historical battles have raged over what, if anything, constitutes a watering-down of black style, and though there is a difference between the smooth soul of late Jubilee-style groups like the Golden Gates and upright-posturing groups like the Fisk Jubilee Singers - who represent a clear and conservative, cautious and legacy-favoring approach - they are all part of a specific if scattered lineage. The question, for me, is less racial "authenticity" than it is musical preference; in other words I would convert any such discussion into an aesthetic one, mindful as I am of the historical significance of the various gospel eras. And though I am less enamored of the Fisks - I actually prefer the smaller Fisk groups, who were recorded early on, to the larger, weightier, full choir - there is a continuum of soul in all of this which is notable. The smoother, more emotional Jubilee style which was passed on in musically meatier ways to groups like the **Southern University Quartet (I'm Troubled in Mind, 1/22/35)** still held a lot of life when this was recorded. A lot is implied in this performance, including what I referred to in Volume 1 as a Harlem Renaissance aesthetic, in its emulation of respectability: harmonies that rarely challenge the harmonic status quo, and a way of singing that *never* challenges the tonal status quo - as though this was a part of the ritual vocalization of faith. Certainly this was true of the most conservative performances of the Fisks, though through the stylistic mediation of groups like the Southern University Quartet - whose performance here is elegant and studied and pat and honest and moving - we get more commercial forms of back vocal singing, with groups like the Mills Brothers, with doo wop, and also in jazz, jazzy, and jivy singing groups, like **The Spirits of Rhythm (I'm Walkin' This Town, 9/4/34)**.

The Spirits included Leo Watson, soon to establish his credentials as the King of Jive (see Vol. 22). As it is easy to hear, groups like the Platters, 1950s hit makers, were listening closely, with an ear to mining this style and form for its ultimate commercial potential. Not that the Spirits weren't popular; *I'm Walkin' This Town* is smooth swing-pop, the jazz elements dropped in like punctuation. Check out their hip hipness - song interpolations (a piece of *Willow Weep for Me* at one point), a very swinging, creeping, fragmented tipple solo (the tipple was a

Spanish, guitar-like stringed instrument) and some of the grooving-est scat this side of the bebop years. That scat solo, presumably by Watson, is its own new language, of notes, words, word-notes, musical doggerel, sly references, and a bit of no-nonsense nonsense.

    I try to avoid the obvious when I write about the blues and other American musical asides, (I figure if my readers want the usual ideas, there are many other sources), but sometimes there are evolutionary aspects of the music that cannot be ignored. The piano/guitar team of **Leroy Carr and Scrapper Blackwell** has long been cited as representing an early and definitive change, from country-scented blues to city-scaped blues, tailored for black lives changed radically by migration and new forms of cultural resistance. There is no lack of down-home feeling in Carr and Blackwell's well-documented duo recordings, but as with a lot of other blues modernization it sounds very different from what we have become used. Carr and Blackwell are relaxed, easy-going, and have what is obviously an urban sophistication, but nothing is lacking in terms of feeling. Clarity does not necessarily mean slickness, professionalism is not a sign of weakness, and the blues remains a vernacular survivor. Through the entire history of American popular music and jazz the blues has stayed constant and resilient, has re-shaped itself with some regularity and resurfaced with new sounds - and yet has always remained identifiable.

    Carr and Blackwell's **I Believe I'll Make a Change (8/16/34)** is like a lethargic version of Robert Johnson's (see Vol. 18) iconic *Dust My Broom*. Neither player is a particularly compelling instrumentalist - Carr is functional on piano, Blackwell stiff and strangely old-fashioned on guitar - but it adds up to what might be described as the new after-hours blues template. Commercially it was more than viable, pointing as it did to a whole range of new, jazz-tinted blues, like early Nat Cole, Ray Charles, and Johnny Moore (see Vol. 23, 24) - all of whom were pushing the old-time blues toward the new-time Cool.

    After all these years, what is there left to say about **Art Tatum**, except to caution about the few voices out there who persist in trying to label his playing as coldly efficient, lacking in the kind of tactile soul that might otherwise make him sound funkier in a "jazz" way? I mention all of this because I find the suggestion that he is less than a feeling, functioning jazz musician to be beyond ridiculous. There are a number of people who have difficulty telling the difference between technical comprehensiveness and cold efficiency, and certainly Tatum challenges many of our assumptions about repetition and improvisation. As a musician myself I have often wondered what it would be like, as an improvisor, to have such god-like powers of conception and execution; Tatum is a clue as to what the right kind of perfection can sound like.

What makes him a great jazz musician and what distinguishes him from those who are merely brilliant technicians is the way in which he uses his massive musical powers to keep the listener off balance - in this way improvisation, even when based on set ideas, is similar to the illusionist's technique of always seeming on the verge of missing a cue but never doing so. But Tatum is more than a circus-like balancing act; that would make him much less interesting. He is a performer who has basically learned everything about the way he wants to play and decided to edit and then re-edit his self-directed re-compositions in increasingly layered and harmonically nuanced ways. In his hands rhythm is harmony, harmony is rhythm, and jazz - and the African American tradition from which it comes - is as much a method as a result.

We can gather all of this from Tatum's recording of **After You've Gone (8/24/34)**. This is an exhibition, a demonstration, a modernist reorganization of anything we might normally expect from this old pop tune (which even in 1934 had a substantial legacy). It is, like most of Tatum's work, a harmonic/structural rebuild, yet ingeniously retains all of its pop characteristics and its jazz feeling - which, yes, begs the question of what is jazz feeling, but as the man said, if you gotta ask....

# Chapter 18 The Minstrel Wound

There is something about the eight bar blues that seems to write itself. It is like the song-form version of the blues. Remember *Trouble in Mind*? Richard M. Jones' plaintive eight bar blues had real commercial impact, and in more ways than one.[13] In the realm of country we have the **Shelton Brothers** delivering an astute version of a different eight-bar blues, the Mississippi Sheiks' **Sitting on Top of the World (12/19/35)**. Not to be confused with *I'm Sitting on Top of the World* (a pop song made famous by Al Jolson), it has had wide circulation in rock and roll, blues, and country circles because it is so instantly memorable, in that eight-bar way. In more recent memory the band Cream Claptonized it, in 1969, and I am pretty certain that I have heard a Grateful Dead version. The Shelton Brothers, part of the new breed of country sound - sonically clean cut, part pop, very professional and technically proficient, with blues integrity and just a little bit jazzy (a preview of Western swing) were an extremely popular country band of the period 1930-1960. They were a part of an end and beginning - the end of the roughneck hillbilly tradition (not quite over but almost) and the beginning of country formula before the formula caught on enough to make it sound like a formula.

Part of that country "formula" was reflected in the development of a somewhat-new type of musical, post-Songster display style, done with neat technical proficiency. This new breed of vernacular musical professional played with what we might call deep musical empathy - the new music, unlike typical technical display pieces of old, had vernacular warmth and accessibility. A new school of folk/blues/country guitarist was emerging, of men who played with smart, slick linearity, of a kind that distinguished

---

[13] Richard M Jones was one of those "all over the place" guys of the early era of jazz and blues, a composer, bandleader, and record producer with a sharp business sense. He was African American, born in New Orleans, and led a band early on of which, it has been claimed, King Oliver was a member. In 1918 Jones moved to Chicago, where he came under the influence of Clarence Williams, which was probably both a good and bad thing. Williams was a shrewd businessman, a black survivor in the white business world, and he was smart enough and slick enough to do for himself. On the other hand, he was also known to steal copyrights.

them from other great virtuosos like Blind Lemon Jefferson and Gary Davis (shades of bluegrass, but more on that later).

**Carl Martin**, black guitarist, member of the Tennessee Chocolate Drops (see Vol. 14, 17) reflected what has been often called the Piedmont style, of ragtime-like finger picking, and his **Old Time Blues (7/27/35)** is a real back-country tune - and, once again, an eight bar blues. Was this format, a short-form blues, a musical move to the center for black players, encouraging as it did a crisper, "cleaner" sound, and one which may have reflected much closer musical ties between black and white musicians than some of the more subterranean, Delta-like blues forms? Certainly the tales of the Piedmont as they are told in stylistic terms encourage such a viewpoint. Carl Martin (who played and recorded into the 1970s) is a powerful musical force in this recording of *Old Time Blues*, a brilliant self accompanist, showy in a self-effacing way. This generation of black (and, we must remember, many white country) players played for what sounded like their own sheer enjoyment, having probably written off, in economic and historical terms, any possibility of legacy, in favor of just having the music as their own.

I hate to evoke the spirit of Forrest Gump; that movie was a little bit like the popular novel *The World According to Garp*: fun, entertaining, but a shallow appropriation of the symbols of philosophical reflection. Homilies aren't existential philosophy; they are Hallmark Cards shredded on the road to the Meaning of Life. Still, when it comes to (classic) country music and the need to discern racial origins, I have to say that country is as country does. If it sounds like country music it *is* country music, and sometimes in this collection, as I listen back and wonder just what I was thinking in deciding to use a specific recording, I find the need to treat the music as though it was part of a Blindfold Test in Downbeat: just listen to it, respond in an objective way, and don't worry whether it meets any particular test of authenticity or historical appropriateness (or even appropriation; but let's close that can of worms right now and seal it hermetically shut).

**Booker T. Sapps** and **Roger Matthews** were migrant workers in Florida recruited by someone in the Lomax gang to be recorded as a duo, and the few transcriptions they made have received relatively wide circulation (one report has Bob Dylan signing on as a fan). One citation describes them as "blues as played outside the recording studio" but I think that's not only insufficient but racially reductive. Their recording of **Po' Laz'us (6/35)** has as much in common with the odd modal mountain blues of Clarence Ashley and B.F. Shelton (see Vol. 7, 13) as it does with supposedly "blacker" blues forms. The single, not-quite-droning chord, the cry/twang of the vocal, and the glowing intensity reflect certain obvious (whiter) country attitudes, though the riff-like unisons (as at 2:22) turn that perspective inside out with black musical attitude and racially-specific rhythm. That description of them, as sounding like "blues as played outside the recording studio" shows, unfortunately, the limits of white racial and cultural imagination. Certainly this and the few other things they recorded - *Boot that Thing* is a perfect example - show, as we noted earlier with Blind Pete (see Vol. 17), that the intensity and relentlessness of black rhythm doesn't prevent country crossover, nor does it impose a categorical straitjacket on black musicians. Country not only is as country (or really a country musician) does, it also a separate space of the imagination, or maybe, more specifically, the conjoining center of a racial/cultural Venn diagram. It may also be relevant that, as Zora Neale Hurston has pointed out, there were in those days pockets of Florida real estate in which black people lived in relative peace with whites; any change in racial dynamics must have effected the music.

Black country music persisted even in the face of record companies that imposed certain kinds of categorical, racialist division. Still, there was a lot of racial overlap, even from as unlikely a source as **Big Joe Williams**. Williams, whose exploits during the folk revival were legendary (Mike Bloomfield wrote a book based on a trip he took with Williams, which was alternately enlightening, frightening, and terrifying, but ultimately quite educational for a young white kid, if something he did not want to experience twice), was the most organic of performers. Both his blues and country-like things seemed to spring from some gruff, wounded part of the soul, with an immediate and powerful presence, seemingly, by the sound of it, available on demand, not appearing to require the kind of pre-psyching that some performers need (and though it will remain unexplored here, maybe this is another useful way of distinguishing some black performance styles from some white; and though I sense that some will construe this as just another racist white interpretation and description of black art as racially primitive and instinctive, it is not. What I am speaking about is a deeper well of expression and style that is so ingrained in certain kinds of black life and so near the surface of certain kinds of black consciousness that it is recallable and summonable with relative ease and with quickly-amplified intensity; which in itself may be related to old Diasporan habits and post-African retentions that themselves are related to not only the manner of black expression but to its communal orientation. Black artists, in their creative life, I would suggest, did not have the kind of compartmentalization that white artists did; expression in sound and rhythm was much more an extension of daily life. And yes, I do think it was just this type of seemingly 'automatic' expression that was taken by white observers as a sign of black racial primitivism, of supposedly primal, untutored expression. Which is a problem that regularly occurred - and still occurs - when whites try to gauge and judge black sound and speech by white standards).

Which takes us to **Baby Please Don't Go**, which Big Joe recorded on **10/31/35**. This is blues-with-a view, unorthodox in its phrasing and similar to that 8 bar blues. Aside from the weirdly-jazzy ride-like cymbal sound of the washboard, this has that familiar country lope, a canter-like rhythm which, in its relative musical innocence, contrasts powerfully with Williams' gruff and no-nonsense delivery. This was a song that had a long and varied shelf life, and that popped up regularly in the 1960s folk and blues revival. The refrain, "baby please don't go down to New Orleans, you know I love you so," in its elongation of the final phrase, is very modern, and so it fit the new blues musical consciousness of the post-60s era with its tinge of rock and roll-like word/rhythm extension.

Country-wise the **Freeny Harmonizers**, more in the traditional country "pocket," were an abbreviated version of Freeny's Barn Dance band, whom Document Records says "came from the music-rich Central Mississippi area around Leake County, hailing from the community of Freeny outside Carthage." Document also describes the larger group (which was broken down into a trio on **10/20/35** for recording purposes) as a show band; certainly **Podunk Toddle**, recorded on that day, makes us yearn to have heard the bigger unit (which apparently included drums, piano, and horns) in all of its glory. *Podunk Toddle* is a constant delight of musical detail. Its sections evoke ragtime's dreamy variations, and its style is pure country string band; what leaps out at us is their technical grace. This is an old-style, pieced-together melodic tour that defies Fair Use (copyrights be damned). There is a seemingly endless supply of melody, an Ives-ian evocation of that outdoors-on-Sunday aesthetic, and a very smooth merging of different American musical grains, from ragtime's slightly funky fiddling double-time to the parlor-like sound of those airy, light-pop/classical-like themes.

And so the fiddle continues, even as the modern era of country music dawns, to carry not just the melodies of country music but the idea (and ideas). This is particularly true in a new generation of players like Arthur Smith who, in the same manner of bluegrass just a few year later, carried the burden of tradition forward with an expansion of ideas and technique. Wayne Erbsen, a musician and internet blogger, explains:

> "Before Arthur Smith came along, a country fiddler's main role in old-time music was playing for square dances. Except for playing a few waltzes, fiddlers mainly played what we call "hoedowns." Their fiddling was propelled along with a rhythmic bow stroke known as the "shuffle." To play this shuffle, the fiddler would make his bow go long-short-short or ONE, two, three, with the accent on the one. This heavy, rhythmic accent played by the bow arm goes back to the early days of frontier fiddling when the fiddler literally played the entire night for a square dance backed up, or "fortified," by nothing more than a jug of moonshine. By the time other instruments like guitar, banjo, and bass began providing rhythm behind the fiddle, the shuffle was so embedded in the tunes themselves, that most old-time fiddlers maintained the shuffle in their music.
>
> Arthur Smith changed all that. He let the back-up instruments provide the basic rhythm, and he simply glided along on top of the rhythm they provided. Although it sounds simple enough, this was a revolutionary new approach to fiddling. It meant that Smith's music was designed not for dancing, but for listening."[14]

Apparently **Arthur Smith (Fiddler's Dream, 1/22/35)** employed what has been called a "long bow" technique, and this long-stroke style produced not only a more flowing rhythm than the old, stroke/stroke as described by Erbsen but also an entirely different, more evenly-tempered sound. Think, of course, in this study, of the old, blues-based fiddle of people like the black Eddie Anthony or the white Earl Johnson, and of how in Arthur Smith's performance the sound of the instrument has been transformed through the stringed equivalent of clear enunciation. As with, say, a comparison of the New Orleans clarinet sound of George Lewis with the modern Swing Era tone of Benny Goodman, the

---

[14] https://nativeground.com/fiddlin-arthur-smith/

difference was, yes, related to training, but came more from cultural habit. Arthur Smith seems to have absorbed all of that old-school sound, and made of it a new kind of technical virtuosity. *Fiddler's Dream* is swift and elegant, unfussy and with feeling. And it swings, without jazz.

As opposed to Western Swing which, by 1935, is a reality, though no one is calling it by that name. To reiterate: Western Swing, to give as loose a definition as possible, was the result of a fusion between certain old time aspects of country music and certain aspects of new jazz, as divided between the Swing Era, the minstrel era, the pop-song era, the blues-era, and the hillbilly era. In its earliest days Western Swing was like a new form of string band music, which is why we have cited groups like the Shelton Brothers and the Lone Star Cowboys (see Vol. 16, 18) as, in musical terms, precursors of the style. To me the ideal of Western Swing is personified in country music's ragtime roots and in its sometimes halting ideas of solo and improvisation, especially as those ideas are filtered through the blues. One can hear Western Swing starting to happen in every white hillbilly shadowing of black style, in minstrel-song remnants, the new blues, and, finally, in early and jazz-like musical emissions.

One of the first and most important Western Swing Bands was **Milton Brown and his Brownies**. Interestingly, on **Down by the Ohio (1/35)**, as in the earliest rock and roll band (that of Elvis, yes, Elvis, and if you want to argue about it send me an email), there are no drums. There is a banjo playing the banjo equivalent of block chords, there is a steel guitar, whose twangy pinging echoes Hawaiian music and black slide playing, and there is a ritualistic, breakdown-type of rhythm. This particular song seems to be based on the old tune *Mama Don't Allow* and its variants. The solos, still very basic, are like a lot of early jazz, by musicians working to adapt to the rhythm with enough confidence to move past simple blues - and other pentatonic - gestures. Technically this music still has a ways, in jazz terms, to go. Feeling-wise, however, it is already there.[15] These guys had found a way in.

---

[15] As long as we are here I want to note that there is a biography of Milton Brown, well researched and written, which does not, to my great dismay, have a *single* word about the historical effects of black music and black musicians on Brown or Western Swing. And I mean it, there is not a single mention in the entire volume of anyone or anything African American. For that reason the book and its author shall remain nameless, though of course both are pretty easy to locate.

Or maybe their own way out. White country music in these years is still a communal gathering of like-minded individuals, people whose basic response to Jim Crow is to just continue to do what they do, in musical terms. Or, maybe, their response to the repressiveness of the Southern system was to find a method of liberation that didn't appear, at least on the surface, to threaten anyone (and it is true that such music, both black and white, though revolutionary it its overturn of aesthetic expectations and even in its subtle violation of professional racial covenants, was not, as far as I can tell, at least in these days, considered in any way to be a threat to the realm).

And yet - one might make the argument that, in increasingly revolutionary ways, black music was not only overtaking white but also that white music was willfully submitting itself to the whims of black ideas and culture. Yes, we know it has always been so, but to picture it in Southern terms in particular, and in the post-Reconstruction era, is to see a white population, even as it willfully submitted over and over again to social and political manipulation of the most classist and racist kind, taking oddly forbidden steps by acculturating with a vengeance to African American sound. Of course the progressive force of such action was felt only in the most subtle and politically ineffectual of ways - at least at first - though there is no way of telling exactly how or if the Civil Rights movement benefitted from the stealth takeover of white lives by black culture. Certainly African American ways of speaking and performing and living had long invaded the supposedly separate Southern social body, but in ways that still allowed for white deniability. There have been books written about this social movement, most concerned with rock and roll and the way in which it accelerated the acceptance of black music by white folks. But it is tempting, though maybe oversimplified, to compare such ways and means to the great aesthetic legacy of Germany in the few hundred years before the rise of Nazi-ism. Music and culture are nice, but they aren't a cure for racism.

So how do we get from Nazis to the quaint innocence of the **Cherokee Rambler's Magnolia Waltz (7/11/35)**? Damned if I know, but I love this charming piece of honky nostalgia, a three-step memory of life after the two-step.

Beg, steal, or borrow, white America in its country manifestation was still ready and happy to raid black music. You can take this in more than one way, if you want to rehash arguments about love and theft (the title of Eric Lott's book on minstrelsy and the way in which it reflected white exploitive admiration of black culture). With white singers treading on the blues in their own overly-careful but determinedly white ways, we might also call this Love and Thrift; as with **The Callahan Brothers**, natives of North Carolina. Their approach to a typical black song - **Somebody's Been Using That Thing (12/22/36)** - is relaxed, smarmy, leering, and funky. The song was written by Tampa Red (see Vol. 13, 25) and is classic hokum, from the school of double-entendre, like Tampa Red's *It's Tight Like That* and other similarly-titled trifles, all of which meant nothing and everything in particular. The Callahan Brothers and their friends would likely not have denied their sources, but they also would probably have claimed it was a Southern thing, musically as much a part of the world around them as segregation and garden-variety white supremacy.

Thinking about that last, I do wonder if it may be about time that we didn't just accept such white acculturation so casually, as though it was just another force - or accident - of nature. It is and was part of a racial/political dynamic that casts distortion all over our attempts at cultural history, though at the same time the recordings - particularly the white ones, like this one - do seem to occupy their own special space of denial and (what appears to be) benign and friendly acceptance of black mores. We shouldn't let it distort our musical evaluations either - the Callahan Brothers were good performers who went through the usual Jimmie Rodgers, blue-yodel stage and came out the other side, blue-eyed soulful. *Somebody's Been Using that Thing* is typical of the style. Mandolin and guitar maintain a quietly effective interaction, as a white call and response with bluegrass implications, and the brothers' drawling vocals are friendly reminders of the way in which such musical ideas were passed back and forth racially. Though we (meaning I) cannot help wondering, while listening to things like this, whether such apparent white passivity and helplessness in the face of Southern racial caste-ing was complicit or simply passive, and whether those, as responses, are actually distinguishable.

And yet, sucker that I am for a really blue piece of music, all my doubts and conflicts vanish when I listen to **Blues in the Bottle** by the white **Jimmy Revard and his Oklahoma Playboys (10/26/36)**. In Volume 1 of this book I made serious reference to the difference in the ways white and black groups handled slow tempos. The truth as I see it is that the slow, walking tempo was one which white groups in his era had the most difficulty emulating, and one that black musicians were able, for various reasons, to maintain with real swing.

By 1936 things are indeed changing due to atmospheric conditions, meaning that whites have learned a thing or two about such tempos. *Blues in the Bottle*, a well-known blues song with some common but effective couplets, was most famously recorded by Prince Albert Hunt's Texas Ramblers, a white country band with some notable pre-Western Swing ideas (see Vol. 9). Revard et al, on the other hand, are considered to be an actual Western Swing band. They are also a string band with old-time implications, but there is a slick professionalism in their delivery which pushes this into the modern commercial era. As with a lot of early Western Swing that slickness is disguised by a genuine sense of deep-funk phrasing and a delivery that is a mixture of sarcasm and eye-wink. This is all in the service of a new kind of blues (and one that has occurred already to black performers like Sonny Boy Williams on songs like *Good Morning Little School Girl*, not in this collection but easy to locate). The new blues is really a commercial expansion of the old, a turn away from the idea of the blues as a vessel of personal discovery, transformed it into something detached from the performer of record. The original country blues was also a format for existential protest; the new blues is more cordial, an invitation to the listener to join in the (sometimes sordid) festivities. Revard et al were the funkiest of white men, adept at this drooling tempo, and good soloists to boot. Revard's lead vocal is in that mouth-full-of-rocks, Southern-white vein, the fiddle solos and backgrounds are bluesy and slinky, and the stuttering steel guitar solo is a nod to (country) jazz.

A slightly lighter shade of pale were **Bill Boyd's Cowboy Ramblers**, whose recording of **Guess Who's in Town (10/27/36)** is also generally classified as Western Swing, though a quick listen tells us that, though Boyd shares certain common musical attitudes with Jimmy Revard (this has got rhythm, and the blues is always lurking around), the cowboy in him is more Saturday matinee than home-on-the-actual range. Boyd's bands are perfect examples of the middle-period of Western Swing. They are capable of good blues playing, but whereas Revard smells of the barrelhouse and late nights, Boyd and his boys seem to be looking for a more family-friendly venue, where their repertoire of Tin Pan Alley-like pop songs with ragtime-like chord progressions can be showcased along with light gospel (they even recorded a version of the minstrel piece *Poor Mourner* as *Poor Mona*) and solid-citizen forms of the blues (and other white-shaded offshoots). This is string band music with jazz overtones, a nice, mid-level guitar solo, good jazz piano in a funky, mobile way (something about this style of piano reminds me of things I heard Sammy Price play in New York in the '70s; Sammy, too, was a Texas musician), and a steady, even swing. This music cleaned up well.

Along the same trail we find the **Blue Ridge Playboys**, whose **Give Me My Money (11/36)** is amiable Swing in the Western manner. The singing is light and fluffy, in the same way that any number of jazz/pop recordings of the day featured throw-away vocals with pre-fab melodies. This is modest but real, performed with basic honesty and country-church faith; these guys are family men, but a lot more than just hobbyists. The fiddle solo swings like mad, and the guitar solo shows that the jazz bug has begun to spread (Charlie Christian was said to have sat in regularly with white bands like this, and there are a number of early amplified guitarists who are starting to sound like real improvisers). If you need any more proof of how rapidly things were changing, wait for the second violin solo near the end. This is first-rate jazz fiddling, modeling itself on country pentatonics and jazz swing. It's 1936, jazz violinists like Stuff Smith, Stephan Grappelli, and Eddie South are out and about, the jazz wind is blowing a lot of good.

    If you want to get the clearest possible picture of where country and blues intersect in technical terms, listen to the opening banjo passage of the black musician **Jimmy Strothers**' riveting version of the country staple **Cripple Creek (6/14/36)**. Strothers was a prisoner when Alan Lomax recorded him, and after his release seems to have vaporized into the mists of Southern blackness; in a region where African Americans, performers or not, were (literally) unschooled (poor facilities or *no* facilities), poorly documented (many could not locate such basic proof of existence as birth certificates) and hounded from birth to death by Jim Crow laws, white courts, and a generalized fear for their lives, it was not unusual for someone to just get lost.

But to the music: I once pointed out (in reference to the great black evangelist/guitarist Utah Smith, see Vol. 22) that the sound of the typical blues phrase was technically close to that of the typical country phrase in terms of interval and rhythmic spacing. Take a typical modern country phrase, stop and balance yourself on the flat 5 interval or the flat 3rd, or hang onto the plain 6th, and you have either a blues or a perfect fusion of country and blues guitar (depending on how you resolve it). It all depends on where you hang your tonal hat. Utah Smith, as a player who predicts the perfect storm of blues phrasing as it morphs into country phrasing and then points toward rock and roll guitar, was prophetic, and in his own way so is Strothers. His repertoire, in the black Songster way, was constantly varying, but *Cripple Creek* is very telling in terms of musical style and habit. That opening phrase starts as a country flag of sorts but then - at about .07 - he bends the note in a sudden, even slightly jarring, blues way; and then rips out a few classic country, or really mountain modal, blues phrases, predicting, as quite a few others did in those years, Bluegrass. At which point he simply goes on his musical way.

    The banjo is a dominant presence here, even, at around 30 seconds in, interrupting his voice. Is this, as I have already suggested a few times in this study, a very particular kind of black country music, in which an African American musician shows how, with that second musical voice constantly intervening (a recurring motif in black music) it can be done with just a bit more kick than in the average white band?

    Who can sing the blues? Muddy Waters once said that white folks could play it as with as much conviction as black folks but that when it came to singing they couldn't match the soul of black singers. I think Muddy had a point but that ultimately he was wrong; check out Jimmy Revard (above), all the hillbilly bluesters were have encountered in these two volumes, and even more than a few white rockers who had the nerve to stand before lots of (primarily) white people and let it rip with varying degrees of blues conviction. Johnny Winter, for one, had a voice like a lawnmower, and it worked (for me, at least). Mike Bloomfield worked a little too hard at the singing side of the blues, but he sounded so much like he believed in it what he was doing (though he apparently was quite insecure about his singing voice) that he pulled it off, somehow, even when it didn't exactly feel like he was pulling it off. (Bloomfield was so personally and musically honest that these qualities showed in almost everything he did, even when his work was not quite up to his abilities or potential; which was not, in my opinion, as often as it was said to be; I am one person who admires a lot of his later work, recorded well outside of the glare of the rock and roll spotlight).

    The point is that white men could sing the blues in the right circumstances. And, as it turns out, Cajun white men were particularly adept at it. Their music, with its basic harmonies and plaintive vocals, seemed a good fit. We heard Leo Soileau earlier (see Volume 13) and now we hear the accordionist-singer **Lawrence Walker**, whose pioneering use of the English language to sing the Cajun blues (**What's the Matter Now? 1936**) is much noted in histories of Cajun music. I hear this as very "traditional" sounding, though it is regularly cited as part of the new school of Cajun "swing;" though I'm damned if I understand why Ryan Brasseaux, in his book *Cajun Breakdown*, describes it as "experimental…Cajun swing," and points out, without argument, that the record company catalog described it as "blues with a touch of jazz and a flavor of hillbilly." While I agree that Walker's use of English in the song is significant (I would assume it was part of an attempt to appeal to a wider audience, though what it does instead is give the song a greater poignancy because of the awkwardness of his diction as juxtaposed with the complete blues conviction in his voice), I don't hear this performance as particularly "modern." Walker's Cajun cry (he was a Louisiana resident and rice farmer) is real, like an emotional 3-D; the most affecting blues performances, like this one, eliminate that third wall between performer and audience. Lawrence and his steadfast accordion, all alone in front of that recording mic, make this an unmediated weeper, and I think Muddy would have approved (and that academics should get out more).

    More to the Cajun blues point was **Les Bleues De Bosco** by **Fats' Raybo Ramblers, 8/10/35**. I don't know much (or really anything) about these guys, but they are essentially a Cajun Hillbilly string band. Yes they swing in their own way, but in the manner of the old-time musicians that they either *are,* or are emulating. This is far from a modern Cajun manifestation of jazz (though yes, there were Cajun string-type bands who were easily categorized as Western Swing); it is about as down-home a performance as you will ever hear in this idiom, though it is important not to damn it with faint praise (as in "good try fellas at adapting the country manner"). No, this is about as "real" a blues as you will ever know. Unlike Lawrence Walker they keep it in their own patois, so though we (well, I) never understand what they are saying, we understand the feeling, which is in the little vocal inflections and tics, in the backing ensemble, small but full of texture and fills. The plaintive fiddle, the somewhat dense, anarchic backing, all keep this grounded as a plain country style, though it is never archaic - which may be a sign of of a different kind of modernization of the Cajun form. For Brasseaux (above) modernization means the application of certain external elements like jazz, but to me the process is (literally) playing itself out quite differently. The Cajuns we are listening to from this middle period are carrying themselves into the modern era by *nationalizing* country music, after a fashion, by making country music an extension of their own Acadian accents.

And they have more in common with the **Dallas Jamboree Jug Band** - whose **Elm Street Woman Blues (9/20/35)** is seemingly washed of apparent "new" elements - than we might have assumed before we decided to compare the two performance. The first thing to notice is the beat, another steady 4, dampened, as with Fats' Raybo Ramblers, by what I like to call a low center of rhythmic gravity - sonically everything seems to grow from the ground up, from the steady foot-brushing (not necessarily stomping) of this group, who sound like they are forming something of a musical pyramid (like those cheerleader formations, impressive but a little unsteady). This is new and this is old. It's a jamboree band, after all, in celebration of a new era, like a parade group marching through the center of town (Juneteenth?). And after all, it *is* 1935, and there is something (or am I imagining it?) in the group's assertive manner which sounds as both hope and frustration, in the guitarist's brief but very contemporary-sounding blues fills and in his broad, floating chords, a clear sign of, musically-speaking, things to come. And yet topically it's still the same-old-same-old; someone is going to jail for no good reason. And overall, though this has a spirit and musical awareness that says otherwise, there is an overwhelming sense that the music - and this recording - are about all we will ever know about this band.

In **1936** the pianist **Meade Lux Lewis** did a remake - or really a reconstruction - of his 1928 piano hit **Honky Tonk Train Blues**. This was a good idea - his earlier version was done for Paramount Records, home of famously substandard pressings on poor materials (and then, of course, they discarded their masters, ensuring that no reissues would ever sound any better). Hence the issue, by that company, of 78rpm records that were noisy - frequently to the point of distraction - by any reproductive standard. Of course the medium probably is the message, and the sound of those early Paramounts really is part of their "meaning." A large part of the legend of early (usually black) performers is in their near non-existence (or invisibility as Ralph Ellison would attest), the lack of any documentation as to their lives and ways, and our struggle to understand not just what they were doing and playing and singing but why. Add a layer of noise to those old recordings that covers them like a screen blocking out the light and you get not myth (that would be potentially enlightening) but blankness. Who were they and what did they do before and after they recorded? There are some budding geniuses on those early Paramounts, and modern restoration techniques have helped us listen and understand.

Meade Lux Lewis' first recording of *Honky Tonk Train* was not only nearly-identical to its 1936 remake, it was an amazing sonic excavation, a matrix of black rhythms and spiritually ancient boogie and blues gestures. Listen for the stomping syncopations, the great triplets (not just eighth note but quarter note triplets, characteristic of Louis Armstrong's majestic solos as well, all over the place in this recording but with particular ecstatic emphasis after 2:00) and the signals Lewis was sending out that the new commercial fad of boogie woogie was just a few years and a rent party or two away. If African Americans really wanted to go back to Africa, this was a convenient alternative to Marcus Garvey.

Lewis' fellow pianist **Little Brother Montgomery** was more playful, a New Orleansian rhythm master who straddled a few different musical worlds. Apparently he played in jazz bands as well as blues groups, though their idea of jazz may have been different from ours. New Orleans in those days was a mess of song forms, and Montgomery wasn't an improviser in the sense that Jelly Roll Morton was, though they both shared a strong idea of the Latinate tinge and the usefulness of the clave rhythm. The clave represented a particularly powerful strain of New Orleans rhythm and music, and can be tied in with the (later) development of rock and roll. Its 3,3,2 line of subdivision was probably African-based and housed not just the classic, commercial Latin rhythms but also the eighth and quarter note triplets that led to the formulation of jazz's peculiar swing (see the discussion in Vol. 2 and 3 of jazz, swing, and its relation to Latin rhythms and Lionel Belasco).

Montgomery had a hard right hand with a beating left, and enough sense of harmony to play the Louisiana party circuit. It wasn't all blues for pros like him, and certainly the dance incentives laid down by bands in that day and in that region were sufficient to bridge any stylistic divide. His recording of **Farrish Street Jive (10/16/36)** is a *tour de force,* of rhythmic and musical gestures that sound like a summary of musical life in the first third of that New Orleans century. Listen for that loping 4 beat that must have inspired Fats Domino (see Vol. 25), and which I have repeatedly cited in this study as an oddball kind of rhythmic walk-and-feint, a steady but hesitant 4 that is directly related to rock and roll's particular kind of delayed syncopations. We also hear the precursor to Professor Longhair's (see Vol. 24) Latin stomp, some driving triplets, and more than a hint of ragtime. But then, at about .41 comes the arrival of some newer and astonishing things - first, in the left hand, a stride-like double timing of a boogie woogie figure, a cascading run in the right, and then a confusion of time and tempo, as though, all at once, Montgomery is filling up old musical spaces in order to leave room for new ones. This is an old-school display of virtuosity, a vernacular flag waver that leaves little in this relatively narrow - but fertile - musical world unreferenced. Things slow down, there is some relief offered with a sudden, breezy interlude (Willie the Lion Smith anyone?) and then the clave walk starts up again with rock and roll intensity. Montgomery brings it home with alternating boogie woogie and light (jazz) swing, before a closing section that seems to drop in a hint of Fats Waller. Was this a pre-modern form of post-modernism?

**The Stripling Brothers** are in the Country Music Hall of Fame. There is even a posted, recorded interview with the two brothers, Charlie and Ira, who died in 1966 and 1967 respectively. Their recording of the instrumental **Mayflower (3/12/36)** is described on various web sites as "traditional," and it certainly is, especially if we define *traditional* as something which, no matter how hard we try to discard it, won't let go of *us*. As I listen back to this recording I cannot quite remember why I included it in this collection, though don't take that as a rejection of the music's value. *Mayflower* is short and sweet, we might say, and musically clean (meaning lacking in loose ends or sharp edges). It would pass an extensive background check and clearly is an upstanding citizen of whatever early cultural world from which it came. The fiddle is plain but majestic, out there, in that modern, Arthur Smith-way, and its variations on the main melody are classics of old-time motif and development. How can you not like something like this, which has a welcoming quality and the kind of familiarity that doesn't require actual familiarity? Like a lot of this school of country instrumental it just sounds like it has been there the whole time, waiting for tradition-loving and history-laden folks like the Striplings to pull it out, like an old-shirt buried in a draw, almost but not quite lost beneath the newer things that we usually wear.

There are times when I feel like I need to patrol public forums like Facebook just to protect the world from the weird emissions of cultural disinformation that regularly appear. No big surprise, but such information often involves minstrelsy, which I have certainly beaten throughout this study like the (almost) dead horse that it is. A few years back a young millennial composer won a grant from a prestigious organization to produce a faux minstrel show, but one in which the performers (all black) sang to us in 21st century terms (because the composer had not a clue about the realities of the times or the performances that he was actually writing about). The songs were bizarre and laughable - "hey you know, even pickin' cotton is better than singing in this minstrel show" went one line (as I recall). Well, when I pointed out, on Facebook, to the young man who wrote it that the whole enterprise was historically inaccurate and in no way captured the complicated essence of the minstrel wound, I was told to "eat shit." This culinary response was, as I pointed out, not really a response, but I let it go at that.

So, some years pass, and I am reading the daily feed, and another expert Facebook witness tells us that he finally appreciates the minstrel singer **Emmett Miller** (see also Vol 4) and realizes that it was through the vessel of minstrelsy that "the blues" was introduced into country music.

Huh?

As I pointed out in there and then, the blues was introduced into country music by *the blues*, as we have seen over and over in this study; there were hundreds of white performances in the country idiom that were specifically in the blues format. And yes, minstrelsy was important to country music, but in much different ways. No response from the original poster.

Well, I still admire Miller and I still stand by minstrelsy as not just a symbol of America's great racial ambivalence but also as a chameleon-like form that has reproduced itself in so many ways as to resist any glib and singular characterization. Yes, it's an embarrassment, yes it's a racist manifestation of America's relentless urge to entertain itself at black people's (literal) expense, and yes, without it we would be, musically, a much different country (and world). Miller himself is a contradiction, a paradox, a charming void into which we might, as historians and critics, dump all of our racist history and racialist baggage. He is the one to blame, for without him and his strange and persistent recordings, which seem to surface no matter how much dead weight we attach to them before dumping them overboard, all would be racially calm and socially well in this country. Right? So he is convenient as an object of derision and even hate. But damn, he is also strangely hip; his phrasing is advanced and always places him on the right part of the beat, and he predicts the kind of sarcastic irony (redundant?) that has animated so much of modern American humor. And he swings. Really. **Anytime (9/1/36)** allows him to mix in a few of his patented yodels, and his Dixie accompaniment involves a few (white) jazz musicians slumming, but not really. So where are we in this argument? When white becomes black becomes white becomes black then we might as well face the fact that we no longer have any way of getting back to square one, or the option of even trying.

  On the other hand, I have to admit that listening to things like **Hittin' The Bottle Stomp** by the **Mississippi Jook Band (1/20/36)** is something of a relief after riding minstrelsy's bumpy mystery train. There is something about a lack of racial artifice and racial controversy that relaxes my ears and my sphincter at the same time. The Mississippi Jook Band was Blind Roosevelt Graves on guitar, his brother Uaroy on tambourine, and the pianist Cooney Vaughn. They build up a real head of steam on this recording. It has been suggested that the sound of this trio in this format was the real sound of the juke joint in those old and now-dead days, and who am I to question the wisdom of this observation? It would be interesting to hear Vaughn in more detail, but it probably doesn't matter. The power (and essence) of groups like this was in their collective momentum, in the anarchic power of relative musical simplicity. These musicians are what they are, to paraphrase a popular cliche; they wear their styles on their sleeves, there is no mystery to their musical sources and intentions. Unlike minstrels they wear no mask, real or figurative. They just stand up there and play with feeling.

  We can defend minstrelsy all day and all night, but it was not really successful, artistically, as a form until it was no longer needed, especially for black performers. Their liberation, won with finality by generations of black men and women, sounds in every note of *Hittin' the Bottle Stomp*. This was freedom, even in the shadow of Jim Crow and even under the watchful, jealous, venomous, and dangerous eyes of white men.

**The Reverend Gary Davis** was a central part of the 1960s folk revival, as a performer, teacher, and powerful, drunken relic of an old-time world of wanderlust, poverty and perpetual music. He performed, he taught, and he influenced a lot of budding folkies, and even some post-budding folkies like Dave Van Ronk, who talked and wrote about Davis constantly. Though Davis was a great singer, the central focus of the legend is his guitar playing and a repertoire, in the deep Songster tradition, that consisted of blues, ballads, marches, rags, some novelties, and lot of religious songs (at this point he was a street preacher). Like more than a few others of his generation who survived the wars (not the world wars but the race wars), by the time he stumbled into the 1960s and faced the new youth movement he was determined to set himself right with god; though he took a few odd turns on the way to doing so, with drunken sprees, the groping of young women, and by pulling out some of his own, and somewhat forbidden, secular repertoire.

Listening to him, from his earliest days, is also an adventure. I waver in my general admiration for Davis, from rapt attention at the interesting guitar figures he is often able to execute to a generalized frustration at his instrumental stiffness and more-than-occasional rhythmic stumbling. He was certainly more consistent in his younger days **(You Got to Go Down, 7/26/35)** but his playing makes me nervous - particularly the clipped notes and near-misses, technically speaking. I find Blind Blake, Mose Rager, Merle Travis, Carl Martin, Blind Boy Fuller and Robert Johnson all to be much more guitar-adept than Davis, though I realize that as I write those words I make myself a marked man. Gary Davis is that sacrosanct, and I don't enjoy chipping away at the legend. *You Got to Go Down* is Davis at full tilt - raggy if not necessary ragged, in the "Piedmont," East Coast, picked style, the Piedmont label a way of contrasting this school with the flailing, neo-Delta method of spooning guitar; and yet, Davis' time is a bit stilted, the internal call-and-response somewhat halting. He just doesn't swing to my ears and my internal clock and I am less impressed than some others by the lines he plays, which are not particularly adventurous or even that well-executed. In his later years he was even more inconsistent, but I will quit while I am behind, because historically he is central - a wandering minstrel (in the true sense of the word) and the real thing, to quote no one in particular but to go with the folk consensus. If you want to listen to him, find his work where it is focused and relaxed - but not too relaxed, if you know what I mean. And no matter what I think of him musically, spiritually he really was very, very, deep.

And at least I know exactly what to make of him, unlike the **Mississippi Mud Mashers**, whose **Moonglow (1/21/35)** (from the old pop tune) is a cosmic dose of slow steppin', quaint, morose vocalization by an African American vocal group who recorded for Bluebird (a subsidiary of Victor). Who are these guys? I can only guess on aural evidence, and truthfully, I don't have much of an idea. They fit into the line of black quartets (though yes, I know, there are five of them) and they have a certain sloppy formalism about them - the charm of the group is in the seemingly random way that they grasp at those old-white-pop lyrics (just as Louis Armstrong did) without a hint of either condescension or Old Man River irony/bitterness (also like Armstrong), and with no sense that they are doing anything but what they like to do. They sing what sound like random bass lines - but which are, of course, well rehearsed - and they phrase so far behind the beat that this may well have been recorded the day before. There are sudden vocal eruptions, as though someone or something has just startled them, followed by a slow descent into that old, sleep walk, rhythm. I spoke earlier about the way in which black performers used these kinds of rhythms - slow and deceptively submissive - as subterfuge, fitting certain nasty white images of African American inferiority; as a kind of cultural defense mechanism, a way of deceiving white people into feeling comfortable enough in their own skin to pay money to someone who was in a different skin.

Listen to those brass figures in the first minute or so of **Coquette** by the jazz band of **Boots and His Buddies (8/14/35)** and you'll get an idea of why I love jazz territory bands. These guys don't phrase together like the Basie band or the Ellington band - to pick just two iconic jazz organizations that have achieved both popular celebrity and musical recognition of the *serious* kind - and yet there is something so entirely satisfying in performances like this that sometimes I prefer listening to these "local" musicians. It's not that they didn't tour and receive some external recognition (they were from Texas), but that the reality of the territory band was that it was somewhat tied to its regional roots and so limited in terms of national exposure. If this sometimes implied a lesser degree of "professionalism," then so be it, because so much of the soul of American music lives in these itinerant gatherings of like-minded musicians. If they sometimes, in their phrasing, lacked synchronization, this was more than made for up by a coordination of spirit and purpose. Take those brass phrasings; in the context of a tune which was considered to be somewhat corny by jazz standards, those little turns and triplets become a declaration of melodramatic profundity.

This whole performance is the equivalent, maybe, of a B movie overcoming its own limitations to reach the level of art by the sheer force of its low-budget ambitions. The music breathes, even if not as one, and the syrupy sectional voicings swing, unlike those of some similar but different white bands (and we should mention that this band is black). And the trumpet solo, at 1:18, is like a final declaration of independence. Once again there is no hint of the band condescending to the material, no sense of ironic distancing.

It is sometimes difficult for those of us who think we occupy the liberal and progressive part of the political spectrum to understand that groups like these (as with the old denizens of the Black Minstrel Show) represent their own brand of national liberation music, as non-political as it was in the most direct of terms. Yes it was, in one important sense, political, because anything black musicians did to free themselves of white expectations was (is) political. But the actual moment, the moment of expression, is one of such pure feeling (listen to the way the sections interact here with the final great swelling of the ensemble at about 2:54) that it is representative of a level of black consciousness that, no matter how hard they try, white folks can never attain to. It is just too far outside the realm of white-defined political dynamics and cultural actions; or even some black-defined political dynamics and cultural actions (like those of Cornel West, who this morning, safely perched on his Harvard throne, was railing against liberals and seemed to be trying to foment his own idea of a post-modernist revolution; in other words, a revolution on paper). This was its own world, of *their* fathers, and *their* mothers.

Many years ago the late alto saxophonist Dave Schildkraut called me up and held the phone up against a hifi speaker at his end of the line. The music playing was that of **Lester Young**, from recording Young made in the 1950s, on an LP that was one of a number of bootlegs released of various air shots (radio broadcasts recorded by collectors). There were a lot of these records floating around when I was growing up, and in those pre-digital download days they were about the only way for us to learn about the essence of jazz, to hear what the music sounded like away from the relative formality and time-limits of recording studios. Dave sighed as a medium tempo recording, probably made in the early part of the 1950s, played. I heard a moaning, slow-motion swelling of sound, a saxophone that was skimming lightly over chord changes and rhythm section, with a tone that was heavenly. Dave put the phone back to his mouth and said "this is where I went to school."

And so it was with Lester Young, one of the deepest poets of jazz improvisation. There has a been a lot of debate about when he sounded the best, and though the general consensus is that Lester was at his peak in the earliest part of his recording career, and that his playing suffered somewhat after his time in the army (when he was courtmartialed and traumatized, a case of adding insult to insult for a black man as sensitive yet ultimately harmless as he was). The key, for me, is not that he was a better player in his later years - I think it's obvious that his glory days were those early days - but that his late playing, even as it reflected a clear decline in his physical prowess, showed an expanded world view and even a new musical consciousness. His late work sounded like survival in motion and in sound, like a man struggling to circumvent objects that constantly stood in his way. Which he did, not with the ease of his younger days, but rather with a type of musical cunning, rhythmic cleverness, and trickster-like avoidance of trouble. And, maybe most important of all, with a poetic beatitude that belied all his suffering and physical decline and determined self destruction.

The moral of the story? Listen to all of Lester Young, though for this study I have picked one of his formative recordings, made in a hotel on **10/9/36**, of **Shoeshine Boy**, with a gathering of some early modernists: Count Base (piano), Buck Clayton (trumpet), Walter Page (bass) and Jo Jones (drums). For the bigger picture I urge you to Google each of these men. For the smaller bigger picture just listen to this recording and try to imagine the revolution in jazz that they led, and in particular the work of Lester Young. If Louis Armstrong unleashed powerful new ideas and forces in American music, Young et al pushed the envelope of these ideas to the next artistic marker. Listen, to begin with, to the sudden accents played by Jo Jones starting at 1:00.

Hear the way in which Young's ideas seemingly skirt the acknowledged conventions of all the improvisers who came before him. Check out the way Basie, in his deep abstraction of the stride/ragtime tradition, escorts Lester in at the beginning with a classic-sounding blues riff, followed by a chorus that is both brilliantly-oblique introduction (in perfect musical balance) and, in a sudden, Tatumesque departure, off centered swing; followed by a perfect paraphrase of the essential melody. And then note how Basie accompanies throughout the tune with the hippest oom-pah chords you will ever hear. The ending is perfect, an accumulation of musical brilliance and off-handed (not diffident; we are talking about the real birth of the coll) meaning and feeling.

    I have been avoiding writing here about **Robert Johnson (Last Fair Deal Gone Down, 11/27/36)**, not because of any nervousness about the way in which some have tried to diminish his accomplishments and significance of late, but because it is difficult to say anything about him which has not already been said. Still, I stand before you discouraged and disheartened at the bandwagon effect (small as that bandwagon might be) caused by writers like Elijah Wald who, in his book *Escaping the Delta: Robert Johnson and the Invention of the Blues,* tries to tell us that we have over-exaggerated and over-emphasized Johnson's accomplishments and importance because the truth was, according to this view, that in his brief lifetime Johnson was little known or celebrated, and because his records did not sell particularly well. To counter this I will refer you, first of all, to Greil Marcus' *Mystery Train*, particularly the last and revised edition, which has an essential chapter on Johnson. As Greil (and others) have said, Robert Johnson was important because he was *important*; the music stands by itself, apart from market analysis and sales figures. I will add that the whole revisionist attempt to downgrade the significance of the early country blues is part of a degrading process that seems designed to ignore the blues as a counterculture of pervasive influence, of a kind that far outlived its relatively brief appearance in that Southern Jim Crow universe. The music has a shelf life of its own.

    I won't even mention the most obvious rock and roll repercussions, the commercial chain reaction that resulted from Johnson's rediscovery in the 1960s by players likes Eric Clapton and Keith Richards (oops, I mentioned it). Revisionists will say that this proves their point, that Johnson's historical emergence was after the (blues) fact. This is nonsense; it ignores the ambiguous way in which cause-and-effect, in cultural terms, function as both cause-and-effect and effect-and-cause. We hear Robert Johnson and absorb his musical lessons and re-apply them. But they are not being applied as either *cause* or *effect* for the first time, because our recognition of his technical accomplishments then leads us back to the days of his first recordings; from where we can clearly see that he was, from an artistic and stylistic sense, central to the transitions the country blues was making in the middle and late 1930s. So effect has become cause - we see what happened and we are forced to trace the effect back to the root (cause). And we see that Johnson was there first, his fierce wrestling with the blues form - a tangle with the Devil, we might add, oblivious as we remain to the mythical implications therein signified - a sign of the classic artist's struggle between present and past, between old, caked-on but fading realities and new visions and hallucinations.

Whether Robert Johnson had a line of disciples lined up to copy his every musical move (a la Charlie Parker) or not is beside the point. The professional world in which he emerged was not like that. It was still an oral culture of musical borrowing and theft and then some more borrowing, in which the ways of stylistic transmission were vague yet traceable (there are a *lot* of records and even some good primary testimony). We know, in basic terms, how that world operated both above and below ground (hence my sense of it as a counterculture), how its legal system made black men and women keep their distance from officialdom (because black life was itself a crime in those days) and that we cannot rely, in our usual white way, upon the normal means of cultural documentation in order to understand just what life and culture were, in those days in and in that place, like or about. As with the writer Bruno Schulz, who lived in a phantom zone between life and death in a Jewish-Polish ghetto before dying in a random yet inevitable way at the hand of a Nazi who murdered him with frightening indifference, Robert Johnson was here and then gone in a way that was both materially verifiable yet eternally mysterious; a death certificate is not real proof of life, and neither is a statement of sales figures. Life is what goes on after death, not in another world but in this one.

# Chapter 19 Religious Connotation

Years ago Dick Spottswood told me a story about watching **Bill Monroe** (mandolinist and the (somewhat) uncontested Father of Bluegrass) at a music festival, standing in rapt attention and listening to the blues singer Mississippi Fred McDowell. I always think of this as I try and navigate the various pathways and controversies of American vernacular song. If the writer Eric Lott refers to the black/white musical relationship as one of Love and Theft (the title of his book on minstrelsy), then this is a witnessing of the "love" part of that equation in action. I won't digress right here into the question of borrowing versus using versus appropriating versus everything else (this whole project is about those things, anyway), but I will note that Monroe is the perfect example of how the whole idea of tradition becomes less an idea than an ideal, obscured by the reality of day-to-day survival. That whole early world of country music (from which Monroe was birthed) was a place of working-class struggle, and it is only in comparison to the condition of black musicians that these white folks seem privileged. Monroe emerged from that same, Joe Dirt world, though the music he played, tinged by black song and songsters and the blue side of musical life, was like a new kind of white hillbilly striving, developed not as any conscious musical alternative but as a more independent cultural strain of white life.

Early on Bill Monroe teamed up with brother **Charlie Monroe**, and as the **Monroe Brothers** they might have, but for personal conflicts and sibling jealousies, together revolutionized country music. That was not to be, but their recordings, like **New River Train (2/17/36)**, are teeming with new life. If they didn't cause a revolution, they certainly predicted one. The vocals and harmonies are what would become the template for the country "high lonesome" sound (itself likely derived from the bottom part of the falsetto, yodel, blue yodel, and blues cry), and instrumentally they (actually Bill, on mandolin) launched a thousand virtuosos, with a new kind of call and response and the rapid deployment of the new, pre-bluegrass instrumental solo. This kind of solo was more brittle than the blues-based one, tense and tensile, and more strictly patterned on pentatonic scales (the flat third and seventh of the blues aura had seemingly disappeared, to reappear later on, as I suggested earlier in this study, in the country/blues fusion that led, with some inevitability, to rock and roll). We will hear more from Bill Monroe in Volume 21. His most acute distillation of certain blues elements, and then discarding of same, was still a few years away.

When I recently posted on Facebook about another post by a wannabe music historian who claimed that minstrelsy was the source of the blues in country music (see Vol, 18 and the citation on Emmett Miller), I noted that no, it wasn't minstrelsy that put the blues into country music, it was the *blues* that put the blues into country music. I asserted that there were literally hundreds of such white-blues hillbilly recordings, after which I was politely challenged to produce some examples, which I did, clearly to the interested surprise of a few observers. It doesn't take a scholar to figure out that if we want to find the real blues thing in the early world of American music we need to look South, which is what I did while writing this and what I have always done.

Of course, if you have read this far you know what I mean. There is a lot of blues in the white way among early American recording, not all of it strictly *country* or *rural* or *down-home* sounding (whichever designation you prefer). In my blues book and collection called *Really the Blues?* I included Al Bernard (see Vols. 2, 4) singing W.C. Handy's *Memphis Blues*, which is an entirely different musical animal altogether, though one I love. Bernard is more in the line of vaudeville blues, or maybe showtime blues, of the kind that bled out from the "let's put on a show" impulse in everything from the Little Rascals to various Mickey Rooney movies. Bernard the white blues man is contagiously enthusiastic in the way he does Handy's little anthem, which was one of the first tunes with a blues form to be copy-written (ca. 1912). Al was the kind of guy who sang the blues with a smiley face, and I can hardly fault him, so enthusiastic was he in the service of the minstrel facade - which of course then begs the question of whether that Facebook claim of minstrelsy and the blues was actually accurate (I don't think so, though in such things the truth often does reveal itself because someone is, as the saying goes, right for the wrong reasons).

As Miles Davis once said "the white folks have the blues so they can keep it," or something to that effect, and as usual Miles, in his off-handed way, was a fount of wisdom. The form was too catching, too glibly convenient, too musically inflationary (financially valuable and growing by the minute) to remain confined to any one commercial - or racial - niche. Early on there were other (than Bernard's) odd minstrel paraphrases of the blues (or really oddly-accurate minstrel paraphrases), in recordings like Lasses White's *Ni\*\*\*r Blues* (pardon the asterisks but I will not type that word), and Morton Harvey's early *Memphis Blues* (both are in my *Really the Blues?* collection), all interesting not just for what they tell us historically, but for how they present musically. The truth, no matter what you may have read on various web sites, is that we have no accurate chronology of the invention of the blues form (though I have speculated endlessly about it), and it is indeed possible (though I would say highly unlikely) that it originated in the work of professional songwriters. This is fun to contemplate for a minute or two, but I wouldn't spend too much time beyond that. The truth is that it was almost definitely invented in its folk form by journeymen - and women - musicians who put 2 and 2 together, harmonically, and got the blues (see Vol. 1 in this study for much of my semi-informed speculation on this); and then it was grabbed by pros who managed to be the first documented on paper and on recordings simply because record companies were hardly ever recording American black musicians - or really any true-folk musicians - in the early part of the 20th century.

Which leaves us with the white blues and its various professional and country mutations. I am regularly fascinated by the way certain early white singers do the blues, less in imitation of black singers than with their own version of white dialect, as a kind of smooth, neo-crooning, vocal massage (think Mose Allison in recent years). So it goes with **Jack Pierce**, white country singer who recorded **Soap Box Blues** on **9/36** as **Slim Mays**. The lyrics are a bit lightweight ("I got the soap box blues and I can't wash my hands") but the voice is very present and in-the-blues-moment, and the guitar playing is remarkable in a very jazz-like manner. The little riff-like fills are seamlessly integrated, and his jazzy chording is another thing altogether. It was, after all, 1936, jazz was a national music and Western Swing was popular. I don't know much if anything about Pierce - was he the same Jack Pierce who fiddled for the Tenneva Ramblers, a country string band from Bristol Tennessee, who briefly backed Jimmie Rodgers and who seemed to have included black-faced comedy in their musical routines? I don't know, but this recording is something of an historical shock to the system. It is like an indigenous, local, professional quirk, deep into the vernacular but too proficient for a hobbyist. And "Mays" is so sharply correct in every aspect of this performance that I wonder at his anonymity. But then there is this citation from the web site Discogs, which describes him as:

"Eugene Debs Mays, born September 7, 1913, died April 30, 1994."

And so now my curiosity is more than peaked. Maybe he's *not* a Southerner; for chrissakes he's named after a famous socialist, something which would not have made him popular in white Southern circles, had that region been his home. So for now we will just live with the recording(s), as a voice and guitar looking for a (historical) place to call home.

In his book *The Beautiful Music All Around Us: Field Recordings and the American Experience*, Stephen Wade includes a section on the fiddler **Luther Strong** and his recording of **Glory in the Meeting House (1937)**:

"In 1937 Luther Strong recorded "Glory in the Meetinghouse" as one of over two dozen fiddle tunes for the Library of Congress. His playing, long admired in his community, became revered nationally through these recordings, with "Glory" among them still regarded as a masterpiece of this idiom. According to his daughter Faye, when Luther played it for his neighbors, "Everybody was wild about it. It had such get up and go." "Glory" functioned not as a dance number, but as a virtuoso piece for listening. This was music made for music's sake. It required, Luther said, the skills that "make a fiddler." Luther's "Glory in the Meetinghouse" brings together the personal and the historical."

Though I could do without that last sentence (what recording or performance doesn't bring together the personal and the historical?) I do love this recording, which to me is not, as Wade describes it elsewhere with (what I think is) intended irony as "way behind his time." I think, for reasons I will state below, it is *exactly* of his time. I tend to find it a futile exercise to try and imagine music as it sounded in the years before it was sonically documented, though I myself often engage in such exercises. But I do so only while offering a disclaimer: we don't know anything for sure about what the music sounded like in its pre-recorded days, and any ideas we have should be approached with great caution. I would say that this especially applies when dealing with an old, traditional, country-modal piece like *Glory in the Meetinghouse*. Would it sound the same without having passed through the musical whirlwind of African America? Maybe. Maybe not; I tend to ascribe the intensity of white fiddling playing (and this is nothing if not intense) to the sometimes passing and often more-than-passing influence of black music making. Strong was from Kentucky so, even without biographical detail, we can assume he had contact with black musicians. But we also know that these white fiddle traditions had their own and independent cultural prerogatives, and it is a mistake to always try and extract black influence from white performance, as though this was a seamless kind of cultural fusion.

Ultimately this is all less important than Strong's great vernacular authority in this performance, his conversion (as his daughter attests) of what might have been a dance piece into a display piece, simply (or maybe not-so-simply) by the sheer strength of his musical presence, even in relative lo-fi. This leaps out at us, and is testimony to *white* cultural preservation and retention of technique and feeling, which we ignore at our own historical peril. After all, it was performances like these, in their 3-D-like sonics, that pushed a lot of vernacular music over the line of communal expression and into the realm of art, art forms, and of art-as-performance, or really performance-as-art.

Equally compelling but, for some reason, much less written about, is **John Rector**'s fiddle-through of **Old Dad (1937)**. This appears to be have been a Library of Congress recording though, surprisingly, John - not Alan - Lomax is listed on the Library of Congress registration card. John was in the field first (though he took young Alan with him), so he may have made a side trip or two while visiting prisons or herding cowboys. This inspires the same questions as the ones I asked about Luther Strong, about the rhythmic - and/or aesthetic - influence of black musicians even on white musicians who stayed within the fold. The best way to describe such fiddling might be as bold; for all the mountain modesty and stoic pride we have traced through the lives of country folk, a lot of assertive music came from up in those there hills (or was it from within those city walls? Or out of those country churches?). Once again we wonder what music like this might have sounded like in early and possibly more isolated times. One can only imagine the relationship of performer and audience in this; could that audience resist the urge to move in time to its old-style phrases? Did they gather around in the same way that the dancers gathered around the Basie band to not just dance to the music but also to watch the musicians who were making it? Virtuosity has always been admired in "local" musicians, but in different ways than, say, an audience might have admired the playing of Arturo Rubinstein or Vladamir Horowitz. Rector's was hands-on music, even when it was only *his* hands that were on it.

**Buddy Jones** might have agreed that black lives matter, if he could understand, I mean really understand, the question. He was a policeman in Shreveport, Louisiana, on the traffic squad, and if this calls forth to you images of "routine" traffic stops of people guilty of "driving while black" you are not alone. Never mind that so much of Jones' music and musical attitude was the sum of black music and black musicians. Surely white country players and singers like Jones exuded the kind of cultural confidence (for lack of a better designation) that filtered out any cultural self doubt or really any reason to question their own (racial) musical independence. It is not unusual to hear white country musicians of that era readily credit black musicians, though often it seems less like giving credit where due than staking a claim to black/white, social fraternity. In other words, yes, the white guys listened to the black guys, but they also felt that they were doing what came naturally. On some conscious level they were correct, and they even, in a parallel world, might have had the right to stake an uncontested claim to their own originality, if, that is, the post-Reconstruction atrocity of Jim Crow had never existed. But, as we know, it did.

This may be a lot to place on the shoulders of one lone country singer who was a friend of Jimmie Davis (later the segregationist governor of Louisiana), a steady and competent blues-like singer, and a musician whose Decca recordings not only predict the blues/pop fusion which, with some instrumental finesse, led to - or paralleled - Western Swing, but also stand as some of the most supremely relaxed of the post-hillbilly new country-hokum. Hokum - a kind of nonsense, humorous song-attitude with all sorts of sexual implication - goes deep in the black tradition, though for white folks, no strangers to bawdy tunes, the mood was usually more fraternity boy than street give-and take.

**She's Selling what She Used to Give Away,** which **Jones** recorded **9/21/38**, is witty and musical. I cannot confirm that the song has links to African American tradition, but the lyrics have a play to them that is similar to much of what we have heard in black blues and black vaudeville:

A redheaded gal lived down on the farm
She messed around but didn't mean no harm

She worked in the fields but didn't make no dough
Still held on to her hi-de-ho
And now she's selling, what she used to give away

She went to the city with a dollar or two
Soon found out that jobs were few
Her money gave out and her spirits went low
But she still held on to her hi-de-ho
And now she's selling what she used to give away

Well, things got better, then she wanted some more
She opened up a honky tonk right next door
Whiskey went up and beer went low
But she still held on to her hi-de-ho
And now she's selling what she used to give away

She started making money, selling gin and ale
The place was raided and she went to jail
She got out and was ready to go
Hangin' right on to her hi-de-ho
And now she's selling, what she used to give away
I mean, she's selling, what she used to give away

He sings it like he means it and he means it like he sings it, if I may be so glib, but then, that is also the new country, getting past the drunken hillbilly vibe to the serious business of near-jazz; just listen to the great steel guitarist **Bob Dunn,** whose skittering solo pauses for a little rip at 1:18 (shades of, yes, Bix Beiderbecke) and who then drops some intervals at around 1:24 that further proves that he's been listening to a lot more than country music (or Western Swing). Dunn was a brilliant autodidact who constructed his own amplifiers and built a style out Charlie Christian and raw musical instinct. All the while Jones sings with an odd, detached, passivity, like he's more spectator than participant.

But then, country was starting to accommodate a number of new things and attitudes in those years just before the War, like **The Sons of the Pioneers**, described as a "Western singing group" by Wikipedia, which works for me. By image the country of the country was expanding, Westward (and Midwest-ward) ho. All kinds of new post-hillbilly scenes began to rise up through the war and post war years, and the new professionalism of groups like the Pioneers was tied in, by necessity, to expanding media possibilities (including film) and mass distribution of recordings. Having a hit was starting to mean having an actual *hit* instead of just a regional marker.

The Pioneers were pop, but they were also gospel of the near-minstrel kind, meaning those kind of tunes written by song writers who dug a shallow musical hole and tossed the remains of old-time spirituals and hymns into it so they could mix and match. The pros polished up the old god-kit and put it out there, and groups like this rose to the occasion with deep, mannerly harmonies, and real feeling in spite of it all. **One More River (12/14/37)** is a perfect example of this type of movie song-of-the-range; god-recognizing but not god-fearing (that would be a bit too heavy for movie audiences). If you can't smell the campfire smoke in this then you are not standing close enough. It is also respectful and pious in its religious connotations, though musically agnostic: like a stealth piece of jazz it also swings; the rhythm guitar playing is supple, there's a nice little instrumental solo, and above it all floats one of my favorite faux-cowboy voices, that of Leonard "Roy Rogers" Slye. Roy always had a nice voice with good time, gave off a low-hanging emotional flame, and possessed a glowing persona that made you feel like he was your friend. Which he was, as his numerous kindnesses to his fans in later years attest. The result for Roy was movie and television stardom and, for the music, a new niche for country, built around Tin Pan Alley skies, Southwestern rhythm, and the new Middle Class Cowboy.

A lot less solicitous but a lot more stoned was **Smokey Wood**, whose **Everybody's Truckin' (3/1/37),** with a cordial leer and easy swing, covered up, maybe, the smell of marijuana smoke and the odor of wise-ass. Around the internet Wood is described variously, but most accurately, as "the Houston Hipster" (note that the old-days definition of the term hipster differs quite radically from our current-day definition, meaning that the old-style hipster was actually hip. To paraphrase - very loosely - Eddie Condon, they didn't wear their jeans, they wore 'em out). How could you not love a guy who would, in the words of one band member, "stay high all the time – sleep in the bus and spend his money on pot." [16]

Smokey was legendary, an excellent pianist ("better than Moon Mullican" claimed a former band member, referring to Western Swing's best-known keyboard player). He marched to a different parade of drummers, and was fiercely independent in an authentic way - he actually lived the life, on the outer frequencies, drinking and smoking incessantly. At first he toured regularly (his

---

[16] https://myweb.uiowa.edu/jwolcott/Smokey/smokey.htm

band was one of the finest in Western Swing) and then settled into occupations from musical sideman to flea market organizer, all before alcohol caught up with him.

At his death the former star, once thin as a rail, weighed 250 bounds. But he did leave a very distinguished series of recordings, some of the most swinging of that era. Though initially categorized as *hillbilly* in record catalogs (they were, after all, white folks from way-out-there), the band was more interested in jazz as jazz and less as string band music. This signaled a major change in the direction of Western Swing, and recordings like *Truckin'* were declarations of these musicians' intent. I might make the argument that in certain ways the form was a more radical twist on *jazz* than a lot of Swing Era music labeled as same. At least on recordings, many such Western swing tunes were not driven by drums but by the dense accumulation of rhythm, and they swung like mad. Plus, *Everybody's Truckin',* with an irresistible twist, had the added "truckin', fuckin'" as a subversive refrain. Such violations were inevitable when the music's most worthy constituents were so damned high and happy.

Equally hip, though nobody left standing knows or remembers why, were the **Alabama Boys**, who don't seem to exist anymore (I can find no reference to them either in books or on the internet), and whose version of **Frankie and Johnny (1937)** is off to the country jazz, or, really Western Swing, races. Clearly a white group, and by sonic outline a Western Swing group, they wring this format for all it's worth. Most musically satisfying are the varied ways in which this recording distorts. We should be glad that some recording engineer, trying to keep the sound out of the red, didn't sit on these guys to moderate their approach. Someone must have figured it was ok to just let 'em rip. The result is very satisfying. The vocal, piano, and fiddle are all fine, but listen especially to the guitar as he goes sharply though his Charlie Christian-like paces. First he bombs his way through the background and then, at about .54, he spits out some very advanced swing phrases, ending with a few chromatically-based ideas that flip the song over onto its back. There's a nicely shouted ending by the singer, which ends the song somewhere very far away from where it started. In non-musical terms this is the *real thing,* that part of country music that was, in those pre-honky tonk days, increasingly defiant and carelessly creative, daring anyone to put the wraps on it.

Country music was on the march and not to be stopped, no matter which direction it came from. Further along the Western Swing front were **Cliff Bruner's Texas Wanderers**, whose **Milk Cow Blues (2/5/37)** was a pointed variation on Kokomo Arnold's blues standard. Note how this band gets the rhythm right; that slow musical march to the sea was now solidly in the domain of *Western white band*. Bruner's fiddle solos are state-of-the-art, expertly phrased, professional presented, and yet completely spontaneous-sounding and tinged with an unmistakable blues/jazz edge. Listen to his budding fiddle chords at 2:12, they way he breaks through the ensemble. This was the new soloist's art, built, in some ways, more on the big band model than the small.

These guys *got* the music (which is not a surprise, as this new professional class of country-swing musicians was now peppered throughout the West and Southwest, professionally speaking, touring and hitting radio and playing for larger and larger crowds). This was the new jazz swing band writ small, but only in terms of presentation. In terms of musical fluency they were, in old-time country patois, the last men standing, observing old-time values in new-time words and music.

New and old, however, are often hard to separate, not just as values but as qualities, cultural and musical. As I have noted in various parts of this study, the pentatonic intervals of country music were just adjacent to the pentatonic intervals of the blues, meaning that a quick adjustment of certain notes, a half musical step here and a half musical step there, could easily turn one into the other. To repeat myself, listen to Utah Smith (see Vol. 22) among others - the fusion of guitar lines was perhaps inevitable as the music spread. This approach linked the modern country style of solo playing, Western Swing, Bluegrass, and even the blues, as retrofit in **Bill Carlisle**'s **Bell Clappin' Mama (2/16/37)**. Carlisle is a classic, historic anomaly, an innovator who probably is not nearly as well recognized as he should be because he lived long enough to stop being an innovator, to become just another face in the musical crowd (he played at the Opry right up until his death at age 95 in 2003). Familiarity doesn't necessarily breed contempt, but it inevitably breeds the kind of passive acceptance that an early death, preferably at the height of creativity, (Hank Williams and Charlie Parker anyone?) discourages. Yes, there are exceptions, but country music is of the kind that tends to bond audience and performer in such ways as to discourage old favorites from taking real artistic chances. Wanna push the envelope, do something different? Well, that sound you hear is the sound of millions and millions of radios being switched off.

Sometimes, however, musical radicalism sneaks in under the cover of a smug, ironic attitude and great technique. Carlisle's *Bell Clappin' Mama*, subjectively typical, about woman-trouble, comes at us with deft finger-style, and blues harmony that is violated by the clipped, flat picked, guitar lines he plays. As has been pointed out elsewhere, this is Bluegrass in more than embryo, and it stands out particularly in relief. It is also the blues in a new country way, galloping through the changes, in the hammered-style, a race, historically, against (blues) time.

Still, time and tradition continued to be on country's side, a close companion when times were hard. I was always taken by a recording Lomax et al made in Kentucky of the banjo player **Pete Steele**, of **Coal Creek March (3/29/38)**. This song comes under the large and sometimes suffocating cloak of tradition - as Charles Wolfe wrote about it, "it is doubtful….if anyone will ever be able to write a complete history of this number's complex transmission." So I won't even try, though Charles, a smart, good guy who died much too young, did work valiantly to get to the bottom of it all.

Let's quote Charles' article which, with its somewhat surprising (for those of us with certain assumptions about the South and its political history) political angle, should be read by anyone out there with even the mildest curiosity about Southern labor history:

> "The Coal Creek March"…is one of a number of songs centering on the troubles at the small mining town of Coal Creek in eastern Tennessee, during the late 19th century. These troubles included a bloody labor dispute as well as a series of mine disasters. The labor dispute was in essence a rebellion by newly unionized miners against Tennessee's convict-lease system; for two years the miners fought a sort of guerrilla war against the Tennessee state militia before the state finally ended the convict-lease system." [17]

Yes, it's amazing what these white folks can do when they put their minds to it. In his rendition Steele, a carpenter who spent time in the mines, plays what we can only guess were certain, but not all, sections of the piece. He also, in later years, characterized it as being a memorial to those who had died for the cause, but

---

[17] Jonathan Memorial Foundation Quarterly Newsletter, Spring 1976

avoided detailing the song's complete political history (for reasons that Charles speculates are related to his audience's lack of memory; I do wonder if Steele just didn't wanted to stir up any new pots). Steels's rendition, aided by the way the room in which he recorded sounded (because, as I have always maintained, acoustics are history too), is notable for its rapid repetitions, its arching melodies, and sheer accuracy. This, in its vivid musical portrayal, caught a lot of imaginations in the years between its recording and the folk-reset of the 1960s, for purely musical reasons, and it took sharp observers like Charles Wolfe to restore it in historical terms. Who says music ain't political?

Well, I usually do; music is social, music is technical, music is a hobby, a profession, an art form, a private activity, a public display. One gets the feeling that country music is all of that, at the same time if in different places. Normally I would use this opportunity to point out that in African American music the lines between performer and audience are often blurred, and that this is one of the things that makes so much of (African) American music so special. It is utilitarian and it is on display for paid consideration, as an occasional art form which you can buy for well under twenty dollars. But the truth is that (white) country music has many of the same characteristics and virtues. And on occasion there are musicians whose lifetime achievements are so devoid of scandal and whose humanity is so clearly on display in their music that personal dignity itself becomes an aspect of their work.

**Wade Mainer** lived to 104, performed for Franklin Roosevelt, recorded in very different eras, and rescued the so-called tradition from preservationists. I am not completely disparaging museum-like musical approaches like that of Buell Kazee (see Vol. 10), but Mainer is a perfect example of how to not just gather the spirit of old time music but to inhabit it, though it does help of course if, like Mainer, you are essentially a primary source. His recording of **Little Maggie (8/2/37** with **Zeke Morris)** is a case in point: this song has been done many times in the country world (by the Stanley Brothers, among others) and it is like a long-meter mountain idle. In a Venn diagram of American music, a song like *Little Maggie*, in the format of what has been called the mountain blues (because of the sad, sluggish droning of their inevitable minor keys and the the way in which the intervals of their melodies arc like blues tones, circular and with very basic, one-chord resolution) would intersect with certain kinds of black sound without representing a direct lift. I tend to think that no matter how independent white song-making was during its recorded and pre-recorded history, it needed the sound of black music to re-animate it, to take it out of the doldrums of the parlor. Still, and given the inevitable cultural crosstalk, singers and instrumentalists like Mainer (who gave it all up when he got religion, and only returned to the stage, late in his life, to sing gospel music) were here and then not really gone, even after the commercial world of country lost track and interest.

Wade's brother J.E. was very much cut from the same homey quilt and his repertoire was very much a songster's repertoire, a mix of home and minstrel favorites and various other music independently outsourced. Or was it? When you hear a title like **Watermelon on the Vine (J.E. Mainer's Mountaineers 6/15/36)** you tend to cringe by reason of its potential racial reference, but the song itself is not quite what you think it will be. Or it is, depending on your point of view. The Traditional Tune Archive tells us that "the song was written by Thomas P. Westendorf as "The Watermelon Smiling on the Vine," copyrighted in 1882." And that it was performed by numerous country performers. Westendorf was white (he lived 1848-1923, was born in Virginia, raised in Chicago, and became a band instructor in Indiana), but we can hear that he had his ear to the ground in places where there were perhaps some people of color. The lines, second hand or not, put the singer in character as a black man, with the same attitude portrayed as that in *Ham Beats All Meat* (see Vol. 8): white folks think they are so damned smart but they don't see the world right in front of them or, in this case, the delicious low-hanging fruit:

> "White folks say I'm foolish
> they should have lots of sense
> or they wouldn't leave it (watermelon)
> hangin' on that vine"

The group harmony is broad and wide and there isn't a truly racist line in the song. Is this minstrelsy lite, or just a line of minstrel cultural query of the kind that showed, on rare occasions, its benign side?

The **Dixon Brothers**, Dorsey and Howard, were like laboratory examples of the conditions that sometimes lead to vernacular expression of the most profound kind. Though the

American vernacular is without social rules of predestination, it is not unusual in the earliest days of the music (as recorded, I mean) to see certain kinds of social friction producing some very specific kinds of real art, in the form of sound and song. So it was with Southern working class culture; even when the songs were not strictly about that suffering, or about the politics of that suffering, they were about the things that led to or out of such suffering, or that transcended such suffering, or, on occasion, avoided such suffering. So while I have regularly argued that music in its final form is *not* political - even if politics led to its composition and performance - it still *lives* in a world of politics.

The Dixon Brothers were products of the South Carolina mills; or were the South Carolina mills the products of people like the Dixon Brothers? The Dixons were in and out of those mills their whole lives (one of them actually moved to New Jersey in the late 1940s for work but soon turned around and went back home). Dorsey was a particularly facile songwriter, and one of his tunes, *Wreck on the Highway*, became a big hit for Roy Acuff, though Dorsey was only paid after filing a lawsuit (which was somewhat successful, though it did not lead to long-term royalties). **Weave Room Blues (2/12/36)** is an amiable piece of labor history, strangely lacking in the kind of urgency one might expect, given the difficult conditions it describes. Unlike with Wilmer Watts, a fellow laborer whose song *Been on the Job Too Long* describes working class anger, frustration, and violence, *Weave Room* Blues has a gentle and fable-like quality that comes primarily from the singers themselves. The lyrics are appropriately desperate:

> Trying to make a living, but I'm thinking I will lose,
> For I'm sent a-dying with them weave-room blues.
>
> Slam-outs, break-outs, knot-ups by the score,
> Cloth all rolled back and piled up in the floor;
> The harness eyes are breaking, strings are hanging
> to your shoes,
> We're simply dying with them weave-room blues

…and the performance is strangely calm, its harmonies translucent in that country-brother team way.

And then there are those odd, off-recordings that are some of the above, the "above" being all of our previous entries - blues, Western Swing, Hawaiian, jazz, minstrel, country, and, most of all, strange. Like the **Rhythm Wreckers' Never No Mo' Blues (1937)**, which first of all puts me in mind of that crazy black-faced white man, the minstreler Emmett Miller (see Vol. 4. 18), he of the disreputable Southern breeze that blew in from the Antebellum era, with the scent of traveling white troupes in black face and then, later, medicine shows, full of insurgents applying the same kind of makeup. I have talked a lot about minstrelsy in this study, and I have tried to balance the positive with the negative, the negative with its ways and means, social, artistic, and commercial. For some of us minstrelsy remains an imaginative construct, a means by which white performers summoned certain kinds of performance personas. Which is accurate as far as it goes, though it has also been asserted with some degree of credibility that minstrelsy also reflected honest and earnest folkloric ideals of crossover culture.

Some days I think I know what's up and what's down with minstrelsy, and some days I don't. When I get done white-splaining I sometimes realize that no one who was convinced before will ever be un-convinced, and vice versa. And then I hear things like *Never No Mo' Blues* by what is obviously (to me) a white band generating its own waves of post-minstrel consciousness, and struggling - I would say successfully - to build its own reality in a musical and aesthetic world in which reality was and remains a relative concept. And they are not only doing so successfully, they are showing how this most self-conscious of forms - minstrelsy with its cultural "slumming" and self referential forms of self-deprecation, in which every vocal pronouncement sounds strangely self-effacing, as though there is no such thing in the world of the minstrel as eye contact - can be used as an introvert's means of becoming, or at least seeming to become, an extrovert. To me the white minstrels whom I have heard on recordings, standing before a microphone in various stages of cultural undress, always sound like they are avoiding cultural eye contact, are fearful of direct communication. It's sometimes the dialect stutter (one of its conventions), but more often it's the cultural mask as worn, the way in which it seems to cover up a kind of terminal shyness and a preference for avoidance of the original - sometimes, and not necessarily accurately, called the *true* - self. This is not, in white hands, as Irving Howe asserts in his book *World of Our Fathers*, a form of alienation identification (Howe believed that Jews in black face were showing a solidarity for *the other,* the fellow social outcast) but rather, I think, a way of burying stage fright, that of the perpetual outsider, who feels that public performance, preferably under the cover of dark-face, is an ordeal, a ritual, a means of cleansing the social palate. Do it once and you can do it again, do it again and you are a free man or woman, finally liberated from expectations, the only ones of which now matter are your own.

How does my interpretation differ from Howe's? I don't think any of these white performers were looking for group solidarity or identification. I think they were, in the most basic of ways, looking to escape the prison of self, and that they found a way in common with others with which to do it.

What does all this have to do with the The Rhythm Wreckers and *Never No Mo' Blues*? Everything and nothing. Listen to that voice, a minstrel variation on the swallowing-eggs sound of some other white Southern singers, the tossing of enunciation to the wind in the interest of language as rhythm (yes, as with black singers and culture; this is another tie-in between minstrelsy and African America). By doing all of this they have learned to *swing*, in that quirky, hip-swaying way that moves from parodic twerking to near-jazz. Start with a Clyde McCoy-like trumpet wa-wa, corny to the core, a Hawaiian steel guitar, and then the Emmett Miller-ish vocal, half yodel and half whiny, white blues, and then add some schizophrenic, cross-cultural gargling from the back of some white man's throat. All the while the band thump-thumps behind with a heavy, black-like rhythm, Western Swing once removed.

Is this Acid Country? I don't really know, but somehow the label makes sense, given the Rhythm Wreckers' determined dissection of the blues, taking it as it both comes and goes, with a steel guitar and the American version of throat singing, as a new category of world music *exotica*. I classify this as country music because it reflects so much of white country music's attitude to music it found so foreign to its own way of life but still figured it could use, even as it felt the need, more and more, to commercially distance itself from this (black) music. One imagines the power structure of institutions like the Grand Ol' Opry, benign by self image, encouraging Opry members to emphasize the white side of black music, and in doing so thinking of its audience and its vast and spread-out social insecurities. **Al Dexter's** very honky tonkish **New Jelly Roll Blues (11/28/36)** is very much of this time and this way of thinking and doing. It predicts, like some of the early things of Ernest Tubb (see Vol. 22), the growing personal restlessness of white folks, whose hands were very much tied by a Southern political aristocracy that patted them on the back while at the same time dangling a carrot and flag in front of the them.

Honky Tonk Music, born in the post-War years, was the music of country roughnecks and rednecks, made as they congregated after work hours to raise more than a little hell. It was not really a thing yet in 1936, but musically we can hear its early echoes. Dexter is a strangely antiseptic performer, though the way he is tracked by the lead (electric) guitar is significant. The amplified guitar connects this to Western Swing (the guitarist actually plays jazz-like lines), but also prepares the music for the kind of volume and impact it will need to compete in noisy, smoke-filled rooms. Of such things, of blues and maudlin tear jerkers and the white way of *lonesome*, were a whole new generation of country honky tonk blues-like singers and balladeers spawned, from Hank Williams to Hank Snow.

Equally ineffectual, but significant in the historical scheme of things, was **Patsy Montana**, whose **Cowboy Rhythm (2/17/38)** sinks slowly into a painted background of Western sky, like low-level film music or, to put it in modern-day terms, like a fake Zoom-call background. Montana's shaky vibrato at once dates this and sinks it with mawkish emulation of whatever it might have been that was the *real thing* in even commercial cowboy terms (I pick Roy Rogers, synthetic as his cowboying might have been, because he was such a fine singer and vivid, welcoming personality). In instrumental terms *Cowboy Rhythm* is perfectly fine; whoever Montana's accompanists were, they were professionals and real musicians. It is her singing that places this on a much lower plain (pun intended), though I need to mention that Montana remained as a significant role model for a later generation of women country singers, because she was among the first and most successful (her signature tune, *I Want to be a Cowboy's Sweetheart*, was something of a landmark in that cowboy/girl category of songs, notable also because it was so gender specific; and please forgive me for using the word *gender*).

This is a silly song, about the rhythms the singer hears on the range, and so probably intended as a vocal backdrop to galloping actors and underpaid, drunken extras. Dramatically it was something that probably did not exist except on big screens, in which the actors were as white as the screen itself.

On the other hand, to paraphrase Richard Gilman, who commented upon hearing someone complain that a character in a play was too unlike anyone in real life that "they live on the stage," these cowboys did, indeed, live on the screen. Had Hollywood contained more ironists, they might have had some fun with the strangeness of "tough guys" like Roy Rogers and Gene Autry, neither of whom would survive a screen fight in the 21st century (or late in the 20th). But yes, they lived - and still live - on the screen, just as a group called **Hugh and Shug's Radio Pals (Sugar Babe, 7/16/37)** lived, I assume, on the radio. The mainstreaming of country radio in this era had a distant (geographically speaking) effect on the music, which continued to absorb all sorts of internal and external influences and which seemed to be either warming itself up or cooling itself down for its post World War II explosion, depending on how you look at it. The radio saturation of country sound was a kind of commercial prep for the mass-cult Nashville of the coming years. Country music was beginning to explore a new kind of instrumental virtuosity, in the service of songs that, more and more, were starting to follow the schematic of post-Tin Pan Alley song. Western Swing was still much more than a passing influence, and you can hear, on *Sugar Babe*, the accordion taking a real stab at jazz-like comping and soloing, the fiddle offering blues-based lines and swing-style phrasing. The vocal is warm and Western-formal, lacking in some of those characteristic, Rhythm Wreckered (see above) exaggerations.

And though I often hear the new Western Swing as an either/or of string band or new-swing ensemble, the band **The Light Crust Doughboys**, one of the originals of the idiom, show on **Stay out of the South** (6/20/37) that it can still be both. This is quite a performance, state-of-the-art in Western Swing terms. These guys clearly had their ear to the ground or to the radio or to the sound of after-hours sessions, and were nearly up to speed in contemporary jazz terms, or as up to speed as they needed to be in that musical environment. Charlie Christian was starting to circulate through gigs and jam sessions, and I will assume, with only minor disclaimers, that he was likely influencing these players, like the terrific guitarist Zeke Campbell, whose solo on this is a very knowing compendium of trending jazz phraseology. Or the pianist Knocky Parker, here in his early, pre-academic days (he later got a doctorate in English), whose solo flows with Earl Hinesian-rhythmic digressions. The song itself is a trifle, but that's the point. If we had an auteur theory of music, such performances would show us that the real authors of sound in those days were those who seemed to know exactly where the essence of any song was.

Further ahead (or is behind) on the Western trail were the **East Texas Serenaders** (see also Vol. 12), whom country music historians are fond of describing in historical terms as part of the ragtime/swing continuum which gave us Western Swing. For me, though I love the group, the jury is still out in this respect, though **East Texas Drag (2/20/37)** is so pleasantly listenable that for the three minutes or so of its duration I worry little about category. This band had a very bearable lightness of being, a parlor-like profundity. There was no musical trickle-down effect here; the band is all straight and professional, there is no Western Swing snark or novelty, and no shallow plumbing of the shallows. First, listen to the wonderful little glissando at .21; and the string unisons, ragged and out of tune, are alone worth the price. *East Texas Drag* has so many of these little gems of detail - the little rise at 1:04, the quaint thirds at 1:16, and then the sudden blues turn-of-phrase at 1:27; the weird way, at 1:33, that the groups seems to have come apart briefly - is someone in the wrong place? - and the way, from 1:50 to the end, they return with ragtime twists to the opening strain but with some degree of ensemble disintegration, like a fireworks display that is starting to fizzle out.

I don't know how different the group was, personnel-wise, in this year from its earlier incarnation in this study (1929) but something has changed. Some might call them less professional now, but I find them to be relaxed and less concerned with so-called precision, and yet in a very white way. Their sloppiness has less gusto than African American musical practices of a similar kind; it is less assertive than the way of black musicians, who celebrate the suspension of certain harmonic and rhythmic rules by making serious music out of casual gestures. Instead, the East Texas Serenaders have a genuinely white way of feeling the musical ground shift beneath their feet. The tremors, gentle but noticeable, are just notes and rhythms.

Country music in those years proved that, in professional and commercial terms, you could take the hillbilly out of the country but you couldn't really take the hillbilly out of the country. There was still plenty of down-home white working class music, some of it drunken and defiant of the established order (as Greil Marcus has pointed out it was, in this way, in prep for the white rebellion of rock and roll, which was, in its early days, politically inchoate yet socially - and even racially - revolutionary). A lot of it resolved around traveling entertainments like the medicine show, for which a likely candidate was **Lester Pete Bivins' Knocking on the Hen House Door (2/20/37)**. This is basically a monolog, sung but accompanied by a talking-blues-like chord progression and with a spoken-word attitude; these were speech-like rhythms, even when they had a melody. It is a series of set comedy pieces with vaudeville-like punchlines, a minstrel veneer, and a layer of self deprecation. This was, even as a new era of country dawned on radio and on record, a winking reference to old times, from which a new and aspiring class of performer and audience could hide but never really run.

  What is it about Cincinnati? From the writer Lafcadio's Hearn's incredible early and revealing writings on the music and song of the roustabouts (unskilled laborers who worked on the docks) to the crazy goniff Syd Nathan of King Records, who showed that even crooks had ethics (he had an integrated work force), the City of Seven Hills (count 'em) has been a thriving force for black music. Why and how? Let us turn to the Chamber of Commerce, because without it we would remain clueless as to Cincinnati's virtues:

> "7 Things You Didn't Know About Cincinnati:
> It has the biggest Oktoberfest in the country.
> It's Steven Spielberg's birthplace.
> We love our chili.
> It's the capital of Cornhole.
> The Music Hall is haunted.
> It's home to America's oldest baseball team.
> It was a stop on the Underground Railroad."

  I will leave it to you to explore the the virtues of Cornhole. But pay attention to the last, because Cincinnati, just across the Ohio River from Kentucky, was, as the C of C tells us, an early stop on the Underground Railroad. So it's not the South but it sort of is the South in that its southern border is a Southern gateway. Today its African American population is just above the national average (yes, even as the Aryan Nation Brotherhood is based in the Ohio prison system).

  Because of some of the above, Cincinnati had a thriving blues and even jug band scene. There must have been something in that flammable Ohio water: Cleveland in the 1960s had a busy counterculture that circled around white nonconformists like D.A. Levy and Peter Laughner and also gave us Dave Thomas and Rocket From the Tombs, a very interesting alt-type rock band that also begat Pere Ubu and the Dead Boys, two of the better punk-

and roll bands of the 1970s. That Cleveland counterculture gave us at least one brilliant, suicidal poet (Levy) and one brilliant suicidal rocker (Laughner) and a bit of poetically-astute social heresy from the likes of Dave Thomas, who appeared to be reaching, in his writing and singing, for something just a bit more socially observant than the usually song and dance of rock and roll. I mention all of this because it tells me that Ohio, for all its political strangeness, is a culturally integrated state (which may be what has scared a lot of white people in it straight, if by *straight* you mean racist-based Republicanism).

    Glib as I sound, there may be something to all of this, a cultural wind that blows east and west, north and south, hot and cold, through that state. The aforementioned King Records was one of the most important record labels of the 1940s and 1950s, feeding as it did on a racially integrated catalog and an owner (Syd Nathan) whose predatory business practices (he was an equal opportunity crook I should add) allowed him to hire both black and white people to run his offices. Without giving you a complete History of the Jews I will offer that, for all the crap that Jews in business have taken and continue to take, there was another side to the scrapping way in which these early entrepreneurs seized control of their economic lives; namely their complete comfort at working with African Americans as musicians, professionals, and co-workers. This was born out of that anti-xenophobic strain in Jewish life, the lack of fear of the "other," of those who were so obviously different or whose lives were foreign to their own. Jews had a social fearlessness that many goyim lacked, to their (the goyim, that is) eternal detriment and damnation. Yes, there was greed and there was unethical behavior (as with virtually all record labels, black and white, Jewish and non-Jewish in those days) but also, within the context of the times, great opportunity for black artists. And yes, we all have a feeling of great ambivalence toward King Records and their business practices, as we do for Chess Records, owned by Jewish immigrant brothers. And I won't try to lecture on the times they lived in, the context, or the American racial structure of those post-War years, because that, though it explains a lot, excuses virtually nothing. I will just point out that, in real terms, some of these Jewish-owned labels and Jewish owners of recording businesses and Jewish record functionaries (like Jerry Wexler, Teddy Reig, Vivian Carter, James Bracken, and Don Robey) did an amazing service for the culture, in spite of their selves (and I throw in Robey, Carter, and Bracken as a form of trick disclaimer;

they were black and crooked as a prize fighter's nose, adept at robbing black musicians with both a fountain pen *and* a gun).

Cincinnati, as I said, had a blues scene and something called the Cincinnati Jug Band. Jug bands were basically musical carriers; they escorted black vernacular song through its various historical stages, from early street jazz of the homemade kind to the land of Songster, then into the blues, all through their odd musical relationships. Now, in 1936, they gave us a kind of blues-songster fusion. One member of the Cincinnati Jug Band, **Walter Coleman,** recorded **Mama Let Me Lay it on You (2/8/36)** (a song later made famous by Bob Dylan as *Baby Let Me Follow you Down* - and much as I love Dylan I think he suffered a failure of nerve. The song was about sex). Coleman gives it an irresistible instrumental pull, with his very basic but keen self-accompaniment. As with many vernacular guitarists of the day he was his own second line - or was he? No one else is credited but I could swear I hear a second guitarist in there. At any rate I love Coleman's voice, Southern basic, and he swings like a breeze. This is blues/no blues, a bit of Songster turf transplanted and then re-planted.

One of the great if rare (and growing rarer and rarer) delights in American music is when something is both first rate and popular. Of course the definition, in sales terms, of *popular* has changed radically since **8/7/37**, when the **Golden Gate Quartet** recorded **Golden Gate Gospel Train**. I don't know how many records they sold for Victor (I was unable to locate sales figures) but their near-perfect fusion of classic quartet harmony, sporadic and more coarse gospel exclamation, as overlaid with the smooth, jubilee style, plus the power of the 50,000 watt radio station which made them stars (and got them a recording contract) led to a perfect storm of popular appeal, sales, and touring. They appeared in John Hammond's famous Spirituals to Swing concert, a clear sign of politically-correct mainstream appeal (if we can call the Left side of Popular Front of those days mainstream; Popular Front referred to the temporarily alliance of Left and Center in those War years, often in service of cultural advocacy and social unity). Their earlier records had a little bit more of the tint of hard gospel (more blatant emotion) with occasional reference to other gospel worlds. Still, performances like this were much more than middle-of-the-road, cultural scale models. The Golden Gates had a sonic depth and harmonic width that gave their performances a level of practiced perfection, but they never ignored the kind of internal manipulation of feeling and time that gave gospel music its good name and made it so appealing to audiences across racial lines. *Golden Gate Gospel Train* has classic rail-motion effects, some human-horn sounds, and a kind of perpetual musical motion that makes it feel like it just goes on and on. This was the jubilee style, densely populated with tiny but intense bursts of feeling.

The **Norfolk Jazz Quartet (Just Dream of You, 7/16/37)** was called a jazz quartet for a reason. They started recording as early as 1921 and showed all the signs of swing and pop by the time they recorded this. We can hear a lot of the ways of black quartets in this - a mobile bass singer whose lines are a combination of non-musical syllables and moveable harmonic rhythm; a jive kind of swing, with finger snapping pauses and feints; vocal harmonies that trace the melody, no matter where other parts of the song may drift. The cured emotionalism of the jubilee gospel style is intact, even as the lead singer bursts into a passage or two of Louis Armstrong-like scatting and phrasing. This was a growing and popular style in this decade, smoothed out by swing (in the generic sense) and shaped by popular image in films and on record. It doesn't take much of a stretch to see how closely related this was to the doo-wop of later years, a smooth vocal style that moved jazz's repertoire to the right, toward a pop - and populist - groove.

Closer to the that doo-wop idea, though still pieced together with a jazz disposition, was **I'm Moaning All Day For You** by the **Five Jinks (2/20/37)**. This has a lot of jazzy gestures, some scat and hipster syllabication, a decorous guitar part (is that a guitar? Maybe some other related instrument) with appropriate fills. The Five Jinks, otherwise undocumented, recorded for Bluebird, a Victor vernacular subsidiary (home of much of its blues and country-related catalog), and they seem typical of the new sound, and not far from the Mills Brothers.

**Oh Lord, Don't 'low Me to Beat 'Em** by **Willie Williams (1936)** was recorded by John Lomax at a State Penitentiary on one of his rambles through the Southern criminal element. I have commented on the Lomax approach throughout this study (see the index to Volume 1) and I have to admit, after many years of skepticism, that I now see the value of what both father and son accomplished. *Oh Lord* is a classic field holler, animated by a pre-blues idea of phrasing and (static) harmony.

I haven't spent a good deal of time in my studies considering the post-ethical issues of the Lomax's method, so I was interested in an article I came across called "How Alan Lomax Segregated Music." The thrust of the article was that the Lomaxes, on their anthropological Southern journeys, ignored a great deal of the popular, vernacular taste of both white folks and black audiences, focusing instead on performers whom they felt had street cred - or maybe prison cred, because that was where they spent a lot of time in search of singers and songs. Which raises another question: were the prisoners who sang and recorded for them (like Leadbelly and Willie Williams and Strothers, to cite just a few) doing so out of a sense of coercion and fear of white power? And if so does this taint the process and the result?

Yes, no, and maybe, to all of the above. Certainly the Lomaxes were consciously segmenting the music they documented by, in many cases (but with exceptional exceptions), race. But this was really a practicality in the South in those days, where whites like Lomax were viewed with suspicion for simply referring to black musicians by the respectful moniker of "Mister" (see Lomax's account in his book *The Land Where the Blues Began* of how a white sheriff takes great offense at his reference to the singer Son House as "Mr. House"). It is not an exaggeration to suggest that a white person delving into the habits and cultural expression of black folks in the South in those days, and doing so with respect and scholarly intent, put their own lives at risk. As to the charge that in doing so the Lomaxes played into certain stereotypes of black folkloric expression and ignored more conventional song and styles, well, it is, ironically or not, to our great historical benefit that they did so. The commercial record companies, if far from perfect, had that other side covered in some essential ways (I think this study proves that) and now that, eighty-plus years later, the cultural dust has settled, we can hear just what the Lomaxes (and their associates like Zora Neale Hurston) accomplished: recordings of black and white country music, black and white ragtime, deep Southern, white and black gospel, local music, neo-bluegrass, black and white string bands, varieties of Cajun music, ring shouts - well, we could go on with our personal catalog of preferences. Now that so much of the music has been reissued (there have been excellent series on Rounder and Document Records) and is also on line (see the Cultural Equity web site: http://research.culturalequity.org/home-audio.jsp_ ) we have the big picture: for all the Lomaxes' faults, they left us, culturally, with a lot more than we knew we had.

Some of us try to keep on top of what we have. **Count Basie'**s band recording of **John's Idea (7/7/37)** is typical of Basie's output, though typical for Basie is ten or so cuts above the average. There is so much here that became (or really already was) the template for the classic Swing band: Basie's piano intro, which was like droplets of musical rain blown about by a light wind, setting the scene, to mix metaphors, like an omniscient musical narrator; a pithy solo, by the Southwestern tenor player Herschel Evans, whose laconic phrasing and funky stops were a nice contrast to the band's other major sax soloist, Lester Young (not heard here) and whose ideas reached well inside the blues; the way in which the band turns the *riff* into an art form (riffs being short phrases of a rhythmic character), alternating these rising phrases with richly stationery harmonies that flow uncannily into and out of these sonic events, punctuated by the drummer Jo Jones' accents, which ring out like a group shout, or a congregational exclamation mid sermon.

Ah the wonders of regional jazz groups, otherwise known as territory bands. As I think I have said before, you can hear in these bands a particular brand of common purpose, an overt, fraternal musical love that is sometimes missing in more polished organizations. And what a wonderful thing is **Moten Swing** by the **Carolina Cotton Pickers (3/24/37)**. This really does swing in every sense of the word. Can one hear even methods of phrasing as soulful? I think so; or at least I can. Every note, every rhythmic time-stretch, pause or feint, every flaccid-toned harmony, says that these are musicians who know each other well enough, musically and professionally, to anticipate each other's every phrase and/or slightly out-of-tune-ness. The intonation really is, as used to be said with pejorative intent, "close enough for jazz," because the sound, the phrasing, the swing, the feeling - are all like a wonderful and free, Jazz Open Swim. They really don't make them like this anymore because no one can *play* them like this anymore.

# Chapter 20: Hillbillies with 401k's: That Low Class Twang

As the 1930 went by country music seemed in search of ways around certain kinds of categorization. The hillbilly label, though still in use, now seemed to encompass a more cosmopolitan musical outlook. Hillbilly was still hillbilly but it was a different kind of hillbilly. This one was still occasionally drunk but now more of a commercial virtuoso - though what's a commercial virtuoso? It's like those guys who used to be on the television show Hee Haw with straw coming out of their mouths. These were hillbillies with 401ks (yes, I know, 401k's were not invented until 1980; I know how to Google, but I am making a point), big houses, accountants, and publicists. And yes, I also know that it was unlikely that a 1930s hillbilly recording artist had any of those other things; the point is that, just as the hillbilly was still a hillbilly, the profession was still a profession. And now, like Minnie Pearl's price-tagged hat, the music was getting real exposure and a taste of mass taste (and by the way I would describe a *commercial virtuoso* as a great musician who, realizing there is gold in the emulation of certain simpler musical styles, is unafraid to emulate).

**Walter Hurdt (Fiddle and Guitar Running Wild 9/29/38)** was another Bluebird recording artist. That record label, which had a tendency in its day to flatten out certain blues styles, seems now, in hindsight, to have done a lot of good work. It was from a major label (it was a subsidiary of Victor) and so the music was well recorded and pressed on good materials. Hurdt, who never achieved great success in the business, was referred with his men as "Walter Hurdt and the Singing Cowboys," which tells us something about the way in which country music was starting to be marketed. And some of the titles they recorded tell us even more: *Hold Him Down Cowboy*, *My Brave Buckaroo*, *Down the Arizona Trail*....and then *Guitar Rag*, a fascinating insertion attesting to the lasting importance of Sylvester Weaver's persistent ditty (see Vol. 3).

Hurdt's recordings attest to the intersection of early, pre-bluegrass ideas and jazz/Western Swing with cowboy music. *Fiddle and Guitar Running Wild* makes reference, by title, to a jazzed-up pop song (*Running Wild*, written in 1922 and frequently recorded by jazz musicians) but is filled with bluegrass-isms - until a smartly calculated insertion of a *Tiger Rag*-like section at about .30. What were these guys thinking? I just like the fact that they *were* thinking, because this section is followed by a chorded (jazz) guitar solo on some classic changes, after which the fiddler enters with some of those great, chopping country-hoedown rhythms, followed by rich jazz chords, *Tiger Rag* again ("hold that tiger") and then a somewhat anti-climactic ending, probably enforced by the recording engineer's red light.

After I heard that one I had to check out more by this terrific band. Another recording which caught my attention, *Honey What's the Matter Now*, is filled with a jazz-like rhythm guitar, a few minstrel whoops (a la Bob Wills, who placed them throughout his recordings) and more country/jazz fiddle, with the emphasis on country sixteenth-note figures and phrasing. Plus a guitar solo that is more jazz than country, cowboy harmonies (if there was such a thing, but their vocal arrangements remind me of the Sons of the Pioneers, see Vols. 19, 20), and a few sprinkled hints along the way that these were jazz musicians who only moonlighted - or slummed? - as cowboy players.

I have probably said this (or something like it) before, but it's only a short skip from groups like the brother team **The Blue Sky Boys (Katie Dear, 1/25/38)** to more "contemporary" (yes, you can tell I am old by my idea of *contemporary*) groups like the Everly Brothers and even Simon Garfunkel - who (like Simon and Garfunkel) were not always brothers but whose way of harmonizing was powerfully influenced by this whole school. This was particularly related to the way in which teams like the Blue Sky Boys modulated themselves tonally, and seemed to ease so gently and *musically* into the harmonized thirds that highlighted their recordings.

The Blue Sky Boys were Bill and Earl Bolick. Both lived well into the modern era (they died in 1998 and 2008). They recorded for Bluebird and their careers were built on radio and touring and they were, in that way of early country performers, rich in followers but (moderately) poor in cash. And they illustrate the complex social distribution of country musicians, who were not always the kind of odd social fits and misfits we imagine them to be. As Dick Spottswood, in his book *The Blue Sky Boy*s, writes:

"…the Bolics were far from being rural throwbacks or idealized folk specimens of an isolated society tied to ancient beliefs and customs. They grew up after World War I in a mid-sized, progressive North Carolina mill town whose opportunities afforded their family a comfortable middle class life."

This explains some of the tensions between old and new in what amounted to the Old and New South, the old representing certain mean social retentions and post-Reconstruction attitudes, the new struggling to re-define itself, even if it had to do so as part of a separate-but-unequal society. The Blues Skies embody this tension, if in genteel ways; they were often saddled with inferior material, and though they resisted recording some of this they had a limited amount of professional power. But it is no accident that the Bolicks, who recorded as late as 1975, come across as decent folk, because they were. They also are the right kind of preservationists because, though they are committed to the careful treatment of tradition, they are not curators of song in any museum-like sense. Their careful harmonies show no antiquarian caution, only a deep understanding of and respect for the material. *Katie Dear* is an old-fashioned suicide/love song, though an odd one; the Katie of the title, asked by the singer to marry him, is told to take the request to her father, who owns a dagger. At which point the singer, on an unexplained impulse, sticks the dagger through his own heart, whereupon Katie takes the same dagger and "plant(s) it through her lily-white breast," singing:

> "goodbye papa goodbye mama
> I'll die with the one that I love best"

Never, since the day of Romeo and Juliet, has suicide and tragedy seemed so logical, even casual, a succession of events.

**Wade Mainer** (see also Chapter/Volume 19) is sometimes called The Father of Bluegrass, a designation that Bill Monroe would probably not have taken kindly to. Still, it's a reasonable assertion, based on Mainer's resonant banjo-picking and the open-air instrumental sound of his groups. Bluegrass had a number of points of departure from older hillbilly instrumental ways. In most basic terms, the line of solo instrument was more streamlined, melodies were stated with a good deal less instrumental melisma, and, in spite of the regular breakdown into group and solo sections (in a kind of organized chaos) it was shy of classic blues and other, blacker, musical gestures. The sound waves of bluegrass instruments in flight seem to clash a lot less than those of black musicians and music, from old New Orleans jazz to jug band music or the blues. This, as I hear it, is a whiter aspect of country expression and performance. Though more than a few early white hillbilly performers absorbed those black instrumental styles and roles, of bent notes, sharp, squealing tunings, blues runs and ensemble anarchy, Bluegrass sounded somewhat more indigenous, more white, more true to certain self (white) identities. Was it an early White Nationalist movement? I wouldn't call it that, because there is no evidence anywhere that tells us that these white men saw it in any way as a method of cultural cleansing. They were just following a different muse, a different tradition, a different internal rhythm.

**Mitchell Blues**, which Mainer recorded in **1938**, sounds in-between traditions. The title phrase, very commonly used in Southern recordings both black and white, is regularly interrupted (as at .30) by a very jazz-like and black-like power riff that drives the message home: black/white musical fusion and white/black musical fusion were, as told in a later musical message, here to stay.

**Molly Married a Traveling Man** is usually credited to Uncle Dave Macon (see Vol.5) but was also recorded by a group under the name of **J.H. Howell** on **1/29/38** (I don't know if it is the same tune). Howell et al recorded for Bluebird, and as I discovered too late for the song as listed here, they went under the name of J.H. Howell's Carolina Hillbillies. There's that H-word again, and though I haven't discussed in this study how some people considered the label to be degrading, it clearly went from epithet to Badge of Honor. Hillbillies seemed to be honoring, by name, their redneck heritage in song and instrumentation, but most particularly by twang and inflection, as with the female lead vocal here. Sometimes when I hear singing like this I think about the jazz/pop singer Jo Stafford, who for some time did a parody of this type of country voice with her husband Paul Weston. It was a nasty thing, and played into Northern snobbery about that Southern sound, that supposedly low-class twang and all that it seemed to represent. Such ways of parody are, to me, about as sporting as the barrel shooting of fish; it's always easier to look down on people than to look at them directly in the eye, to try and imagine that they have their own ways of living life and of making art.

Suffice to say that I love this kind of sound, the flattened vowels, the tight-mouthed syllabification that in the South, in spite of its multitude of sins, stood for a lot of poor and downtrodden white folks who for generations allowed themselves to be manipulated and exploited, but still managed to preserve their own essential dignity in song. And yes, there is a dignity to this kind of presentation, a country formality that few if any revivalists have been able to replicate either vocally or instrumentally. I think of it as a very white-postured style, as something that draws meaning from a way of life that, from the beginning, and at the hands of too many folks with both good and bad intentions, has been denied purpose or artistic value.

That twang, nasal and stretched thin over classic string band instrumentation, was a signal to audiences in these years that their lives still had some connection to an older way, even if no one cared to really define what that older way was or what it really meant (it worked better as something symbolic and spiritual, like that figure hanging from the cross in church). The **Coon Creek Girls**, for example, were a 'traditional' string group from Kentucky, and their popularity attested to the hold that those old-time sounds had on audiences, and not just in the USA; when King George and Queen Elizabeth came to visit the United States FDR invited the Coon Creek Girls to entertain them at the White House.

**Sewing on the Mountain (1938)** is a classic *Christian Warning* song, commanding sinners to get their act together in preparation for the arrival of a savior (or two), to be ready for the time when not life but the afterlife was in the balance. It has something of that amateur ethos I refer to from time to time, a sense of performers who saw this as less a profession than as a way of life, though even that may just have been part of the act.

Maybe only country music could take us, in the space of two performances, from the sublime and unselfconscious reality of professional amateurs-in-essence to a newer, more image-conscious model of country and *Western* music as it strived for the inauthentic. Think **Roy Rogers (When the Sun is Setting on the Prairie, 1938)**, who always retained a paradoxically honest sense of image-as-reality. But Roy was from somewhere, and this is probably why, even at his blandest and most middle-of-the road, he came across with complete and unfeigned honesty and sincerity. I once described him as a "right wing mensch," after his Republican politics, and anyone who has ever observed an interview with him or watched him with his fans knows what I mean. His deep and caring personality is a big part of what made him a star, proving that sometimes the real thing is as effective as the fake.

And he was born in Cincinnati, that amazing musical gateway between North and South - or was it between South and West? - where a lot of musical feeling was expressed, both black and white. Remember Lafcadio Hearn's early observations of Cincinnati's black working class music and culture of the 19th century? In his early years in the early 20th century Roy Rogers was a purveyor of *white* working class music, after a fashion, as country music was talking hold in Ohio's bi-racial melting pot. Roy sang and played a number of instruments and moved between there and his new home in California before becoming part of the great and permanent country-fed migration Westward; radio, record, and film stardom followed. By the time he recorded *When the Sun is Setting On the Prairie* all hopes of a true emulation of the sound of working men and women of the West had been lost to the class-invisible, amorphous drift of Hollywood-cowboy mythology. Roy's cowboy was earnest, laconic, faithful and honest to a fault, and, though I love him and the horse he rode in on, as unreachable and false as a holograph.

It wasn't long after this that Roy was **Heading for Texas and Home (4/18/39)** which is just one more exceptional exception to the old cowboy rule of dirt-deep reality, working-man's pessimism, and days spent wading in cow shit. John Lomax, who early on collected actual cowboy songs, would not have approved, but his was already a lone voice echoing in a museum-like and virtual cowboy wilderness.

This song teamed Roy up with the **Sons of the Pioneers** (see Vol. 19), a cooperative group. Roy's name, however, was already above the marquee. Both Roy and the Sons had started appearing in movies in 1935, and though there was never any great schism (Roy was too nice a guy for that), his star could not long be contained. The song itself is a perfect little analog to the cowboy action film, beautifully sung (or is it galloped?) by Roy, whose wobbly and effervescent yodeling brings that skill to the next stage of its useful musical life. The song is filled with an accordion, references to lucky buckaroos, post-Depression optimism about fellowship and friendship, and a very good violin solo with a real jazz pedigree.

As bright as Roy's outlook was on life, country music from these days is often never more than a step or two from its own version of going over the edge - toward death, as it happens, even as the end of life is accomplished with bright eyes and bushy tails - because such was the typical imagery applied, in Southern white gospel, to death's inevitable invasion of your (living) space. In this way endings become beginnings and loss becomes recovery, of parents, friends, and other vanished relations. As **Smith's Carolina Crackerjacks** tell us in **Your Soul Never Dies (9/29/38)**:

> "To Canaan's land, I'm on my way
> Where the soul of man never dies
> My darkest night will turn to day
> Where the soul of man never dies"

It is not hard to see the appeal in the idea of such heavenly excursion, and I have to admit that as the aging process sets in and as the casualties around me mount even I, a practiced cynic, occasionally succumb to what I regard as compassionate expressions of false hope. I would suggest that, though it was expressed racially in radically different ways, gospel music's entire appeal, both black and white, was based on such promises, on the ethical carrot and stick dangled before the multitudes mortally wounded by life. Still, the musical differences between black and white are significant, and not merely stylistic or aesthetic challenges to each other. Try as we might to make the reasonable point that white Southern life had its own matrix of pain and suffering, its own (literal and figurative) crosses to bear, nothing in that life could compare to what amounted to the physical, political, and legal crucifixion of the black population, the black nightmare of pursuit and capture. Even the Pentecostal aesthetics of white religionist were different from the black religious equivalent; whites of all sects, unlike blacks, were able to separate fear of bad moral actions from fear of political actions and irrational and unpredictable consequences; whereas African Americans of Southern geographical extraction had good and rational reason to fear the result of any and all actions they might take in the course of a day or a lifetime.

And yet given all of that we have to admit and recognize that, by any true measure, *Your Soul Never Dies* is a stout and substantial musical accomplishment. Even false hope settles on those who believe in it, and these hillbillies clearly and with absolute faith trusted their own (final) judgement. There is just something about that twisting, and maybe even twisted, rural twang that works so well musically; put two voices with that off-white Southern inflection together in harmony and what you get when things go right is the most sublimely dignified representation possible of *the moral life* in song.

In this way black and white music did have its own kind of compatibility. There was public music and there was private music. On the private side this meant everything from inter-racial violations of the local social code (the late guitarist Steve Bruton - of Kris Kristofferson's band - told me that black and white musicians often met to play together in graveyards in order to ward off intruders who might not approve of such things) to single and double entendre ditties sung by both blacks and whites with heavy doses of sexual symbolism (like Lucille Bogan's screamingly funny and obscene *Shave 'Em Dry* or even Gene Autry's private recording of *Frankie and Johnny/Bye Bye Boyfriend*, with it's quite direct references to male and female organs. Really). Sometimes (or maybe a lot of times) singers were both sinners *and* saints, like **Cliff Carlisle** (Bill Carlisle's - see Vol. 19 - brother), who recorded his share of dirty ditties along with songs of clean-cut country sentiment, like **Footprints in the Snow (1939)**. *Footprints in the Snow* is classic country balladry from the days before it was classic, with a humble baritone vocal, love-as-found lyrics, and polite instrumental interruptions perfectly spaced apart (listen at about .49 to the way in which the steel guitar rises with a mood of pleasant melancholy behind the mandolin, offering little whoops of stringed affirmation).

Even Bill Monroe, of bluegrass intentions, recorded a version of this, six years later, which tells us how compatible the tune was with several generational ideas of country performance (it was originally written in 1880 as an English music hall song). Monroe's performance offers an instructive contrast to Carlisle's; Monroe stretches out the syllables of certain words - "some folks like the summer TIIIIMMME" - in a way which puts the high and lonesome into it, whereas Carlisle keeps these phrases under wraps (the difference is instructive, showing aspects of bluegrass singing as a very canny white version of black vocalism, with a kind of stationery melisma).

**I'm Not Angry With You Darling (The Four Picked Peppers, 8/22/39)** is awash with country sentiment, with rich, smooth harmonies (not unlike the idealized vocalizations of the Sons of the Pioneers) and occupied with a new kind of country orchestration: add a bunch of stringed instruments like mandolin, fiddle, banjo, and guitar together, find three or four crooning, polite, sincere voices singing in multi-part harmony, place them all together, up front and, sonically speaking, in your face, and you have the Phil Spector Wall of Sound well before anyone called it that. It is full and dense and comes at you like a great, rising and sinking wave, of sound as both motion and emotion.

We can admire how much recording engineers did in those days with pretty much nothing but microphones and direct-to-disc recording, which allowed no interruptions or overdubbing. The Peppers are smooth and soothing in service of what might be called a forgiveness song, a declaration of slightly tainted love of the kind that was starting to pull country music into its modern love-song era (soon to be known as Nashville). This type of song had the advantage of lending itself to assembly-line musical methods; one can already hear, in this finely-tune performance, future songwriters, producers, and studio musicians sitting in a circle in a studio and awaiting their next instructions.

Of course religion and secular country singing always intersected, first in rough, emotional terms, and now, in the immediate years of pre-bluegrass, with smoother, friendlier, and more harmonious forms of singing, as on **Farther Along** by the **Pine Ridge Boys (8/22/39)**. This was smooth gospel quartet singing in a string-band format, not for the first time, of course, but with an additional, possibly middle-class purpose; it may have been more consumer friendly for groups increasingly dependent on radio transmission for sales and touring. It's one thing to enter someone's living room after dark, it's another to enter and scream bloody religious murder, splashing Jesus' blood around the room in life-saving ecstasy, even if it's done with indoor voices. The Pine Ridge Boys are modulated, moderately-inclined and friendly visitors, and that translates over to their method of religious singing - done with pious congeniality, over subjects that merely suggest, in everyday terms, that life is a mystery solvable by god-fearing optimism and patience ("we'll understand it all by and by"). By this time, post-Depression and pre-War, audiences were probably a little weary of death, hell fires and divine punishment. Been there, done that, as they might have said.

By the time **Roy Hall** recorded **Orange Blossom Special (11/7/38)** bluegrass was, with or without Bill Monroe, very nearly a thing. Listen to that long, train-whistle bowing, that *peppy* tempo (I hate that word but there's no other way to describe it), and that sense of breezy virtuosity. These guys were enjoying themselves. I once compared the rise of bluegrass and Bill Monroe's leadership as being to old-time hillbilly music what Charlie Parker and bebop were to swing. I still stand, somewhat, by that comparison. As many holes as there are in the analogy, it holds up in relative terms: hillbilly instrumental style was like a big circular saw, cutting through the mix with many rough edges; bluegrass, which had its own untamed quality, was smoother around the edges, its virtuosity, relative to old-time music, in service to a seemingly less earthy musical aura - but only seemingly (at least in its infancy). Like bebop in relation to swing it had a different emotional compass, a different emotional range, a less-obvious depth of feeling (compared to prior styles), sometimes masked by the technical requirements of musicians who played in the style; it's not that such facility dampened the music's effects but rather that it deepened them, fused sound with effort and emotion in such a way that the extension of line tapped into newer and more complex aspects of musical reflex, consciousness, and association. As with bebop bluegrass inspired a new king of classicism, a skimming of tradition in ways that masked its sources, but which used them just the same (though another comparison with bebop might make the point that eventually bluegrass settled into repetition, a schematic rehearsing of certain musical gestures and patterns; though I might add that the problem was greater for bluegrass since, even at its height, it relied upon a relatively set series of scales and rhythms; bebop ultimately, in the right hands, had much greater musical flexibility and still had room for non-technical virtuosos who had, instead, virtuoso minds and ideas).

Roy Hall, from North Carolina, was another whose reputation was made by radio exposure, along with his Blue Ridge Entertainers. Though overall their recorded output was mixed with a lot of poor material, *Orange Blossom Special* was a pioneering display piece. Their version of the tune was only one of several released by different country groups, and this recording captures the essence of the new Bluegrass idea, with spirit and technique. This was the so-called *tradition* as it was being hijacked by an ambitious generation of musicians; for a sense of the somewhat schizophrenic way in which this kind of string band music was advancing, listen at 1:33; the fiddler, who is at the center of the piece, alternates old-style hoedown phraseology - which is like a vertical, musical pause and effect - with the new linear approach that is at the heart of bluegrass melody, making a quick re-reference or two to the train-sing which is at the center of this performance before driving the hoedown home with increasingly spiky leaps of (modern) rhythm.

Bluegrass, in its steady acceleration, almost always tends to sound like a race to some musical finishing line; listen to **Byron Parker and His Mountaineers' Up Jumped the Devil (2/9/40)**, with the influential banjoist Snuffy Jenkins. Parker didn't actually perform; aside from lending his name he seems to have presented and/or introduced the group. This kind of relationship wasn't that unusual in country music, in which sponsors names often popped up to let audiences know just who or what product was behind their musical favorites. Jenkins was known as the first banjoist to perform what is called the three-finger roll, even before the pioneering Earl Scruggs (see Vol. 24), and though here he is a bit buried in the mix he can be heard throughout, particularly at 1:25 and afterwards, driving the band above and beyond the call of the rhythm guitar. Though a contemporary citing of the group refers to them as "an Appalachian string band" (on the Country Sales web site), they were a bit more than that, as part of the driving force of bluegrass' ruthless usurpation of country technique; not to mention that, at the same time, they were entertainers. Gospel music, breakdowns, nostalgia ballads, weepers and even a bit of blues (or something resembling the blues) were all starting to creep into the bluegrass tent, and the Mountaineers presented it all with post-minstrel dignity and pride (because even white folks, inadvertently or not, were victims of minstrelsy's persistent trivialization of repertoire and musical gesture).

**The Sons of the Ozarks (Plantation Blues, 12/8/39)** are, in terms of any ideas we might have about tradition, a little more complicated. What is that opening riff that establishes the tune, with its oddly-modern sounding ("modern" meaning that it sounds to my old ears like this recording was made during the '60s folk revival), deftly-phrased rhythmic signature? I immediately, while listening to this, started singing along with it as *Bottle of Wine* ("Bottle of wine, fruit of the vine, when you gonna let me get sober; leave me along, let me go home, I wanna go back and start over"), which I first heard folker Tom Paxton do many years ago but which was replicated in more than a few versions after 1960. I can find no information on this group, but they are remarkably relaxed, and the song has the kind of novelty-over-blues feeling which perfectly fits the folk revivalist musical spirit of old-time fun and trad-based seriousness. It's a white band, I am sure, and they may indeed be trying to harness a musical wave of nostalgia, as even in those years there was a recognized stylistic dichotomy between old and new country music. It is quasi-jazz, with a steady rhythm guitar not far from the kind that lurks in those Roy Rogers tunes we talked about, and there are some game attempts at a guitar solo, most of which come off with knowledgable proficiency. I will add that the somewhat heavier two-beat time on this ties it in with old-time African American blues ritual, though without much of the emotional - or musical - baggage.

Obviously these musicians are not oblivious to all that is happening around them or even unaware of how transitional a period this is in country, as the music navigates some deep blue and quasi-jazz waters while steadying itself in preparation for the commercial wave to come. Still, I have heard nothing from this time period that stands as a musical equivalent to *Plantation Blue*s. Even without knowing how close the sound of this will become to modernist (post 60's) folkie imaginations, it still appears like a form of premature nostalgia.

Professionally **Bob Wills**, singer, bandleader, and fiddler, was something of a country music franchise. His career crossed several generations, starting with the first generation of Western Swingsters. Wills' bands were string bands, medicine show/minstrel touring orchestras, dance bands (closer to the conventional swing-jazz idea of the day), square dance groups (well, with some imagination) and pop bands, depending on the year, the record label, or the event. They were slick without the usual sound of slickness and they were musical everymen, with good sidemen, good singers, some exceptional soloists, and a way of sounding very much of their time no matter what year it was.

It is difficult to find a song that sounds like a representative sampling of Wills' music (see also Vol. 23), but **Pray for the Lights to Go Out (5/16/38)** will do. From its first strains of violin backed by muted trumpets, to its full-chorus vocal, spritely jazz guitar, and faux/jive gospel lyrics (this is an oddly-spaced minstrel preacher sermon but not really, which makes it a real minstrel preacher sermon), this is a world-music hybrid (if by world music you mean the big and culturally-complicated world of South and Southwestern folks from which this grew). It is hard to do justice to this somewhat impenetrable sex song (no pun intended), with its multiple entendre verses and its consistent comedic/minstrel attempts as meaningless meaning. If you want to know what *I* mean check out the lyrics:

Father was a deacon in a hard shell church,
Way down South where I was born.
People used to come to him from miles around,
Just to hear the holy work go on.
Sister grabbed the deacon 'round the neck and says,
"Deacon, won't you sing this song?"
The deacon tells the deacon that she didn't have time,
Felt religion comin' on.
Just then somebody got up, turn'd the lights all out,
And you ought to heard that sister shout:

She hollered, "Brother, if you want to spread joy,
Just pray for the lights to stay out."
She called on Deacon for to kneel and pray.
You ought to heard that sister shout.
She pulled off both shoes,
She pulled off both socks
She got low down on the eagle rock,
She hollered, "Brother, if you want to spread joy,
Just pray for the lights to stay out."

    I did a little splicing, but you get the idea; and your dirty-minded guess is about as good as mine. Add Wills' patented - well, borrowed or stolen - minstrel/vocal oohs and ahs, some warnings about all the crap shooting going on, and you have a nice, old fashioned and typically racially-slanted Sinners' Sermon. Did such a song, like Wills in general, straddle racial traditions? There certainly are plenty of black songs which belittle religion in ways similar to this one, which use similar minstrel-convention language and images, at least partly as a concession to the times in which they were written. Whatever the source, this was neither quite the end of one era nor the beginning of another. It was just white country-string-jazz musicians - Bob Wills especially - working from a place that they called home.

    Someone posted the **Night Owls**' version of **Memphis Blues (1938)** on Youtube and not only apologized for the language but also advised listeners that it was recorded in the 1950s. Such things keep me, if not employed, at least busy, writing books like this. By now, as I write, the basic description of a band like this goes out like just another APB - or a call to grab the usual suspects: "White country band, identities unknown, very well recorded (not just for its time), good musicians, sincere and idiomatically adept; armed with a few racially-charged lyrics, so approach with caution."

Is this Western Swing? Yes, I think so. Are these racist lyrics? Yes, I think so, though not written by W.C. Handy, who wrote the melody, but by George A. Norton, presumable a white man who was hired by another white man (George Honey Boy Evans) who ran a minstrel troupe. Handy provided the song - which was an early blues copyright, in that one of the sections used a blues chord progression - to Evans. The piece was originally composed for a Memphis mayoral candidate; Norton took Handy's melody (registered in 1912) and added lyrics about Handy's band, to white folks listening while the "darkies" play the music that only they could play. Interestingly enough, as I perused the internet for different lyric versions I usually did *not* find the "darky" reference included. I don't know if the lyrics have been sanitized in general or if this represents our current sensibilities, but even Bing Crosby's version whited-out (pun intended) this section of the song. A clip of Bing singing *Memphis Blues* in the 1941 film *Birth of the Blues*, does, however, instead of having him sing about those darkies, show them: one from a prison cell with a huge, toothy grin (reacting with delight to Bing's vocal and jazz group performance of *Memphis Blues*; these white boys, he seems to be telling us, can really do it), another who is shining a white man's shoes, and still another who dances with, yes, colored abandon on a balcony.

On the other hand, Al Bernard's wonderfully animated 1918 version informs us, without embarrassment, that "while the white folks sway, all the darkies play." And then Louis Armstrong, about 40 years later, changed this to "all the boys begin to play."

So the song does, as the saying sometimes goes, carry some baggage with it. It is almost as though it was all part of *The Memphis Blues*' journey through the 20th century - first as an early carrier of the blues form as composed by a pioneering entrepreneur of black music, next as a popular vessel, through various distinguished and perfectly reasonable instrumental mutations by mostly white bands like Prince's Orchestra and the Victor Military Band, then the song as carried through a minstrelized version faithfully done (faithful, that is, to the commercial re-positioning of the song) by Al Bernard; followed by Western swing adaptations like this one, done with an apparently sincere and respectful recognition of the song's seeming recognition of black musicians (who, we are told, were the only ones who could do what they could do), and then screened as Bing

Crosby's movie-ized version (no longer referring to those darkies but actually inking them out of the actual performance of the music, substituting a white instrumental group and reversing the prior order of things, so now, in the movie and as he sings and plays *Memphis Blues*, the darkies are swaying while the WHITE FOLKS are playing), and then, like a final judicial ruling, closing with Louis Armstrong's perfect 1950s version, which effectively says "this is the final word on the *Memphis Blues*, so let's give it a rest."

Should we saddle the Night Owls and their 1938 version with all this negative history? Oh, why not. It's a fine version, with a nice, neutral tone (are these guys just innocent bystanders? Well, as Henny Youngman used to say, sort of, "It's a living").

The organ that briefly introduces **I Can't Give You Anything But Love (Adelaide Hall, Fats Waller 8/28/38)** is, yes, by the inimitable Fats who, it turns out, was not only a great soloist but a great accompanist. Does his parallel tone poem (to Adelaide Hall's slightly arch but gentle, out-of-jazz paraphrase of this famous melody) have the characteristic Fats humor, his sardonic detachment from the grittier affairs of life? I mention this because that's how I hear Waller's music, as an avoidance of life's practicalities, a way of holding reality at bay. Would that we all had the ability to do it in this way, with all of Fats' resources and angular approach to reality; it always sounds like he's looking at life from under a table, peeking out at the strange goings on. On this it's a little more complicated, since the organ doesn't have the expressive nuance of the piano. Everything on it is, in terms of touch and dynamics, like one big wave of sound. Still, Fats loved the instrument, maybe because it brought out the formalist in him or reminded him of his original training, of the days when life was less complicated and music more an orderly matter of exercises and etudes. Still, he can't resist injecting some personality into it; note the the way he so artfully and conservatively shadows the melody here but then suddenly drops, at .053, a chromatic anchor into the proceedings.

Adelaide Hall is a good singer to trot out whenever we need to make the point that African American music and singing is far from the uniform march of blues and vocal twerking it is usually made out to be. Hall is a gentle escort of songs like this, which she phrases with careful rhythmic drops behind the beat, subtle lyric variations, and the slightest of melodic paraphrase (jazzy in a narrow way). She weeps, she sighs, and she squeezes the melody with more and more liberty, and Fats, as either cause or effect, answers her with a few brief verbal jibes, as he begins to walk the time, almost forcing her to swing. Hall, a warm singer with a somewhat cold exterior (she was memorably cast as the vocalist on Duke Ellington's early version of *Creole Love Call*), sounds like a symphonic pop singer here, someone more at home in the concert hall than in a jazz joint, and Fats, ever the trickster with the heart and soul of a gentleman hipster, sounds like he wishes he was back in Harlem.

Of a decidedly more funky and exhibitionist bent is **Sister Rosetta Tharpe,** whose recording of **I Looked Down the Line (and Wondered) (1939)** is not exactly typical of her work, and yet feels like just another way that she could sound and be. Tharpe started her musical life on the road with her mother, performing for Pentecostal meetings, and though there is not a lot available that speaks to whatever conflicts it led to, she surely must have stirred things up in that movement by doing material like this. *I Looked Down the Line* is about as straight a blues as you will hear from those days, seemingly lifted right out of the world of old back-country black-country music. And yet - the lyrics tell us that maybe Tharpe was trying to put something over. The sound and the whole aura of the piece may place it down-home in a heretical world of flesh and then blood, but the lyrics say something a little bit different:

> I looked down the line and I wondered
> Oh I wondered, yes I wondered
> I looked down the line and I wondered
> Just to see how far that I was from God.
>
> And the line looked sad and lonesome
> Sad and lonesome, sad and lonesome
> And the line looked sad and lonesome
> Just to see how far that I was from God.
>
> I buckled up my boots and I started
> Oh I started, yes I started
> I buckled up my boots and I started
> Just to see how far that I was from God

So the blues had room for religion, something which we already knew, though maybe not in this way. Tharpe is a bit cagey about the way she approaches musical form here (which itself shows how hip and musically aware she was) - she stretches it out to the limit but her final rise to the five chord puts this in blue territory, as does her interactive guitar (and nice, pace-setting intro, with its clear Blind Lemon Jefferson reference).

Tharpe was a major figure both in her own right and as an influential, interim gospel figure relative to the development of black pop in the 1930s and '40s. In our time she seemed suddenly to become a *thing*, particularly in the middle of the first decade of the 21st century, as an obligatory citation for academics (I will say with pride that I wrote about her in my first book, *American Pop*, back in 1995), with a biography (which came out around 2007, though unfortunately it is a sociological mish-mosh which never seems to put its finger on the essence - or even the nuts and bolts - of her life and work) and then a bit later the American Masters documentary treatment by PBS (a program which was dumb and strange in its own way, but I will get to that in a little bit). Suddenly she was recognized as the major figure she was, but more important was the fact that now various culture scribes had found a *hook* - Little Richard and Elvis liked her, so hey, there's our selling point, we've found another black originator of rock and roll (who was inducted into the Rock and Roll Hall of Fame in 2018). So it's safe to write about her as long we drop in the obligatory assurances that this was black music and a black heritage, especially in relation to rock and roll. Never mind that most critics hadn't a real clue as to what she actually did and with whom and why; and that the way she was presented, as just another cultural example of white theft, represented, maybe, just another racist way of reducing black music and musicians to near-passive social symbols.

Rosetta Tharpe performed and/or recorded with Cab Calloway, with the Lucky Millinder post-swing band, and with the great pianist Sammy Price, which never seems to really enter into articles about her. Yes she was a fine guitarist and maybe Chuck Berry lifted some things from her (or maybe not), and she was a fuser of pop and blues and gospel before Ray Charles (though writers never seem to realize that, just as importantly, jazz was part of the equation too). In my opinion her ties to rock and roll are less significant and interesting than her ties to what I call the blueing of American pop - the way in which the blues and its offshoots, like gospel, so permeated the American sound and style that they became their own form of cliche (repeated into the present day with repetitive, vulgar melismatic fervor) and, ultimately, a wing of soul music. But in order to realize this writers would have to dip into American musical history with much greater depth and fore-knowledge.

Take the American Masters documentary. First it talks over and over about her deep respect for gospel heritage, and then, without awareness or irony, it shows her singing a song written by a white Jewish guy (Nat Shilkret) and his white, gentile, crooner partner (Gene Austin) called *Lonesome Road* (a typical, catchy, post-minstrel category-2 fake spiritual). And then, in the middle of describing her pious dedication to spirituality they show her, without, once again, any sense of awareness or irony, singing the pop song *Four or Five Times*, which is about nothing but sex:

> "Just four five times
> (Four five times)
> Baby, four five times
> (Four five times)
> Maybe tonight
> Done things right
> Four five times
> (Four five times)
> Maybe I'll try
> (Maybe I'll try)
> Maybe I'll die
> (Maybe I'll die)
> If I die, I'm gonna try
> Just four five times
> Oh, four five times"

So....Sister Rosetta Tharpe was an incredible performer, a powerful singer bridging gospel and pop music, who predicted the combination punch of the newer style called Soul Music. As for piety: well, read the above, and then *you* do the math.

Piedmont, shmiedmont I want to say from time to time, but sooner or later I have to face the real thing, the musician or musicians from that region whose playing puts the depth into the depth of that music. In basic terms the Piedmont guitar style, which placed the blues and other black country song into post-ragtime territory, was in contrast to what we call the Delta format, which also used fingerpicking but was less particular about its rhythmic meaning. In heavier Delta-country blues such picking and plucking was more like an uncharted counterpoint. This is not to say that the time factor in Delta picking was unrelated to the pulse of the performance but that it more freely related to the overall line of the song, was more a second, freely applied, roaming voice (though you should feel free to find exceptions to this overly-generous stylistic rule). The Delta blues seemed to carry a heavier weight, philosophically and so musically-speaking; the Piedmont players had plenty of depth, but they expressed it much differently; there was something jivingly insinuating about the bopping rhythms of Piedmont things like **Blind Boy Fuller's Jivin' Woman Blues (1938)**. This was another of those tunes and performance, like *Plantation Blues* by the white Sons of the Ozarks (see above), that, in its profound lightness of being, became such an obvious stimulus to the modern American folkie (as in 1960s) imagination.

This is ragtime guitar playing, yes, with its own relationship to other aspects of black and white guitar playing, like that of Blind Blake or Sam McGee (see Vols. 5, 9), but with its own clipped rhythms and brittle swing. I have complained before about some of Gary Davis' (see Vol. 18 ) lack of musical elasticism, but though some of it is related to late-in-life technical issues, as much of it is probably related to the powerful influence of the school of rag-related musicians he came up with (he travelled with Fuller). Combine this with the playing of Mississippi John Hurt (see Vol. 9) and you have 1960s folk music in essence. Maybe the Delta blues aura of conflict and non-resolution was just too much for those (mostly white) kids to absorb; Fuller and Hurt were calmer and more user-friendly sources of inspiration, even through surrogates like Gary Davis and good-time bands like Spider John Koerner's. [18]

The **Alley Boys of Abbeville** were, according to a web site called *Early Cajun Music Blogspot*, "one of the last Cajun string bands to record before the war." The implication, of course, is that things were changing and that Cajun music, despite its deep and traceable folk roots, was just as susceptible - or should the word be adaptable? - to changing commercial ways. Their performance of **Tu Peus Pas Me Fair Ca (6/30/39)** communicates the fact that they were far from a Cajun trad band. This relates, with obvious intent, to the jazz-injected music of Western Swing, which was busy infiltrating itself into a lot of different commercial lines of country-type song (including the work of another Cajun string-based band, the Hackberry Ramblers, who added electricity). The

---

[18] Spider John's band was an amazing revivalist evocation of old-day pep and swing and new-day good time/ragtime. Read about him here: https://en.wikipedia.org/wiki/John_Koerner

rhythmic and sonic basics of the song (I don't have a translation of the lyrics) imply a relaxed good time (compare these chord changes to Commander Cody's song *Lost in the Ozone*). The jazz element seems like an added starter, but comfortably applied. Listen particularly to the way in which the fiddle solo, starting at 1:47, eases its way into the front line, with a solo that quickly discards the old sound in favor of slinky, jazzy, phrasing; the solo has the prerequisite blues dips but a smoother delivery. The overall performance, in all of its earthiness, shows that, if swing and stomp were never that far apart, they were, in the modern era, going in different musical directions. In Cajun music, however, as in a lot of country and country-related music from this era, the coexistence of certain musical elements - blues, jazz, folkish recitation and new-vernacular slang - was a musical and commercial fact of life.

If white music of this era was struggling to face the demands of both a newly-determined national demographic and the narrowing of commercial category, what of black music and black bands?

**St. Louis Stomp Speckled Red 12/17/38:**
I have written more than once about the delights of Speckled Red's playing, and I will continue to try and explain his significance until at least one of my feet (and maybe the rest of me) is in a grave somewhere. It may be hopeless for me to continue to insist, especially to the the jazz world, that it was Speckled Red and the piano school he represented, and *not* James P. Johnson, who were *the* pervasive influence on Thelonious Monk's old-school distillation of near-stride piano, Monk's own testimony notwithstanding (he once commented, upon hearing back a passage he was playing in a solo piece, "well, that sounds like James P. Johnson"). *St. Louis Stomp* is an astonishing case in point. Right out of the gate Speckled Red tackles rhythm in the varied, circus-style manner that predicts the Monkian time-knots of the bebop years: a rollicking yet very conservative gallop based on riff and variation; triplets that have the effect of creating a sense of accelerating tempo, even while the time remains unchanged; rolling, high cascades of notes that are like trills, but uneven trills with uncertain tonality; and, most Monk-like, the way Red makes the notes of the piano, not strictly alterable like those of a horn, ring and bend with polytonal implication. Musical momentum in this is based on some

kind of internalized, uncanny and personalized rhythmic clock, variation based less on a linear sense of line or conventional motivic development than, to paraphrase the critic Max Harrison, emotional transfiguration and mood shift.[19]

    I understand that it may be a mistake to couch Speckled Red's importance in comparative language, especially as related to jazz piano. To me, Monk or not, Red represents that line of ingenious eccentricity that continually animates black music making of the 20th century. With such figures as Red comparison to other musicians is instructive yet of limited utility, distracting as it can be from his own accomplishments and evolution. If you can, go to Youtube and listen to his performance from the 1962 University of Chicago Folk Festival; it is part jazz, part ragtime, part blues, a little bit of stride, with plenty of jive, a comprehensive musical tour of black America of the 20th century:

https://www.youtube.com/watch?vzNYOE-rrHtA

    This performance is astounding. If the African American Museum in Washington D.C. is reading and listening to this (which I highly doubt, as I cannot seem to get their attention) please open up a new exhibit for this man. Or name a hall after him. This is black music from front to back, back to front; as with the jazz pianist Jaki Byard this is real, educated sound and art in the deepest sense, educated in reality, learned from both the inside and the outside of life. Musicians like this crossed social boundaries regularly like a raiding party on American life; supposed outsiders in the larger historical and social picture, they were really the most *inside* of Americans, more aware, and in greater depth than a thousand sociologists and academics, of what America was and had been. On their way through life they lived intensely in a world which had supposedly been denied them and which kept them perpetually at arms length, but in their wake nothing about this country was ever the same, neither perceived reality, social dynamics, or sound. Everything was different after they'd been here and gone, whether or not Americans (both black and white, because in truth they were that far outside) realized it or not.

---

[19] See Harrison's discussion of Charles Mingus in his book *A Jazz Retrospect*.

**Streamline Train Cripple Clarence Lofton 1939**

On a somewhat more primitive level - yet still acutely central to the sound of American musical location - is the pianist Cripple Clarence Lofton. Like another so-called primitive, Cow Cow Davenport (see Vols. 9, 11) Lofton has an internal rhythmic clock that doubles as a musical compass. The music takes a lot of small detours yet ends up, in an odd and un-ironic way and with full intention, back where it started. Maybe this is a good way to look at music like this, as a whole *other* category of other, of American vernacular music, black and white: it isn't classical or "serious" music, with their grand designs and calculated if effective emotions and emotional transitions. It is feeling-in-real-time, love and hate by the seat-of-your-pants, action and passivity on the fly.

One of the reasons old recorded *black* music like this is so appealing is that it does not contain that layer of guarded truth and racial distancing that still characterizes (if less so than in the past) a lot of what black people say directly to whites about race, whether whites (who are often very deluded in their sense of racial camaraderie) believe and understand it or not. Records like this represent the rare opportunity for whites to look *behind* the mask (not the minstrel mask but the one spoken of by Paul Laurence Dunbar in his poem *We Wear the Mask*):

> We wear the mask that grins and lies
> It hides our cheeks and shades our eyes
> This debt we pay to human guile;
> With torn and bleeding hearts we smile,
> And mouth with myriad subtleties.
> Why should the world be over-wise,
> In counting all our tears and sighs?
> Nay, let them only see us, while We wear the mask.
> We smile, but, O great Christ,
> our cries To thee from tortured souls arise.
> We sing, but oh the clay is vile Beneath our feet,
> and long the mile; But let the world dream otherwise, We wear the mask!).

The more we listen to this kind of music the more we realize how much we *don't* know about black consciousness. Sure there have been a million powerful and revealing words written by African American writers, but somehow nothing gives us the essence of black reality (and by saying this I am *not* assuming that we really understand this essence, know how to interpret it, or really feel it in a profound way; I also am not saying that we *don't* understand this essence, that we don't know how to interpret it, and don't really feel it in a profound way; the jury, hopefully not all white, is still out) like *the music* - even some of the white of it - I have been writing about in these many chapters.

*Streamline Train* is typical Lofton, and of course I mean that in a good way. It has that lean-to rhythm which pushes the steady four beats of this in a way that clearly (at least to me) presages rock and roll's even yet syncopated lope (the left hand on this is a series of rhythm pushes: one-and-two-and-three-and-four-and, implying a syncopation of those weak beats yet very crucially withholding it).

(Digression in re: what I have just thought and written about, it also occurs to me that the appeal of black music to us white folks is not merely in what it reveals about black lives but, in our own selfish and self-directed way, what we hear in it that reveals so much about our white selves, and not necessarily in a racially-specific sense. If the music, as I have suggested, in spite of its original source of inspiration, is, at its moment of creation non-political and instead synthesized out of experience and life and from the core of our unconscious, freely-associating selves, then the power of black music is in not only how freely and convincingly it does so, but also with what unmediated daring it accomplishes all of this, how it tells us what we have been thinking without knowing we are thinking it, what we have been doing without being aware that we are doing it. And it does all of this by providing us with a complicated pathway into our individual and collective memory and consciousness, by showing us a way to combine past, present and future creatively, giving us aggressive access to all we are and, because it has been gestating in the USA for over 300 years, doing so in an amazingly fused Western-Diasporan way. This is no longer the life-mapping of rational man or the careful, compassionate detachment of Transcendentalism, nor is it lofty contemplation or kitchen-sink rationality and realism; it is another way entirely, the way of *the other*, of those who survived the middle passage only to become enslaved, who were led down one political garden path after another and exploited and abused with awful regularity. And because not just the culture but the entire way of life is so damn convincing and enlightening, so persuasive in a supra-rational way, we follow it to the ends of the creative earth like cult members who have given up on exercising our own free will.)

**Tiger Rag Jelly Roll Morton 1938**

In his interview with Alan Lomax for the Library of Congress Jelly Roll Morton brilliantly explains, personally and musically and through the vehicle of the song *Tiger Rag*, the evolution of a certain kind of American song and rhythm, by way of early American dance, ragtime and then jazz. There has been some argument about the song's provenance, about authorship, which has inevitably devolved into a racial argument (Morton's disagreements were with Nick LaRocca, leader of the Original Dixieland Jazz Band, who claimed to have written *Tiger Rag*; some recent scholarship tells us that, though known for some troubling racial attitudes in relation to jazz's origins, LaRocca may have actually been telling the truth about the song itself).[20]

Morton, who for various and strange reasons was often underrated as a pianist,[21] is an amazing musician and cultural resource. His historical memory, as both spoken and performed, is astonishing. The way in which he performs *Tiger Rag* here, no matter who wrote or rescued it from the cultural dust bin, is nothing short of miraculous. Like an old-days Jaki Byard he has a way of evoking a distant musical past through the surface of a porous musical present. Every note and turn of phrase is like a sideways-glance at some different and distant musical day, shaded by a very personal, present-tense, intellectually and aesthetically active cultural worldview. As with Jaki he combines the two perspectives seamlessly, like a patchwork quilt in which the patches, distinct and noticeable, still seem like uninterrupted extensions of the original design. If this *Tiger Rag* is somewhat instructional, Jelly's piano playing is the opposite of pedantic. It is live history, the opposite of dead history. This is no lecture hall and all of Morton's virtues as a pianist are on display - even his somewhat simplified yet brilliant distillation of the stride tradition (Jelly is no flag waver in the James P. tradition) becomes more a matter of

---

[20] This becomes a somewhat hopelessly complicated racial issue; this article, though containing some cluelessness, is overall a very good piece of research on LaRocca, and very worth reading: https://narratively.com/jazzs-great-white-hype/ One thing I would add, about the allegation that calling something a "Dixieland band" is racist, is that Larry Gushee, the most knowledgable jazz historian ever on the subject of early New Orleans, pointed out to me once that the old New Orleans black jazz musicians referred to their music as Dixieland.

[21] Truthfully I think it's because in his arrogance he just pissed a lot of people off.

reducing - no, transforming - the heavy classicism of that style into a new kind of vernacular, one built on a more subtle bow to barrelhouse tradition and outlined with a mannerly respect for certain kinds of cultural and musical decorum. And Jelly's funk is a new kind of funk, derived in part from certain obscene and salaciously embroidered black traditions, as filtered through an amused and somewhat outsider (by way of class) sensibility. Hence his blues, played with non-barrelhouse flourishes, or this *Tiger Rag*, done with ragged aggression yet accented with near-delicacy, novelty effect, and converted, through the sheer power of Jelly's musical personality, to a very advanced form of stomp. The right hand variations near the end, the odd tinkling piano, the finale, like a musical fireworks display, tell us exactly what we need to know about this tune, so elastically adaptable to the art and craft of jazz. But more importantly they tell us what we need to know about Jelly Roll Morton, who *was* the art and craft of jazz.

**Hear De Lambs Plenty/Good Room Roland Hayes 1939**
**De Blind Man Stood on De Road and Cried Morris Brown Quartet 8/23/39**

At one point in my writing life I was something of a constant advocate for the understanding of what I (and many others before me) called the Black Cultivated Tradition, a way of making sound which violated certain of our assumptions about black style. Lacking in tonal ambiguity, swing (in the conventional sense) and what we also often call, correctly or not, blues feeling (because I would argue that such a feeling was really representative of much more than the blues, of centuries of black sound and movement), this tradition followed a different cultural path, though it had its own cultural unities. I felt it was especially important to point this all out because of the way in which certain kinds of black performance had been routinely condemned as representing the supposed taint of European form and style. It just felt all wrong to me; people should be allowed to play and sing and dance as they want to play and sing and dance, and criticizing them for doing so with supposedly less than historical and cultural purity was reminiscent of all sorts of Fascist and authoritarian artistic directives, from the Nazi's suppression of abstract art to the injunction of Russian Socialist Realism during the Stalin era.

Certainly things have gotten a bit better in terms of acceptance and stylistic accommodation. Whatever your opinion, there is no need for apologies for Roland Hayes, whose 1939 recording of *Hear De Lambs/Plenty Good Room* is instructive. Hayes, who successfully toured Europe throughout the 1920s (though he was still subject to the subtle and not-so-subtle insults of supposedly post-racial Europe which, as we know, was in those days often but not always accurately described as an island of black liberation), has a beautiful voice, and he embraces the ballad side of this medley with a reach and range that is tender and artful. Though he is a much better singer than the more recognized Paul Robeson, Hayes has a similar outlook on the black spiritual musical legacy (and I do think that nearly all performances that I have heard in this style are self-consciously concerned with legacy). The sense of balance in this is like a social reclamation of certain values, especially as these values exist to counter degrading white images of black artists; maybe. Certain black ways of being and performing (as with this recording), in their resolute dignity, represented to some an acquiescence to white social expectation, to others passive resistance. I will say that Hayes does present a picture of social ambiguity that is best evaluated - and judged, if such judging is necessary - through recognition of his great poise and unyielding dignity.

Follow-though in that cultivated tradition has often been the domain of vocal quartets. The Morris Brown Quartet recording of *De Blind Man Stood on De Road and Cried* (8/29/39) is a thing of great beauty and impeccable honesty (and as with the Hayes recording above we will refrain from speculating on the source of the word *De* in place of *The*, though if you have read this far you probably have some idea; like the occasional use of the present-participle of *gwine*, such things were casual black accommodations to the *body cultural*).

One of the things I like most about *De Blind Man*, aside from the sheer density of the vocal harmonies and its subtle harmonic transitions, is the terminal patience these singers have with tempo, an ease which comes across as not just a deep expression of black dignity but as a way and means of piety and respect for the song's subject. These are hackneyed topics, poverty and blindness, but black expression in this form, especially when coupled with certain implied minstrelized uses of language, hits my ears like a very subtle and distinct declaration of cultural independence .

### Matzoh Balls Slim Gaillard 10/11/39

There is not a lot that we know for certain about Slim Gaillard. He was an extremely good musician on multiple instruments and, like Leo Watson (see Vol. 22) he took a new language and made a newer language out of it (jazz-to-jive we might say). At first it was for the hip, for insiders only, but before long even the non-hip were hip to it, buying jazz/pop records with strange things happening in the grooves. Some of this jive was a bridge between old and new, walking the vocal mannerisms of Louis Armstrong via Cab Calloway into the modern world of bebop, where hipsters were permanently encamped. Bebop was a serious business, but its highest-functioning artists - like Charlie Parker and Dizzy Gillespie - had much more than just a passing professional acquaintance with the vagaries of black vaudeville and even minstrel mugging. These guys, while assembling some of the most complex music of the 20th century - bebop was like the new musical math - knew from whence they came and understood the racial ambiguities of black entertainment.

In Volume 1 of this study I spoke about the Jenkins Orphanage Band and the more-than-passing resemblance of Dizzy Gillespie's antics in a short film called *Jivin' in Bebop* to the Orphanage's minstrel-like convolutions in a film they made a few years earlier. In black terms we might say "that's entertainment," or really a reclamation by black musicians of certain negative mintrelisms - a reclamation that either proves that, in black terms, there was more to minstrel humor that was close to home than we may sometimes want to acknowledge, or, possibly, just the opposite. Black creativity has a sponge-like tendency to soak up anything it fancies and to use it for its own purposes. So it is very possible that black entertainers grabbed, as a matter of creative principle, at something that was racially counterintuitive and turned it into something that worked to black professional advantage. Another possibility is that the history - of black legacy, minstrel distortion, and black reclamation - is so inextricably intertwined that we will never untangle its insane web, will never really know how far the minstrel apple truly fell from the African American entertainment tree.

Do we really need to weigh Slim Gaillard down with all of this social rationale? Well, it doesn't hurt to know where he came from, though in some ways it doesn't really help either. A lot of this music is good, clean, hip fun, and *Matzoh Balls*, with its very funny recitation of the culinary benefits inherent in this simple yet unique food, done with a distinctive growl that is neither dialect nor accent, recalls a time when the unity of African American and Jewish culture, if somewhat loosely defined, was in their shared view-from-the-bottom. By legend Gaillard, who was abandoned at age 12 on the Island of Crete and who never saw either of his parents again (this is a strange and long and unconfirmed story, best to Google it), was the child of an Afro-Cuban mother and a Jewish father; though somehow I don't think that's what got him to this song, which is like listening to the hot side of cool.

# Chapter 21: Old Music of the Future: Separate and White, The Hard Country

Country music on the gospel side seemed, in the old days. to sometimes struggle with subject matter. Normally we divide a lot of this music into categories of sinner or saint, but a lot of songs were more ambiguous. Death was a given, but how to approach it was not. By the time country was ready to enter the modern era, the Pentecostal approach (emotional, pure, humorless) seemed to have been replaced by the jive sermon (cynical, sexual, jaded and sarcastic); hence, in Volume 20, Bob Wills and friends' strange song of priestly flirtation and congregational sex, *Pray for the Lights to Go Out*, and now, from **Buddy Jones** (with the amazing electrified steel guitarist **Bob Dunn**), **I'll Get Mine Bye and Bye (3/4/39)**.

As a singer Buddy Jones was nothing if not amiable. He tends to sound, in songs like this and *She's Selling What She Used to Give Away* (see Vol. 19), like someone singing phonetically, who doesn't really know what he is singing about, though this may be a form of white signification (ie, fake innocence). The lyrics don't make a great deal of sense, touching as they do on lost love and concluding each verse with what seems to to be an assumption of and reference to heavenly justice. Or is it, and is Buddy a lot less innocent than we think he is? The "bye and bye" is heaven, but getting *his* seems to be a lot more reflective of earthly physical resolution than heavenly. The joke is on someone, but I am not sure who or why, though ultimately this seems to rest in the domain of inoffensive country humor, with a little bit of sex and a lot of pious feint in the direction of assurances that god, too, may be in on the joke.

So the more things "modernize" in country music the more they seek their old level of fake godliness and comic/minstrel punchline. Or at least so says the title of this song. But Buddy Jones is no hard-line hillbilly, but rather a singing monologist, of country humor standardized by flat syllables and a kind of moral shrug. That was the future of this music even as Bob Dunn, one of the great country instrumentalists, really straddled different worlds. Dunn was a musical progressive, amplified and harmonically jazz-conscious, more of a true interval player than even some of the relatively advanced country guitarists of the day, with their blues-based phrasing and pat tonal resolutions. Dunn was more in line with Charlie Christian, jazz's first truly great guitarist, whose new ways of phrasing echoed all over the Southwest and had by this time filtered even into Western Swing recordings. Which is why Dunn was both old-and-new school: his idea of a good time was to swing like hell with challenging phrases and big harmonic skips. At the same time the rest of the country music world was beginning to sever ties with this idea of music, which was both too old (string-band like) and too new (as in jazz) - (or was it too black? Not for me to decide, but certainly something to consider as country music begins its own version of Sherman's March to the Sea).

And yet that march was filled with pauses and detours. I wrote earlier about **Bill Monroe**'s love of the blues and of how, at a folk festival in the post-'60s era, he was seen listening with rapt attention to the blues performer Mississippi Fred McDowell. Bluegrass, we might argue (and argue and argue) in its classic/new music form was Monroe's invention - well, if not his invention, his child. Say what we will about various manifestations of the bluegrass impulse in earlier country music, it was Bill Monroe who took the ideas of Bluegrass' earliest expression as they were in musical utero - that spidery mandolin, the pentatonic line of country scale, the clipped rhythms which replaced the soft, back-in-line passive swing of hillbilly blues and ragtime, the ragtime double beat, the hoedown fiddle wave which became the bluegrass breakdown of solo virtuosity - and realized that these were not just varied elements of old-time music but rather unified musical ideas with new possibilities; and also symptoms of an emerging, white burst of independent musical thinking. Yes, we can trace a lot of this to black musical expression and instrumental thinking (and we will and have; see Evans and McClain, Vol. 15, and Nathan Frazier, just ahead in this chapter). So while some of this sounds as business-as-usual (black origins, white adaptation) in reality bluegrass in its gestation and birth was a progressive and complex series of instrumental events, resisting glib or racially-skewed big-bang origin theories.

Just listen to the accompaniment on Monroe's pointed take on the blues tradition in his recording of **Six White Horses (10/7/40)**. This is a new kind of call-and-response; instead of the interactive push we hear in the black world of blues song the instrumental responses here to the vocal feel like stops and bends - like interruptions in the flow of musical feeling, not so much like the detours of black blues, but more as rest stops where the instrumental interlude is projected like film onto a (white) screen.

Has Monroe, inadvertently or not, found a way into a new white musical world of feeling? The lyric imagery he uses for this blues is classic and black - the six white horses, the train he is riding, "sixteen coaches long" - and yet it is re-injected with white substitutions of feeling, swapping the depth of blues tragedy for an oddly breezy white sense of mere misfortune. What was suddenly most important was not wallowing in past tragedy but instead reveling in novelty and optimism, because the new Bluegrass, for all its trappings - and traps - of memory, was a thing of relentless progress.

Of course, **Muleskinner Blues**, recorded by Monroe at that same session, was both less and more of the same - meaning, it was a blues, a Jimmie Rodgers tune and, to my ears, an even more radical re-statement of whatever Monroe was telling us that was new. Years ago, not long after I first heard this recording, I likened it to the early recordings of Charlie Parker, as a rude announcement to much of the rest of its musical world that the times were not *about* to change but had already changed. In a way even more immediate than *Six White Horses*, *Muleskinner Blues* is a declaration of intent and of a true white way of feeling all of those feelings that coursed through the veins of American - and in particular American country - music in the first half of the twentieth century. This doesn't mean, as I have said, that we have discovered some new, pure white strain of expression, but rather that we have discovered some new and radically independent strain which, having absorbed multiple black ideas of sound and articulation, has found such an original way around imitation that musical precedent is suddenly much less important. *Muleskinner Blues* is like a musical diagram of this newly-radicalized high lonesome sound. Related as that "high lonesome" was to black ways and means (check out some of Blind Lemon Jefferson's vocals), the bluegrass high lonesome had its own isolationist world view. Its cries of existential panic were drier, more detached and more determinedly protective of the self than those of the black country blues men and women who, pushed up against a social wall, became defiant but shrinking resisters. The white bluegrasser, on the very other hand, still had some reasonable and workable alternatives.

Still another way to go was **Riley Puckett**'s, with **Nobody's Business (10/11/40)**. Puckett is more often cited as a guitar pioneer of country music than as a great individual singer, and certainly his guitar accompaniments in various groups like the Skillet Lickers (see Vol. 15) cast him as a having a very personal sense of time (though strangely not as radically odd as some country music critics have claimed. What he did was simply subdivide the basic rhythms of country in somewhat eccentric but clearly discernible ways; and though I hate to say it, this is another example of the inherent disadvantages of having critics with little or no technical musical knowledge). To me Puckett was just as important, and maybe more so, as a singer. From his lips to those records that hillbilly twang was flattened out and basically eliminated. His diction was clean and open, accessible in a very basic and rhetorical way. In other words, this was country crooning, but not of the type that later became depressingly dominant (think: Jim Reeves and Eddie Arnold). There was no saccharine emotional dip, no catering to the matinee-cowboy crowd, which is not to say, of course, that Puckett and the label he recorded for (Victor) was unaware of the need to sing for the people. Still, check out some of what he tells us is *Nobody's Business*:

>"Sunday morning gonna wake up crazy,
>Slay my wife and kill my baby,
>nobody's business if I do....
>
>Morphine's gonna run me crazy,
>cocaine's a gonna kill my baby,
>it's nobody's business...."

It does make me wonder, just which people was he singing to? Is this Gangsta Country? No, it's actually another fine country singer observing the tradition which was, yes, in this case, one of (country) drug and alcohol abuse, petty offenses, poverty and crime and domestic and other casual forms of violence. Really. There was no way to sugar coat it *except* with amiable reminders like this, which let audiences have it both ways - he's a rebel, yes, but he's also your neighbor and church companion who atones ever Sunday for all the bad things he has done during the week. In other words he was *country music,* all things to some people and a reminder to us pale folks that white crime was acceptable and a reasonable alternative to black crime - though not necessarily black music. But miscegenation, even of the cultural kind, had its limits.

Another country crooner, but also of the undeniably soulful kind, was **Johnny Barfield**, whose 1939 recording *Boogie Woogie*, was, apparently, the first country boogie recorded, and a juke box hit. A lot those books about the first rock and roll record will insist on telling you it was the *country boogie* that was the true precursor of rock and roll, in its white-ish adaptation of the (by now) classic blues form, as retrofit for white voices and time. I don't doubt that there is truth to this (though as I have already discussed and will discuss later, I think there is a lot more to the rock and roll dream than just the odd sum of various parts, rhythm-wise and racially-speaking), but I should mention that while Barfield's recording of *Boogie Woogie* (not included here) is certainly very good, it is really a song *about* boogie woogie rather than being an actual boogie woogie; the distinction, musical and otherwise, is important.

First of all, the difference points to an important development in the modern era of country music, one that would have incalculable impact on the music and its audience. As with bluegrass, the new mainstream of country crooning was becoming, more and more, its own indigenous white movement, a declaration, as I have said in regard to Bluegrass, of racial independence. Though just about anything American and musical will always have some connection to African America, it was becoming clear in the modern era of country singing that the market was changing, the commercial targets were changing, and the musicians were changing. From Jimmie Rodgers on the blues was served in ways that distanced it more and more from its sources. Barfield's *Boogie Woogie*, very much in debt to Rodgers, was a very important record, though for reasons much more substantial than its ties to boogie woogie as an historic form: here was another path to *white* soul, driven not by racism or any idea of racialist separation but by a very logical evolution of country sound. In the long term, hillbillies were being driven back into the hills, figuratively speaking, to be replaced by urbanized vocal bots, many of whom, particularly in the early days, still had a human soul (which never disappeared altogether, lest we forget George Jones, Hank Williams, Lefty Frizzell, Willie Nelson, Merle Haggard, et al; these were more than remnants but a rather representative line that went back to the blues through the rough soul of honky tonk music and forged various alliances with other musical progressives of their day and afterward).

Barfield, whose best commercial days were already behind him, recorded what should have become something of a new-day Western anthem, **Gonna Ride 'til the Sun Goes Down**, on 2/5/40. I assume he is being ironic, because this new-day Western Man is riding, not an animal, but an automobile. He has also decided to "quit my rowdy ways," (a Jimmie Rodgers reference) but it is too late, as the girl he is riding in his car to see has already left town with someone else. He then threatens to kill himself with his "44" but he doesn't sound overly serious about it and that's not really the point, anyway. Here, within the musical envelope of old-time country sound (guitar and very bluesy fiddle accompany Barfield in a sparse and soulful way) was the essence of modern country soul, a white man singing a white song about life among other white men (and women); separate and and white; next stop, Nashville (and what could possibly go wrong?).

And yet some things out of the tradition never entirely went away. **The Carter Family**, gone today as a professional entity, lives on, remaining popular and even the subject of a documentary (and book). But think of them, instead of as distant icons, as plaques on the wall of country music's strange hall of mirrors; as living, breathing history, never merely symbolic, always humane and dignified in song. There truly was a greatness about the musical spirit of this clan, who were given the *American Experience* treatment (not to be confused with the *American Masters* treatment) by PBS in 2005. They deserved it, and though it's been a while since I watched the show, it did, unlike the PBS sacrifice of Sister Rosetta Tharpe (see above), actually ring true. Maybelle Carter, the musical fulcrum of the group, in addition to being an influential guitarist (her playing continues to echo throughout the prostrating realm of white folkie revivalism), was also a constant and dignified presence in the 1960s (one of the nicest things about the movie biography of Johnny Cash is how well she is portrayed as a steadying and humane presence amidst the country music maelstrom). She was a non-controversial symbol for white counter-culturalists, and never seemed to suffer from any taint of Southern racial legacy.

The Carter Family recording of **I Never Loved but One (1941)** comes a bit late in their careers, from a time in which their mountain music perspective was starting to fade in overall influence, and yet during which they thrived in the popular country image by sheer musical conviction. Border Radio, a multinational phenomena, spread their music far and wide by the sheer power of Mexican radio broadcast transmitters, which pushed a number of old-school country singers to the forefront with a subscriber-like audience (and yes, those of you who see the irony in this Mexican welcoming of American culture are more than correct).

The Carter Family is central in the history of country music simply because they existed; if they hadn't, to re-coin an old saying, someone would have had to invent them. Their records remain like the lives they lived - respectful and carefully calculated yet never slavishly observant in an historically stilted way, distinguished in their detachment from the perversely vicious tendencies of the political world that surrounded them (politically and racially I would say they achieved profound deniability), and preservationist in the truest possible way; they had the *feeling*, the sensual connection to those aspects of life, real or not, lived or merely imagined, which stood for the most humane aspects of their Southern world. And they were wonderful performers. *I Never Loved But One* rings with that unmistakeable, off-kilter mountain vibe, of twisted vowels and two and three part harmonies built on the tangled consonance of untrained voices. It is the beauty of that twang, once again, which offends certain liberal sensibilities but stands for a heritage carefully preserved and guarded.

One always wonders at the private racial lives of people like the Carter Family. It has become fashionable to label all white social expression and advantage as standing for nothing but white privilege, and this begs the question of Southern complicity in not just slavery but the 150 years of collusion between whites and segregation that followed the Civil War. Even a lack of active collaboration doesn't mitigate guilt, just as Germans who remained aware of Nazi crimes yet remained silent must, even if not acting directly, be considered as participants in evil. Was the right to remain passive in the face of Jim Crow and all of its attendant atrocities a privilege afforded specially to Southern white folks? Well, yes, without question; I just have to admit that it is hard to judge people for not taking certain kinds of actions, because any white person who advocated for African American humanity in that day and in that place exposed themselves to great risk. Most likely an absence of such activism indicated a sense of acceptance rather than support, though technically they may have been one and the same.

From a cultural and musical standpoint I do wonder how aware they were of alternate currents in that Southern musical stream. A.P. Carter, the family's patriarch and song collector/arranger, worked with the black Leslie Riddle to learn and collect songs, and certainly had the collaborative advantage. But the Carters without a doubt had their own thing, separate from if not really completely independent of the racial divide. I have much the same question about Bill Monroe, and wonder how aware he may have been of music like that made by the black **Nathan Frazier and Frank Patterson, (The Eighth of January (8/42)**. This was not a commercial recording, but the music made for this field transcription was unlikely to have been an isolated cultural act. Would Monroe have recognized it as something related to his own ideas or, really, as something directly connected to those ideas by way of sound and rhythm? As something he had heard before? The internal and internalized repetitions, the ritualistic use of phrase, all seem to relate to some earlier stage of the bluegrass impulse. The (black) singing voice throughout has a much different sound than contemporary blues singers from that region, and has much more in common, in its density, to a Songster like Jim Jackson (see Vol. 11). This really is present and past in one, in black music as isolated and separated, segregated and saved. It is absent the blue-isms that we customarily associate with black musicianship, though ultimately it holds our fascinated interest not because of novelty but because it is so deep and dense, musically speaking.

I have written elsewhere that one of the most notable differences between white and black vernacular instrumental performance is that black music in this realm tends to have a lower sonic center of gravity (compare, for example, rhythm and blues and early white rock/rockabilly). So it is with black and white country playing, especially in the rock-hard consistency of performances like *The Eighth of January*. The saxophonist Julius Hemphill used to refer to the "hard blues;" well, this is the *hard country,* rising out of a much more complicated and turgidly-expressive layer of country music than we normally hear. It is not the under-side but the *other* side.

Black vocal groups persist in recalling the basic unit of the vocal quartet, as in **I'd Rather Drink Muddy Water** by **The Cats and the Fiddle (6/27/39)**. Everything from the black vernacular seems to flow through such units - the soft-focus harmonies of the new black pop, the hard harmonies of deeper Southern-bred gospel groups, the square-wave harmonies of black barbershop-type groups singing post-minstrel pop tunes and post-vaudeville jazz; and the coy, somewhat sarcastic drawl of those accepting and resisting, at the same times, certain kinds of racial categorization. The Cats and the Fiddle were a popular group with a number of hits over a 15 year period and, once again, as with some other such gatherings we have heard in this study, they show, in the way the vocals are so openly exposed and dominant, the way to the future of new kind of black popular style. There is something in this style that represents a black aesthetic as it works against certain sociological assumptions. The sexually ambiguous falsetto voice which we discussed in Volume 1, the pliant and docile dynamics of these groups - based to some extent on jazz's need for tonal mobility, its rhythmic and sonic plasticity - imply an ambivalent phonic motility, an effeminate cool which defies dominant images of black aesthetics and sexuality. And yet nothing about it seems contradictory. It stands quite comfortably next to the harder styles of black blues and tougher strains of rhythm and blues. And it even has a common musical bond with figures like Louis Armstrong who, in his more outrageous re-orchestration of pop song (and whose influence this reflects), presented such things as, in essence, black life in (stylistic) drag.

A little more rhythmically mobile was the **Lewis Bronzeville Five**'s version of **Laughing at Life (4/11/40)**. This is more of the same as above, in a category which I have mentioned before but which I call, once again, black pop. Black pop is a post-1935 way of singing, a broadening of black song performance to include not just cross-over but cross-over/crossover, whites and blacks listening to blacks and whites who have clearly listened to blacks and are now playing and (mostly) singing in ways which, if they are not directly black, show a powerful black influence. This also includes the phenomena which I call the blue-ing of American pop, in which the commercial and aesthetic prerogatives of the blues begin to force a lot of non-jazz singers into certain categorical imperatives - in other words *do aesthetically unto songs as that which you would have the songs do unto you*. Make your song the blues and maybe the blues will make you a blues singer. Of course not all black pop was blue pop, though I know some historians and critics (and, yes, musicians) tend to talk about the blues as though it is a form of surveillance: always there, always watching, and always throwing shade at very nuance which might be interpreted as blues-ambivalent.

*Laughing at Life* has more than a little corn in its soul, but swings in that typical casual 1930s and 1940s vocal group manner, with what seems like the obligatory unidentified picked solo (is that a tipple? Probably). The solo itself is swinging in that pop-jazz, pedestrian way, simple and a little bit stiff, really just an interlude, followed by the merging of voices into those typical broad harmonies, then a bit of scat, lead singer vs ensemble, and a Mills Brother-like conclusion. Maybe this *wasn't* the blues or its close relations but just another black performance style. And maybe, in ideological terms (because the way some people talk about the blues makes it feel like an ideology) we should leave it alone, like the sacred tomb of an Egyptian pharaoh.

And yet the blues, per country, still walked musicians back to home, though to one viewed increasingly, by new generations of black urbanites, as quaint and old fashioned. In truth it was anything but, and even the most country of the 1940s country blues showed an awareness, a new perspective, that was like the vernacular-in-motion. One sign of this was the new lyric sense; in its new incarnation the blues was being drawn away from the internalized drama of the Delta, to be replaced by an urban theater-in-the-round, the sound of new city life. Singers, like **Big Joe Williams** (see also Vol. 18), with **Big Joe and his Washboard Band**, were pulling out simplified verses like those heard on **I'm Through With You (12/17/40)**. The lyric story it tells is a relatively benign one, a typical lover-rejects-lover tale, but the musical story is something more. Its two-beat motion is a predictor of early rockabilly rhythm, as in Elvis' *That's All Right Mama*, though the two-beat, easy swing also reminds us of Sonny Boy Williamson's *Good Morning Little School*. Still, *I'm Through With You* carries with it a verywhite-ish gospel-like beat and vocal harmony.

There was a new convergence in this country-in-the city era. As in **Key to the Highway (Jazz Gillum 1940)**, which is a blues of a different kind, sort of. This is an early stage in the life of a blues standard, and though many blues melodies are the same they tend to create variation in lyric and rhythm. The lyrics tell the story here, and it is new, after a fashion:

I got the key to the highway,
Billed out and bound to go.
I'm gonna leave here running
Walking is most too slow.
I'm going back to the border
Woman, where I'm better known.
You know you haven't done nothing,
Drove a good man away from home.
When the moon peeks over the mountains
I'll be on my way.
I'm gonna roam this old highway
Until the break of day.
Oh give me one, one more kiss mama
Just before I go,

'Cause when I leave this time you know I,
I won't be back no more.
I got the key to the highway,

    Direct and deliberately indirect at the same time, it gets its currency from the new distance of singer from song, as part of the trend I spoke of earlier in which the blues secularized its own secularity - the personal, inside story was becoming the personal, passing story, a vanishing act of sonic image; at song's end we have something of an empty stage. This was a modernist credo: I will tell you all I want you to know about me in the course of the performance and that is all you need to know. Good night. And (maybe) that's how the new commercial blues was born.

    Though, like in those creches that multiply every Christmas, it was being born in a lot of different places, some of them not-so-sacred. For example: we love Robert Johnson, but by the time Alan Lomax discovered the almost-as-great **Muddy Waters** living in a tiny shack in Mississippi and recorded him **(You Got To Take Sick and Die Some of These Days 7/42)**, Johnson was dead and gone and the world was ready for some other new and emboldened carriers of the blue torch. There are many startlingly new things about this performance; what leaps out first is Waters' vocal personality, the assertiveness of a man who had never before heard his own voice in this way. Now, in recorded playback, it was projecting like a movie on a screen, and this was all the affirmation, as he recounted later, that Muddy needed. Though he had not been lacking in confidence beforehand, he now knew exactly what he was and what he had to do. So yes, the medium was the message, as any musician of any kind who has ever recorded knows. There is just something about hearing the rising sound of one's voice from a mechanical source. It immediately changes, for better and sometimes worse, one's own self-perception. Either self confidence comes of it or the ego shrinks. Muddy's rose, and it was perfect timing because his was a voice for a new age; think about Son House, equally great, but whose time had, if not actually passed, come and gone with the Delta twilight. House's sound was the sound of the sun setting on a particularly nasty and old way of life; Muddy's was of a whole new day and place.

    **Jimmy Yancey**, pianist, was a groundskeeper in Comiskey Park in Chicago, where the White Sox played. He was a master of that strange rhythm which moved slowly through the Southern blues and which some called the Latin tinge a la Jelly Roll Morton, but which is the clave beat, subdivided as it is in the classic breakdown of 3-3-2. Think ahead to pre-rock and roll (as in a lot of New Orleans rhythm and blues) and then rock and roll (Elvis' *That's All Right Mama)* and you will get the picture. Yancey's playing was strong and basic, elemental in his isolation of certain key tonal and rhythmic elements. He played mostly blues, but within the borders of that sound he found a lot of room for personal variation.

**Yancey's Bugle Call (9/6/40)** is somewhat typical of what he did and how he did it. Yancey had been a dancer in vaudeville (which was a surprise to me; in pictures I have seen of him he appears heavy set and sedentary), and each section of the song sounds like he is calling a new step. The fanfare on this sets the image, of movement across a very funky sound stage. One can hear the curly-q time twist of boogie woogie, the gentle Latin syncopation of his left hand, and the constant shading and re-shading of blue phrases. Yancey was a master of rhythm and dynamics. Listen at 1:03 to get an idea of the intricacies of his art: the sudden abandonment of the rhythm as set just prior to this in favor of a new section of stop-start time, complete with a left hand that plays what sounds like a Latin embroidery, reconciled immediately afterward by a snaking boogie woogie beat.

As a kid Yancey toured with a minstrel group, yes, a minstrel group (remember them? Time to face their definitive professional role for a lot of early black musicians), and travelled all over Europe, singing and dancing and acting. At age 15 he took up the piano, though there is not a lot of information available about his direct influences, or where or how he got his style. It may not matter, but it is fascinating how original he is, working within a very simple format that depends on constant variation to keep it fresh. And yet - there is a letter he wrote in 1940, to the jazz historian William Russell, that, in its way, tells us much more than we already know about black keyboard music of the early 20th century, lax as early record companies were about recording black musicians in those years. After touring Europe Yancey came home and met the blues singer Ida Cox - and Cow Cow Davenport - about 1915. He also ran into Jelly Roll Morton on the road, and Pine Top Smith (pianist and early boogie woogie player). He knew Albert Ammons and Meade Lux Lewis "since they were kids" and met Cripple Clarence Lofton "at house parties." By 1940 Yancey had been working for the Chicago White Sox for more than 20 years, but he kept up his playing. So here we have a classic black musical journey

- from minstrel troop to vaudeville hoofer, with time, as a child, spent theatrically as a "piccaninnie" (a category of young black-vaudeville extra, placed on stage as part of a crowd scene with other young black performer as "cute" filler between bits; "they were always a hit" reported one contemporary black performer about these young crowd scenes of stereotypical, kinky-haired negroes). And then a day job, self-tuition as a performer, and an unassuming moment in the sun recording for Victor. There was nothing antiquarian about the Jimmy Yancey of the 1940s, no taint of nostalgia in his playing but just the opposite; this was old music of the future, in the country of the city.[22]

Significantly more of the same is **Robert Petway**'s **Catfish Blues,** which is one of the most remarkable and telling recordings of the new era **(4/28/41)**. When I first started to write about this tune, striking as it is, I decided to do a little internet research, though I was soon sorry I did. It turns out that the history of *Catfish Blues* is long and twisting; it links back to the songster Jim Jackson, through Ma Rainey, and then seeps into the modern Delta blues era by way of a version by the stunningly rough and original Tommy McClennan (see below). Writers seem most interested in the animal/sexual imagery, though some of the association gets, if you will pardon the expression, waterlogged in the analysis. Apparently, and according to academic analyses, there are fish in the sea and so sex on land and…well, honestly, my eyes began to glaze over at this point. There are significant versions of *Catfish Blues* by both Muddy Waters and Jimi Hendrix. But as much as I idolize both of these men, their versions seem to miss the point that Petway makes so well: this is new and rangy *musical* material, with a drive and direction that immediately removes it from the material meaning of the lyrics. First, consider McClennan's version from about the same time; he transforms it with the knife-edge of his own voice, tinged, as it is, with some kind of deep-set anger but softened, if only somewhat, by the control he has over his own *musical* instinct. His self-accompaniment, disciplined and consistent, helps, though his overall performance is like a glass of water being continuously filled and refilled under a running faucet, as the liquid bounces on and over the top of the glass, splashing off and away and never quite smoothing itself out.

---

[22] For a fascinating examination of what little is known about Yancey read this well researched article: https://www.jstor.org/stable/25046011?seq=1#metadata_info_tab_contents

Petway seems to have taken McClennan's version as a point of departure, but he has so much more patience with the whole of the song that he gets much more out of it. One aspect of what I consider to be the musical genius of the early country blues is the way, amidst a sea of repetitive performance and composition, so many of its performers managed to twist blues melody to their own original uses, to craft new melodies from old by the most subtle of variations of rhythm and verbal emphasis (and so unifying those two in a way which would make any modernist advocate of form-as-content proud). Petway chops *Catfish Blues* up into smaller and shorter musical cells, and he rises to the top of the melody at each key point in a way which makes this sound like some sort of post-Robert Johnson musical variation. Even as the lyrics resist the secularization of the secularization that I discussed above (in which the personal remains personal but also becomes public) they remain open to not just interpretation but also to reinvention. The blues now fragments itself in professional and commercial terms for reassembly by a new generation of singers. Now it's not only everybody's business what you do, but anybody is now entitled to do the same business, to repeat your words with a different meaning.

So where does **Leadbelly** (see also Vol. 17) fit into all of this? Though it is true that he was initially "discovered" by the Lomaxes on one of their searches through the prison population for things as they *used to be* (they guessed, in some ways correctly, that men who had been confined were less likely to be effected by the commercial trends of the "free" world and so more likely to offer musical examples of a an older and uncorrupted style), his music and his attitude turned out to be a bit more complicated. His career is a perfect example of the caged-performer who starts out, of necessity, as an exhibitionist-on-demand, but who ends up, upon liberation, angry and defiant, sponsors-be-damned. He was released from prison in the custody of the Lomaxes, and his eventual conflicts with them, over song rights and patriarchal attitudes and their attempts to domesticize him for public consumption, have been well documented. Still, the end result is an amazing maze of songster creativity as Leadbelly, on display, in effect says "I hope you white people enjoy this because this is what I *am*." **Gallows Pole (1941)** is a thing of great power, rhythmically and lyrically, a plea by a poor man to be spared the hangman through the financial largesse of his friends. Is the powerful double-timed rhythm of this a remnant of ragtime? Probably; the way Leadbelly uses it turns *Gallows Pole* from a song of self pity to a declaration, no, really, a demand, for life, leaving any quaint notion of those old-times far behind.

Leadbelly's professional life, viewed in a certain light, is a matter of either guilt or innocence by association, depending on your point of view. He was a beneficiary of the crusade-like new-folk movement, a movement whose spirit was both embodied and transfused by the personality of Pete Seeger, a charismatic figure with a repertoire smartly tailored to both the patriotic spirit of the war years and the new sense of hope fostered by the Popular Front (which was essentially a social, cultural, and political movement to unite the Left and center in American politics in service of a broad, politically-inspired, war-solidarity imperative). Leadbelly personified the new movement. Through no fault of his own he was everything that white, liberal America required in its spiritual time of need, most particularly as a representative of a heretofore (to them) hidden heritage, and even more particularly as a symbol of something white America had, just maybe, finally done right.

The **Almanac Singers**, very much a white product of that era, were that lucky and unusual phenomena, a group of sincere, deeply principled and uncompromising musicians who, through no fault of their own, became famous (as a result of a hit with a song which Leadbelly had introduced and over which copyrights and authorship became a flash point on race and exploitation, *Goodnight Irene*). The Almanacs included two figures who were key to the radicalization of commercial American song, Pete Seeger and Woody Guthrie. Guthrie is a fascinating figure, a California-born folk singer who early on became very popular as a radio performer but whose instincts and principles and ego told him he had better things to do than end up as a regional, proto-country, cult figure. So he abandoned his first fame, went across country, wrote a series of songs which uncannily captured the proletarian folkie spirit of the time, hooked up with Pete Seeger, among others, and then had second fame.

Truthfully, as I listen to a lot of his work I end up scratching my head at the breadth of his reputation, as he was a mediocre singer who seems, at least on recordings, to have little performance charisma. Surely this was different in person, and I can imagine, from accounts, how well and honestly he played the part of workingman's cultural icon. A good example of his mediocrity is the lead he sings on the Almanac's version of **House** of the Rising Sun (7/41). His voice has little personality and very little going for it other than an earnest but undistinguished attention to the lyrics. Still, this was f*olkie state-of-the-art,* courtesy of the War years, and what *I* think of Guthrie as a performer doesn't really matter to anyone for whom this style and movement of song and singer altered the whole idea of the historic aesthetic in American music. Every bland folkie who stands up in front of an open mic today owes their ambition to Guthrie and friends, who seem to be telling us on these old recordings that if you want to be a real American folk singer everyone has to be able to understand the words.

As with whites, many good black singers flared only briefly in the pop and blues field and either never produced enough "hits" or, in the modern era, never had enough social cache to capture the imaginations of academic critics. The singer **Georgia White**, for one, is little known today. Her name doesn't seem to merit insertion into any available feminist blues theses (Angela Davis, are you out there?), which goes to show that fame is fame even for those whose mission is, at least on paper, to ignore such things in favor of artistry and history.

White was performing in Chicago from the 1930s on and recorded (in 1930) with the New Orleans-born clarinetist Jimmy Noone. That recording - of *When You're Smiling* - is instructive. She sound like she is doing a take on Sophie Tucker (see Vols. 1,10), down to the phrasing and texture of her voice. The result is a little odd, and she is much better a few years later on a series of recordings she made for Decca with, among others, Lonnie Johnson (see Vol. 8) and Les Paul. Her voice has lightened up (texturally that is; there is no racial ambiguity to it) and she sounds more herself, or at least what we imagine her self to be. The whole process is light but not fluffy. She swings, and she seems much more comfortable than on the Jimmy Noone recording. By now she is a regular in black Chicago blues clubs, working with Big Bill Broonzy, among others. She exudes an easy confidence (on **Mama Knows What Papa Wants, 3/41**) that sums up the way in which black song had changed and matured, at least in the commercial sense. Decca would not have recorded her if they didn't hear her as a mainstream singer, and for once the designation was a compliment and a vision instead of a crime against aesthetics.

The new piano blues was changing, smoothing itself out and adapting a more laid-back, mellow posture. A leading exponent of this was the pianist Leroy Carr whose playing, with the guitarist Scrapper Blackwell (see Vol. 17), carried the scent of urban, late-night alcoholism, something prevalent in that nightclubbing, social milieu, where alcohol was still the drug of choice. Jazz was implied in such things, the lighter beat carrying the idea of swing, if not the idea, of actual jazz. I will, for once, agree with the conventional depiction of this as a decidedly new and urban phenomena. It was a product, directly and indirectly, of the great northern migration of African Americans, the new incarnation (though more literal) of the Underground Railroad. It started around the time of World War I, and by 1950 it represented not just a major influx into Northern cities but a radically altering cultural movement. As Nicholas Lehmann writes in his book *The Promised Land: The Great Black Migration and How it Changed America*:

"The Great Migration was one of the largest and most rapid mass internal movements in history—perhaps the greatest not caused by the immediate threat of execution or starvation. In sheer numbers, it outranks the migration of any other ethnic group—Italians or Irish or Jews or Poles—to [the United States]. For blacks, the migration meant leaving what had always been their economic and social base in America and finding a new one."

The rest, as those annoying narrators on cheesy documentaries in which a locomotive is racing across the screen tend to say, is history. A lot of the new that is happening in black music in the post-War years traces back to these new black immigrants,[23] who fled the violent anarchy of the South for new opportunities which, if not exactly emblematic of complete liberation, certainly beat the Deep Southern alternative (and it was in these Northern and Western cities that they encountered some of the Jews who were merging their own lives with the independent record business, strange and scrappy, socially wounded people like Phil and Leonard Chess or Syd Nathan of King Records, Morris Levy of Roulette Records, and of course the leading goniff of them all, Herman Lubinksy of Savoy Records).

You can practically hear the changes as they happens on these old records. Regionalisms were being flattened out in favor of a new kind of urban character. Muddy Waters made the next train to Chicago and was now about to break locally in a way equivalent to national stardom; he was perfectly suited for this temperamentally and took to it like a prisoner to parole. Others migrated with a greater sense of trepidation, sneaking out to catch trains in the middle of the night to avoid their current cracker overseers, who held them captive in Southern sharecropping hell and still regarded them as property. People like Major Merriweather (**Big Maceo**) went from Georgia to Detroit to Chicago, where there was a new and growing audience for the new blues. Maceo himself was a gentle soul on the evidence of his recordings, like **Worried Life Blues (6/24/41)**, which used the Leroy Carr/Scrapper Blackwell template as a jumping off point but with a more concentrated, if gentle, funk. The guitarist was Tampa Red, and it was an appropriate partnership; Tampa Red was a leading composer of the new blues who, with a great generosity of spirit, acted, by greeting them, feeding them, and finding them work, as a one-man welcoming committee for the new musical immigrants.

Already arrived was **Sister Rosetta Tharpe** (see Vols. 20, 22). She knew her way around the blues side of gospel music and wasn't, in spite of some potential issues with the Pentecostal world from which she came, fazed by any of the materiality of the material she sang. Sex, religion, and rock and roll might well be the proper mantra for Tharpe's regimen of religio-sexual fusion, which in itself was not, in a musical sense, a novelty. Black religious and sexual imagery lyrically combined was nothing new, hence the promiscuous African American use of the phrase "rock me" to signify not just the bosom of Abraham but actual bosoms; rock me in church or rock me in bed. And watch out for the orgasmic gyrations of Holiness Church-ites, who were literally rolling in the aisles in what was, I would assume, a process of sublimation of one kind of troubling urge or another. Tharpe's **Stand By Me (3/41)**, only mildly suggestive, tells us how much she knew about the old Southern blues, down to her pinpoint guitar phrasing and its distinct vocal/guitar echoes. Her voice on the other hand was more a noisy fusion of city pop and country style than just a plaintive country wail.

Though born in Arkansas, by the 1920s Tharpe was living in Chicago and staring to sing for church conventions. It is more than a little exaggeration to say, as many sources do, that she was a pervasive influence on the modern blues guitar through her use of electricity and (mild) sonic distortion; she played artfully and with what would in those days have been called, yes, a man's command of the instrument, a silly and sexist terminology that, in its refutation, still doesn't tell us that she was a strong instrumental influence on others. I see no testimony from other guitarists to this effect; more important was the way in which she superimposed, in a manner that was not new but not yet nationally prominent, religious emotional elements onto mainstream pop style, leaving clear, even in white productions as they followed, the overwhelming power of gospel-fueled black music.

 I love electricity in music. Much as I love acoustic guitar it tends, at least in practice, to lack certain kinds of resonance and sonic clash. Unless it's Charlie Patton, with his plunking, search-and-destroy style of guitar playing, or Son House, with his steely and slightly-drunken slide, I tend to get bored at the sound of just plain guitar strings (though yes, Robert Johnson is a whole other matter). Of course numerous Delta/Piedmont/country players solved this problem by creating a fluid kind of vernacular rhythm (eg, Blind Blake, Carl Martin, Blind Boy Fuller, Bill Carlisle, Sam McGee, Merle Travis, among others) that was devoid of the stiff finger-tipping that mars a lot of late 20th and early 21st century guitar playing. To me certain kinds of virtuosity have been the death of acoustic-guitar soul: in the modern folkie universe virtuosity equals cleanliness, which is next to soullessness. The older masters (as above) achieved their greatness with a nasty precision, an angry raggedness of execution that implied, in its starts and stops, more soulful and/or sinister worlds of sound.

 But I digress. There have been numerous discussions of and arguments about who played the first electric guitar, and though I find these to be endlessly fascinating I will avoid them here. I believe that the electrification of the guitar, particularly in the early days, was not only liberating on a sonic and even rhythmic level but also inseparable from the technology which permitted it. Without getting into all of it, suffice to say that the production of sound with vacuum tubes, as in all those early guitar amplifiers, was a singular thing. If you were a guitarist in those days you worked harder than you would today - tubes and early amp technology were temperamental things - but the sound you got, as expanded and compressed by that electrical circuit and as powered by those tubes, was a brilliant thing in itself. It breathed, it distorted, it faded, it extended itself with great plasticity, and it *revealed* itself like the phenomenon of nature that it was, like a flower blooming or a mushroom cloud. Almost all of that has been lost with solid state technology in the production of sound, in the substitution of convenience for musicality. Of course each musical generation strives for its own ways of doing; I just happen to love the rotting beauty of old technologies stripped sonically bare, in a way that exposes the elegance and grace of nature's decay.

I bring all of this up to introduce Muryel Zeke Campbell, early country/jazz/electric guitarist for various Western Swing bands, most particularly a pioneering one called the **Light Crust Doughboys**. There is a shocking lack of information on Campbell on the internet (there *is* a chapter in a book somewhere, but I cannot locate it). Still, the Doughboys are one of my favorite country/Western Swing groups, from the early days when country jazz got most of its ideas from its strings. They are relaxed, they swing, and one can feel the edges of the music as they play it. On **Slewfoot on the Levee (2/27/41)** Campbell is musically right out front; this is the thing to play for your friends who wonder just what country jazz is or means. Listen, for a start, to his perfectly executed triplet at about .58. By 1941 Charlie Christian has emerged as everyone's favorite guitarist, though I am reminded of the racialist exclamation of a well-known white critic who, when I asserted on an internet group that all of these guys had to be listening to Christian, demanded to know "why do we always assume the black guy was the first?" Good question, oh Grand Dragon of the critical fraternity, though as someone like Fats Waller would have responded, if you gotta ask…..

That same critic probably would have had some trouble with the country-nee-city blues guitarist and singer **Tommy McClennan**. Want to know what black music is? Well, here it is. There is not a lot of information available about McClennan, though at some point we know he left his home in Mississippi and settled in Chicago where, as accommodating as that town was for blues singers, he was, despite his worst efforts, a fish still looking for water. He did record for a major label - Bluebird, like a lot of the Chicago blues crowd - but in day-to-day professional terms he remained on the margins. Why? Because he was unreconstructed country to the core, working in a crowded field; the problem was that to a new generation that field too-closely resembled one filled with cotton. Still, McClennan's records were popular and sold well, maybe because his voice burst out of them like someone rising from the dead (and he was the clear exception to the acoustic rule I just cited, uncouth and like a house on fire, and pissed-off enough to provide his own electricity).

McClennan was living on a Mississippi plantation when Bluebird producer Lester Melrose, representing the civilized side of Jim Crow economics (he was a thief who pilfered copyrights and cash), came and convinced him to move to Chicago. There McClennan recorded (**Blues Trip Me This Morning, 2/20/42**) and did his best to fit with the blues club and rent party crowd, but it did not always go well. One story has him being chased from one such event at knife and gun point because, in the midst of singing one of his better known songs (*Bottle It Up and Go*), he used the "N" word. The rest is a blur of alcoholism, until he died from bronchial pneumonia in 1961. But McClennan is important - he stood out in that relatively polite Bluebird Blues crowd; their eyes (they being Tampa Red, Washboard Sam, Bill Broonzy, et al) were on a certain prize, on the new-song blues and an expanding urban audience. Tommy McClennan, just out of the South, was Mr. Natural to their somewhat sedate, living-room reorganization of the music. But maybe there was one in every black musical crowd in those days, one man or women who just stood up and belted and bashed their way through a world of black sound and image, without consideration of "taste" or tact. Without arguing the details, I might theorize that this is what kept the music alive.

**David Honeyboy Edwards** may have lived just a little too long (he died at age 96 in 2011) to get the full blues respect he deserves. He wasn't on any early commercial label, but he did record for the Library of Congress (**You Got To Roll, 7/42**) and did finally make records for one of the small record labels that were starting in those days to appear and then disappear just as quickly (Arc). Pete Lowry, one of the unsung greats of the blues industry, also recorded him, in the 1970s, for Trix. Some limited fame followed (Edwards was especially popular for not only knowing Robert Johnson but also for having a credible account of the night Johnson died). And it's not that he didn't get some final recognition; even the New York Times eventually realized that he was an important link to a ghosted way of life, and he was written up accordingly. He also wrote a very good autobiography, though little I have read of him seems to show much understanding of his musical importance.

Edwards was one of the more radically changeable instrumentalists of that second generation (or so) of Southern bluesman. His guitar style was a re-thinking of the blues' instrumental physiology. It flowed and had a new kind of Delta-swing, was partly linear and partly not; it interrupted itself often. Strangely enough I have not read one word written about Edwards that mentions in any way his unique musical approach. By becoming something of the Grand Old Man of the Blues he seems, through no fault of his own, to have lost his historical edge. Blues journalists, like a lot of music writers, tend to not really understand music at its most basic, though it is hard to see (or hear) how they could miss Edward's radical reorganization of the old-style blues on performances like *You Got To Roll*. From the beginning Edwards sets up a very special kind of counterpoint between voice and guitar, inter and yet in-dependent. His lines feel like they are stretching to somewhere, but then not. Listen at about 1:42 to a classic multi-stop riff that he alters ever so slightly at 1:52 with the implication if not the letter of dissonance. Edwards knew how to smooth out the rough edges of the music, but he also knew how to play those edges into blue musical shapes.

Of course, this being black music, sometimes those edges stayed edges. To each their own in this incredibly tolerant tradition, which almost never seems to police itself, to draw stylistic lines that it forbids others to cross (of course this is not completely true, as one hears later of Northern migrants who rejected the blues as being a sad remnant of plantation Negro-ism; and of Harlem Renaissance-era bourgeoisie folk who strived to be "better" than jazz or the blues and so expressed much different cultural ideals. Still, these attitudes were eventually drowned out by the sheer volume of music that contradicted their assertions).

One such edge was **I'm Gonna Lift Up A Standard for My King**, recorded by Alan Lomax on **8/41** at, according to a catalog card from the Library of Congress, "Moorhead Plantation near Lulu, Mississippi" by a group of singers from the **Church of God in Christ**. This is music as part of that Sanctified tradition which we have visited regularly in this study; the hard-four of its handclaps gives it a sound derived directly from the ring shout. It is a particularly notable performance because it goes on for a long time (in recording terms), lasting nearly 6 minutes, significantly longer than a commercial recording would have allowed. So thank you Alan Lomax; these people are clearly making it up as they go, prolonging the freedom and ecstasy principle of real-time performance. Surely this was both a worldly and extra-worldly alternative to the tortures of plantation life, that version of slavery.alt created by the those whose images of reality are coming down these days like their statues.

A little bit more perfunctory, but just as heartfelt, is the **Paramount Juniors** version of **Old Ship of Zion (11/10/41)**. This is 51 seconds of pure feeling, in a vocal style for which it is hard to do justice in words. Talk about ebb and flow - this is more of the periphery of the black vocal tradition, harmonized in more formal ways than *I'm Gonna Lift a Standard for My King*. *Standard* has ad-hoc harmonies, dependent on sudden and transient inspiration, as the spirit wills itself. *Old Ship of Zion* is more arranged, quartet style, both old and new, re-fitted to a larger chorus of sorts. The unison harmonies - which sound like someone pounding a hammer into clay - drift in and out of focus, with little emotional epiphanies that sound with slight variations of vibrato and pitch. This is, in my opinion, another black relative of the white Old Regular Baptists. It is emotionally available yet aesthetically reticent, seeming to encompass its own religious world of private prayer and public exhibition.

A friend of mine, a brilliant jazz pianist, expressed the opinion a few years back that **Charlie Parker** could and should not be discussed and analyzed in worldly terms, because, quite simply, he was not of this world. I would tend to agree, and it is interesting to contemplate, because, great as Parker was in his earliest recordings (non-commercial, on broadcasts and in private sessions) there is something different going on, an explosion of realization, that begins right around 1945, when he is fully revealed to the world. All that comes afterwards is, compared to his earliest and seminal work, not just more developed but transformed. Does this prove that genius is not necessarily fully formed from birth but requires some period of gestation? I leave that to the neurologists and astrologists among us; because in spite of what I just said, Parker was great from the recorded get-go. If he had been killed in a car crash in, say, 1942, we would still have enough to describe him as a great seer of modernist jazz, though perhaps robbed of his best years. But he wasn't robbed, and neither were we.

As early as 1940 we can hear this youngster, Parker, age 20, proclaiming a new jazz age, via some older ideas (Lester Young anyone?) and a completely new kind of jazz consciousness. I think that sometimes we worry too much about describing jazz in evolutionary terms, for the purpose of respecting the elders who preceded the revolution that was bebop in 1945. All due love to Lester Young and Coleman Hawkins and, of course, Louis Armstrong, but as Joe Albany told me one day, hearing Charlie Parker led to a kind of temporary evolutionary amnesia: "he made everything else sound old and out of date, even Lester Young," Joe said because, yes, this is the effect of certain geniuses. They crash onto our aesthetic stage, charging out of what seems like some historically-hidden space in the wings of art. But metaphors can only get us so far. Charlie Parker learned from the past, but he *was* the future. So, really, no metaphor needed (sic).

On **11/30/40** Parker made some transcriptions (recordings for radio release) with the **Jay McShann** band, out of Kansas City, and I dare say that I prefer this particular band to that other great KC big band, Count Basie's. This was still a small big-band sound, compact and roughly synchronized; Basie's band, fantastic as it was, had already rounded out the edges of Southwestern swing. McShann in 1940 was still old-school. On **Moten Swing**, written by Eddie Durham, Bird, as advanced as he was, is still part of the ensemble, which is a compliment to the ensemble. They don't sound like they are struggling in any way to keep up with this stylistic upstart, who glides through his solo like Lester Young on new skates (yes, another metaphor). Parker was in a constant rhythmic dialog with himself, with the band and, ultimately, with history. Trite as this sounds - and is - it is just the way that Parker constantly forces us, as we look to find new ways to define him, to resort to older and blander ways of doing so.

As does, sometimes, **Duke Ellington** (see Vol. 7). I face, with such a unique yet highly exposed historical figure, the dilemma of how to say something about him and his music that has not already been said a thousand or more times already. This version of **Koko**, an ingeniously designed blues, was recorded live in concert on **11/7/40**, and while one hears from such things how routines were repeated from performance to performance, one also learns that a large part of the art of jazz is in violating the norms of conventional expectation, even in the face of the presence of certain conventional elements. Duke and his men do so in such a convincing way as to make certain kinds of repetition seem instead like development and variation. *Koko* is a maelstrom of sound on the edge of cacophony, built from Ellington's typically peculiar way of dealing with the internal and moving parts of his orchestra. Sections rise into it, fade out of the ensemble, and then move over to let others in. The result is a highly-exposed work in which you can hear and even see the sound and the elements of its production - colored as they are by unusual harmonies and combinations of instruments - but in which nothing, in terms of process, is ever really clear. How did they do that? And that? And that? It involves phrasing and sonority, fragments of music and solos as played by young black men who were, consciously or not, thereby expressing all that white America did not really want them to express, because in doing so they were a threat to the overall dominance of white ways. These men had *personalities* of the kind often resisted by (white) popular image, a deep and aggressively assertive, consciously artistic, bent, and it was all there in the music. And it is worth noting that aside from their fractious relationship with the world of whites, they were perpetually dissatisfied on a personal level with Duke as a boss (based on implications which I have read into various historical accounts and interviews with band members). It is just possible that, in the long term, it was this irritant that produced such greatness, which we might describe as the love-hate aesthetic of personal relationships. But it worked, maybe because these men were used to the daily struggles engendered by double and even triple levels of consciousness.

As we go through this fragmented musical study I feel compelled to deal with the continuing claim that white music is but a shadowy rip off of black music; the controversy is an inevitable result of America's bitter and racialist intellectual and aesthetic history. Arguments pro and con are inevitably skewed by economics and racism, by issues of access and institutional cultural nearsightedness. Which doesn't answer any specific question, but does allow me to divert attention from the difficulty of trying to assess aesthetic achievement as it it is tainted by racism on every level of consideration. And to further obscure things, this difficulty is fed by the incredibly complex factor of America's paradoxically closed open-ness; meaning that never has a society allowed so much room for not just truth but lies, for aesthetic and creative freedom as tempered by legal and extra-legal forms of bondage. America will let you in, but only if you can scale the wall.

Why all of this occurs to me in relation to **Louis Jordan**'s **A Chicken Ain't Nothing But a Bird (9/30/40)** is anybody's guess, but I can drop a few clues. This is 1940, when rhythm and blues is not yet even a thing. And yet many aspects of that music, or what it will become, are in view: the hokum of black word play, the essence of the riff (which in its rhythmic distillation of melody is so essentially black and, something tells me, African or really post-Diasporan), and the transitional lightness and even triteness of the blues as it goes on display for the masses. Jordan was on to something, and it was related to things that Lucky Millinder and Buddy Johnson were also figuring out, which was that the (black) public still wanted to dance and relax to the music. Analysis was to be left to a new class of (mostly white) historians and critics, and though bebop was in the air it had not yet arrived. Modern jazz's expansion of black aesthetics changed everything, made an *art form* out of an art form, inspired a generation of both black and white intellectuals, and was an irresistible force for black liberation or, at the least, the idea of black liberation through modernist transformations of consciousness (because as funkster George Clinton said some years later, "free your mind and your ass will follow"). Louis Jordan didn't lead this movement, and he probably didn't even think he was a part of it, but his music was one of many signs that, in a categorical sense, American popular music was about to split like an uncontrollably mutating cell.

And it was significant that as black music as a way life and as an aesthetic expanded it also contracted, allowing for the kind of eccentric and even impenetrable niches that art, as a fluid and plasticized form of creativity, requires. Meaning: sometimes the new appears as something strange but accessible, and sometimes it feels like it's covered by a cloud, obscuring the details of its means and method. As with **Thelonious Monk**; much as he has, eighty years hence, become a household word, a symbol of quirky genius, this was not only not always the case but often very far from it. From the beginning he was not just misunderstood but one of those "principled" personalities whose single-minded dedication to a single and unwavering purpose was, in reality (and this is just my opinion) just the way it had to be, and not necessarily representative of some great and principled stand. Some artists have no choice; ask them to "sell out" and that blank look you receive will be not a sign of principle but of complete non-comprehension.

What matters most, however, is that by certain critical standards we could ignore Monk; say what you want, he had very little influence on other musicians, though by saying this I will raise many hackles and a chorus or two of protest; but think of it: yes, eventually everyone heard and came to understand his importance. Many played his tunes, and Dizzy Gillespie, for one, remarked on his harmonic innovations. But name me a single pianist who sounds like Monk except in a referential, sidelong-glancing way. Quoting and citing and even paraphrasing for effect are not really influence (and, I will note, the fact that he *effected* so many musicians is not really the same thing as having influenced them). And yet, look again at Monk and realize what a really idiotic standard I am (well, not really) proposing. Monk was great because he was great (shades of the Robert Johnson argument, see Vol. 18), and he was his own man from what appears to be the very beginning, as from this excerpt from his solo on **Nice Work if You Can Get It (5/41)**, recorded after hours in New York City during what we might call the pre-bop years. All of 24, he has already assimilated the elements of his mature style: an odd kind of rinky-tink, on-and-off-the-beat manner of accenting, a way of jump-starting the chords of the tune with percussive dissonance, a sound of constant asides and apparent musical digressions, and a means of constant compositional forward motion (as the French pianist Marital Solal remarked years later, "he was always composing"). The hell with a musician like Oscar Peterson, who in later years argued that Monk was a composer but not really a pianist. Oscar was all surface. Monk, on the other hand, was beyond Peterson's comprehension, neither surface nor strictly depth, but an uncanny merging of the two, of complexity in the service of clarity and new perception.

American record companies, in the historical sense, are like the benign evil seed of American culture, weird and vampire-like structures that do both a lot of good and a lot of bad. Without them we would be like those empty houses owned by Raleigh smokers who, on television commercials years ago, failed to clip their Raleigh coupons; as a result they were denied what they needed for a happy and fulfilled life, denied possessions and other impulsive needs. With them (the record companies) we, like those Raleigh smokers, have a lot of what we require and which makes us feel much better, despite the health risks.

What inspires such over-the-top moralizing on my part? Well, my over-reaction comes from listening to **Lil Green**, a black, woman singer and composer whose modest yet intensely personal approach to singing and song may be said to have had a vast effect on American popular singing. I have spoken here of what I call "the blue-ing of American singing and song," the sometimes subtle but always decisive effect of the new, post-1940s blues, compositionally and vocally, on the American song industry. A large chunk of American singing was, in those years, converted, gradually (though in essence it had been happening from the 1920s on) into a school of blues and post-blues warbling of various and odd stripes and mutations. The impact the blues had was on phrasing, vocal timbre, inflection, and lyrics. Some of these singers leaned toward the jazz side, some toward the blues side, and some stayed in the middle, in the nebulous and forever changing land-of-pop.

    Lil Green was a central figure in all of this, through compositions and recordings like **Why Don't You Do Right (4/23/41)**, but also in her manner of singing, which was gently stylized, yet still all-blues with a feeling. She had a small voice, but it filled all the right blues spaces in and around the songs she wrote. Her records sold well, but it was left to Peggy Lee, who had an even bigger hit with this song, to spread the word. We will not do a recount in racial terms here, because the implications are obvious, but it also matters that Lil was dead by age 35, after having signed with Atlantic Records, which tried to re-create her in the image of Billie Holiday. The results were dismal; she just did not have that kind of voice, and her death completed an unfortunate commercial cycle. Hence my meditation on record companies and their sins, because Lil, who could sing, who wrote great songs, and who had a real and lasting impact on the musical world around her, was soon forgotten, erased by the perpetual curse of the industry's inability to just let an artist be an artist.

# Chapter 22: A Trap Set For Squares; Gospel in Drag

Some revolutions turn the word inside out; others have a calming effect, as in "gee I never noticed that before, but it's perfect. It's just the thing I - I mean we - need."
Such was the world of song and music as the depression came to an end and the War in Europe reached its midpoint. Let's take a look at some of the newer things happening in sound:

**Born To Lose Ted Daffan 2/20/42**
Country balladry, as I have mentioned, was now in thrall to some of the more compromised (as in blander, less harmonically interesting) streams of post-Tin Pan Alley song craft. Ironically or not, while in the big picture American pop singing was showing the broad effects of the blues, in the realm of the realm of country things seemed to be going in the opposite direction. Or were they? Harmonically things were sticking close to those three or four (arguable blues-based) chords which Harlan Howard later on associated with reality and honesty ("three chords and the truth" is how he summarized a good, basic, working-man's country song). The songs themselves often had a bluesy cry - or really whine - to them, and the result was something of an industry of tuneful homogenization, a la Tin Pan Alley, not devoid of feeling but often exclusive of the black/white tug of that old hillbilly sound. There was, of course, plenty of variation, but the preponderance of country balladry was like a new line of heterosexual designer clothing, revealing and sometimes a little too tight, but all-man just the same. Not that the blues were un-manly, but that these were very white folks and they were, intentionally or not, declaring cultural independence under the umbrella of Nashville banality.
But at the same there was honky tonk and its furies, all predictors of rock and roll, which signified, in its crossover, the hardening of country music's muscles at the same time that some of its songwriting was growing more flaccid. There was steady and good-paying day work in war industries and oil refineries, which led to the invention of disposable income which it appears was primarily disposed of on alcohol and, if we believe the songs, women. *Born To Lose,* of the crying-in-your-beer and leaving-it-on-your-sleeve variety, sentimental with a slice of indifference and sung on an instrumental cushion of steel guitar, embodies some of

these tough-guy contradictions. The instrumentation on this was suspiciously close to that of Western Swing, including electric guitar and slinky accordion, showing the convergence of a few different production ideas, all of which pointed to the near future. This was one side route to Nashville, a city where the music took its place on an assembly line in search of certain and profitable common denominators.

**I Be Bound to Write To You  Muddy Waters 7/24/42**
**Joe Turner Blues Son Simms 4 (Muddy Water) 7/24/42**
What more can I say about Muddy Waters, who I think rivals Robert Johnson in importance relative to the musical and commercial expansion of the blues? Maybe it's the musical conservative in me, but I've always preferred Muddy's early work, including the few things, still confined as he was to that one-room country shack, he recorded for Alan Lomax. In the sides from his solo and trio days (his early recordings for Aristocrat and Chess) there is a stark muscularity that, great as his later work is, sometimes gets a little bit lost in the blues band sound that became the standard for that era (the 1950s). *I Be Bound to Write to You* is basically a blueprint for his first Chess hit, *I Can't Be Satisfied*. Thanks to the fact that it was recorded outdoors, it has an usual and (literally) airy sound. His guitar playing is more than complimentary to his singing voice; it is like a circuit wired in parallel, part of, once again, the typical black double voicing of instrumental and vocal, the internalized call and response. Muddy has incredible presence even on this somewhat primitive recording, which is very well preserved and preferable in so many ways to studio perfection. I saw Waters in person in 1969, with his 4 or 5-piece band, and yet I remember mostly the sound of *him*, of his voice and guitar. This is aesthetic charisma: all eyes and ears focus on the center, which was and remains Muddy. Nothing on record that I have ever heard of any blues performer (including Waters) since matches that direct experience (it helped that I was sitting about six feet away from him. This was in one of what the Newport Folk Festival then called the "concerts on the lawn"). In a way, if less radically, it is like my experience, as I discussed in Volume 1 of this book, with the Cajun Balfour Brothers. There was something so visceral in the live-action of Waters' voice versus band that nothing, detached from the in-person experience, can ever really match it. This was an in-the-body experience, totally dependent on the air and the sound waves and the absence of

anything mediating between me and Muddy. Ironically this early 1942 recording, made out-of-doors and with no commercial frills of any type, on a very simple disc recorder, comes closest to what I heard and felt that day.[24]

While Lomax was in the neighborhood he also recorded Muddy, on the same plantation, playing with the group of Son Sims. Their version of *Joe Turner* Blues is stunning, most particularly for the way it points us in the direction of a means of black sound that is largely ignored and misunderstood, even today (even with the various and somewhat de-natured advocacies that seem to float around in discussions of black country music. Someone should play *this* one for Rhiannon Giddens).[25] From the first, slightly disoriented, notes, this can and should only be called from the *black* country of black country, an informal yet deadly serious gathering of black voices in the service of a very specific tradition, as they lived and breathed and walked it, every damned Southern sharecropping day. It is precise, it is ragged, it is a formal recitation of legacy turned out without any trite consciousness of "tradition" as we (of the white and, as I see things happening, the black middle class) think of it today. It is just another day in the field, with instruments that are basically extensions of these black lives, a day made of black Southern consciousness, defiant and resistant (and this is where the political basis of black music lies, I think, in the persistence of those who kept on keeping on under the most vicious forms of social surveillance, revealing so much of themselves in essence yet never showing their true social cards; what makes it even more interesting is that the strain of this hardly ever shows. They just keep doing what they do).

---

[24] Consumer alert: on the official release of Waters' "plantation" recordings the sound is, quite literally, destroyed by horrendous restoration and de-noising. I mean *destroyed*; it sounds like it was recorded in a water tank with all frequencies above, maybe, 1000 kilohertz deleted. If you want to own it, get the Document issue, which is un-tampered with.

[25] I have caught some flack for my public criticism of Giddens who, to me, McArthur or not, has not a clue about black style and the vernacular tradition. At best she has a very pleasant singing voice, but is nowhere near to grasping the ways of poor vernacular folk song in any way. Her gospel singing is exhibit A of this, and really the only exhibit we need; you want cultural appropriation? Here it is: https://www.youtube.com/watch?v=KUdNZ7kHea8

**Mean Old World T. Bone Walker 7/31/42**
Listen to this one, and I mean listen, from the beginning. First, hear the descending chords of the introduction, which immediately tell us that this is a brand new kind of blues. And then listen at how, over a heavy, steady walking bass, surrounded by a trilling piano and brushes, T. Bone Walker enters on guitar. First there is that unique sound, which the guitarists among us might know is produced by having the guitar pickups (which are basically the microphones that amplify the sound of the guitar strings) wired out-of-phase. As is noted on something called The Gear Page on our friend The Internet:

"Out of phase means that one pickup is connected backwards -- either the hot and ground leads are reversed or the magnet has been flipped. The magnetic polarity determines which way the current will flow in the coil, and if each pickup is connected with respect to its proper current flow, the pickups will be in phase."

The result is that flat, thickened sound that T. Bone has, which is made, as well, by combining two of the pickups on his guitar, the neck and the bridge. But more important, listen to the way the rhythm section implies the value of swing; but mostly there's Walker, the notes he plays and the way he phrases them, not as jazz but as blues powerfully influenced by jazz. Walker was from Texas, definitely knew Eddie Durham (brilliant arranger for the Count Basie and Bennie Moten bands who played both trombone and guitar and who early on was experimenting with ways to amplify the sound of the guitar) and most certainly was aware of Charlie Christian, who had taken the concept of jazz guitar to new levels. Walker is smooth and relaxed; in conventional terms this is usually (and correctly) cited as representing a new approach to the blues, as a wartime and post-war signifier of a new musical sophistication; and played in the style which will become commercially dominant in the next few years through both pop-blues and jazz vessels (like Nat Cole, not to mention the early Ray Charles), signifying a new level of social sophistication and a new style of post-vernacular night - and day - life.

**The Honeydripper Part 1 Joe Liggins 1945**
There is a very interesting book I read a long time ago about a subject which has become more and more popular in the last thirty years, as more and more early and mid-period music has become available on reissues and the internet. It is called *What Was*

*the First Rock and Roll Record?* and was written by Jim Dawson and Steve Propes. And though I have certain disagreements with some of their points of emphasis (I take a very unpopular position on the invention of rock and roll, which I think is very distinct from its black predecessors and very much a white medium and which, as I have said, represents a white meditation on black forms. But more on that later), the book is a wide-ranging and interesting examination of many of those recordings which preceded rock's musical explosion in the middle 1950s, some of which I was previously unaware. One in particular, *The Honeydripper (Parts 1 and 2*, though I include only part 1 in this collection), recorded by Joe Liggins and group, has always stood out for me.

First of all, and most interesting to me for its cultural imagery, Propes and Dawson tell us that *The Honeydripper* was a huge hit locally in Los Angeles and that, as they tell it, one could walk down the street on a warm night in black neighborhoods there and hear it played continuously on record players through open apartment windows. And certainly this tune, with its stripped-down instrumental sound and very basic lyrics, was in its odd way a predecessor of rock and roll and a departure from the typical (black) rhythm and blues sound. It was something of a novelty, with its repetitions, unison vocals (almost jazz-like, as in the black vocal group sound), jive vocal riffs ("hoy hoy hoy hoy hoy"), its (sorta) jazz interludes ("Swing it on, swing it on, swing it on up there") and, finally, a classic rhythm and blues tenor sax solo, which takes it back home to a more traditional r&b sound. As Propes and Dawson make clear, they are only speculating on whether this (among many others they name in the book) was the first rock and roll song. I have to admit I find all such speculation fascinating; just asking the question and failing to really answer it tells us all we need to know about such origin stories, which are irresistible yet inherently false. But the song remains.

**I'll Remember You Cecil Gant 1945**

Cecil Gant was just out of the army when he recorded his big hit, *I Wonder* (which we will hear in this collection in an unexpected but strangely effective performance by John Lee Hooker, see Vol. 25), a tune which, as such things sometimes do, both summed up and predicted changes in the body-culture of America life. We won't belabor the various historical events that led up to the decisive urbanization of American music, but suffice to say that the exhilarating effects of World War II (segregated army and all) on black veterans led to certain great, post-War expectations, not all of which were quickly or completely dashed. The usual factors - war industries, returning soldiers, the exhilaration of American victory - all brought both white and black together, sort of, and the results were probably not what the war-propaganda machine was expecting or, really, depicting. There was little lasting harmony in racial relations after the war, and the new social intimacy inspired by the war itself, amplified by mass media like radio, the recording industry, and even film, produced the peculiar sensation of segregated integration. People might work together, walk together, ride public transportation together, but at the end of the day (actually at the *beginning* of the day) certain things hadn't changed; the racial and racist hierarchy remained. The vicious inequities of the American system were still built into that system, especially in terms of professional pay and promotion (for an unrelenting examination of all of this read Chester Himes' searing novel *If He Hollers Let Him Go*).

I always remember something that Dizzy Gillespie said to me years ago in a phone conversation. "They never let you forget you're black," he told me, his voice dripping with anger (this was over a major if unintended insult he suffered while performing at the White House). The point was that the more things changed the odder they got in terms of racial and professional dynamics. Still, a performer like Gant had something of an integrated approach to performing. There was nothing compromised about his sound or style, it just represented what we might call a more middle-class musical perception, less aesthetically disruptive, more settled, a kind of calming of the seas of black performance art. And he was popular, though sadly his career was shattered by his drinking (he was dead by age 35). *I'll Remember You* is typical of his compelling yet very elemental songwriting and vocal technique. It's not really the blues, but the blue implications are obvious. The chord changes on the A section are all 1-4-5, with a few substitutions dropped in, and his piano playing is very pleasantly and appealingly jazz-like (the bridge of the song is what jazz players calls *Honeysuckle Rose* changes with some variation); this guy had real jazz chops, and his voice, if limited, is amiable and accessible. This was the blues with benefits, with a tinge of actual sophistication and no artifice, and so perfectly suitable for the begrudging social optimism of those colored folk who were on their way to becoming, instead, white resistance notwithstanding, people of color.

**Shaw 'Nuff Charlie Parker Dizzy Gillespie Al Haig 1945**

Now *this* was a real revolution. Try as we might to fit bebop neatly into some older and more traditional jazz boxes, the music, seemingly sprung from the head of some crazed agent of Zeus, was maniacally complex, speeding toward its own musical conclusions. Despite this it was, in certain ways, a disturbingly soothing thing. It was new and it was fantastic in every sense and it was also strange and forbidding, with its difficult tempos and the way in which it required a command of instrumental technique perhaps only seen before, in this musical universe, in Art Tatum (see Vol. 17). We talked about Parker (see Vol. 21) in the last chapter; by 1945, when this particular performance was broadcast, he was teamed up with fellow revolutionary Dizzy Gillespie and, among others, the pianist Al Haig. Here they were in California, on bebop's first real commercial journey.

(And I guess I should quickly and at least partially define *bebop*, which was a re-working of jazz's harmonic and rhythmic elements. Though not the first generation of jazz to emphasize certain kinds of rhythmic parameters, of eight notes, rapid triplets, lightning-fast harmonic and rhythmic resolutions, odd intervals and certain kinds of chord intervals - often inverted for effect - it *was* the first to build a style on these things).

*Shaw 'Nuff* is an apt introduction to this music, with its brilliantly abstract introduction, sharply-pointed melody, and comprehensive solos. Parker is Parker, a musical lightning rod of melody and rhythm, the supreme genius and logician of bebop. Dizzy has an equal aptitude for rhythmic spark, and an amazing technique unparalleled (and essentially un-imitated) in jazz; Haig, the pianist, an old friend of mine who told me years later that "Dizzy showed me how to voice chords," is, as Bud Powell remarked a few years later, a "perfect pianist," already acclimated to the bebop line, which was a thing of linear wonder. On drums is another white disciple of the new music, Stan Levey, about the only drummer in bebop's history who could match Max Roach in steely intensity. He is all of 19 here, and he keeps up with the music's accents and and crazy time without appearing to break a sweat.

As Haig told me years later that this band, contrary to legend, was not, in its West Coast debut, met with anger or hostility but with confusion. "They were just flummoxed," he said of local audiences, who had little idea of what they were hearing. Certainly they had no idea that this was, in spite of my general aversion to cliches, real and living history being made right before their eyes and ears. Yes, there had been sounds like this in the air for a few years already, but bebop in its final form, as on this live version of *Shaw 'Nuff*, was so essential and necessary a movement of change that hearing it was like watching an underground movement in plain sight, shielded by technique yet, sonically, completely exposed.

### Walking the Floor Over You Ernest Tubb 1942

By now anyone reading this study has probably figured out my own musical and aesthetic prejudices. Though I worry that someone will challenge me to give a definition with more depth to it than I am inclined to give, I will say that I like my music *real*, to sound like life itself (though my idea of *life itself* should not be assumed to reflect what I think is the fake-ness social realism; If you asked me, which you didn't, I would say that you will find reality more readily in what you don't see than in what you do).

Vernacular music is a different kind of complex. In country music, at its best, what we hear in record grooves are graven images that come at us in three-minute sequences, easy to understand in the basics and yet with a whole lifetime of subtext. These were more than simple snapshots of Southern life, they were sonic life studies. This gave them a sense of spontaneity and, yes, reality. As much as things like *Walking the Floor Over You,* as recorded, were set pieces, they still implied other spaces and other audiences, peaceful and troubled, reactive and passive. This was one of the beauties of working class music in those far-away days, when it was the music of the real folk - it was all the same over and over again and yet made different at every turn by the changing consciousness and perceptions of its audience. The music stayed the same but the audience changed, internally and externally. They were its means of variation, even as the one hundredth quarter was dropped into that jukebox, or as the singer took the same request he or she took night after night; it was all the same but different; the message became something imaginatively relative.

*Walking the Floor Over You* is a glorious example of this kind of reality as counter-reality. It is not surreal, not part of any parallel universe. But it was among the foundation recordings of the honky tonk style, built for those roadhouses where white rough and rednecks gathered to shield themselves against the changing political and social realities of American life - which doesn't make the song or the genre political. It is actually counter-political, really a shield of sorts against encroaching human beings of a different color, against life itself and certain American social inevitabilities (like the beginning of the end of segregation, not to mention the massive federal New Deal aid that pinned the South to the American map). It is, in its basic-ness and simplicity, with its functional electric guitar and man-of-the-people vocal, like a small chamber of blues pastiche, almost completely white it in its subtle musical deniability. This was just those guys and the night and that music, a story told over and over and over again.

**East of the Sun Sarah Vaughan Dizzy Gillespie 12/31/44**
This was a different night and yes, different music, though no less meaningful to its audience. Made something like 24 hours before bebop was officially born (I am, without authorization, dating bebop as having started on New Year's day 1945, and this appears to have been recorded the day before), several of bebop's sharpest advocates were present for the pre-post-labor rituals of setting it down on disc. Sarah Vaughan was barely 20 years old, Dizzy Gillespie a ripe but refreshed 27, and yet they had already changed the world (though the world didn't know it yet). There is something about the work of revolutionaries at first flush that I find essential and educational, a refreshing lack of self consciousness in their early and sometimes most revolutionary utterances, and I find this to be particularly true of Sarah Vaughan. She did incredible work at all stages of her career (particularly in the late 1950s), teaching the jazz-vocal world a lesson it could never really fully assimilate, about not just melodic and rhythmic paraphrase but also about how to re-build a popular song in radically assimilative ways (meaning, the song was still recognizable). No matter how she executed her vocal acrobatics - with scat-like lifts in the melody, broad stretches of interval or real-time rebuilding of the time, getting new melodies from old - she always landed on her feet. Most compelling is that like Gillespie she spawned almost no real imitators, because her way of singing was literally inimitable. It was more than just a matter of being technically compelling. She lived in a realm of radically shape-shifting aesthetics, with techniques that were almost not copyable by other performers, so forbidding were they in techno/aesthetic terms. You might learn one or the other, the technique or the art, but you could never fuse them like they were your own. This was more than someone else's ideas, it was their *reality*.

Listen as Dizzy steps in at 1:25. I love the way this is recorded, in a dry room which projects the sound. The trumpet is in your face, as though Diz has just stepped right up to the microphone (which is exactly what he has done). He delivers a temperature-controlled solo, perfectly paced. But he still has to remind us that this is bebop - hear the flatted fifth he delivers right at 1:35/1:36, its dissonance like a trap set for squares - and he quickly resolves the tonality and any doubts anyone might have have had that these musicians, in the modernist theater of change, were conducting the orchestra.

**I Want Two Wings Utah Smith 1944**
**God's Mighty Hand Utah Smith 1944**
Just what the hell is Utah Smith up to on these two recordings, both made in the same year and both mighty candidates for the distinction (and this is just my opinion) that I discussed earlier, of being the first rock and roll records? Let us examine the elements of Smith's style: an electric guitar, fluid, technically precise, rhythmically driven by some dynamic inner, divine voice. It is played out-of-tempo, as the free jazzers like to think of it, but it has a consistent and deep, elemental pulse (as the free jazzers *don't* like to think about it). How do you keep time while not keeping time, swing while not swinging? Utah Smith is how, by keeping a lid on certain linear impulses even while bringing out the kind of linearity that does not depend on (conventional) continuity. In this way his music is classically *black*: thoroughly modern in its emotional development of certain lyric and musical motifs, thoroughly free in it is surface abandonment of inhibition and self consciousness, thoroughly and spiritually liberated in its other-worldly-ness, thoroughly traditional it its free-form association with community and worship, and thoroughly conservative in its attempt to gather all of that strange and compelling aesthetic baggage and drag it all back down to earth in order to address the concerns of common folk.

Is this the beginning of rock and roll, and if I think so, what is my justification for saying so? Well, start at the beginning. Though we tend to persist in looking in certain directions for the things that birthed rock, at the blues and rhythm and blues, I think we are lost on a a circular trail. After Darwin, I would posit that the blues and rock and roll are not direct antecedents but rather have common ancestry, in the direction of what has been called the guitar-playing evangelist, for starters, and certain, religious/ emotional aesthetics. Note, I am not merely citing gospel music in general, I am looking at form and style, at the way the gospel, guitar-playing leader of the flock led with his fretboard, driving the time through the contrapuntal rhythm of his voice and guitar. Utah Smith does this plainly; in the African American manner, yes, his guitar is the drum that drives the sound, but it is also the voice-lead that drives the congregation. This phenomena, of guitar-led congregational singing, was both black and white (Elvis' congregation had a guitar-playing leader) and pointed both forward and backward, historically speaking. In this study see Blind Willie Johnson, the Reverend E.W. Clayborn and Brother Claude Ely (Vols. 6, 9, 28), all men of the moveable cloth, roving evangelists who settled down for the occasional congregation and recording session. The sheer drive all of these men had was a pre-rock and roll premonition, and it was the guitar that did the driving. Rhythmically this was *not* the rhythm and blues shuffle, it was a relatively straight-4-beat ministration; different audience, but same basic emotional outlet. And as I will continue to point out, sonically it had a higher center of musical gravity, a spirituality derived from the trebly center of its being. [26]

And listen to Smith's motile guitar playing, a perfect mix of emotional stops and precise, emotional, defaults - for the people in one place, for god in the next. Listen to the intervals he plays, which are a unique, recognizable and compelling fusion of country pentatonics with the blues, using intervals - the flat and major third, the flat and major 7th, the sixth and fifth and flatted fifth - that combine modern country solo tonality with blues phraseology. That is what probably makes *these* the first rock and roll records, because if rock and roll was, as I have claimed, a white meditation on black form (with electrical implications), then it is fitting that the first to person to offer a primer on how to do so in a truly compelling way was a black man.

**What is This Thing Called Love? Lennie Tristano 1946**

Back in the middle 1970s I was doing the occasional jazz journalism piece and, after months of pursuit, managed to land an interview with Lennie Tristano at his home in Jamaica Estates, Queens, in New York City. Lennie, in his musical dotage at the time (well, he didn't think he was at this stage of life but there was something odd and off-putting about the way he held himself out

---

[26] This, by the way, might take us in an entirely new direction. As Dave Schildkraut told me, speaking about John Coltrane but applicable here, the search for the highest note was a spiritual search for God. So, it may be said, was the increasing screech of blues, and then rock, guitar.

as the last great defender of artistic principal, in a way that made it all seem like the final ravings of a faded revolutionary), was still, in his way, holding firm. He was vain about the money he earned teaching ("this is my price," he said, pointing to two adjoining 9-foot Steinway grands that took up a large, two-room living room) and he was overweight and sedentary looking. His favorite word was "cocksucker," with which he labeled everyone he felt had somehow insulted him in the music business through both omission and commission - this one wrote about him but didn't understand his music, this one ignored him completely. Sadly, Lenny didn't have long to live (he died of a heart attack not long afterwards or, as Paul Bley said, by way of an attack of Chinese food, with which, according to Paul, a series of girlfriends stuffed him).

    I mention all of this because Lenny, if content to tie himself to the mast of modernist principal, was not altogether incorrect in picturing himself as a lone model of artistic virtue. He had devised, in its earliest days, one of the true alternatives to bebop's strangely schematic, yet freely interpretive, language and syntax. He had taught its essentials to a few others (most particularly the saxophonists Lee Konitz and Warne Marsh) and really done something that had to be done as jazz, post-bebop, juggled new-modernist impulses by digging into "contemporary" composers like Stravinsky and Webern in harmonic terms. The result on some early and sincere musical attempts was melodic/harmonic exposition and composition that stretched the bounds of tonality, followed by solos that, instead of taking these ideas to any logical conclusion, fell back on conventional bebop phrasing and harmonies (a good example of this is George Russell's brilliantly imaginative *A Bird in Igor's Yard,* written for the clarinetist Buddy DeFranco and big band. The beginning is adventurous and expansive, and then DeFranco steps in and plays, beautifully - but in a very conventional bebop way, sidestepping Russell's intentions and the tonal implications of the piece).

    Lenny changed all that, and he changed it before anyone else even thought about doing so. From the beginning, though steeped in the playing of Art Tatum and Bud Powell, he was interested in more adventurous harmonic extensions, in constructing odd meters of line, in exploring intervals that were ends in themselves - as on his 1946 solo version of *What is This Thing Called Love*. Beboppers all played odd intervals, but they also almost always insisted on resolving them in consonant ways. Listen first at the beginning of this as, almost Eric Dolphy-like, Tristano constructs the line based on chord substitutions that make it sound like he is having, musically, an out-of-harmony experience. From there he goes even further, punctuating chords with whole tone intervals, flat ninths, and other assorted varieties of moveable tonality. At .35 he twists his way through the changes in ways no one else was doing at this time. Add some amazing abstractions of Tatum-like harmonic cascades and extended lines, some perfectly executed block chords, some machine-gun clusters of notes, and you have bebop unlimited; and, yes, the messenger is a white guy.

**Indiana Don Byas and Slam Stewart 1945**
The tenor saxophonist Don Byas wasn't exactly part of the revolution that was bebop, but he wasn't exactly *not* part of the revolution that was bebop. Early on he recorded with some of bebop's prime sources, including Dizzy Gillespie and Charlie Parker, Al Haig and Max Roach. In the parlance of the day (well, any day) Byas tore through the changes, meaning he approached chord sequences like they were harmonic mazes set up to be circumnavigated, mathematical puzzles in need of solution.

The conventional wisdom tells us that anyone who soloed in the style of constant eighth notes was a bebopper in those days, but Byas, who does just that, tells us otherwise. Like Coleman Hawkins, one of the other great saxophonists of early and mid-period jazz, Byas played those eights with just a slight hesitation on the first of every pair, an old style of phrasing derived from Hawkins but turned, by Byas, into bebop-derived Swing, a more linear, horizontal linearity. Byas' method was more in line with bebop's contours of melody, the harmony navigated like a trail that led through the upper and lower partials of those chord changes in a constant and steady stream (Hawkins approach was more stop and start, of ready detours leading from horizontal to vertical; in metaphorical terms it was as though he kept pausing in mid-hike to gaze at the view).

Byas was old-new, or was it new-old? Either way he signaled a new sense in the music, that tradition was relevant simply because there was now a tradition that was clearly defined in its contrast to *the new*, and yet which overlapped. To wit: Louis Armstrong and Jelly Roll Morton played like they played and, yes, their music was timeless but still very much of its time. They may have fiddled through the fire that was modern jazz, but they were always purely themselves. When it came to change, in the modern jazz sense, they largely, in their playing, avoided the issue. But Don Byas heralded the arrival of a new generation of jazzers by fraternizing with those who some might have considered the enemy. In this he, like Hawkins and Lester Young, signaled a new movement, or really maybe just a new trend, in jazz, of certain key and creative older figures who just naturally synthesized certain older and even out-of-date musical elements with the new. By doing so they sometimes negated themselves in critical terms (because critics and historians often have problems with artists who wander, ghost-like, between warring aesthetic camps); Byas helped lead us to a whole new way of seeing jazz history, in which musicians were no longer viewed as either/or but as part of a non-linear continuum. Trite as it may sound, the past was now *officially* the present, the present the past.

**Coquette Leo Watson 1/24/45**
Someone who is much better equipped than I to lead the discussion will tell you why black word-play is related to not only hip hop but old styles of black argument like The Dozens, the talking blues, and any number of of life-narratives a la Jelly Roll Morton et al. I will only say that the African American talent for improvisation, built, in the North American version, into a life-survival technique and method of self and group-entertainment, was verbal as well as instrumental. Saxophonists, pianists, trumpet players and drummers were just following a well-worn trail that lead from slavery on, and hip hop, one of the most logical extensions of that trail, is also one of the most highly developed, fearless, contemptuous, braggadocios and, when necessary, just plain nasty.

And then there's Leo Watson, one of the inventors, in the modern, jazz, sense, of the style of vocalese, a method of fitting words to music in improvisational ways. The challenge of vocalese was syllabic, the fitting of language to phraseology that was driven more by musical imperative than spoken, and yet was really an intuitive combination of both. Watson recorded as a soloist and with vocal groups (like the Spirits of Rhythm, see Vol. 17) and was a leading purveyor of the *real* American hipster ethos in its actual phase, of free association in the material sense; meaning the scattering of images knitted together by a hipster logic and consciousness (substitute, if you will, black for hipster any time that you feel like it). The trick was to make language and music fit together naturally and poetically, and yet as logical contradiction.

And so I offer to you *Coquette*, which has all of the above. It has now been reset from its original meaning as a song about elusive love. In Watson's mouth it is a song about food, chicken croquettes, mustard greens, and filet mignon. It's all delivered with a mop-mop logic and insertions of syllables determined by sound more than meaning, or, really, sound-as-meaning. In this sense it is a truly revolutionary thing, a radical realignment of reality in a very black, hipster (there's that word again) way. It is as though Leo Watson and friends are outlining the future, a world of post-representative reality in which reality is whatever they determine it to be, in the moment; is this an Afro-Futurist manifesto and declaration of independence? Probably; because American reality was never, in the truest sense, and as much as white people may have tried to impose it, black truth.

What is smooth as silk, slick as pup shit, yet very rough and even knife-like around the edges and hard for your average man-and-women-on-the-street to digest?
If you answered "Black Sanctified religious music" you win a get-out-of-hell-free card (though it would have been ok to answer "White Sanctified religious music, because there are white fundamentalist sects that follow the black example with screaming, flailing, arm-flapping hysteria; see Youtube for examples). Play something like **J.H. Terrell and Congregation**'s **Missionary Sermon (7/23/42)** and odds are your average American will either hate it or love it; when it comes to this kind of religious, love-hate passion there is little in between. Terrell hits the ground growling, his entire sermon a warning, as tough love. There really is a detour ahead and that detour is death, though, maybe, it's not to be feared but rather welcomed; or maybe it *is* to be feared:

> "You promised me a long time ago
> You'd make up my dying bed
> Come on, stop crying!
> Don't let me come into your kingdom crying!"

The congregational response is nothing short of hysterics and hysteria, frenzy on the edge of panic, though it's panic as a form of self-medicating. As crazed as these preachers were, as blinded by the light, they really saw not only the American present, beat as it was, but also the American future: death as an exchange for freedom, and earthly existence as a mere transitional state. But a transition to what? Some things, in this light, are beyond death; the American contradiction was all tied up in these hellish versions of the existential middle passage, which were both liberating and terminal.

As I write this and remain exiled in my house during the Pandemic I am about to do a Zoom session on black country music. I have, especially since I started this project, been critical of the way most entities, from documentaries to journalists, treat the subject. Most such efforts seem to me to be tainted by a well-meant tokenism. The effort to praise African American contributions is usually reduced to almost nothing by intellectual laziness, an unwillingness to do anything more than give lip service to a tradition which is incredibly complex and diverse. So we hear of mediocre contemporary singers who are trying to fill the historic void, and then, always, about the banjo. Hey, it came from Africa, did you know that? Hell yes, but tell me something more, something that connects black men and women in this country and within the last century to *country* music. Hell, tell me what country music *is*, and then tell me about black contributions.

The problem is that most people who work that side of the divide - of historical reparations - don't actually like country music. To them it is just another offensive American twang, racist and separatist, white and violent. So this banjo thing is a convenient rescue, since it restores the old-country to country music, ties it to old insults that need to be redressed. So far so good, but not good enough. Black country music is more, much more, than some old guy flailing at a banjo somewhere in some forgotten place; it is part of a shared tradition, not necessarily dominated by black musicians but animated by them, given a new life that extends beyond the Scotch-Irish, Appalachian whiteness of the sound. Yes, this means the blues, but it also means a lot of things that happened before and after the blues. It means that my original definition of country music, as I stated in Volume 1 of this study, as a music of passive sophistication, has a broad, and particularly Southern application that is bi-racial, united by the way in which white folks learned sound and rhythm from black folks, which was then applied to traditions that, in their own white Diasporan way, survived hundreds of years of exploitation and poverty. The writer J.W. Cash wrote about how the white man and the black man entered into each other in these years, and nowhere was this more obvious than in the intersection of white and black country and hillbilly music.

So…we have already heard in this study from the likes of Stovepipe, James Cole, Carl Martin, Peg Leg Howell - all of whom reflect different stages of black country music of the Southern sphere. All had different ways of staging the blackness inherent in the country and hillbilly sound, of reflecting the traditions from which they grew. Black musicians played the fiddle differently, their time sense was different, their music, to cite myself, had a lower musical center of gravity, it was heavier to the touch but also had more motion to it, more tonal mobility; it is no secret that white hillbillies were heavily influenced by the sound and that it completely altered the way most white hillbillies played. And yet some *black* country music was closer to *white* than others, as we can hear in **Soon in the Morning** by **Sid Hemphill (8/15/42)**. From the beginning, this performance's repetitions and rhythmic rituals seem to mirror white dance postures, though I think it's fair to say this group leans on the time a bit more than white bands with similar repertoire, and that the singer's exhortations are just a little bit more passionate, as he leads a chaotic, internal call and response.

That call and response is more direct in **Rev. McGhee**'s powerful if somewhat ritualized and (maybe) less spontaneous (than some religious services) performance of **I'm a Soldier in the Army of the Lord (7/42)**. McGhee was a popular reciter of sermons in those years, though this particular transcription was made by Lomax in the field, and it sounds like it. Outside of the studio things are definitely more spirited; we hear the ring-shout clap on all four beats along with the requisite rhythmic accents, the screams of the flock, the passion of men and women whose Sunday release must have been an incredibly necessary pressure valve, as material suffering was sublimated to spiritual relief. Was this country music too? I hear such things, in their strangely constricted yet open-air quality, as occupying a similar emotional space. And by "open air" I mean open and rangy, as though this performance echos in spaces away from urban constriction, at least as a state of mind; it doesn't, in my imagination, get any more "country" than that.

I was recently browsing Youtube when I came across a clip of the old Mike Douglas television show with a fascinating appearance by the singer **Ethel Waters** from 1976. Waters, who we talked about earlier (see Vols 4, 6), was a pop figure exiled, by that year, by time. She was about a year from death and was appearing on the show with Fred Astaire and Gene Kelly. She certainly had, in terms of her own fame, seen better days, but was by then deeply religious in the way of some performers who (both black and white) had already dealt with both the frustrations and the sins of show business, the violations of privacy and modesty, the debilitating demands made upon them by the physical and psychological exertions of touring and performing (made even tougher when you add race as a factor). She had become a fellow traveler of Billy Graham's traveling Christian crusade, and she seemed, in this interview and in others from around that time, settled and resigned. Black show business veterans, even when successful, rarely had the security and continuity of fame that white ones did. But Waters, whom I suspect had a lifetime of racial grievances (see James Weldon Johnson's hint of same in his book *Black Manhattan*, in which he make clear that she had a streak of independence that bordered, in terms of temperament, on the violent) seems very well adjusted in these late years, though I have to admit, watching her in late interviews, that I sense an edge of anger, camouflaged with charm and smiles and regular and repeated, self-reassuring expressions of faith.

To his eternal credit Mike Douglas is clearly aware in this clip that the sedentary-looking septuagenarian sitting with him is much more than just a historical curiosity or monument to pop nostalgia, but rather a great artist who is an essential part of the black-and-tan showbiz legacy that fed his own generation. He is never condescending in that weird, white, racist/aeg-ist way, and is so conscious and respectful of her greatness that one can see, watching her, that she feels, as a result, relaxed, respected, and understood, which was probably, in combination, something of a rarity for her. And, of course, it is obvious from their comments and responses that Kelly and Astaire know exactly who she is. The result is one of those great and rare moments in American entertainment/racial history when all due respect is promised and then actually given.

In this clip, and at Douglas' request, Waters, sitting, sings the song *Cabin in the Sky* from the movie of the same title, made in 1943, which was a showcase for black entertainers and actors and in which she starred. She proceeds in a kind of elegant slow motion, her voice a little bit trembly with vibrato (after all she is in her late 70s) but still possessed of that crystalline quality, that purity of tone and casual directness of phrasing, which had made her one the deepest resources of American popular singing. In her hands, as it had in her earliest days, the pop gesture took on jazz overtones. She swung in the same non-jazzy way that Frank Sinatra did, with an emotional directness that infused each musical and lyric phrase with a hard-won and judgmental sentimentality that, in it's clear-eyed sense of reality, contradicted any implied melodrama. The integrity of the phrase, the logical way she permitted it to expand, is (also as with Sinatra) what gave the song its emotional power and swing, even as it very specifically avoided the digressive time-stamp of jazz.

So it is on her **10/42** recording of **Stormy Weather,** a great Harold Arlen tune from a different movie, also titled after the song. Waters expresses a great deal of emotion in this performance as well, though at each juncture she seems to pull back from the ledge of complete emotional release. *Stormy Weather* was one of a number of tunes Arlen wrote with essentially the blues in mind, and which he implied here with the repeated shift of one-to-four chords and the repeated intervals of classic blues; and yet Waters, never really a blues singer even when she was singing the blues, seems content to suspend the time, take her time, and let the song become, instead of a rumination on blue suffering, a pop reflection on the universal melancholy of experience.

Still, the pop-principled avoidance of the hard blues was not the only way to go. Witness **Betty Roche,** a great and under-recognized singer whose recording of **Trouble Trouble** from **1943** is a perfect example of the new jazz-vocal state-of-the-art, even before there existed that state-of-the-art. Clearly she wasn't influenced by Sarah Vaughan and clearly she is a much different type of singer, but they have, at least in my disordered mind, a musical relationship.

When I spoke, earlier, of the bluing of American popular song and American popular singing, I was thinking in terms of both black and white, and will take this opportunity to further develop the idea. Lil Green (Vol. 21) was the singer/songwriter who, to me, in her occupying of both camps (blues and pop) personified the origin of the idea of blue pop and the way in which it infiltrated the mainstream, phrase-by-phrase, melody-by-melody, arrangement-by-arrangement. Jazz was something of a parallel movement to this, and yet - to hear Betty Roche sing this, to hear the crystal clarity of her enunciation, in which the King's English is replaced by Common Sense-Vernacular, is to see (hear) that a new era of spoken-word transparency had arrived, in which the emphasis has switched from a kind of garbled-blue syllabication and syntax to one in which the very basic simplicity of the lyric is a point of vocalistic departure (and it was only a short step from here to vocalese, see Leo Watson, above). So it was with Sarah Vaughan, if to much different ends.

Betty Roche's singing is really, really, funky, but in a completely different way than with the country blues singers or the so-called vaudeville blues singers or the gospel singers of her day, not to mention the soul singers of future-pop years (which are sometimes like dog years in the way they seem to represent such an acceleration of time). This is blues for the new-age, elegant with more than a touch of after-hours feel, of forbidden body parts and life itself. *Trouble Trouble* is on the cusp of bebop, though her backing musicians are a very canny combo of swing and proto-bop (the trombone player is Mr. Dixieland, Lou McGarrity, the trumpeter the high-note, neo-bop maven Al Killian). A few years later she recorded the same tune with Earl Hines, Johnny Hodges, and Ray Nance, and it is interesting to hear, in both settings, that there is no conflict or contradiction between her new-music impulses and the in-between modernism of a prior generation of players. For once the blues was all its advocates claimed it to be, a unifying historical force with universal musical meaning. [27]

I will go out on a limb and say that on some levels the new style of country music, heading into World War II and coming out if, represented a calming of the Southern waters, at least for white audiences, who had fought the war, migrated in and out of cities, joined unions, and adapted to a changing life. As the American Historical Association tells us in a discussion of these migratory changes (https://www.historians.org/teaching-and-learning/teaching-resources-for-historians/teaching-and-learning-in-the-digital-age/the-history-of-the-americas/migration-and-the-american-south/migration-and-the-twentieth-century-south-an-overview):

"There was also an internal migration within the South with large numbers of people leaving rural areas and migrating to the small towns and cities of the

---

[27] When I say "for once" I am lodging an official complaint with the way "the blues" has been stamp as the end-all of jazz feeling, as that without which jazz, as a force and purpose and style, does not exist. I find such aesthetic requirements, as externally imposed, to be unfair and destructively coercive.

region. Although reliable figures are simply not available on this migration, probably the majority of white migrants were involved in this intra-regional migration."

What set people in motion in the South either as migrants **out** of the region or migrants *within* the region? The transformation of agriculture was a major "push" factor. People had been leaving farming for decades by the 1930s because for many farming was a sure route to poverty. Too many families pressed on on a limited amount of land; the typical farm shrank in size decade by decade after the Civil War, and the typical farmer by the 1930s was not a landowner but a tenant farmer or sharecropper who tended someone else's land and could never seem to climb out of debt. To make matters worse, a rural depression had afflicted agriculture since the early 1920s and only worsened with the onset of the Great Depression in the 1930s. Declining agricultural prices year after year for over a decade thus drove even more sharecroppers to the cities and towns in search of better paying employment."

So the Great Southern Migration worked its way out in more ways than one, in a certain homogenization of white style and country-music manner. Some of this was resolved in unsettled ways, but within each regional grouping of styles there seemed to emerge a camaraderie and social consensus, eased by the growing sense of American (white) immigrant opportunity. And at the same time, I would add, the calming of these social waters led to a roiling of those waters, as whatever optimism that had been fed by the war changed to a more mixed worldview for those left behind or those who still found themselves on the social fringes, drunken and frustrated in a land that was racially charged with fires ignited by the internal and the external pressures engendered by a new form of blackness - musical, social, and legal (Brown vs the Board of Education, anyone? And think Thurgood Marshall, a one-man Civil Rights movement). Country music seemed to become less of a working-class social adventure and more of a "middle"-class counter to the unpredictability of life, though there were more than a few old-style shit-kickers still shaking things up, like **T. Texas Tyler**. The style of honky-tonk had more than a few remnants of hillbilly's bashing aesthetic, anti-social and rebellious in that unique, conformist, Southern way ("we hate life, our fate, and all the rules, but we LOVE America"), and Tyler's own life, hardscrabble, marijuana-stoned, defiant yet brotherly, was a perfect parallel. And, unlike a lot of "hat acts" we hear out there today in the synthetic heartland, Tyler was the real deal, if authenticity still means anything (and it does, at least to me). Tyler's **Remember Me**, from **1945**, is a compelling example of what I am talking about. His voice leaps out at us with conviction, the acoustic guitar playing is shrill and precise, and the ensemble is gradually integrated into the performance in a way which is intensely revealing. And certainly we can hear the relationship of this to, at the least, the *idea* of rock and roll (because another of my pet academic peeves is the way in which academic - and other assorted liberal approaches - ignore the clear country footprints that lead to rock), in the hard way the electric guitar enters at .48, with a strangely jazzy yet countrified and ultimately funky set of riffs and phrases, closing with block chords that would have made Elvis' Scotty Moore proud. Of course this was a different thing, but listen through and hear that blues-vocal growl of Tyler's, so perfectly *white* as applied here, and the little funky phrases (as *country* as they are) that the guitar inserts throughout. Everything, in the post-War, bi-racial Disapora, having come apart in the wartime setting of death and industry, was coming back together, and in much different ways, during the peace.

**The Blackwoods Brothers** vocal/gospel group was formed in 1934, and had a long and varied legacy. They were white and subject, in their early years, to the whims of radio audiences, for whom they performed and who made up their base. Radio was not, by itself, especially lucrative for country performers in those years, except as it led to gigs and songbook sales. The Blackwoods were associated with another long-term white gospel group, the Stamps Quartet, and franchised themselves out to sell song books under the Stamps brand. In later years the Blackwood Brothers received all kinds of awards and made all kinds of commercial breakthroughs, especially after they began broadcasting from Memphis (in 1950). Though scarred by tragedy (a plane crash in 1954 wiped out part of the group), they established themselves, in that country/gospel way, as standing for God and Country, even, in 1969, using the airwaves to organize a petition-signing protesting the judicial banning of prayer in schools. Hmmm; was this a conflict of interest? Well, God schemes in mysterious ways; in 1971 the Blackwoods were forced to rescind their own their victory and apologize following the annual issuing of the Dove Awards by the Gospel Music Association. Apparently the Blackwoods had been selling a lot of memberships in the organization, according to the Southern Gospel web site, "which skewed the final results of the Dove Awards in their favor (and in favor of groups they recommended to their fans). James Blackwood, who was on the

GMA's board of directors at the time, issued an apology to the industry on behalf of the Blackwood Brothers."

Oh well; we know from our own History of Moral Transgression that God forgives all Christians who recant their sins (not sure about his attitude toward wayward Jews - redundant as that description may sound). In their early recorded days the Blackwoods were a small wonder of harmony, which they produced like a mighty, flowing river of sound. This is real sonic whiteness, but listening to it I am struck by its recurring blackness, by the somewhat strange way in which it flows back and forth in a disconcertingly white/black, black/white direction. Historically this should, of course, come as no surprise, as it is more than just a premonition of the new white Country Gospel sound, which, as the years went by, thickened with age. The Blackwood Brothers recorded **At the End of the Trail** in the **1940s** (there is no exact date of attribution) and it starts in that Sons-of-the-Pioneers (see Vol. 19), Sunday-chorale way, but it soon ripens into something else (which makes me think, chronology of this collection be damned, that it was likely recorded in the *late* 1940s). There are fat traces in this of black vocal traditions we have encountered before, as the group splashes around in a soulful pool of both pop and jazz. Listen at 1:30; shades (well, the opposite, in a manner of speaking) of the Platters (and other black vocal groups, of course), with those drippy tremolos and sagging vibratos. All of this speaks to some legacy which will perhaps remain mysterious, but which immediately bring to mind the gay/drag/falsetto birthright of certain sides of black singing and performance (and which I discussed in Volume 1 of this book).

If this is gospel in drag here, all the better, because if there *is* a god, I imagine him/her to be a great connoisseur of irony in all of its forms.

There is an Old Testament legend about the Hebrews who, constantly on the run from various plagues of both nature and politics, always left some remnant of their presence in the place from they had last fled. Such is the way of black vernacular music, which always had a powerful and life-altering effect on the places in which it originated.

We continue here, as usual, to examine the music, and we won't even attempt, in most cases, to determine what happened to the men and women and made it. As I wrote in the very first book I published about 20 years ago (*American Pop*), we cannot even begin to understand, in our current, Everyone is An Influencer for 15 Minutes world, the intense anonymity of so many of these old musical figures. To us their abilities run the gamut of genius to ordinary, but never without some edge of interest, some point of entry into lives lived primarily, for our purposes, in recording studios. Though some of these people were, indeed, white, the shroud of race covers a great many whose very creations were the stuff of art and craft; art in the execution and realization, craft in the itinerant way in which they were forced to live and die.

But still, the remnants of those lives are everywhere, if we only take the time to seek and then find. Richard Gilman said, of certain mysterious and elusive theatrical characters, that "they live on the stage," and I would say the same of so many old-time old-time musicians, black and white, who, like those old wandering Hebrews, were subject to the deepest insults life can offer and yet stayed alive (though, yes, in the studio). Like the mystery duo of **Skoodle-Dum-Do and Sheffield**, who made four sides in, of all places, Newark, New Jersey, on **11/6/43**, including the spiffy, snappy, and irresistibly swinging **West McKinney Street Blues**.

What is this thing they are calling a blues? First, it is a wonderful anachronism, and you can almost hear them singing it as street buskers on what was apparently placed as an actual Newark Street (where, it is guessed, they were living at the time). It's old-timey cache is achieved by its Piedmont-like musical accents and the lead vocalist's old-timey voice, in the style of what I call Black Operetta, and which came from the pre-blues singing mandates of the Songster, the minstrel crooner, and then, just maybe, the traveling-show blues in all of its strange popular (re)formulations. That voice is broad and dense with vibrato, emotionally tinged with audience-pleasing effects. Fused with dance-like instrumental effects, this record really feels like a Southern vernacular leftover, but one that was not merely well preserved (because these guys weren't revivalists) but lived and re-lived, as often as necessary. Like some old Hebrew notes carved in ancient stone it comes to us, so many years later, in the here and now or, really, the there and then.

What became of the old, stage-like mainstream of black and white song as bebop and other assorted post-War black and white musics eased their way into the mainstream? Out of the leftovers of swing came the early danceable ministrations of rhythm and blues, as well as the formulaic pop of post-War balladry (not to mention more rhythmically-mobile forms of country music like honky tonk, and Nashville's new manufacturing method of interchangeable musical parts). The old, if somewhat misleadingly-labeled, vaudeville blues had a long shelf life, and was not about to disappear into the blue mists of black time. Effected and changed by jazz style and form, many black pop-blues singers adapted to times and taste, easily assimilable as their music was to post-swing styles.

**Viola Wells** was otherwise known as **Miss Rhapsody**, which is the name under which I saw her sing in New York City in the 1970s. She was born in Newark, and did some religious singing early on before settling into traveling shows like that of Mamie Smith's. Wells' recording of **Downhearted Blues (11/21/44)** is a good example of just how comfortable middle-aged jazz musicians of the day were with something which we may now think of as commercially compromised, but which may just as well be considered as part of That's Entertainment (Black). The trumpeter Frankie Newton, card-carrying political radical (according to what I have heard from reliable sources like Dan Morgenstern), accompanies Wells on this with a lovely opening phrase, sounding like a flower in bloom, and interjects throughout with his accustomed deep-blue lyricism.

(Digression: just to note; I have known a number of jazz players who worked "commercial" blues-type gigs, and the truth of their attitude was usually far from from reflective of blues-fan myth about great and deep traditions. These jazz players tended to be merely tolerant of such things, and saw them as a necessary financial distraction from the music they really wanted to play).

Wells herself is a great proponent of that in-between world of blues (of stage or vaudeville or traveling show genus) and jazz, and this is the kind of performance which is typically of *two* worlds. It's just possible that neither really understood the other, but that like an old married couple they stayed together for the sake of their bank accounts. And as luck would have it, they still made some beautiful music together.

*Commercial* and *folk music* may not seem to be terms that should be associated with each other, but there was a moment in time - mid  to late 1940s, maybe - *before* the so-called folk revival, when folk or folk-type acts were making a mark in the record business. Those were, indeed, the days - when a lone singer or instrumentalist selling 10, 20, 30, 40, or 50,000 records could drive a profit in the industry, particularly among independents like Savoy

Records (run by a thief named Herman Lubinsky) or Folkways, run by that communist of the capitalist class, Moe Asch - who did everything on the cheap, pressed the results on sub-standard materials, and then sometimes forgot to pay musicians what they were owed in royalties. But what's a little graft between comrades?

As with all such discussions of the independent record business, we balance fiscal reality (were these guys making that much money?) with ethics (doesn't matter, they still had to honor contracts) and capitalist reality and history (they were doing what no one else would do. This is true). Not privy to the balance sheets, I can only say that yes, we have a lot of music - and hence, history - that we might not otherwise have without the larcenous license of these scrappy entrepreneurs.

Certainly they were enabled by the remnants of the Popular Front, a term that refers to the unification, for practical political reasons, of the center and the left, in those days, for the express purpose of defeating Fascism (not dissimilar to the current alliance between the Democratic Party and Lincoln Project Republicans). We have heard, in this collection, auspicious beneficiaries of this movement of political (and other) capital, like Leadbelly and the Almanac Singers (see Vols. 17, 21). So it was with the real-country duo of **Sonny Terry and Brownie McGhee** (**That's the Stuff, 12/12/44**) who, we are told, didn't speak to each other off the bandstand but did always manage to show up on time to sing and play and record. They were a potent match of modern-day folk sophistication (Brownie's sharp and tight guitar playing) and country memory (Terry's deep and down-home harp and primal blues screams), tempered by a little bit of hokum and blues. This may be history to a lot of liberals and political progressives, but it's music to me.

The pianist **Brun Campbell** is a fascinating figure, a student and disciple of Scott Joplin who lived long enough into the modern era to go on record (literally and figuratively) about ragtime and life in the early hand-to-mouth days of the American musical vernacular. His autobiography goes well with the few recordings he made; both have a distinct voice, a sense of the pulse of life in its American transitions, through the days of aural culture as it transitioned into the mechanical age. He is also somewhat representative of a new class of musicians working their way out of the economic and class bondage of folk life, asking, in effect, "how do you make a musical living while remaining true to the things which made you want to be a musician in the first place?" Some gave up, fled the sources of their music, and left the profession, and some remained on the edges of the life, with the misnomer of "hobbyist." Some did both, looking for ways to stay alive but keep the hunger. Campbell was one of these.

Fortunately he chronicled his own experiences throughout. Though he was white, he was *there*, in Sedalia when Scott Joplin was alive and composing and teaching, when ragtime, a new art of both performance and composition, was rising from the ashes of black life's intensely pressurized, post-Civil War sense of possibility - soon to be dashed in many ways, but also the source of a new black and educated class, whose professional ambitions were no longer necessarily confined to white expectations. The piano, so self-contained as to permit a new kind of independent self-definition and self-sufficiency (it was a band-and-orchestra-in-itself, and it did not need white patronage to be so) was the vehicle of liberation. Scott Joplin knew this and Brun Campbell, white and looking for a different kind of emancipation, recognized immediately that this was the way to achieve it on a personal level, to find a place for himself in a revolution of black aesthetics.

And he did so comfortably, traveling through the West and Southwest and then later offering himself as a witness to all that he could see and find in American music in those years and in those places. His very short version of **Tent Show Rag**, from the **1940s**, jaunty and open-ended, was a kind of *ragtime redux*, dated but fully functional, like a quick tour of the past.

And we conclude Chaptorial festivities, with, once more, Our Lady of the Gospel Facade, the great **Sister Rosetta Tharpe**. As we mentioned before, a PBS documentary on the Sister spoke piously of her piousness even as she sang some songs by Jewish-revisionist gospel composers (and others) about multiple orgasms. On a **1940s** radio broadcast she tells us she wants **A Tall Skinny Poppa**, who has to work all night and do his best to satisfy her. But not too late into that night, as we all have to get up early in the morning for church.

## Chapter 23: Where Folk Dreams Live and Die: Surviving in Their Heads

Sometimes the years line up like our stars, as perfect purveyors and predictors of our fate. In this case 1945, and the few years afterwards, are like calibrators of new music style. Of course this is no accident of time. The end of World War II, like many such events, signaled an era of varying kinds of licentiousness. Was this the inevitable aftermath of survival-against-the-odds? Well, watch all of your friends die and you, too, will likely rail against the gods and do what you want without worrying about consequences. Life goes on for some, but not for those bodies strewn about several continents.

Sometimes the music reflects this and sometimes it does not, though we tend to try and avoid the strain of trying to fit numerous square pegs into not-so-numerous round holes. So I will make little attempt at sociological justification as we reel in the years in musical terms; that connection (or disconnect) I leave to the reader.

For a start: the tragic arc of **Texas Ruby**'s life is well known among country music observers, especially as it seemed to symbolize the awful hazards of itinerant, if decently-rewarded, musical life in America. Much as we see many of these old, gone country singers through an aura of legendary, angelic frame, in the early years of country media they themselves mostly lived with considerably less than pop-star glamor. Some achieved fame that took them just a little bit beyond the reach of arbitrary material poverty - think Hank Williams and Roy Acuff, and though of course Hank never quite escaped his highly-internalized, alcohol-fulled personal impoverishment, there was nothing arbitrary about it - but most were grunts in the culture struggle, underpaid if still able to make a living, of sorts, touring and on local and national country radio. But a national platform on something as big as the Grand 'Ol Opry didn't mean you could stay home and collect cash. The shows paid little and though mail-order was already a thing, no one had web sites or the means to translate, in an instant sense, listenership into dollars.

Texas Ruby (Ruby Agnes Owens) died in a trailer fire in 1963 at a nexus of country tragedy; the Palladium Item, a paper out of Richmond, Indiana, notes in its story about her death that

"Texas Ruby's death followed by about a month the deaths of five other Opry stars in accidents," in the plane crash that killed Patsy Cline, Cowboy Copas, Hawkshaw Hawkins and Randy Hughes and, two days later, the death by car crash of Jack Anglin of the country duo Johnny and Jack. It would take an actuary to put all of this in perspective but it does tell us something about the country music life - not as destructive as the blues life or the jazz life, maybe, but with its own difficult mortality rate.

Ruby herself was known alternatively as "radio's original cowgirl" and "the country Sophie Tucker." The Tucker comparison is based on her deep voice and active phrasing, something which she likely also picked up from the older classic blues singers. **Don't You Lie to Me (1945)** is a perfect post-War country music blues takeoff, firm and tough and, in a very honky tonk way, portraying the victim as aggressor, as one who won't take any of it sitting down. In this she was both reality and symbol, as the new country women who was as liberated as she could stand to be in that professional world, which was managed by men, programmed by men, and financed by men. The art of the lady country singer in those days was to resist in a non-threatening way, to stand up to her man and the world around here while still projecting an image of relatively passive domesticity. Ruby's whole manner of singing pushed this whole image a little further than most. She was artistically aggressive in ways to which country music was unaccustomed though, as far as I know, she didn't encounter industry resistance. And the image she projected made her a role model for succeeding generations of women country singers who showed that passive resistance could become both a personal and professional strategy.

*Don't You Lie to Me* is a significant recording on multiple levels. It was written by Tampa Red, one of the first and best of the new-blues composers to cross, with finesse, the vernacular line between the obscurely-personal poetry of the blues and the blues of mass distribution. The blues was still a story medium, full of tales of sad fate and defiant resistance to same, but now its rough edges were increasingly smoothed over, as if to show that white folks not only had it, too, but were able - and permitted - to express it in that post-War, liberated way. And Ruby certainly did so in this recording, with a determination that was a signal to country women that life as they *really* lived it could now be a thing of public witness. All one needed was the decoder ring of personal experience.

Because the jazz world, at least up until about 30 years ago, tended to be nervous about how or how much it praised white jazz musicians, it always helped for any white jazzer to have the stamp of approval of some established and iconic player of African American origin. I know how this works, because I have done it myself (I always cite Dizzy Gillespie's lavish and unhesitant praise of Dave Schildkraut, and then I add a dash of Jackie McLean's comment that "he was one of my favorites"). Things have changed somewhat, I think, for the better - which is not to say that we are living in a post-racial society, but that many of us, liberals or not, have learned to separate aesthetic and political issues. Black lives matter, black musicians matter, and black music matters. But reality matters too, and ideology should never overwhelm what we see and hear with our own eyes and ears.

So it is and was with the singer **Kay Starr**, whose work I love and who had much more than a blue-eyed soul (which was the phrase first used to describe white soul singers, back in the 1960s, like the Righteous Brothers). There was nothing imitative about Starr's singing, though of course she had a certain way of phrasing and making sound which derived from black traditions. It's just that, like any great performer, she made something of it that was much more interesting than second-hand interpretation. And she did it in the most honest and forthright way, and one which brought her to the approving attention of the saxophonist Lester Young; from an interview with Lester done by my old friend, the late, great Chris Albertson:

"In a 1958 interview with the jazz writer and producer Chris Albertson Prez was asked if he had ever heard the blues singer Bessie Smith in person. He had. And could he think of any singer who reminded him of Bessie? "Yes," said Young, "Kay Starr." Not the answer Albertson was expecting. Surely, he suggested, someone like Dakota Staton might be closer? Prez urged Albertson: "Listen to her voice, and play one of Bessie's records. See if you hear something."

Lester knew of what he was speaking, and we know that he would not have mentioned Starr at all if he thought she was nothing more than a repeater pencil. He understood, in a manner of speaking (and here I am citing Charles Mingus in reverse), that she went to the same church as he and other black musicians. **Love Me Or Leave**, Ruth Etting's (see Vol. 8) anthem and signature tune, which Starr recorded in **1945**, is all we need to hear in order to understand what Prez was getting at. Though not directly relevant to my point here, I am struck by the abstractly appropriate intro, with a somewhat wooly piano and a shadowing bass (who arranged it? This reminds of some of the things Pete Rugulo was doing in those days) and then Starr's poised entrance, which occurs as though nothing untoward, musically, has already happened (this is a little jarring and maybe typical of early jazz experimentalism, which was sometimes tempered by conventional resolution, as though, as with some writers in old Hollywood films, arrangers were sneaking things in past the censor). Starr has a wonderfully swinging, flat-footed way of phrasing in a blue manner, especially as the lyrics, along with the song's flirting with minor tonality, hint at the blues and its moods. Starr closes this on the edge of shouting, at least in the blues sense, but keeps it emotionally under control, in the jazz sense. This was one important direction in post-war white singing, particularly with certain women who crossed over, in the modern sense, between pop aesthetic and jazz feeling (and I kept hoping the ending would somehow revert back to that uncommon intro but, alas, it fades conventionally).

Some years ago Rounder released a CD which they called *Altamont: The Black String Band Recordings from the Library of Congress*, and which featured two black, essentially country, bands recorded in the 1940s. One group consisted of Nathan Frazer and Frank Patterson (see Volume 21) and the other was **Murph Gribble, John Lusk, Albert York**, who recorded **Across the Sea** on 9/46. The reaction, at least in collector/nerd circles, was of alternating delight and astonishment, as this sounded like a fantastic and missing country and bluegrass link. Not only was the music wonderful, but some of us wondered, immediately, "what else have we missed?" Those of us who have long-pursued the history of white and black music have known all along that things are seldom what they seemed to be in American song, but to hear such intense and vital music coming from the margins was still a pleasant and clarifying shock.

I have tried to employ all of my revisionist knowledge of black country music in doing this study, annoyed as I have been lately by the way in which *The Banjo* has become something of a one-stop label for all black country music. Yes, that instrument, which came out of Africa, is important, but such knowledge is usually, in my experience, expressed by people who really have no interest in country music except for the political leverage it provides in order to allow them to lobby politically for the importance of *black* music. I don't think we need such leverage, and the fact that such examinations of black country usually begin and then immediately end with *The Banjo* (because by the time the dust has cleared the person bringing it up is usually onto more important things, like wine and cheese art openings) is something of a racialist gaffe. Yes, this is black country music, and yes, we need more of it, but let us at least have the respect to linger on the sound and the musicians who made it.

*Across the Sea* is a good place to start, to contemplate all that we consider to be black in the American vernacular. The shrill fiddle at the top of it comes at that black/white intersection, black in origin but, by this time, having come through the hillbilly years, it is a mixed thing. The time feel on this, as a matter of fact, is very close to a lot of old white hillbilly recordings, comfortably conversant, in what was now something of an anachronism, with its ritualistic repetitions. This has a black feel and a white consciousness, and then a black intensity; so it is one chicken and one egg which will continue to feel interchangeable.

**Ivy Anderson** may be my favorite of all the Duke Ellington-associated band singers. Duke had good vocalists but they often felt like an afterthought, though his way of integrating them into the orchestra was sometimes very unique. In those days the "girl" singer was a necessary appendage for big bands, something of a commercial sop to audience demand. As *jazz* as many of these bands were, there was nothing like a national radio vocal hit to attract sales and bookings. In this respect Duke was a little more circumspect than most, in an artistic sense; witness his early vocal accommodation of Adelaide Hall (see Vol. 20) in *Creole Love Call*. Hall, who was not a "jazz" singer per se, was, in that arrangement, like another instrument in the band.

Ivy Anderson fit in in more conventional ways, not because she was a more conventional singer but because her talents were more in the mainstream of the jazz/pop interchange. She was clearly, with her tight, Southern vibrato, an influence on Dinah Washington, and, through this crossing, a central influence on a whole school of jazz and pop crossover. Anderson sang in a way which put her in both camps, with a tough anti-sentimental attack and blues over-ride. The blues aesthetic represented, if nothing else, a confrontation with life itself on the level of everyday experience. Add to this sort-of formula an expansion of orchestration heavily weighted toward blasts of bebop-inspired brass (without a doubt Dizzy Gillespie's big band had a major influence on all of this) and some great soloists, and you have the elements of a great pop performance, like Anderson's **Empty Bed Blues** from **10/46**.

When we talk about country music in this apparent middle period we often (as I myself have done) refer to the venues it was employed in, honky tonks, white jukes, and other assorted dives. Like Ivy Anderson and mid-period jazz, country was jockeying in these days for commercial position. Never completely abandoning (or at least not yet) its hillbilly/mountain legacy, the folk-instrumental techniques and non-verbal communications of old-time howls and minstrel whoops (akin to both the vocal falsetto and yodel/blues yodel which Jimmie Rodgers had made so prominent), country was like an artist in search of a new and reliable patron. Nashville had not yet established its commercial hegemony, but radio was king, as the first form of social media (in the sense that its effects were felt instantly, its means of communication immediately translatable to response and reaction).

**Bob Wills** was a perfect and representative example of country's search for itself, rising as he did from the still-hot ashes of traditionalism (he himself was a good old-time fiddle player) and still searching, for material and ideas, through the rubble of early jazz and country string band music, but also browsing through Tin Pan Alley and then jumping head-on into the Swing Era. Wills' bands were a mix of old-time, tongue-in-cheek country charm and improvisational nerve, through the medium of string band music but also jazz and then the pop tunes and then the pop-inflected folk and minstrel songs of the day and earlier. By **1946**, when he recorded **I'm Talkin' About You** on a radio broadcast, he was a full-fledged country celebrity. *I'm Talkin' About You* is a good summation of where he had been musically in his professional career and where he might also be headed. It has a fiddle-based bounce, a hoe-down like atmosphere somewhat violated by its air of showbiz-blues, mixed with a bit of jive and a background vocal chorus (which is the the band chanting its part in the general call-and-response). Then Wills does his accustomed "ahs" over a jazz-like piano solo, followed by a fiddle solo that outlines itself in conventional pentatonic terms but which really swings. A pedal steel follows (and this instrument is really *the* signature instrument of the upcoming era of padded country arrangements and soft-focus vocals) and then a very good if jarring trumpet solo (I have to admit here that I hate the sound of trumpet in Western Swing). And then, the *piece de resistance*, a guitar solo by the great Junior Bernard, and one which asks, again, the musical question: what was the first rock and roll record? Well, this might be it, folks, though we know it will not put an end to all of this conjecture; but's it's in the remarkable way in which Bernard, a white man and great jazz and blues guitar soloist, drives his amp to the point of distortion in a way rarely if ever heard on record in those days.

The legend is that the technique of distorted, neo-rock and roll guitar originated in black blues sessions, caused by low-power amps pushed hard; or was produced by the deliberate damaging of guitar amp speaker cones in later, also black, rock-like rhythm and blues sessions. Well, *this* is the white Junior Bernard, a few years in advance of all that, and he brilliantly pushes the line along, playing a perfectly paced and voiced blues solo that starts with an audacious bounce, continues with a few country-like twists, and concludes with a sudden and final, fuzz-infested jazz line. Did he come up with this idea himself or was Junior, like a lot of other white musicians of the day, a habitue of black clubs, where the idea of this may well have been in utero? I would guess the latter, though it does him no less credit in how audaciously he uses it, how he fearlessly puts it right up front, on this sedate radio show, like an anarchist bomb thrower during cocktail hour. Which might, anyway, be one logical explanation of the methodology of rock and roll, of the *how* if not necessarily the *why*.

In a very folk-like, American way, **Hobart Smith** was neither a professional nor an amateur, or at least not in the way that we normally think of them. He was white, played the guitar, the banjo the fiddle and the piano (and maybe a few more instruments), and he was the poster child for the Vernacular, an active if largely unpaid performer who did it for the love of the music. It was a family thing and it was a community thing, even though he occasionally made a living at it; thereby showing that not all of the communal aspects of American singing and song derived from the African American diaspora. In Smith's case the habit of music was passed on by seven generations (as he told interviewers) of family, originating in England. And yet…well, you know what's coming, sort of. He was initially taught music by a black man who boarded with his family (in Virginia), he absorbed black banjo techniques along with other old-time ones, and he toured, early in his life with, yes, a string band in minstrel and medicine shows. In the big picture of vernacular America Hobart Smith was a one-man band, combing strains of old English/American song, the burgeoning popular music industry, some blues and mixed-songster material, all in the new profession of Professional Folkster. The latter happened as a result of his appearance at one of the early music-heritage festivals produced courtesy of the New Deal, at which he was seen by Eleanor Roosevelt, who invited Hobart and his singing sister Texas Gladden to perform at the White House.

Yes, this is a very American story, no snark intended. **Railroad Bill**, which Hobart Smith plays on guitar **(1946)**, and which is very close harmonically to Libby Cotten's (see Vol. 30) *Freight Train*, is a speedy and smoothly-executed race through familiar chord changes. Like Sam McGee (see Vol. 5) Hobart Smith is a rapid picker who, at the least, predicted the dominant style of folk guitar in the soon-to-be 1960s folk revival. The playing was crisp and clean, with technical snap and a lots of feeling. It steered itself clear of the blues except on those occasions when it felt the urge. The war and post-war years were good to Smith, leading to recordings by Lomax, radio shows, and appearances at the Newport Folk Festival, the place where, it seems, folk dreams went to live long and prosper.

I have to admit to being a fan of drug and alcohol songs, along the line of the old one that tells us "what's the use of getting sober if I'm only gonna get drunk again?" **Jo Jo Adams**, taking a different tack in **The Reefer Number (11/11/46)** tells us:

"If it's rainin' I don't mind
Because I'm as high as a Georgia pine"

...and we're off to the stoner races. The virtue of songs like this is their slacker informality, the clear sense that they are writing off anyone who doesn't understand or feel the virtues of a particular, high lifestyle. And this was truly an *alternative* lifestyle, especially back then, before Wall Street analysts were snorting cocaine and high school teachers smoking pot. As old as it makes me sound, drugs of a certain kind actually meant something back then, when a subculture was really a subculture and a hipster really a hipster. You can't synthesize the preternatural cool of Lester Young or the slow-motion life of the hip jazz druggie, try as you might by snorting and inhaling with all of your might. And this, the drinking and drug use, was all in step with a classic sense of *black* cool, and even probably related to the slow-stepping of characters like Stefan Fetchit, who, as I tried to explain in Volume 1 of this study, were very likely showing off their sharply-honed defiance of white standards, even as they seemed to reassure the white folks of their passive and non-threatening inferiority.

"I'm so hip and high as I can be."

*Stealth* is the word for this, for the invasion of the white world by a new kind of black cultural activism, through what at least *seemed* like inaction and the appearance of social inertia - because before you knew it every black entertainer, from the black minstrels of the 1890s to the new jazzers of the 1930s and 1940s, or the tap-dancing men and women of every era, had essentially taken over the world; even if white people did not realize it until they were outnumbered, out foxed, and out-stoned.

**Tex Ritter** was the actor John Ritter's father. He was also something of the quintessential folksy crooner of country myth, the voice of the kindly old storyteller and keeper of the country faith, locked up as it still was in its mythical mountain lair. He was also a very popular singer, a reassuring country father figure of the type that, in country music's history, makes regular appearances, with a *voice* and delivery and the wisdom of the sung-spoken word, put across with wit and dignity. Tennessee Ernie Ford (see Vol. 23) had a similar aura, of country legacy tweaked occasionally by mild forms of self deprecation, performed with family values and self-knowing humor. Ritter was, at the same time, both old hat and new testimony to country's continuing view of itself, against some but not all evidence, as pious and socially virginal.

He recorded **Trouble in Mind** on 12/11/46. This is an eight bar blues composed by the African American composer and record producer Richard M. Jones, and it had, by the time of this recording, become something of a popular blues standard. Ritter had quite an interesting career - law school, Broadway chorus singer, and then host of a local children's cowboy show and appearances on radio cowboy dramas on the East Coast. By the time he moved to the West Coast he was well established, starting his recording career in the middle 1940s. One of his best known recordings was the theme to the movie *High Noon*, with its famous and unforgettable, beggar's opera-like country opening, "do not forsake me oh my darling," which he sang with an emotional catch in his throat. Here was another singer, like Ernest Tubb, who had a vocal *sound* rather than a true singing voice, and it carried him through his career. If I had more time I might even dub this Folk-Pop, as slick but heartfelt music that gave a good name to a very synthetic form.

*Trouble in Mind* is early period Nashville, hinting at that city's country production excesses, as the sap, even at this stage, was beginning to run from the country music tree. Still, the horns are arranged with taste, mixed at a distance, and the accordion/brass unison takes a piece of late Western swing and applies it to middle-of-the-road country balladry. A little more jarring is the female chorus, dropping a hint of Andrews Sister corn and dominating the last half of the song, even as Ritter himself, suddenly and strangely absent, seems to have left the room.

There is a school of white female jazz singer which seems to have descended, with strong musicality, swinging phrasing, and some emotional diffidence, from Anita O'Day. O'Day set the pace and the sound and the cool emotional temperature for this school - not to mention the sandpaper vibrato - and the others followed, with some popular success, even outside of jazz's exclusive and excluding sphere. This was an important strain of white-girl jazz singer connected, in its way of relating to song, to singers like Peggy Lee and even Helen Merrill. They proved that ice melts at a temperature much lower than we might have thought, that smooth doesn't necessarily equal shallow, and that all that is cool is not cold.

Such was **June Christie**, who sang with Stan Kenton and recorded for Capitol Records. Early on in her jazz association **(1/46)** she made **What's New**, with an unidentified studio orchestra, and I gotta ask: what is it with these crazy intros? Abstraction, abstraction: a piano intro that tells us something is about to start, but not what; a tenor solo that is clearly written out and sounds like a narrator trying to set a stage he cannot see; and then Christie and group ease their way in. She has a perfect jazz sound, a tight vibrato that veers in the direction of going-out-of-tune but always saves itself in time, and a calm, deliberative, yet very swinging way of phrasing. This was medium cool, post-bebop style, with that intro as a strange interlude meant to signal that there were more possibilities in the air than these players could freely express - compare it to the introduction to Kay Starr's *Love*

*Me or Leave Me*. Such was the perpetual condition of American and jazz modernism as it strained to stretch the limits of the popular imagination; only so much strangeness was permitted.

**Merle Travis** was a great enough guitarist to have an entire genre of guitar playing named after him, Travis Picking, though its lineage wasn't hard to trace through contemporaries and predecessors like Blind Blake, Sam McGee, Mose Rager, and Ike Everly. What set Travis apart was how brilliantly he adapted these country-picked forms to a pop-song sensibility, how easily he moved between the worlds of country heritage and glacier-smooth pop. But such was the way for figures like himself, who were suspended historically between their own personal history and the commercial world they grew up in, the sometimes - but not always - opposite pull of country pop song, jazz, and folksy authority. Travis was all of that, a reassuringly folk-like voice in the commercial storm that was brewing in country music, an able singer who knew how to croon a country song. Still, even at his most pop-song dedicated he swung on the guitar, with a richly-voiced musicality, wide chords, a comprehensive picking technique, and a rhythmic stability that made him essentially a one man rhythm section. Like a few others we have talked about he was an old-time musician proselytizing in modern times.

**Pigmeat Strut (4/8/46)** shows his purely instrumental/musical side, a Travis Picking showcase of the kind that established his virtuosic hegemony in middle-period country music. Other guitarists, like Chet Atkins, had similarly comprehensive technique, but Travis' playing had the aura of true spontaneity, a jazz-like momentum that, even on set pieces, gave the music gravity and swing. It was fun and it was heavy, two things that made him utterly unique in the new country era. And he had a powerful influence on generations of players, from Doc Watkins forward, though few could play with Travis' degree of calm and collected speed and precision. I don't really know how much influence Travis had directly on the new *folkies*, but he surely had the attention of the growing community of folklorists; I remember from my reading through issues of the publication of the dedicatedly folkloric Jonathan Edwards Memorial Foundation (named after the late Jonathan Edwards, an Australian who was one of the first to seriously begin to collect American folk music and its artifacts) that Travis was a correspondent, writing regularly about country music's history. So he was part of that part of the underground which was just beginning, in those early days, to expose the common roots of American song. It changed a lot of lives, including mine, and I know that without that dedicated movement I wouldn't be writing this, and you wouldn't be reading it.

    The movement of black song and black singers is strewn, particularly in the 1940s and 1950s, with would-be opera singers who, excluded from the classical world by racism, turned to popular music. Lucky us: listen to the way **Gatemouth Moore**, recording for Savoy Records on **12/26/47**, leans into "wellllllllllll...." at about 1:20 of **Did You Ever Try to Cry?** This is a weeper, saved from the maudlin by Gatemouth's dense-pudding mass of a voice. It's also something of a middle-of-the-road template for a style of post-War black balladry that seemed to be trying to rescue jazz from itself, commercially speaking. Though it's not true that bebop was completely anti-dance (I remember more than one of the older jazz musicians I knew in the 1970s pointing out to me that they had, indeed, worked bebop dances in the 1940s and 1950s), it was certainly not as user-friendly as the blues and related balladry. This growing repertoire, of ballads and blues, was not just fine and mellow but more congenial for certain nighttime activities. And it helped that many of that current jazz generation had learned their craft in the world of jazz/pop; the studios were now filled with jazz musicians who were on the clock, and they turned these songs into small musical gems.

    It was great, professionally, for singers like Gatemouth or Big Maybelle and Big Joe Turner, reintroducing a style based at its root on the old, solid blues, from Bessie Smith and Ma Rainey forward (and Gatemouth had not only toured early on with a black minstrel troop but also with Rainey, Ida Cox, and Chippie Hill). Stylistic lines were blurred but not eliminated. Jazz was part of this particular blues equation, but there was a deep-blue thing in action: rock-hard anti-sentimentality on the edge of teary regret, with the added and essential ingredient of jazz-like micro-phrasing, which didn't avoid the beat but sometimes only hinted at it. Jazz instrumentalists phrased ahead and behind that beat, and blues singers in the post-War world of blue pop, with less ornamentation, did similar things with much the same effect, of a displacement of time and emotion; the blues singer with jazz understanding was expert at masking the unorthodoxies of the jazz phrase, with emotional directness and bombast as needed.

Another side effect of this changing commercial dynamic was the growing dominance of small group neo-swing, a la the Nat Cole Trio. Cole first achieved popularly in the late 1930s, and his vocal style, drawing from Leroy Carr (see Vol. 17) but continuing to smooth out the edges, spilled over very quickly into the commercial mainstream. By legend this was the new sound of not just after-hours but of the new nighttime, nightclub business. This was symptomatic of a growing West Coast jazz and pop and nightclub scene (and the two, jazz and pop, were, unlike in our current day, rarely strangers to each other). It was populated by not just city folk but by slumming movie stars who, as ever, sought ways to publicly affirm their hipness. Even Ray Charles (see Vol. 24), in his earliest days, mimicked the Cole trio, to the point of sanding off the bluesier points of his voice.

One of the most popular groups of this kind was **Johnny Moore's Three Blazers (You Won't Let Me Go, 1946).** Moore's brother was the guitarist Oscar Moore, who was not in the Blazers but who worked with Nat Cole in the trio and who was one of the best guitar soloists of the day, in what was essentially a swing style with bebop tint. The pianist for the Three Blazers was Charles Brown, later a star from his solo version of the hit *Driftin' Blues*, and his smooth croon on *You Won't Let Me Go*, along with a sparse and mellow instrumental commentary, was something of a signature for black blue balladry in those years. The blues shouters were far from extinct (they were, as a matter of fact, commercially ascendant) but there was clearly commercial co-existence and crossover. And in those brief years of post-War racial optimism (short-lived but presenting a kind of psychological Reconstruction Era) this was one sound of liberation.

In those days you could take the blues out of the country but not necessarily the country out the blues, though that would happen soon enough. For now the rapid northern migration of Southern blacks created new communities and, along with them, new markets. Between 1915 and 1940 Chicago's black population more than doubled, and the result was a multilayered black music scene filled with blues, jazz, and a lot of sounds in-between. This coincided, not coincidentally, with the growth of independent record labels like Aristocrat and then Chess and also many less successful if significant regional ones; and of course there was also, by way of Cincinnati and New York, King and Savoy.

Digression: yes, these were all owned by Jews, and though I am exhausted by my own personal efforts to root out anti-

Semitism on Facebook, which seems rife with such things, let me point out that, as marginal as some of their business practices were, the ironic point of their success was that it resulted from a social fearlessness, a willingness to do business with African Americans at a time when many others of the white persuasion would not. This was very much related to their outsider status as Jews, to a sense of social equality which, if it did not necessarily carry over to business/financial practices, is important to note as the reason for their business dominance - in other words there was nothing inherent in their Judaic background that caused them to cheat black musicians, though of course this is not an attempt to explain or rationalize away such things - except to note that black-owned labels like Vee Jay and Duke/Peacock were equally venal; at least the Chess' paid their contractees, well enough for them to remain loyal to the label (even Chuck Berry, who left briefly, came back). There was enough cheating and hypocrisy to go around, yes (and even the self-righteous management of Atlantic Records had, eventually, to give back-royalties to many of its black artists), but the reality is that Syd Nathan of King actually had an integrated staff and did sign (thanks to Ralph Bass) James Brown.

Which is all by way of introducing **Little Walter**'s version of **I Just Keep Lovin' Her** (with **Othum Brown, 1947**), an early harbinger of the new blues changes then circulating. Walter, who also played guitar, became famous for his groundbreaking harmonica playing, though you would barely know *why* if you read his notices. Such things tend to be filled with pointless descriptors of his style, comparing it to saxophonists and even Charlie Parker, which all misses the point. What made Walter so singular was the way he adapted the old-style country blues to swing-era rules, playing his (eventually electrified) harmonica in a way which showed a real grasp of the jazz-time roots of that earlier music, but swamping it with urban-blue waves of blues accent and classic blues intervals. Listen to the opening riff on *I Just Keep Lovin' Her* - which is straight Swing Era. Walter (see also Vols 25, 27) was gifted with a knack for creating snappy, catchy melodies; such things were increasingly popular with the greenhorns who were still arriving daily from the South.

There was recently a discussion on my Facebook page about singers which evolved into a sub-discussion of whether or not **Frank Sinatra** was or was not a jazz singer. Though there was little consensus, my own belief is that, much as I love his singing,

Sinatra was not from the land of jazz. Some of it is a matter of *time*, the way he preserves the written integrity of the melodic phrase - and in this way we can compare him to Billie Holiday, who Sinatra loved and who undoubtedly had an influence on him. But whereas Holiday completely reconstructed the American songbook, re-did its melodies and re-staged its rhythms - all the while, in a miracle of musicality, keeping those songs recognizable and even hummable - Sinatra stayed much closer to what we might guess were the songwriter's original intentions, re-phrasing, yes, but with a greater adherence to basic form. None of this is a value judgement but rather an attempt to put into words certain non-verbal intellectual values, to show why Sinatra, much as I love his work, is not, in my opinion, a jazz singer.

But there is more to it than that, I realize now, because Sinatra often employed a direct kind of jazz-like phrasing. I think what ultimately separates him from jazz singing is his employment of the kind of emotional and dramatic verity that escapes most jazz singers - or which, really, they, in a typically rebellious jazz manner, escape. This is done (by jazz singers) through different kinds of distancing - through irony, anti-sentimentality, cold observation, defiance, blues phraseology, instrumental imitation, humor and ironic separation - in any number of musical ways, including the insertion of certain kinds of sub-textual verbal and musical excess. Helen Merrill, one of the coolest observers of song convention, was a jazz singer, even as her phrasing contained only the slightest alterations of phrase and accent. But she took the opposite tac to Sinatra - she burrowed deeply into the emotional depths of a song to the point of near emotional self-immolation, but stopped herself by a constant if subtle reversal of temperament, by a calm but determined defiance of the rules of emotional engagement. She was in the moment and yet apart from it, with out-of-body, observational detachment; on the edge of that emotional precipice, she refused to jump or even lean over and contemplate the vast empty space below. This was a kind of dance-and-defiance that Sinatra avoided, not through irony but through a calculated, commercially appropriate presence-of-mind. Jazz and bluesters were willing to flail away at misery, to wallow in self hate and pity while angrily denying, in the face of what seemed to be reality, that they were victims of self or social sacrifice. Sinatra, emotionally speaking, completely avoided the issue through a new kind of pop self-possession and an introspective, yet conventional (because that is what still made him accessible in a pop way), rationality.

Of course the early Sinatra was not quite the same as the later (1950s, Capitol Records-era) Sinatra. Cool as a cucumber, he was, in these early days (as in his deep and warm recording of **It Never Entered My Mind**, from **11/5/47**) closer to, but never a victim of, sentimentality. The voice was not as plainly emotive as it became a few year later. It still had a slightly weighted, edge-of-maudlin depth of the kind he discarded in his best work for an off-handed and haughty self pity, sometimes disguised and even camouflaged, in that pop way, as self-reflection.

Some people think that country humor is to country music what military music is to music, to borrow from some long-lost source. The work of **Rose Maddox and her Brothers** is studded with canned laughs and off-hand comic remarks. This is part of the acquired-taste side of country, but matters little once the band gets down to musical business. Rose's voice is one of the glories of post-War music. I could mention that, as with some other women singers of that era, she was a strong and important example and role model, but it's obvious from hearing her sing that she needs no special categorization. Still, she'll get it, because it is interesting to compare her assertiveness to other women singers of that era and just before and after. She had an aggressive quality to her singing that was unlike anyone else's, even that of Texas Ruby (see Vol. 22), tough and uncompromising as Ruby was. Still, Ruby set up something of a largely-ignored template for country ladies, which Rose followed to some extent - though she had a more complex singing voice, filled with bluegrass twang and capable, in the same breath or two, of both broad-toned balladry and down-home bluntness. Rose Maddox was something of a school unto herself, arriving in the business just before singers like Kitty Wells and Jean Shepard (see Vols. 26, 29), strong women who were just a bit more demur, who put themselves forward with a modesty and patience that Rose lacked - or rejected.

Maddox and her family migrated West during the Depression, and she and the family band began performing on radio when she and the brothers were in their teens. In **1947** they made their first records for Four Star, but also did regular broadcasts and made transcriptions like **Milk Cow Blues**, a song performed regularly in the blues and country/Western Swing world, and written by the bluesman Kokomo Arnold. Trite as the opening of their version is, it has a certain silly charm, though Rose's entry makes us forget about everything but the music. She could rip through a lyric like this one with finesse, all the while making asides to the band, who were all excellent players and whose output from that era is only vaguely categorizable and, if nothing else, drops hints of the way rock and roll was, in addition to some of the other things I have mentioned, a white way of adding raunch and alcohol to the blues in a very white, country-brawl way. The steel guitar in this gives it more country emphasis; Maddox's whoops and laughs were not unlike Bob Wills' minstrel cries, and the occasional guitar solo adeptly hinted at jazz. Most notable, of course, was Rose Maddox's blues-bouncing acrobatics and beautiful sinewy voice. And truth be told, though people wondered in the succeeding years why she was not as famous as her talent deserved, I would suggest that she lacked the kind of front-person good looks that tends to chase mass popularity on various mass media platforms. That's to our discredit, not hers; still, it helps to make the point that no singer of her day or afterwards, male or female, had as much country soul or depth.

We all live in one big, over-sized country, and maybe that's why every region of it was able, by the middle and late 1940s, to offer musical sacrifices to the gods of country music. **The York Brothers** were born in Kentucky, raised in Denver, and ended up on the radio in Ohio before moving to Detroit to become a local phenomenon in a city dominated by auto workers. The blues was a strong entity in what would seem like a natural, urbanized, black setting, but so, apparently, was country music; in a match to black migration, thousands of working class whites moved North during this period. The Brothers' first single, *Hamtramck Momma*, sold 300,000 copies, though the slightly suggestive lyrics incited some of the more pious locals. It helped that the Brothers could plug the tune in local taverns, where they were regular performers; though by the time they recorded **New Mississippi River Blues (9/1/47)** they had decided to follow the old monetary trail South in the direction of Nashville. The new/old Southern Strategy of country music was much like Nixon's: create your base in the South and then broadcast, in one way or another, your white family values to the rest of the country in order to catch the runoff. For country music this meant boosting broadcasts like The Louisiana Hayride and the Grand Ol' Opry, all of which begin to infiltrate the (largely white) frontal lobe of the American psyche.

*New Mississippi River Blues* is in a category of populist bluegrass. It is part two-part country harmony, part Delmore Brothers family hoot, part old-country instrumentation, and two parts country pop-song template. Hear them sing, re-that river, "I can hear you callin' to me," and note the way the melody is harmonized with an obvious and old time, Tin Pan Alley cadence, and you know we are crossing a commercial river of sorts. Is this country music's middle passage? Very likely; the Yorks maintained their popularity for a number of years, and their work had an impact on important crossover brother acts like the Everly Brothers, who took that somewhat bland country format and rocked it, ever so melodiously.

By the time **Big Joe Turner** recorded **Nobody in Mind** (11/29/47) the former Kansas City blues singer had established dual blues citizenship of a kind later applied for by singers like Bobby Bland and even, to some extent, B.B. King. The blues was endlessly adaptable, as we know, and could go, pretty rapidly, from lascivious lip licking to contemptuous shout to sentimental balladry; it, like Turner, was also poised to cross over into a new and so-called (with white, liberal, blind-spot hindsight) rock and roll market, which at this point was merely a twinkle in some hillbilly brawler's eye. And though I have argued and will continue to argue that rock and roll was a completely different musical and racial animal than the blues (even if both, after Darwin, had related ancestry), the blandification and slight dumbing down of the blues in this era (think *Shake, Rattle, and Roll*, a hit for Turner, and a host of other rhythm and blues shouters), was a blatant and largely successful attempt by the independents to field a team for the purposes of garnering what appeared to be a new youth-music market. Joe Turner did what he had to do, and he was great at it, with a strong ballad sense directly descendant from the women blues balladeers we discussed earlier who, like Turner, infused somewhat self-pitying lyrics with a seemingly new and modern kind of defiance; though it was, in reality, an attitude descendant from a long line of professional cynics (otherwise known as blues singers).

*Nobody in Mind* is really a sub-standard (no pun intended) ripoff of the tune *Trouble in Mind*, and it is not known whether the composer or record company, whoever they were, got into any kind of difficulty for it. Would they have pleaded Public Domain and made the claim that the blues' harmonic format was so pliable as to make such distinctions of originality pointless and unenforceable? Ask Richard M. Jones, who wrote the original. For our purposes *Nobody in Mind* is typical of the blues' middle period, between swing's secession from bebop after World War II and rhythm and blues' usurpation of the audience's casual, pro-dance agenda.

I will defer to others much more expert in Latin music to completely assess the work and influence of the great percussionist **Chano Pozo**, Cuban born, imported to the United States by Mario Bauza, and then introduced to Dizzy Gillespie, for whom he filled a rhythm gap that had clearly begun to suggest itself in the trumpeter's musical consciousness. In many ways the Afro-Cuban fills and gestures of Pozo's music were the missing link in jazz's Diasporan journey from Africa and through the Americas, where it picked up bits and piece of localized and exoticized (to our ears, of course) melody and time before settling in the actual America.

Pozo's life was brief (he was murdered in a Harlem bar at age 33), but he embodies a brilliantly inventive type of post-African cultural methodology, a way of forming, practicing and expressing culture in street-wise ways. I have long suspected that, at its best, Hip Hop is the last remnant of such a thing, the last frontier of randomly created yet precise musical culture juxtaposed with blunt and violent lyric themes, sudden violence, and an artistic community almost willfully at risk. Chano Pozo had a lot of the same angry spirit. Early on he learned the religious practices of Afro-Cuban worship, which were powerfully drum-centric; later he absorbed the Nigerian-originated religion of Santeria, which was taken by Afro-Cuban slaves and converted into something quite different through a combination of West African and Christian ritual. Out of his teens, Pozo began to gain local fame as a street composer and dancer in the yearly celebration of Cuban Carnival.

It is here that his early life becomes not only most interesting but also begins to parallel that of Louis Armstrong, whose youthful tutelage in street culture made him uniquely suited for the kind of transcendent artistic vulgarity which makes jazz (and all of American vernacular music) so unique and, I would say, appealing on so many levels, from its uninhibited rhythm practices to its unfiltered knack for verbal release. At these lower frequencies (to cite Ellison) the lewd and violent eloquence of street performance - think of Black Benny in Armstrong's autobiographical telling, a brute of an artist, a great drummer and rhythm man - achieves its own level of dangerously threatening artistry. The idea of risking one's life for art is, except in certain authoritarian cultures, almost dead in the modern world. Only in hiphop today do we see equivalencies to this, even as the music has been co-opted and monetized endlessly; violence and death are still violence and death, and I would guess that threats of same are real factors contributing to that music's sense of heightened aesthetic release.

Pozo recorded **Placetas** on **2/4/47**, and it has the sense of deep ritual which I pull from music of this type, clueless as I remain in relation to the music's deeper social meaning symbolism. Still, the visceral impact of Afro-Cuban rhythm sections (and this is basically only that) is much deeper in relation to my sense of soul than garden variety Latin tempos and styles like Salsa seem to allow for. This music has less of a sense of escapist pleasure, is less flighty or fleeting than the entertainment music of popular Latin culture. Do I feel it as t*he real thing*, that loaded phrase, with no precise or even correct meaning, used to described cultural expression which we cannot, on occasion, otherwise quantify? I leave that to the reader, but I hear in this a reality otherwise missing from typical pop appropriation of any color.

**Big Maybelle** recently came up on Facebook, where she was described as a "blues belter." With my customary tact I begged to differ, because she was a lot more than that. It is fascinating to hear her singing, from **12/47**, **Sad and Disappointed**, commercially poised as the song is, as in the work of Big Joe Turner (see above) to ride what certain record companies perceived as a new wave of commercial blues (created, at least in part, by jazz's seeming abdication of its consumerist role in black American music). Maybelle was typical of the type of singer who could handle such things, yet more than a few cuts above a lot of the rest, in talent and artistic weight. Listening to her sing produces one of those indefinable moments of *meaning*, much as I hate the term; one hears immediately in her voice a different kind of talent, a deeper soul, a more meaningful comprehension of the material being performed. How does this all happen? Some of it is mysterious; listen to two singers with comparable control of pitch and time, sing the same song - and then try to explain why one holds your interest and absolute attention and the other does not. Well, any time Big Maybelle's voice comes out of a speaker - even one as small as that built into my laptop - I snap to attention and listen. She commands such fealty.

This is blues with a popular feeling, and the impulse which produced such feeling has long disappeared from American musical life - there are still singers who attempt such things but I cannot name one who rises above show business gloss like Big Maybelle does. This, among other things in our musical life, is definitely a lost art. Too much of this particular community has vanished through time and death, though not necessarily in that order.

**Bill Nettles** may be right for the wrong reasons when he tells us, from 1947, that there are **Too Many Blues**, though you will have to forgive me for picking such an easy target. Of course he wasn't speaking from the standpoint of the consumer; I am. Still, though he is not a great singer, and even though this starts with a weirdly nostalgic Bob Wills reference (listen to those ghostly minstrel whoops), it quickly segues into certain signifiers of the modern country ballad, with a parallel steel guitar and weepy fiddle chords. This was, as I have said in reference to other such things, a middle period in country music song, of song and sample. Nettles didn't record a lot, and few details of his life are known (he lived 1907-1967) but he acquits himself well enough on what is actually a non-blues ballad. The title is both a throwback to the old days of inserting the word *blues* into a song for the sense of cultural cache it provided, and a look forward to the new country ballad world of the post-War years. The song itself has sincerity going for it, the kind of lyrics about sweethearts and the inevitability of abandonment that fit it neatly into the emotionally-blunt template of honky tonk music of the day. And whatever I think, this was all real to a lot of those lonely men crying into their beer, as they epigenetically passed their sorrows and fates on to succeeding generations of weeping country crooners, not to mention their happily self-pitying audiences:

> "Too many heartbreaking letters I've read…
> Too many times I wished I was dead…."

Jazz instrumentalists and jazz singers have, historically, had an ambivalent relationship. What annoys jazz musicians about (some) singers is an occasional lack of musicianship; many jazz players, secretly or not, have historically harbored a prejudice against vocalists as not being real professionals. I am reminded of this as I listen to **Babs Gonzales** who, it appears, was well-liked by jazz players for both musical and extra-musical reasons. What a life he lived, hipper than hip, speaking two languages fluently, those of jazz and the straight world. He navigated the USA's racial caste system with sarcasm and straight-on, bitter comprehension, sometimes, on the road, donning a turban to pass as something exotically non-negro in order to avoid both official and unofficial segregation. And he was obviously a cool guy who understood the street life of the music and found a way to describe it with some of the hippest words and syllables around, a lot of which he seemed to just seize out of the thin air of the English language and fit into into song with a unique sense of Diasporan phrasing. As the late pianist Joe Albany told me, with an authoritative sense of finality and just the right amount of emphasis, "Babs was *hip*."

  **Weird Lullaby**, which Babs made on **5/47**, is like an abstract expressionist tour of the mind. Babs just seems naturally able to align verbally with the contours of the harmony here, with fill-in-the-blank terminology, made up and fit to the song like the words on a page torn out of a book of private poetry. The minor-key makes the point that this is a nighttime excursion, and it's modulation to a major key - and then back - is handled with a surrealist's deeper and more direct sense of life. I talked earlier about what I think are the emotional distinctions between jazz and non-jazz singers, but there is even more here which pinpoints Babs as a jazzer. He doesn't have a great voice (like Sinatra) but he has the *right* voice to make his musical points. It's like an amateur aesthetic converted in real time to professional, a snapshot of an odd and informally-arranged scene transformed into c*inema verite*; the very informality of the technique and pose put it into a world of its own, though it is a world we immediately recognize as jazz, no questions asked.

  There's an old quote from Hank Williams, to the effect that, after god, the most popular person in the South was **Roy Acuff**. Until I read that I had no idea that Acuff, whose music I have always liked, was that big a country music star. And though I tend, in writing these types of studies, to pay less attention to popularity than musical value, I do have to regularly juggle quality and popularity as value judgements. Every pop music historian has their eye on sales charts, even if it's mostly a matter of using peripheral social vision to put things in perspective. Meaning: try as I might to place everything in aesthetic terms, to hold the *quality* of the music as the ultimate historical standard, I (meaning we) cannot ignore the question of economic impact and popular influence.

In terms of what I like to call country music's middle period, Acuff really represents legacy, a moveable respect for country's musical heritage, though it's also clear that he doesn't necessarily follow the roughneck hillbilly order. His is a more genteel look at those backwoods.

Acuff began his career in medicine shows by working in blackface, progressed to radio (where the crystal clarity of his mid-twang of a voice appealed to audiences) and ended up, from performing to the business itself, covering virtually all aspects of country. What made him rich was the forming of a music publishing company, Acuff-Rose, which was successful for a number of reasons, not least of which was their signing of Hank Williams, whose song rights, in which they thus shared, made several generations of Hank's family members wealthy as well.

Acuff is not only an excellent singer, he is a hard-working one, which may account for his extraordinary appeal. There is something earnest and honest about everything he does. He was old-time country music without the hick stigma, new-time country music without Nashville or new-age slickness, or any sense of the abandonment of a rich, rural heritage. His own band had great dignity and a knack for earnest cleansing of old-time sound; it was a matter of interpretation and near-religious respect for the world of their fathers and mothers; and now you could actually understand the words.

Acuff recored **Unloved and Unclaimed** on **11/19/47**, and it's typical of the type of things which his audience loved to hear. It has a solemn religiosity; the song is about a sad and anonymous girl who drowns, unknown and apparently without family affiliation, and is pulled from the river with a note that says "blame no one but me." It's a weeper yes, but also a thing of some hope: "I know when she reaches those golden gates/she won't be unloved and unclaimed." The music is calm and reassuring, the small-group hillbilly format bisected by a yearning harmonica, which, because of all that we know about the coming era of folk music, makes it sound modern and contemporary (for which we have to thank, yes, Bob Dylan, who turned this weird, dragging whine of a sound into a style). Acuff's voice resonates with the tragic aura of death's inevitability, overlaid with that poignant twang and a strong dose of faith. His way of ending certain phrases with a tear in his voice, the dignity of the brief guitar solo, the hints of a dobro slinking its way through - and, finally, the way in which the song tells the story of the dead girl with such documentary patience - makes this one of the more beautiful and poignant artifacts of the life of the old hillbilly, as sung by the new hillbilly.

When **Sister Ola Mae Terrell** died back in 2006 at age 95 I was absolutely floored to learn that her life had intersected, chronologically, with mine. I had listened to her music for years, had written about her, if only briefly, and had considered her to be of the category of street guitarist - well, evangelical guitar playing preacher - who most directly connected to not just the heat-seeking sanctified strain in American music but to the earth shaking guitar-origins of rock and roll. My idea of rock and roll's origin as a white, epiphanous movement, of its condition as a white music with black antecedents, a white way, as I have said, of thinking about black music, positioned early white rockers as active witnesses to early and mid-period gospel (both black and white; Elvis had a guitar-playing preacher). Talk about rhythm and blues and the blues all you want (did blues really have a baby named rock and roll?); I see a more complex series of events leading to rock and roll's white, soul-churning beginnings. If Elvis was the musical sacrifice who not only died for our sins but cleared a path for generations of white rockers, then those guitar-playing evangelists were the ones who talked him into making that ultimate sacrifice. But if only I'd known that Sister Terrell was still among us! I felt like I had lost my one chance to connect to that old, gone, sanctified world.

These street preachers were not all the same, but they weren't all that different either. They had skills, at playing the guitar, at coordinating prayer with song and even, yes, at singing the blues. I would suggest that the spiritual world from which they came started and flared with slavery, simmered like a low flame from the spirituals of the the post-bellum and post-Civil War period, began a slow burn with the heresy of secular, sinful vernacular music, and burst out like the fires of the sun with the rise of the Holiness movement and Sanctified religion. The moaning intensity of this style of singing, the active counterpoint of head-butting guitar, the ritual repetitions (often accented with the depraved twang of a steel slide over the guitar strings), were of a piece with a new kind of down-home religious witnessing. In that wider world groups like the The Fisk Jubilee singers were a formal chorus who scolded as much as they preached; early religious vocal quartets in general presented a succession of sermons with only creeping anger. Few of these seemed to be in real touch with what was happening in much of the outside world. On the other hand the guitar-playing preachers had a vantage point on life as it was actually happening; they were *there*, as witnesses, on the spot, where and when they were needed. They knew how much of a struggle real life was between the devil and the details, and they made it clear, as Sister Terrell does on **Life is a Problem (1948)**, that the heat of the moment was a matter of more than just the blues. Because they were so basic and spiritually ecumenical, white country boys identified with them and followed their example; this was a new way to use the blues, compatible with honky tonk bluntness and other types of white-country, post-mountain, religious and post-religious anger.

In Stefan Wirz's invaluable and beyond-essential continuous, on-line discography of the blues he tells us the following about the singer/guitarist **Manny Nichols**, who would otherwise have remained, at least to me, a biographical blank:

"Manuel Nichols
b. March 15, 1906 in Cuero, DeWitt County, Texas
Nichols lived at Victoria when found by Chris Strachwitz in 1967
d. November 25, 1970 at the Victoria Convalescent Center in Victoria, Victoria County, Texas; buried at Woodlawn Cemetery in Victoria, Texas"[28]

Thank you Stefan, without whom we would remain in the dark about more than a few old African American musicians, each of whom is essential in some way. Some of the most important

---

[28] Visit Stefan here and give him some money; tell him I sent you: https://www.wirz.de/music/america.htm

things we hear in American music, Elijah Wald notwithstanding,[29] happened in so-called "local" settings where musicians, deprived of the usual "professional" credentials, just did their thing. Though they might have failed the tree test (about whether that thing unseen and unheard really existed) they do confirm the impression of that philosopher who might have said, about musicianly existence, "I play therefore I am."

The point is that these people lived real if unclaimed lives. If those lives seem incomplete that is our fault not theirs, for our general lack of cultural curiosity; but we do know that Manny Nichols recorded **Forgive Me**, a heartfelt blues about love and loss and the possibility of redemption, in **1949**. In musical terms it's a return to the land, to a world that Nichols lived (and died) in. It is not a time capsule but a time stamp from a survivor, powerful testimony to a culture that was still thriving, at least in his head. Empathy will only get us so far in this particular world of culture; documentation (and cash) is better. *Forgive Me,* despite out worst efforts, *does* exist, as a test pressing and a cut on an old LP. [30]

At this point, in the matter of black vocal groups, it is best to refer you to the first twenty or so chapters of this study to see how things have evolved - from early quartets singing faux spirituals and minstrel tunes, gospel songs, pop tunes and even a bit of what we might call, after Julius Hemphill's work, the Hard Blues.

As we move away from World War II a new and popular black-group style is emerging. One question we might ask (or really answer) is, is it really black enough, even as it plays down the blues

---

[29] Wald has attempted to defend his downgrading of Robert Johnson's place in blues history by telling us that, in order to understand why Johnson is insignificant, we only need to realize that our understanding of the blues would still be the same if Johnson had never existed. Aside from the unintended racism of this statement (because it reduces history to a sequence of documented events that favors not only white persons but white interpretations of those events, by ignoring the brutal social circumstances that lead to the continual cultural and social isolation of African American performers), it is irrelevant to our considerations. And by saying so Wald makes himself seem totally oblivious to the difficulties of documenting and tracing early black music, as though it existed and competed on a level playing field with white music At the end of the day Robert Johnson was a great and important musicians because his music was great. End of story.

[30] Once again Stefan Wirz to the rescue, and of course it was Arhoolie Records which issued the LP that included this song.

connection we so automatically associate with black music and musicians? Or is the new style of black-harmony group singing, especially as it explores avenues of deep sentimentality and heart-on-sleeve emotion, a legitimate expression of a legitimate black musical consciousness? Well, it is black, and it is an expression of black artists; so, question answered....

**The Orioles** (**It's Too Soon to Know, 1948**) were one of the most popular of this musical species. Wikipedia describes the Orioles as "R&B's first vocal group," which I would question as a matter of origin; there were a lot of groups working this way in this era, in a smooth pop/jazz fusion that soon purged its jazz effects; the moment of initial crossover is impossible to determine. More seriously incorrect is Wiki's further allegation that the Orioles were unique because "they made vocal music with limited orchestration and accompanied only by the guitar of Tommy Gaither and the bass of Johnny Reed." The very basic kind of accompaniment they used was, as we have heard in this collection, extremely common. Still, this *was* the beginning of something new, of a soulful fusion of dense black-ballad style with sentimental design, drawn from the turgid drama and sound of gospel music, and secularized with pop spectacle and lush vocal orchestration.

And now I ask the musical question: why is garden-variety, formulaic black music still, with regularity, so effective and listenable - as opposed to garden-variety, formulaic music of the white kind? Maybe it's the *way* it's done, the communal effect and racial unity in black music. With exceptions, black groups emulate, while whites seem to copy. There is a difference, at least to my ears.

**Sister Matthews** inciting version of **Stand by Me (1948)**, in which she appears to be cloning Sister Rosetta Tharpe's method of big-vibrato shout, is a case in point. This strikes me as essentially a copy, but a copy with feeling. Listen to the way she circles the melody at 1:29 with a sudden, dynamic twist, ringing just a little bit more emotional feeling out of the song and taking the vocal from its obvious tracing of previous work (by, most obviously, Tharpe) into, if only temporarily, a new emotional realm (she does this again at 2:05). There is not a lot more to say about this performance, which is reassuring in its reaffirmation of the guitar evangelist model of black singing, and tells us that the African American *continuum* (a word which academics are fond of using, and which characterizes the particular way in which black culture represents a succession of common and related gestures; and which also explains the differences, as I cited them above, between copying and emulating) is and was real, as a point of both reference and cultural exposition.

And so was, in a much different way, **Tennessee Ernie Ford's** version of **Milk 'em in the Morning Blues**, from a **1948** radio broadcast. Ford, accompanied by that ubiquitous country accordion (an instrument which, like a lot of country music, gets an unfair and undeserved bad rap) was, like Tex Ritter, an inheritor, for the modern age, of all that country music thought it was trying to preserve in the post-War years. These were country's alleged family values, of collegial humor and smiling sincerity. This kind of performance, non-threatening, amiable, sincere and even soulful, might have been seen as an antidote to the rise of country-slick, even though, in its own way, it was just as smooth and surface-skimming. The blues as a country music descriptor was by now just another conversation starter, a way of referencing mild forms of personal malaise without any implication of greater social or psychological depth and meaning. Television was waiting in the wings with a series of pre-Hee Haw country hootenannies, hosted by warm-voiced men like Ford and then, later, Jimmy Dean, among others.

The music was excellent and professional, a mix of honky tonk blues, proto-bluegrass, and some new country-pop balladry. *Milk 'em in the Morning Blues* was like a quaint memory of some of the old country ways from down on the farm, wherever that was, mixed with modern instrumental techniques, including a brief guitar solo in the mode of Chet Atkins, finger picked with a few jazzy notes sprinkled over a few jazzy chords. This was the new commercial reality for a whole set of country performers, but it was a reality based on what they seemed to know best. In their minds a few new hooks and some blatant folksy posturing about ways of life that may never have really existed except in Southern white fantasy were acceptable and expected. They were in no way betraying their heritage, just making it a little safer for Democracy.

## Chapter 24
## Black Bleeds Through

As I said a few paragraphs back, you could take the country out of the blues but you couldn't take the blues out of the country. Or was it...you can take the blues out of the country but you cannot take the country out of the blues? And are those two different things? In 1948, we find ourselves, pun intended, at a crossroads in the blues profession. I spoke earlier about how Robert Johnson represented a near-complete shakeup in the blues form and format, re-animating, as he did, a relatively young yet throughly-examined music - suffering from not just the same repeated chords but from similar melodic rhythms, similar accompaniments, similar methods of call and response and repeated themes. Johnson was like blues lightning caught in a bottle, jump-starting a music in danger of running out of creative oxygen.

After the war years newer forms of mass media like radio, juke boxes, and national networks of independent record distribution accelerated these changes. Those independent labels that sprang up as the opportunity arose were - like that of the Chess brothers - the bearers of new and primary blues documents. As I have claimed many times before, after Richard Gilman, one of the essences of modernism is in the ability of certain artists to tell us what we will be thinking next, even before we know ourselves. So it was with certain kinds of musical expression, as with Robert Johnson's ability to encapsulate certain newer and more persuasive forms of existential anxiety, to predict the electro-acoustic properties of ideas that would necessitate new technologies like the electric guitar and amplification. It was as though Johnson just knew, in his instinctive, genius way, that the new blues (and later rock) would require more of everything: more volume, more sonic clash - and yet also more musical organization. All of which would not just liberate the music in new ways but broaden its audience.

The effects of Robert Johnson were both direct and indirect and, I would guess, spread even to musicians who did not know his work. Black performers of his stripe were still socially and professionally marginal, but the movement of cultural change which they led, shaded by the veil of racsim, rippled throughout the entire country and its music. The oral/aural spread of black music in the first half of the 20th century is still largely misunderstood; from our historical perspective there is a lot of guesswork involved. But it's there, in the stealth movement of certain kinds of electrified poetry and rhythm. Take **John Lee Hooker**. In the early years of his professional life (before he plugged in) he was just another obscure Southern figure, yet possessed by a strangely retro-approach to the blues, a sound which was both very new and very old at the same. The way he played the guitar, his whole cave-like presentation, spoke of a resonance and consciousness that was as old as black American song itself - or at least as old as the term of its inadvertent underground confinement. **Grievin' Blues**, one of the first things he recorded, from **1948**, is as turgidly meaningful and *real* as anything you will ever hear in American music. From the beginning the vocal-guitar unisons, melodically and emotionally identical, are perfect, parallel voices, part of that dual-voiced tradition of black music and sound that I have spoken of before. They exist as call and response and yet as abstract counterpoint, with complementary yet independent tracks of meaning. They are subjectively personal, yet objectively separable as representing a material response to the world, buried as they are in mounds of unconscious yet clear-definition verbal poetry.

Aesthetically the blues at this stage, as occasionally electrified, sometimes crossed paths with gospel music. Take the **Elder A. Johnson**, of whose work I am so enamored that I not only used a recording of his in more than one collection but also named a book after it: **God Didn't Like It**, from **1948**. Now, please note: this version of this screaming gospel tune was never officially released, and it is only through the grace of some obsessive collector that we are aware of it at all. And what a thing it is, one of the most intense recordings in American music. Though Johnson made another take, and though that other was released because it was not saturated with so-called distortion (I say "so-called" because this kind of ultra-driven guitar and over-vocalized breakup, here in its naked state, is really the opposite of distortion, with an absolute and startling clarity of sound and feeling), this is the one you need to hear. It is another of those fly-on-the-wall moments in modern American music, with a kind of unmediated passion that is so rarely visible, in its unfiltered state, on even vernacular recordings. He screams, he yells, he plays the guitar at max volume and beyond (yes, to number 11 on this amp), and he does it all with analog finesse, with the amazing sound of pure and plain and unvarnished sound-waves, clashing.

The Elder returns to administer another dose of the truth in **Lord Will Make a Way** from the same year and probably the same session. As the lady said in that movie, I'll have what he's having. As he sings this sound meters all over the world are smacking the red, but don't go for your limiter so soon. If you want a sense of why black *music* matters, then listen at about 1:29, where the good Reverend picks up what I believe is a slide and delivers hell's fire in a way that just might convince you that there really is a god, as unlikely as, in the light of day, that may appear to be (because to paraphrase Hank Williams, there *is* no light of day).[31] Remember my assertion that in looking for rock and roll we need to turn away from glib recitations of blues and rhythm and blues antecedents and turn toward those evangelists who picked up guitars? Well, here is one such performer, and if you combine Johnson's approach with that of Utah Smith you might just be able to identify the very moment, the exact point at which gospel music liberated itself from the strict outlines of the blues, mated with country music (because there is nothing more country than the sound of Utah Smith and Elder A. Johnson, both of whose work embodies the passive sophistication that to my mind characterizes country song and attitudes) and landed in the faces of white country boys like Elvis. Just as water seeks its own level, passion seeks its own way of reconciling itself with reason and form. And in this, and in that, you have it all.

But still, the tendency in black music in these years, with the blues and related sounds on the cusp of mass commercial explosion (the second such occurrence for the blues, post-dating the original, 1920s blues craze), was to expand itself sonically and so market-wise. Blues shouters were the rage, as they seemed to channel the operatic impulse in American music. Opera you say? What does that have to do with anything? Well, think Louis Armstrong, who always acknowledged the effect listening to arias and other operatic forms had on his glistening tone and gloriously new and open sense of phrasing. In the American grain there is a

---

[31] Near the end of his life Williams' friends were singing to him to try and cheer him up and out of a drunken stupor; they began a chorus of one of this songs, *I Saw the Light*. In the middle of it Hank exclaimed: "Wait! That's just it! There IS no light!"

strain of middle-brow admiration for "elevated" forms which regularly translates itself into art in ways that transcend and even exceed the originals. So, yes, Armstrong (who admired Guy Lombardo as well) made, of those remnants of operatic oratory which he may well have picked up off the streets of the New Orleans of his boyhood, something which far outlasted, in impact, the originals.

And speaking of opera; we talked earlier of those scattered black singers who might, but for racism, have looked to the academy to train officially, and who might then have joined troupes to sing old and tired forms of vocal music. The opera world's loss is our gain. We might even hear the new dramatic shout of all of those big-voiced men and women as our own form of domestic opera; **Roy Brown (Looking for a Woman, 1948)** had that kind of vocal range.

Early in in his singing career Brown was hired to sing pop standards as, he said, "a negro singer who sounds white." It would be interesting to hear some of that, as his early training was in church gospel music, and one might compare his later instincts to those of Ray Charles, to focus that sanctified idea of soul, time, and phrasing onto popular song. Brown became a major blues star with his hit *Good Rockin' Tonight*, soon to be picked up by every rocker or near rocker of the day. In 1948 he shows the effects of hoarse-voiced belters like Wynonie Harris, with a vocal which swells with technical pride and agility. *Looking for a Woman* has swing-band riffs and even a neo-bop trumpet solo, which interrupts only briefly and to little good musical effect, but which also serves as a signal that this is a new kind of expanding blue universe.

Of course, as soon as we attempt to "type" black ways of making music something comes along to defy not just expectations but established, commercial, hopes-and-prayers of predictability. **Nellie Lutcher (There's Another Mule in Your Stall, 1948)** might be heard as coming from the perspective of jazz, because everything about her performance here (and most of her other recordings) rings with the true idea of improvisation, of impromptu changes of musical direction and unpredictable, broken-field ways of playing the piano. In a prior book I described her method of piano playing as being like someone playing pinball; notes seem to careen off side and center bumpers, return to where they started, or suddenly land in odd places like explosions of light. For all the strain in that musical metaphor, I think it still holds up. She also occupies a rare, strange and unaccustomed (unaccustomed, that is, in our day) sphere of commercial success, as an artist who combines popularity with unorthodox gesticulations of time and phrase, odd-ball instrumental performance and vocal. In a very "black" manner her voice, crystal clear and well-defined, fades off on certain phrases, which de-materialize into mumbled non-syllables that are, momentarily, sacrificed to rhythm. And yet nothing about the song - melody, rhythm, accompaniment - suffers in the process, nothing is lost to these small abstractions, integrated as they are into the "text" and meaning of the performance. This itself is a fascinating aspect of Afro-modernism as it inserts itself into the world of American vernacular and popular music, and is one of the prime reasons why these ways of (black) music, unlike some other radically abstract forms of modernism, remain accessible and popular. Even as certain kinds of black modernist work depart the world of representational shape they still leave form as as clearly visible in outline and contour. They rarely, even in the process of re-shaping reality, lose sight of material essence, which is helpful and assistive to audiences otherwise lost in other new and modern artistic worlds (which, please, is not to be read as an attack on other forms of artistic avant garde-ism, or as a criticism of freedom of expression and free jazz, free music, abstract expressionist painting, stream-of-consciousness writing, or really anything, but rather an observation of the odd and off-kilter but consistently recognizable reality of African American music and art). This, in particular, is something entirely new, neither religious fish nor secular fowl.

Though, speaking of the devil (literally) here comes **Ray Charles** in his early, early years who, in this rare 1948 recording of **I'm Wondering and Wondering**, has successfully cast aside his early obsession with Nat Cole and replaced it with something which we might assume was closer to his own heart. Though maybe not, as his later forays into popular and country song attested to not only the catholicity of his tastes but also his ability to treat everything thrown at him, musically speaking, with taste and a calculated (in a good way), mass sensibility. More power to him, as we say; *I'm Wondering and Wondering* may have been something of a commercial experiment, a drift away from smoother pop in the direction of the hard(er) blues. This performance is from the new school of slow, solo, long-suffering blues, and yet very different. Think Leroy Carr and Big Maceo and the way in which the old, blurred lines of country mumble and slur had been displaced, in these urban times, by clearer and broader frames of diction (as in those blues shouters we have mentioned) without sacrificing soul and fire and without any sense of psychological dislocation. This was still the real thing, but it was a *different* real thing.

Of course we don't need a lot of explanation for Ray Charles, who was soon to become one of the great phenomena of back-American music, with a crossover appeal that plumbed the mystery of American audiences and their shifting ideas of what was cool or hip or had social currency. *I'm Wondering and Wondering* is cool, calculated, and raw, with Ray Charles' characteristic blue cry as overlaid at the end of certain phrases (very close, I should say, to the white-country way of ending a phrase with a teary vocal tic; check out a number of country singers before and aft, including Lefty Frizzell, Vol. 25). Like just about every other performance in this collection this was the new-old, the road, to contradict that very annoying poem by Robert Frost, that *everyone* was now taking.

Sometimes that new road didn't lead anywhere, but just as often it revealed new things about the musician who was taking it. Like **Memphis Minnie**, whose voice was also new-old, a throwback to be sure, but one whom modern recording techniques revealed to have a sound that really was bigger and better than some of the equipment that had, early on, been used to record her. It really is true in her case that such types of intense soul never date musically or otherwise, and it helps that in **1949**, when she made **Night Watchman Blues**, her voice sounds like it is as new as the tape which was being used to record her. Say all you want about the supposed digital revolution; the old analog ways of doing things had certain visceral advantages, a depth-of-field and sonic immediacy that still retain their impact. Though to add or really subtract from my argument, digital technology, when properly used, has been the best means of analog recovery, in that analog originals digitally transferred often have a stunning immediacy and presence.

So it is with *Night Watchman Blues*. From her electrified double stops (and Minnie had recorded on electric guitar as early as 1942) and great whooping vocal to the way in which the whole performance just *goes*, with that nice, slow-tempo amble, to Minnie's way of soloing on guitar (taking true advantage of the electric *idea*), this really is something to behold. And then there is her cosmic vocal cry at about 1:35 - sounding like joy *and* pain - and the way this, from its old-world blues feeling to its stabbing, new city assertiveness, is, in ways that tell us about much more than inspiration, just another day at work.

Was **Julia Lee (When Your Lover Has Gone, 1949)** the third side of the professional coin, the other two of which were, at least for the purposes of argument, Memphis Minnie and Nellie Lutcher? Lee's singing showed great thematic versatility. Wikipedia calls her "an American blues and dirty blues musician," an unfortunate turn of phrase prompted by double-entendre hits like *My Man Stands Out* and *King Size Papa*. Still, in terms of comparison she actually evokes another singer, Ethel Waters, whose blues singing had similar pop/sex impulses but was restrained by a prim, show business restraint. Either way it might be a good time to try and revive Lee's reputation, which faded with the 1950's and the end of her hit-making years. A few years back I heard a radio DJ in Maine refer to her as "the obscure Julia Lee" and I got on the phone immediately to inform the jockey that Ms. Lee was a member-in-good-standing of the Capital Records club, for which she was something of a mid-level star throughout the 1940s and '50s.

Julia Lee had or looked for cross-over audiences at a time when such a thing was still possible for this style of would-be pop, splashed as it was with jazz attitude and accompaniment. Her own voice, phrased with pop precision, was flexible and jazz-oriented more than it was jazz-like, though she had a sure way of spacing things rhythmically, a boldness that sounded "jazz." And she was from that home of Southwestern swing, Kansas City, and her brother was the bandleader George Lee, which closes the circle of jazz pedigree. *When Your Lover Has Gone* is a perfect, if modestly done, recording, a model of pacing and pop overlay of clarity and slow-motion feeling. It feels like a little *recitative*, and her voice has a thickness and depth which betray a somewhat more pop-gospel orientation than they do, once again, jazz. This is the kind of record (and singer) that inevitably gets ignored in both pop and jazz histories, which are sometimes a bit too concerned with the compromising sins of crossover.

Well, whatever, as they say. Music is as music does, and it sometimes seems like it's my job to explore the things that fall between the stylistic cracks. Pop is Nellie Lutcher and pop is even Memphis Minnie, whose 1949 recording betrays a depth of vocal accessibility which is both a contrast to and extension of her older and more country-blue work. For some others singers of that day black pop draws less from jazz and more from gospel. An old book refers in its title to "gospel blues," but I tend to shy away from cliches, especially as they draw on certain references without really explaining or understanding them. Though at certain points gospel and blues seem intertwined, we can separate them and their history, especially if we consider how the blues had its own formal origins, and if we are willing to avoid labeling every similarity between the two as proving that the blues is the beginning and end of all American music.

**Annie Laurie** is a singer who has suffered needless obscurity, which may have been the result of late-in-life conversion (likely as a result of a combination of religious repentance and disgust with the music business). She had a typically smart career with territory bands, with jazz bands who were branching off into blues and pop, and then with commercially-based rhythm and blues. She was said to be a favorite of Dinah Washington's, and there is nothing in her singing which makes me think otherwise. As with others of her type we can hear the gospel in her voice, in that way which buries the gospel impulse in pop cordiality but then allows it to erupt, as needed, with great dramatic effect. Her **Cuttin' Out** (from **1949**) is fairly routine in terms of composition and musical intent, but she keeps rescuing it from the garden variety for which it seems, by virtue of harmony and accompaniment, to yearn. She is too uncommon a singer to satisfy the generic goals of such songs, too direct and self aware and in-tune with the blues and both it's possibilities and (sometimes self-imposed) limitations.

**Floyd Dixon** runs in a similar circle (or, maybe we should say, in similar circles) on **Dallas Blues** from **1949**. This was an extremely popular format in those years, the piano trio with guitar, as an after-hours template with the blues as signifier of jazzy, late night sophistication. At the center of this musical word were Nat Cole and Leroy Carr, though it was surrounded by the early Ray Charles, Charles Brown, Johnny Moore, et al. They ran the course, from the ultra-smooth Cole to the rough-around-the edges Dixon, proving once again that imitation sometimes succeeds. There's enough room in this sound, filled as it is with space and easy tempos, for variation. In this case that means Floyd Dixon's Joe Turner-like slurring around the ends of words, as part of a stylized blue diction. It also signifies Dixon's apparent naïveté, a city-out-of-country innocence. For a lot of black music the pull of these geographically opposed ties remained at the center of the tension in the early post war blues, between the instinct for music and the instinct for economic - and artistic - survival.

For me, learning that **Blind Willie McTell** - a country blues icon - had recorded later in life, at the cusp of the modern era of the recording industry, was jarring. There is nothing as satisfyingly time-bound as those early blues recordings, not just from McTell but from that whole blues generation, documented on record with surprising detail. It all sounded so much like a lost way of life; what would they sound like if they were found again? And how well-known were they anyway, how well did their old blues records sell? I am not aware that there are decent accountings anywhere, and I would tend to distrust the official numbers. Even those regional scouts - like the legendary H.C. Speir, who, as cited on the web site The Mississippi Blues Trail:

"made (at his store) test recordings which he would send to Victor, Columbia, OKeh, Brunswick/ARC, Paramount or Gennett, and if a company approved the artists, Speir would sometimes accompany them to recording sessions in New Orleans, Birmingham, Grafton, Wisconsin, and other cities. During his travels he also scouted for talent in the South and Midwest and even in Mexico. At other times record companies called on Speir to organize sessions in Mississippi...."

...and who were noted for their relatively benevolent dealings with these Southern black men, played distinct and ultimately racially-reenforced roles in that Southern system. Royalties were low, there were no audits, and the relationship between black and white assured that there would be no challenge to the established power relationships through formal or informal challenges (like litigation). Men like Speir made their real money through publishing the materials produced by these itinerant geniuses, little if any of which has been successfully restored to families and estates in the years since. If challenged they might have pointed out what a marginal and obscure music the country blues was, though this would have begged the question of why, if the market was so limited, they kept seeking out and recording a population of poor and indigent people.

But back to the original point, which was that the deep, Songsterism of the hard blues and other things, as represented by McTell, seems, to our modern ears, to be so much of its "time" (the 1920s) that any attempt to transplant it into the modern, post-War era feels like anachronism. And yet - like Memphis Minnie just before this - the reality is completely different. In **1949** McTell recorded **I Got to Cross the River of**

**Jordan** directly to tape, and not only is this a significant step of historical documentation, the music is stunning and immediate, like a process of complete rediscovery. Revivalism, in this light, pales; McTell is not just the original, the primary source, but he has an internalized energy in his late performances and a sense of aesthetic progress that is usually missing from those who try, sincere as they might sound, to re-create the era from which McTell originated. The voice - well recorded on the 1920s originals - is, if not crystal clear in 1949, gloriously nasal and indelibly direct, movable, clinging, *real* (there's that word again) and infused with the kind of feeling that defies not just our assumptions about the life men like McTell lived but also the stereotype of Blues Victim. Here, once again, is that alternative history Richard Gilman wrote about, constructed with a supreme independence of spirit, aesthetic and poetic form, of the kind that resists schematic attempts to caste artists like McTell as passive social objects.

And McTell was not alone. The bits and pieces I hear from these post-War years, of the country blues as reformulated and preserved (but never in a museum-like way) by the men and women who originated it does make me wonder at how much, as the recording industry re-calibrated itself for new markets, was missed. These "old" bluesmen were still, relatively speaking, young men, through their attrition rate was high. Still, when we can find musical examples, especially as documented by newer technology, they stand as much more than just remnants of an old way of life, and instead as something too vital to be considered to be near death. Clearly that great Southern subculture, of black life and music, was not just active but creatively alive.

As with the guitarist **Curley Weaver**, who was known as an accompanist and musical busker, though before **1949**, when he recorded **Trixie**, we have almost no examples or true indicators of his individual ability and style. But here it is and there is no more mystery: he is a musical force, a brilliant technician of the guitar in what we continue to label (for want of a better term) the Piedmont style, of crisp, varied/complicated guitar picking in a sort-of ragtime way. We praise Gary Davis and others for carrying this sound into the modern era, but Curley Weaver was more than just his equal. Listen to Weaver's easy and unhesitating swing (unlike with Davis, who always seems to be fighting the guitar), the bass lines he plays in smart harmonic counterpoint, and the way in which the time gains forward momentum throughout and never feels rushed or forced. And then at 1:40 he inserts a series of picked chords whose density contrasts with what came before but which fit the design of the piece, so perfectly are they integrated rhythmically; as in so much black music, works like this are unified, not necessarily as melodic theme and variation and but as *emotional* theme and variation (which reminds me of the jazz critic Max Harrison, who remarked that the work of Charles Mingus, sometimes criticized by classically-oriented writers for not observing classical rules of thematic unity-and-variation, was united and divided and segmented *emotionally*, as in a series of musical vignettes that observed and then broke rules of dramatic unity for the sake of personal expression. As Harrison clearly understood, black music was not to be confined to or limited by such Western definitions, derived as they were from outdated, classical aesthetic assumptions).

How many of these musicians were still out there, in the Piedmont or elsewhere, in America, where the sun only occasionally shone in their back door? I hear **Ralph Willis (Goin' to Virginia, 6/8/48)**, a great picker and master of folk/harmonic transition, with a central-casting blues voice, and it makes me wonder where I have seen (or really heard) this guy before.

Well, in discussing black music we often talk about a continuum, a tired reference by now (especially as over-used in this book) but one which I cite by necessity, as I find little in the way of alternatives (and because "tradition" is an even sadder word, reeking as it does of language fatigue). Willis is all of that and more, a symbol of not just himself and all that his important work means in its own time and place but also, in this weird period of musical adjustment, of other rapidly-vanishing (black) worlds. Where I have heard him before? Well, everywhere in the world of black blues and Songsterism. He is not just an individual of tremendous talent, he is the tail-end of an era in which black folk performers, after the blues, tell us, in every phrase and note of music they play, that history is alive even as those who make it are dying. Music like this is not some antiquarian phenomena; as I said about Curley Weaver and Blind Willie McTell, these musicians were more than just still functioning, they were thriving in a way that defied their chronic invisibility. Some part of their consciousness was able to overcome neglect, indifference, and obscurity and permit them, in the face of highly destructive odds, to create some of the most vital music out of this style that we will ever hear.

Willis was a bit of a chameleon, instrumentally speaking, but his connection to the world of Piedmont guitar is obvious. In terms of his own survival it is notable that he was part of that brief but significant folk revival of the 1940s, that gave new life to both black and white performers, like Sonny Terry, Brownie McGhee, Gabriel Brown, Leadbelly, Woody Guthrie, Pete Seeger, et al. We are long overdue for a detailed *musical* study of this era, of how it effected music and audiences and how it linked itself, politically and aesthetically, to the 1960s run of folk-commercial rebellion. It also helped, I am sure, that Willis recorded for some important, major/minor labels like Savoy and King, who had distribution and radio play. But what finally made the difference was the artistic end of it, the power-guitarist that he was; this kind of playing, gymnastic and artful, was a school unto itself, crossing over from black to white, racially and historically: Blind Blake, Mose Rager, Ike Everly, Gary Davis, Blind Boy Fuller, to Merle Travis, Scotty Moore, Doc Watson, and a whole procession of younger musicians. Later folkies picked it up through first and third parties and converted it, with white conviction and naive ambition, to their own somewhat quaint purposes. In the 1960s this way of guitar occupied one whole side of the folk and folk-rock street.

We also, by the way, know that Willis died young because, as Wikipedia tells us, with blunt finality, he succumbed "in June 1957, a week before his 48th birthday. His cause of death was unknown." As the man said, 'nuff said.

Throughout every era of American music, blackness, as a form of both active and passive resistance, bleeds through. It seems, especially in the years I am covering here, to be a constant, an unending theme. And though I will stick to my assertion that African American arts are not, in their essence, political - because at that moment of true feeling, of sudden creation, when the light of discovery shines on some heretofore hidden sound, all politics and social conflict fades to background - the essence of that essence is somewhat harder to explain. And the very act of trying to explain it is obscured by politics; though I would argue that that doesn't make the act or the production political. It only means that the politics which surround American life are distorting factors that obscure a lot of our attempts make sense of everything *else* we do.

But yes, blackness bleeds through. Just listen to **Professor Longhair,** whose every note of rhythm - from the great gliss that opens **Hey Little Girl (1949)** to the audible foot stomp which helps to guide the song throughout (like an underground metronome), to his pleading voice - tells us that his is a life lived under the cover of certain forms of racially-guarded inspiration. What do I mean by that, especially as I deny the music's political ties? Blackness and responses to blackness shape lives like this, as the external world tries to marginalize them, failing through success; marginalization breeds independence and ingenious forms of resistance, as in Black music. This music was a threat to the White Southern (well, to the White American) way of life, and the very act of forcing black culture to the margins highlighted all of their racial differences, of speech, rhythm, and sound, in such a way that made it even more attractive and desirable to whites. The parallel to the old biblical story, of forbidden but nutritious fruit, certainly hastened black/white cultural miscegenation. Think of the way that even the most racist of white kids today imitate black talk and dress and movement and you see the historical inevitability of it all: blackness just inevitably bleeds through into all of American life. Try as some might to fight the "contamination" of such things, the history of black and white aesthetics has become too intertwined, in all these years, for denial, reversal, or extermination.

Listen to Professor Longhair's conversion, here, of that clave-rhythm breakdown, of 3-3-2, to a rock-like (in more ways than one) drone and drag, and you are hearing a corruption of form and time which is as American, well, not as apple pie, but as racist anger and resentment. And make no mistake; this whole process, of black blood seeping through every aspect of the American aesthetic, represents, to many white Americans, a corruption of all that is pure and dear. And yet they covet and even celebrate this corruption, if in their own way. Though even as white people learn this aesthetic, this music and dance, to either love it or use it, they tend to forget the source, with a cultural amnesia that is more than simple denial, but rather a kind of self-rejection. So, ironically, the only thing preventing a lot of white folks from appreciating their own crossover accomplishments, and even mastery of black forms, is the specter of self hate. They will never look in that cultural mirror for fear of what they might actually see.

When it comes to Elvis Presley there are those of us (or, really, *you*) who tend to spend too much time trying to tear him down, like he's one of those Confederate statues that recently ate dirt in the wake of the BLM movement. "Elvis," it goes, "was this,

Elvis was that, he was a racist, he stole this and he took that"... well, you get the idea. Many persist in this kind of posthumous character assassination even though none of it is true. Elvis did no more, in terms of cultural adaptation, than any rational, intelligent, and talented singer would do. Even as he was, in a cultural sense, flying blind (this was, after all, the early 1950s), he just knew what he had to do and he did it, after a fashion. And let us not forget that he was forging a new musical path as he did so; it's not that other white Americans weren't clear in their admiration and willingness to work on and with black music, but that Elvis, in a very new and individual way, did so with an uncanny and mimicking originality. He was no more a copyist and a thief than the saxophonist Sonny Stitt, who clearly admired Charlie Parker and found his own complex path within Parker's own twisting creations. So it was with Elvis in relation to the black music that surrounded him as he went through life, in Mississippi, in Memphis, on records, in the streets. I would note two important things in this regard: a guy I worked for years ago, African American, once said to me, "I never thought Elvis Presley copied black people; he doesn't sound like anybody black that *I* ever heard." And yet Sam Phillips, the pioneering record label owner and producer who first recorded Elvis, commented: "Elvis Presley was more like a black man than any other white man I ever knew."

What Phillips was referring to was Elvis' humility, his fascinating mix of assertive vanity and artistic and social subservience to the music he played. He was a Southerner and he was politically conservative (though, yes, a cultural radical) but he was not racist in either his personal attitudes or in his sense of cultural magnanimity. And though he didn't really have to, he was always quick to credit his sources of inspiration, from Arthur Crudup (see Vol. 25 ) to the pianist/composer **Ivory Joe Hunter**. As noted in the book *A Change is Gonna Come: Music, Race, and the Soul of America* (by Craig Hansen Werner), when Hunter was in Memphis in 1957 he was invited by Elvis to Graceland, where they went over some songs for Elvis to consider; as Hunter said later:

"He is very spiritually minded...he showed me every courtesy, and I think he's one of the greatest."

Hunter, a gifted and prolific songwriter, was also a good singer and pianist, fusing a pop and blues aesthetic to the formal revisionism of those post-Tin Pan Alley years. This was the blue-ing of American pop song which I have referred to over and over again, a technique of adapting the cadences and phrasing of the blues to a more expansive harmonic vocabulary, especially as defined by standard song form (something which would also, I should mention, strongly effect film music in the work of composers like Elmer Bernstein, Alex North and Henry Mancini). The blue gesture that so effected post-war pop and jazz-inflected pop (think, once again, of Nat Cole, Charles Brown, early Ray Charles, Johnny Moore, Floyd Dixon) even seeped into rhythm and blues and (in a different way) early rock and roll. Certainly Elvis felt it, though he was not really typical of the rockabillies, preoccupied as he was with his own ideas of sentimental balladry (though that's another story).

In this way Elvis and Hunter were a good match; Elvis eventually recorded a song that Hunter made, on **10/21/49**, called **I Almost Lost My Mind**. Hunter was clearly, at this point, in a Nat Cole-vein, recording in those years with a variety of jazzers, including various Duke Ellington alumni. He just had something compositionally that worked, that was mellow and sat well musically, in its blue re-stating of colloquialism and in its gentle match of word and rhythm. Vocally he had that sound, of thick, liquid phrasing, which covered the gospel impulse with a veneer of pop reductionism, and which so effected modern soul balladry. *I Almost Lost My Mind* is ingeniously constructed and an actual blues, not just a song with blues reference. It masks its blues with a chromatic, arcing melody, something which Elvis, a hidden bluesman to the end, must certainly have noticed.

No white singer was more adept at consolidating the blue-pop impulse than **Peggy Lee (I Ain't Got Nobody, 1949)**.

In this study and others I have done (and I got some justified criticism for this relative to my first book, *American Pop*) I have, I admit, avoided bland, mainstream popular music. I tend to ignore certain, All-American, singers starting with the 1920s pop era and extending into the sorta-rock and pop sound of some of the whitest of 1950s song. I don't just mean Georgia Gibbs, whose copying of black hits was just that and little more (if strangely defendable), but also the likes of Dean Martin, Alan Jones, Tony Martin, Perry Como...well, you get the idea. The justifiable aspect of this criticism of my work is that I have thus ignored performers who, whether I like them or not, have had real historical impact on popular music through sales and pop influence. My response is to argue that we don't write literary histories by citing pulp and popular authors just because they sold in great numbers and influenced other pulp and popular authors. On the other hand, in American song we have Bing Crosby and Al Jolson, who were not just great singers but extremely influential and who sold a lot of records. But those two, who I have indeed cited in my books, were chosen because they were artists and had artistic impact.

So we have, for your consideration, Peggy Lee, and though I seemed to have pegged her racially, I have no intention of thus diminishing her talent and significance. Certain things are just *there* in American life, and until there is a level playing field in racial terms in this country I will continue to make distinctions based on color, because such distinctions instructively point out differences in style, approach, influence, image, and professional access (with an emphasis on the latter). Peggy Lee needs no such introduction, but here we are: a graduate of Benny Goodman's big band school of hard knocks, right out of the box she had an easy and politely swinging way of phrasing, with an insinuating tone of voice and a talent for subtle melodic paraphrase - of the kind that, while not diminishing her jazz talents, gave her work an accessibility that a stricter jazz perspective might have denied her. I cannot say exactly how much she learned from the singer Lil Green (see Vol. 21), but she had Lil's talent for taking a modest vocal instrument and making it work. *I Ain't Got Nobody* is more strictly out of jazz than some of Lee's post-1960s work, and it is pure silk, musically-speaking. "I sing sweet love songs," she tells us at .35, in a way that would have made Billie Holiday proud (or pissed off), and the way she slurs her words from 1:57 to the end is like a hipster tag to this old and still (musically) relevant song. The swinging intimacy of this is a sign of what was lost in Lee's "star" years. The bigger the groups they put her with (or that she put herself with) as her celebrity ascended, the more she seemed to be drowning in accompaniment, and a voice that had always seemed small (but to good effect) now seemed tiny, lost in a cavern of orchestration.

And now for something completely different, as I ask the musical question: what is it about speed and virtuosity in instrumental music which satisfies something in our souls, evokes responses ranging from wild cheering to stunned amazement? Is music an athletic event, something to be viewed as though from the cheap seats, from which we squint at and pity the losers, who slink by in the distance and hit the finish line like after-thoughts? I think of all of this as I listen to the pianist **Bud Powell**'s glorious version of **Sweet Georgia Brown (1949)**, in which he negotiates the chord changes with flash, yes, but with flash of a kind to which we, as spectators, are largely unaccustomed. His playing on this, as on much of his work of the 1940s, sounds and feels like fogged lightning, with a certainty of execution veiled by what seems almost like a form of hesitancy, a series of almost-discernible pauses which create odd rhythmic spaces between the notes. In this way the line of improvisation is converted from one of train-like momentum to that of a more human machine, to a method of internalized stop-start, executed with a sense of constant motion. The notes Bud plays have definition, but it is not the kind of definition we hear in classical - or even in most other jazz - pianists. His tone has its own rhythm built into it, and the effect of these notes and chords multiplied is of a continuous web of sound. I would say this is a black thing, but that, especially in the context of this book, might be redundant. And it also might obscure the complexity of the jazz argument about virtuosity; compare the speed and continuity of this, which is like human locomotion, to the way in which the pianist Oscar Peterson turns every run and series of runs into *just* runs, like a hail of musical locusts. They rain down on us from a material world; and they are *just* material, not substance. For Oscar Peterson notes were just notes, strung together to impress audiences; think of a circus act in which a man dangles from a wire, creating the illusion, but only the illusion, of daring. Like that circus act Peterson worked with a net, with the sense that everything would always be resolved safely; the net was Peterson's way of turning out pat little twists of safely-accommodating, "bluesy" phrasing. Powell was just the opposite - his music is so exhilarating because there is always a sense of danger in it, of human consciousness on the edge of sanity and irrational resolution; such, also, was the jazz movement which he helped to lead. *Bebop*, criticized as a label by some for its supposed trivialization of a great art form, to me perfectly encapsulates the sound and effect of the new music, which, at its best, was like a mind constantly at odds with itself.

   And now, Country Music in some of its growing ways and means:

   Remember Al Bernard? My old friend who we discussed in Volumes 2 and 4? Well, back then Al took the *Last Train Through*

*Arkansas* and I cited his recording as a prophetic look at what country music might still become, as a canny, sideways musical view at the idea of the *idea* of rural music - or really the idea of the idea of *country* music (though no one yet called it that). Al Bernard was a cultural and musical prophet in many ways. He predicted, with his own cheerful sing-song demeanor, the way the pop dream - to not-quite-quote the late great film critic Stanley Kaufmann - would inflate our opinion and understanding of new kinds of Afro-White fusion in this *American Century* (and apologies for sounding like a bad Public Television documentary title). But Bernard really was all that, a benevolent minstrel who co-opted that old blackface form for the benefit of a new era, in which the actual black began to show through the fake black and in which the white started to assert itself as deserving (at least in its own mind) its own music and its own market, undisturbed (or untroubled) by race. And though such a dream was wholly unrealistic and unattainable, its very existence created a new force for musical change, and one which paradoxically was a new declaration of white independence at the same time that it established a permanent racial *co-*dependence. As soon as white people began most vehemently and categorically to deny their connection to blacks and black music, the connection became not just more obvious but completely irreversible. This was the exception that proved the rule, the irony that proved, when it was laid bare, to be absolutely lacking in irony.

So along comes **Wayne Raney**; the year is **1948** and the song is **Fast Train Through Arkansas**. Coincidentally related to Bernard's *Last Train*? No, this is the white continuum; I do believe, in spite of what I just said, that such a thing exists, even if it's a tailgate attached to the black continuum. Raney is recording for King Records, an unlikely but perfectly appropriate vehicle for the modern country era, stocked as it is with black artists, black composers, and now a new generation of white post-Western Swing, neo-Bluegrass strivers (and with the shrewd if only semi-comprehending Syd Nathan at the label helm). The new music that they are making is far from the growing Nashville school of syrup-laden balladry and dramatic re-statement-of-the-emotional obvious. King's music is energy music, correctly traceable to rock and roll (and almost always ignored as such by the bevy of liberal critics and assorted listeners who cannot be swayed from the belief that rock and roll was just another confused white disciple of the blues). That moaning harmonica is now perfectly focused and no longer just a musical side bar to a hillbilly moan, swallowing this straightforward melody as it accumulates some blues points along with its bluegrass fast step. The tight harmonies, very bluegrass, and the brief guitar solo, give us enough to prove that this an actual white thing and not just a passing commercial fancy.

In spite of all the changes country music is going through, god is never far away. **The Sauceman Brothers**, radio stars of the middle years of country broadcasting, assure us of that god is still on the water, in spite of all that is moving through country's field of focus, with **Hallelujah We Shall Rise**, which they recorded in the **Late 1940s**. Country faith is one thing that never faded, but it is interesting to realize that in many ways it adapted to the new sound of the new music. Bluegrass gospel, whiter than ever, was now a major force. Even Bill Monroe was fond of his little bluegrass prayers; *Hallelujah We Shall Rise*, observant of that Southern Christian thing, is a quick trip through bible country with a very black sense of internalized vocal call and response, reshaped by white voices, who reach for and then flatten out its blue intervals. We might even say that the bluegrass sound and format, with its strange formalist veneer, was more appropriate for white religious observation than the sanctified method. It required less overt emotion and matched the Southern mountain temperament - think of the tight-jawed formality of country/mountain singers, the stoicism which stood like a musical and spiritual gatekeeper before the Golden Fence. A few quick interludes of finger-picking in this remind us what it has all come to; no more blue bends for these folks. Bluegrass, in some if not all ways, was a prim and proper re-posturing of country music, a statement of country virtuousness. Though I don't think it was a specific or even conscious rejection of blackness, listening through this, with its protean and very black bass voice, I get the sense that although black musical supports are still part of the edifice of old-time country music, the weight of the building has shifted to support a more white (and white-Christian) point of view.

Is the bright and perky piano intro to **Hard Times Will Soon Be Over** (**The Blue Ridge Quartet, 1948**) telling us that what is really over are the old days of fearsome gospel warnings about the fires of hell? In claiming that hard times are nearly at an end (and this is only 15 years or so after the end of the Depression) are they speaking to post-War optimism (and I *don't* mean the Civil War), the sense, like in a bad marriage after a reunion, that this time we'll do it right, we'll get our act together, and really make the South safe for Democracy (aka white people)? I really don't know, but there is a sense in this of all those things that the new gospel stands for in parallel to the new country. The rhythm section is slick and the piano sounds like it is returning to the traditional country fold (unlike with the near-black, godless excesses of Western Swing). It has an optimistic gospel bounce, the new-time gospel rhythm that derives from old-time black piano a la Arizona Dranes (see Vol. 5) but which has largely jettisoned any signs of black heat. This performance is all-white emotion, but measured, with an underlying sense of reflective relief. We have none of the depraved tension of the white sanctified movement; gone is the idea of spinning in church, of grabbing all that is the holy and hanging onto it for dear life, like it's a bucking bronco. Which is not to say that the white sanctified tradition did not live on - see Brother Claude Ely, Vol. 28 - but that even the mainstream of white religious performance was mainstreamed.

The Blue Ridge Quartet is, in the most essential way, a descendant of black quartets, but the whole emotional temperature has been lowered. The voices blend with harmonic symmetry and the lead voice remains tethered to the group even as it occasionally slides, with great care, away from the ensemble - listen to the high voice as it begins to depart in a lead way from 1:35 to the end. This is as close as this performance gets to getting back in touch with its emotional roots ("lord I'm tired" he sings, while sounding completely rested), but it never crosses the line, and that last chord - well, it sounds like someone splashing bright white paint on a wall that is *already* sparklingly white.

More satisfying (to me at least) is **Hank Williams 1948** solo transcription of **Lost on the River**. What can we add here to the legend that is Hank? Well, we can look more directly *at* him, away from the legend and in more specifically musical terms. There is strain of solo male voice that we hear in country music of this era, led by Williams' example, containing what we might describe as a Southern tinge, a slight and ever-urgent twang, applied to the blue-twisted syllables of Southern speech. Tonally it is white over black, a very racially individual form of inflection that would not exist, paradoxically or not, without the model of black speech. The writer J.W. Cash's once-controversial claim that the southern black man entered into the southern white man is no more obviously confirmed than in this whole school of singing, from Hank Williams to Lefty Frizzell to Merle Haggard. It is the white version of the Southern cry, or maybe more a teardrop than a cry, and part of what I have referred to before as a new movement in country music of white musical independence; though, as I also have said, the more white musicians cleared their own individual paths, the more those paths seemed to lead, in reverse and absentia, back to black culture. This is not to take anything away from white singers. It's just that their lives and music were hopeless intertwined with the lives of black folks, whose halting approaches to Southern white people were self-preservationist actions forced by necessity and amounted to a kind of ghosting-for-survival.

Hank Williams was one of the biggest stars of country music and for good reason. He had a beautifully expressive voice, a great sense of dramatic shading, and he wrote *songs* - songs of love, of loss, of thinking about - if not necessarily owning - the blues. This was a renaissance period in honky tonk composition, a time of great personal introspection, of reflection on the ups and downs of life, on the transitions between poverty and fame, public presence and private alcoholism (which is what finally did Hank in at age 29, in the back seat of a limousine on New Year's eve), hope and hopelessness. And as always there was god and religion for fallback, to try and ease the chronic pain of existence. *Lost on the River* is not quite gospel, but it reshapes its own story of human tragedy into religious-like form. It is a fairly standard recitation of life's difficulties, but in the manner of a great artist Williams converts it to a riveting tale of moral confusion and then, finally, the end to possibility and so to life. "Out on the river where sorrow creeps...thinking of you and how my heart weeps...tomorrow you will be another man's wife..." he tells us, and admittedly the tragedy of this situation is augmented by our knowledge of the awful fate which awaits Hank. Still, he was Hank Williams, and by his example country music was forever changed, by subject, voice, and the sudden and simultaneous elevation and descent of tragedy into a condition of spiritual elevation and drunken inevitability.

**Merle Travis** (see also Vol. 23) gives us another song of biblical proportions on **Little David Play on Your Harp (3/20/48)**, recorded for a radio show. Though Merle is a much different kind of performer than Hank Williams, the effect of Williams' brand of white soul shows clearly in Travis' singing. Listen to the half-falsettos, paused for emphasis, at the the beginning of this, for a mulatto style of singing which fuses the old Hawaiian cry, the minstrel whoop, the Jimmie Rodgers yodel and the African American field cry - all happily compatible with each other, and all part of a strangely user-friendly method of vernacular singing. Travis has a deeper voice than Williams and is more of a crooner - at lease as we define crooning, a smooth and soothing style of pitch-steady singing, cushioned by a comfortable and soothing depth-of-voice. But Bing Crosby he's not, and that's a good thing. Travis swings in a way that Bing could not, overcoming the crooner's natural tendency to sentimentalize and so neutralize. This is an unsentimental telling of the tale of David mixed with Travis' signature way of fingerpicking, as he executes a complicated and difficult accompaniment. The song sounds like another of those *gospel* tunes written in the minstrel style (I don't know the actual source), a pop secularization of the old black spiritual. As such it is religion-lite, perhaps a more acceptable way, for certain musicians, to express faith, at a certain arm's length, in public. In this they avoided the exposed public piety of some of the heavier forms of white gospel practice, and showed how useful minstrelsy, this far into the 20th century, remained: the minstrel model, strangely utilitarian, still had a purpose, to distance the singer from the song while bringing him closer to the audience.

Country gospel, in this era, sounds like a very distant echo of the old-time sanctified groups (like the Phipps gathering, see Vols. 9, 10, 11). **The Cavalry Quartet's** version of **What You Gonna Do? (1948)** is more of the same, as part of the new, friendly, congregational form of singing. Listen to this next to the Blue Ridge Quartet's *Hard Times Will Soon be Over*; this is, again, religion with a smile. Though white Sanctified singing always distanced itself from black Sanctified singing - both were essentially like warning voices, but the black was Dostoyevsky to the white's Stephen King, real life versus shallow and shadow fantasy - the new middle-of-the-road Southern religiosity was more tolerant of sin, treating sinners like misbehaving children. *What You Gonna Do* certainly suggests the bluegrass model in its instrumentation and accompaniment, but it uses the layered voices of the vocal quartet model, with, once again, a deep bass voice, which sounds here like a lone black man lost in a white wilderness. And this is certainly the most cheerful accounting I have ever heard of what things will ultimately be like "when the world begins to burn."

Closer to the source is **Roy Lanham and his Gospel Quartet**'s version of **We Will Know (1948)**. The subject is basically the same as before, with the after-life template that was used to scare and then reassure men, woman, and children for hundreds of years. This quartet is, accompaniment or not, its own rhythm section, which places it even closer to old-style vocal-group tradition. These well-tempered voices don't strike the kind of dynamic, hectoring pose we are becoming used to in the modern country gospel era of good god/bad god religion. They smile and shake your hand, all the while whispering sweet warnings in your ear.

In re: country music there are certain terms I use and references that I make which are technically incorrect, come as they have to signify certain kinds of country music sounds and poses. One of these is "mountain," which has come, at least in my mind, to equal a certain isolated twang, like the soulful and heartfelt nasality of singers like the Carter Family, BF Shelton, et al. I don't honestly know if these were all mountain folk, and if they were I couldn't tell you which mountain they lived on, or what constitutes mountain-living (is the valley *next* to the mountain a conveyor of mountain life?) or whether, as in my head, such a thing signifies country isolation and loneliness of the most profound kind. It certainly does all of that in the popular image, and I have a feeling that such singers encouraged this. Like Bob Dylan presenting himself as the Wandering Jew of Modern Hobo Times, mountain singers presented themselves as gatekeepers of a tradition characterized by honesty and obeisance to neighborly values. Far be it for me to question such country (or is it mountain?) authority.

I hear all of the above in the singer **Molly O'Day**'s work (**Poor Ellen Smith, 4/4/49**, recorded on my mother's 22nd birthday). Kentucky born and raised on a farm, O'Day changed her name from Lois Laverne Williamson, became well-known on radio (singing first with her brothers and then with a band called The Forty-Niners, where she met her husband), met Hank Williams, had a an actual country hit, and was signed to Columbia Records, before giving it all up in a religious spasm of guilt and spending her remaining years singing in church and at evangelical events. One can admire the principals involved if not necessarily the implied politics of such a typical Southern way of life, and one can admire the mountainous sincerity (no pun intended, sort-of) of this whole school of country singing and singers. Their way of verbally caressing the word-phrases of old-time mountain music certainly implied the kind of religiosity that eventually took over O'Day's life, though in the early days she used the act of piety to sing of secular scenes of tragedy and regret (two words which should probably be sewn into a giant country quilt or placed on every old country singer's gravestone). *Poor Ellen Smith* is nothing if not typical of Southern, white, mildly regretful remembrance of things well past. If there is a strangeness to such songs, a nostalgia for old-time death and disease and certain forms of mental derangement, it is probably due to the Hallmark-card formatting of white Southern commemoration in general. Audiences ate it up, and O'Day sang it from the perspective of a slightly judgmental, passive observer rather than as any challenge to authority. Her voice had the intense, spoken/sung sound of uprisings past, a kind of active-passive (in that strange white, country way) yet defiant acceptance of fate. This was a mild protest against, well, *things*, but only for the duration of a song.

On occasion public cultural wars can be a form of self entertainment. But even more interesting, if ultimately petty in the most petty ways, are those cultural wars which are fought internally, between members of a particular movement. In something like jazz (whose battlefield I am most familiar with) the struggles tend to be over a shrinking amount of territory, though I will warn you not to use this limited perspective as cause for minimizing the importance of such arguments. These are intellectual fights we are fighting, and jazz's small sphere of influence makes them, if anything, *less* petty because we are fighting less over territory than intellectual rights. In the great tradition of the intellectual battles of the 1940s and 1950s, over everything from Abstract Expressionist art to modernity in general, jazz people argue over issues of form and expression and commercial exploitation. These are good fights, I think, even if they sometimes go bad.

I was thinking of this as I listened to **Flatt and Scruggs'** recording **Cabin in the Caroline (1949).** As the form of country music called bluegrass emerged and, more importantly, became popular (because in most musical forms, jazz notwithstanding, fights over things for which no money is at stake are rare) there were not just arguments but bitter rivalries over origin and development, over who did what first and who pirated what musician from what band (which made it even harder to determine who did what first).

To make things a little bit easier I am going to stretch the definition of Fair Use, and quote, inadequate as it strikes me, from Wikipedia's definition of bluegrass music:

"Bluegrass music is a genre of American roots music that developed in the 1940s in the United States Appalachian region. The genre derives its name from the band Bill Monroe and the Blue Grass Boys. Bluegrass has roots in traditional English, Scottish and Irish ballads and dance tunes, and in traditional African-American blues and jazz. Bluegrass was further developed by musicians who played with Monroe, including 5-string banjo player Earl Scruggs and guitarist Lester Flatt. Monroe characterized the genre as: 'Scottish bagpipes and ole-time fiddlin'. It's Methodist and Holiness and Baptist. It's blues and jazz, and it has a high lonesome sound.' "

Like most such things, the inadequacy of that description (with the exception of Bill Monroe's short but pithy summation, which leaves out a lot, but at least gets to the point) is ripe for the picking by half-baked critics like myself. But it will do for now, except to add that bluegrass was like a musical formalization of hillbilly blues and ragtime, a neater and tidier instrumental expression of hillbilly's ragged sense of improvisation, as overlaid by vocals that adhered more closely to the rules of standard triadic harmony, as derived from the (white) gospel and black and white quartet tradition. And though some have claimed it represented a de-emphasis on blues phrasing and blues semiotics, I would say instead that it represented a reclamation of the blues idea in a specifically white way. Was this another white way of thinking about black music, as I have described rock and roll? In some respects yes, but in a less acculturated fashion. And so we are off to the races, as derivation battles with credit and credit battles with personnel. Hence, from the web site of the Bluegrass Heritage Foundation:

"While some bluegrass music fans date the genre back to 1939 when Monroe first appeared on the Grand Ole Opry, most believe that the classic bluegrass sound came together in December 1945 when Earl Scruggs joined the band. Scruggs, a 21-year-old from North Carolina, played an innovative three-finger picking style on the banjo (which came to be known as "Scruggs style") with such drive and clarity that it energized and excited audiences. Equally influential in the classic 1945 line-up of the Blue Grass Boys were Lester Flatt (from Sparta, Tennessee) on guitar and lead vocals, Chubby Wise on fiddle; and Howard Watts, also known by his comedian name "Cedric Rainwater," on the upright bass."

In professional terms these kinds of jockeying for historical position caused great friction between Monroe et al. Truthfully it's silly and (yes) petty to claim anything other than that Monroe was the founder of bluegrass or that others got the sound "together," in ways he hadn't, after his initial efforts. Nonsense; listen to Monroe's early Columbia recordings, his late 1930s and early 1940s Victors, and the records he made with his brother Charlie as a duo (see Vol. 19). This was all more than just bluegrass in gestation. It was new and it was stylistically particular; more important, both Lester Flatt and Earl Scruggs initially worked for Monroe before splitting off from his band. For many years they and Monroe were not on speaking terms, though the music continued to make its own claims.

The phrase *high lonesome* has emerged from this music to describe its vocal range, and the beauty of its higher-pitched vowels comes through on even the earliest of recordings. *Cabin in the Caroline* is classic in it's whining vocal and interactive meshing of guitar and banjo. Scruggs' three-fingered banjo picking did become a definition (or, really, re-definition) of the bluegrass sound, in its peripatetic outlining of bluegrass harmony and rhythm (it had been Monroe's mandolin which was the initial signifier of bluegrass' instrumental style; while it continued to be central, it was slowly overtaken by the banjo, an instrument of greater resonance and volume). *Cabin in the Caroline* has the wonderfully understated modesty of the best of bluegrass, a form which has tended through the years to rest on its technical laurels, to become so formalized in its instrumental execution as to become frozen in a variable time machine of technical dazzle (do, however, look ahead in the next few volumes of this study for some of the newer bluegrass players of the next ten years who, before the style became rigidly defined, injected it with localized and regional heat).

I have emphasized country music's ties to the emergent form of rock and roll, and it is fascinating to examine even some of Elvis Presley's antecedents, who were (way) out there whether or not Elvis was aware of them. **Bill Haley** was born in Michigan and raised in Pennsylvania, and his father was a traditional country musician from Kentucky. It didn't get any more American than that, especially as country music spread itself around like a regional weed (I was going to say pandemic). As far as we know Haley left home as a teen to pursue a musical career, became involved with a a form of quasi-Western Swing (which had some broader pop and country elements), and ended up coordinating the music programs for a Pennsylvania radio station. Before trying his hand at rock and roll and succeeding, most particularly, with *Rock Around the Clock*, Haley was a (regionally) well-known yodeling cowboy singer, taking the post-blue yodel to another and very different level, though one which lined up with the Hollywood-Cowboy example and with role models like Roy Rogers (see Vol. 20).

In **1949** Haley recorded **Yodel Your Blues Away**, and his opening yodel is startling and wonderful. This is essentially a country-pop tune, with a dominant accordion and a solid and rhythmically assertive accordion solo, shades of Western Swing's odd but observant compromise. The whole recording is peppy and spry in an almost silly and overly-optimistic way, but it works because the band is so together and Haley's singing is so clear and plain. And his yodeling is fantastic - listen to what amounts to a yodel solo from about 1:17 on. He trills and and trembles his way through a series of intricate warbles, and then comes right back in with a bright-boy vocal. *Yodel Your Blues Away* is blues/not blues, though it is *about* the blues and its offshoots, and ends up as country-populist pop of sorts. It doesn't quite fit into any known musical category, though it does match, roughly, a number of Hollywood soundtrack confections, as a smiling, rover-on-the-range, insert. As a matter of fact this whole performance sounds like it might be the last word on country music's infiltration of the old-time cowboy mainstream, just before it left such things to Hollywood and television (where Roy Rogers consolidated his cowboy bona fides in the 1950s). After this there was nothing really left for country-revisionist performers like Haley to do *except* rock and roll.

# Chapter 25  A White Spy in the House of Love: An Overdose of Reality

It has always bothered me that there is, in the literature, little deep writing about the heavier sources of Bob Dylan's work. Not that there has not been some excellent writing done on it - by Greil Marcus in particular, but also a number of narrower but illuminating studies of certain aspects of Dylan's life and work - but a bit too much of the literature beats around the bushes of the blues, ignores a little too much of country music, and maybe even makes too much of Dylan's lyric poetry, which to my ears alternates between brilliant word association and doggerel disguised as poetry. Paul Simon sang of "words that tear and strain to rhyme," and nowhere was this more evident than in some of Dylan's best songs, done during his mid-period of post-acoustic, anarcho-electric, epic composition.

A lot of this worked brilliantly even as it did, indeed, strain to rhyme, though some of it sagged under the weight of Dylan's growing hipster arrogance. There *was* something happening, but plenty of people knew what it was, not just Bob and his entourage. The self-superiority expressed by this in-group way ("you and I are the hip ones, the ones who really *know*," it seems to be saying to a growing yet "exclusive" circle of fans, "and everyone else is on the outside looking in)," appealing at first, wears a little thin. And it was to the detriment of some of his work.

I say all of this out a sense of tough love toward a man who had the canniest way of assimilating so much that came before him, out of the vernacular and into the popular, picking and choosing without appearing to pick and choose and just simply coordinating it all into a personal and starkly original musical viewpoint. To Dylan's credit none of it sounded as though he was showing off his origins, even as his own personal vanity flared obnoxiously. But his humble "act" wasn't really an act so much as it was a reconciliation of contradictory desires. He may indeed have absorbed this attitude and point of view from Woody Guthrie, who combined working-class humility with the ego-centric impulse and instinct of celebrity. Certainly Dylan learned a lot from Guthrie in terms of image and the technique of sideways communication of ego, of how to grab the spotlight while feigning indifference to all that being in the spotlight meant.

The most obvious source of a lot of Dylan's work and charm was a counterintuitive form of self deprecation, of the kind that was self promotion, but that really did let him have it both ways: *I am so smart and charismatic but still a man of the people* might be the slogan that sums it all up (yes, as it does Woody Guthrie). And though this was a particular condition of *modern media man*, Dylan shared this perspective with a number of old time musicians like the mysterious **Dan Pickett**, whose **Baby Don't You Want to Go (1949)** is Dylanesque-before-Dylan, in its arms-length and slightly contemptuous, judgmental approach to personal relationships. Pickett, who was born in 1906 and died in 1967, presumably lived some kind of life in between those years but, as is the case with a lot of black musicians from his generation, we know virtually nothing about him, except - and this a big except - the fourteen fascinating recordings he made. I hear a lot of Dylan (yes, I know, really the other way around), though I think it is unlikely that Dylan actually heard Pickett. The playful repartee here with an unseen woman, the nursery-rhyme rhyme scheme, and the melodic wordplay; but mostly the attitude, the very title of the song, are of a late-vernacular, post-Delta blues levity, not far from *Good Morning Little School Girl* in the way they both predict and define the newer populist lyricism of what will, yes, become the stuff of rock and roll. This is less that old dusty personal poetry than it is a newly-composed epistle to the world, an announcement that the ego of the vernacular musician is as healthy as anyone else's, as secure as any respected member of the middle class. Dylan, steeped as he was in a quirky but malleable tradition of ballads and blues on 78, surely had his ear to the speaker, in one way or another.

One of his Dylan's most redeeming qualities was that he didn't, unlike a lot of the folkies, let himself sink into the mud of traditionalism. This may, ultimately, be what kept him alive and what made him not just of interest but a great artist. It certainly made him stand out in that crowd, made him most noticeable in the great wave of tradition that swept, tsunami-like, out of the first folk revival of the 1940s and seeped into the rock and roll era of the 1950s and 1960s. There was a salt-of-the-earth quality in Dylan's music that offset the hip snobbery and sense of self-love. Would he have been listening to things like **Rockin' With Red** - recorded by **Piano Red** in **1950**? Once again, if not this particular version, he knew, we might say, the "literature" that fed performances like this one, whose ultimate "simplicity" and near-primitivism rings through Dylan blues heads like *Rainy Day Women*. The straightforward lyricism, the odd repetitions, the way in which the blues was now an even more pliant and song-friendly structure, still ripe for strange and modest but tasty variations like Piano Red's, all gave a good name, in the post-War era, to commercial music. Piano Red, to paraphrase Duke Ellington's comments about the trumpeter Ray Nance, may have had only a limited musical range, but he explored that range like no one else. This record is a tribute to simplicity, just Red and his piano and (I think) a snare drum of sorts, a portrait of a strange and personal musical world in less than three minutes flat. The song itself is an old story - his baby is waiting for their rocking assignation, and the wait is accompanied by a country-like two beat on the piano, some assimilated blues runs, and a big, easy on the ears, beat. The rhythm on this is key to its deeper charms; it never exactly starts and it never exactly ends - it's just *there*, from the very beginning, like a sound we hear whenever we open a particular door.

    And speaking of Dylan by way of Elvis (because I think that one of the most lasting effects Elvis had, inspiration-wise, was on "fringe" hipster, white figures like Dylan, most of whom, unlike Dylan, went straight to rock and roll and skipped the folkie stage), let's look, quite literally, at the record. No matter what you may think in 2021 in the comfort of you own living rooms, wallowing in sophisticated musical strategies (should we listen to the Brahms tonite or the Gilbert and Sullivan?), the early Dylan was wired in parallel to the early Elvis. What sane guy wouldn't like to have been like Elvis, especially given the crowds he drew of young women and their jealous boyfriends? And this is what made Dylan different, I think: a taste for youth forms that were not politically accurate (I was going to say *correct* but decided better of it). Sure he admired *the folk*, like Woody Guthrie et al, but one sign of his real destiny was his fearless willingness to piggyback on the rock and roll giant who, with awkward, lurching, steps, was (literally) threatening the countryside. Dylan, most simply put, had a rock and roll imagination (it's apparent, I think, even in his pre-electric work), and that rock and roll imagination was bound up with the Elvis-fantasy of stadium-sized stardom.

    But where did that whole musical wave start, aside from with the idea, as I have asserted, of the guitar-wielding evangelist? The spirit of rock and roll was found in a lot of places in those years, many unexpected, but the most obvious was in the composing, singing, and playing of **Arthur Crudup**, a rock and roll pioneer if there ever was one, and the true grail for those who are still searching for it in rock and roll terms. Listen to Arthur on **My Baby Left Me (11/8/50)**, and if you have been wondering until now exactly what traces of blues and country music Elvis was working from when he made his first startling recordings for Sun Records (in 1954) you can end your search. What is it about Crudup that so caught Elvis' ear and which still sounds so deftly and cleanly creative and musically cognizant, in a very self-aware post-blues way, even 70 years later? I have often claimed that one of the prime ways in which white rock distinguished itself from black blues and rhythm was in its raising of the sonic center of gravity, from the rhythm section outward. Rhythm and blues was bottom-heavy, pounded with deep bass and thick-toned drums, while country, as it withdrew into itself, was high-strung, trebly, weightless and propulsive rather than deep-swinging. And, yes, we might claim that that all started (or was at least synthesized) by and with a black man named Arthur Crudup, who beat "that box" (as Elvis described it) which he called a guitar like it was a drum, worked with a different kind of rhythm section (as far as I can tell only a drum here) and left the open musical spaces around him open. This is airy and free, like a hillbilly jamboree minus a few hillbillies, and that guitar solo! Played, as far as I can tell, by Crudup starting at .054, this is the blues/country fusion that Scotty Moore (Elvis' first guitarist) learned from. And there is more in this performance that pre-echoes Elvis, in particular Crudup's vocalized "dee, dee dee dee dee" at 1:37, which was, of course, mimicked almost exactly by Elvis some years later. This was a new rhythm, a new way of taking the open-air sound of country music and subverting it with drums, electricity, a bit of the blues, and an aggressive sense of decorum. And yes, the rockabillies were watching and waiting in the wings - I think. Because the truth is that I have never seen anyone else from that era, other than Elvis, cite Crudup in any way. Which goes to show how enlightened Elvis was, how original in outlook - and interpretation - he was.

Of course, other beneficiaries of this new enlightenment were the black blues singers whose idea of a better commercial day was stoked, just a few years later, by the relatively sudden emergence of a white youth culture which seemed to hunger after their *realness*, their authenticity and their true sense of having lived the music. The question of the racial benefits and deficits in this relationship - between the young, Southern white boys, most of whom in these early days were not, except by comparison to their black neighbors, particularly privileged, and the black music all around them, feeding their hunger - was not heavily discussed in a public sense in these early years of new blues and rock, though one cannot help but think that after Elvis the topic was on everyone's mind. Though I don't agree that, as Muddy Waters famously said, rock and roll was the blues' baby, I do think that, especially at this mid-stage of country blues (treblized by the sound of the guitar as pushed by low-powered amplifiers), the white country boys who made up the first generation of rockers knew the blues, knew its sound, its power to radically transform the honky tonk shouts that were their raw material. So it went with the imitable yet perhaps copy-worthy **Howlin' Wolf**, whose **Cryin' at Daybreak (1951)** is a deep and shattering warmup for the style-shattering riff of his later record of *Smokestack Lightning*. Wolf was like no one else in those country-blue days, monstrous by image and forbidding and yet not some freak of country birth. As crazed as he sounded, in his tortured elocution and fire-breathing blues mania, he fit right in with this stage of the blues' commercial rebirth. There was room in the music for more than a little bit of his type of sincere kitsch, especially with its deep bursts of emotion, theatrical vocal transitions, and intense riffing. And yet, like Crudup, he left a lot of musical space in his mad meanderings through the blue landscape, with heavy repetitions and fiercely contrasting dynamics. This was something, from proximity, the white boys understood.

And yet the "tradition" was never far away from all that they - white musicians - played or sang. The black blues was still more than capable of becoming the hard blues, in ways that the rockabillies might imitate but had trouble replicating (though not always; twenty years ago I played a gig with Billy Lee Riley of Sun Records/My Gal is Red Hot fame, and he was an amazingly pure blues singer when he wanted to be; and of course there's also Wayne Cochran, Roy Head and Mitch Ryder). In our current-day historical rear-view mirror, as I listen to **Johnny Shines** sing **Joliet Blues (10/23/50)**, I see Robert Johnson. The secular fervor which ignites *Joliet Blues* may be attributed to learned religious intensity, to the gospel tradition that was all around Shines, or it may be heard as an escalation of Johnson's emotional techniques (or both). The emotionalism of this is a step beyond - or beside - the kind we hear in the country blues of the 1920s, re-cast in a stark and more inflammatory way. It feels harmonically sedentary, even as it navigates old-time blues changes, making it feel like *Mississippi*

*Jailhouse Groan* (see Vol. 11) in it's static dynamics and sense of spiritual seance. In the new world of commercial blues performances like this were old-time survivals, with a familiar, modern sense of dread and loathing.

    Sometimes the nicest thing about those early Chicago blues recording sessions is the sense of their being thrown together with little if any premeditation, played in a way which was about as close to the personal and after-hours reality of these men as we, as spectators, will ever get. Record companies working with city bluesmen in those days were flying blind from a commercial standpoint, and so often just let things, in the studio, happen. The results were sometimes fantastic and fascinating; you cannot get any deeper and immediate and "real" than **Little Walter**'s version of **Muskadine Blues,** recorded in **1950**. Little Walter was a very original harmonica player, but even on things like this, where he plays only guitar, he had a knack, an ability to convert his own musical ideas into disjointed but swinging time frames. This one lopes along with a country feel but a free-form sense of casual indifference, to organization and verse beginnings and endings. There was no audience and yet there was. Walter preaches, as the old saying goes, but like a street preacher at the end of the day when he is too tired to worry about making much sense. The group takes its cues where it can find them, with sudden guitar riffs, background commentary, and such a sense of relaxation that I do get the feeling, as I listen throughout, of being a White Spy in the House of Love, lost in another world, where middle-class values are about as relevant to life-knowledge as Saturday morning cartoons.

    Though Little Walter et al did eventually try and meet the rest of the world, white and black, half way, at this stage they were trying to please mostly themselves and the people of their immediate world. And thank goodness for that, because without *Muskadine Blues* we would have that much less a sense of not just what happened to the blues in those years but why; *Muskadine,* like some other things (see, just below, *Rollin' and Tumblin'*) is what these guys were doing when they thought no one else was watching.

    I wrote in Volume 1 of this book of how significant a song I believe *Rollin' and Tumblin'*, in the history of the blues, from its early Delta manifestation to its final resting place in the hands of the genius blues-Phoenix Johnny Winter (see Chapter 12) is. What was there about this tune that seemed to inspire all kinds of reconsideration of not just the blues but the blues as shape shifting modeler of modern music? There have been times I have complained about the fetishization of the blues, at the way in which emphasis on the blues as a kind of all-purpose social and musical shaman has distorted our sense of black musical and cultural reality. The blues has, in my view, become a bit too much of a literary cottage industry, its study a substitute for looking at all that preceded and followed it. But just when I feel the most negative about t*he blues*, along comes something like the recording made by **Little Walter, Muddy Waters, and Leroy Foster** of **Rollin' and Tumblin' (1/50)**, and all bets, pro and con, are off.

I have reported on this performance before (in my study of the blues) but everything I might have said about it then bears repeating and then some. I consider this performance to be the Rosetta Stone of modern bluesology. It is something for blues archaeologists, past and present, to (re)discover, as a new language and system of cultural symbols. If, like me, you consider the strength of vernacular music to lay in the way it restores us to reality on a second-by-second basis, the way it flattens and then eliminates tiresome metaphors through a hard dose of reality, diluting white fantasy and replacing it with an alternative universe of poetic dreamscape (which is hammers home like an overdose of reality, destroying, in its path, the overgrown weeds of white symbolism), then you may understand why I am so enamored of *Rollin' and Tumblin'* and all that it stands for (sic).

From the top the music just bursts out at us, overwhelms with feeling. It sounds, once again, like something we are dropping in on, uninvited; we feel like we have arrived in the middle of a work that is already in progress. It's like - Action Painting in sound? Once again we are in the presence of something strange but not-so-strange. And, yes, it is like someone has opened a door into a room that we should not necessarily have access too; but there it is, in all of its epiphanous glory. To paraphrase Dick Katz about the Miles Davis group performance of *Walkin'* (which Dick wrote about in the old *Jazz Review*), it is as though a group of musicians got together one day to discuss and review all that they had learned in their musical lives, to sum it all up and then give us an idea of things-to-come. The stomping foot rhythms, the knife-like harmonica (in the days before Little Walter amped up), the actual drum - which drops a little snare-like bomb at .046 - the sheer cumulative musical weight of all of this musical knowledge gathered around a microphone - well, the revelatory wonders of

*Rollin' and Tumblin'* never cease in this three minute excerpt (there is a second part to this which is available in various blues collections, including my own). Finally - well, not finally, because this never really lets up - Little Walter lets out a chilling harp trill at 1:46 that should set your hair on end, followed by a very *electric* electric guitar - the final *coup de grace* for the county blues as we might have known it - at about 2:04. What we learn from this is that even in a form which we might think of as settled and static - the country blues - change was not just inevitable but necessary, as the music had long been sagging under the weight of repetition and formula. It helped that this change was happening in an organic way, the new style flowing out of the old, even if, as in this performance, it was coming out like musical rapids. As I have always insisted even the vernacular arts behave like *art*, are subject to the aesthetic, *artistic*, pressures of change. This is living proof.

The opening, echoing saxophone solo on **Take Out Some Time**, by **Laverne Baker** as **Little Miss Sharecropper (1950)**, followed by some effective, burrowing blues piano, takes us firmly into the post-Bessie Smith world of female blues singing. We've been there before in this study (see Annie Laurie, Vol. 24) but there is a commercial finality to Laverne Baker's whole manner of delivery that tells us where we are and what is just starting to happen with this kind of song and this kind of music. Like Dinah Washington's, Baker's tightly-wound voice seems to hold the lyrics of the song in a benevolent death grip. The song is hers, the blues are hers, and there is no going back to the country of the country of old timers who were, at least in the view of some of the new generation, just too passive in the face of racial intimidation.

How do I read all of that into one three-minute recording? Well, I really read it *out* of this record. The old Southern blues had a self effacing quality that was at least partly a matter of self preservation. Some of that old-time singing sounds as a sonic parallel to the street requirements of the Jim Crow South, where even black-white eye contact, if initiated by a black man or woman, was seen as defiance. There was a growing resistance to this restriction in some of the early country blues - hear Charley Patton's death-defying twists and blues turns, or Son House's "I am a man" declarations of fear and even self loathing - but as always there were limits to what a black man and woman could say in the old days in the old places. But now - there were fewer such restrictions. It wasn't, of course, the end of racism or even the end of the physical and psychological Jim Crow of northern segregation and cultural separatism, but it was, as on *Take Out Some Time*, the first of the last steps toward cultural independence and social redemption (and how do I square all of this with my frequent claims that music was not, in its essence, political? Quite easily; see my prior discussions. But we should add that Baker, as Little Miss Sharecropper, performed early on in a sack dress, as a reference to the the new-bondage profession of black tenant farmers, a way of life imposed by the Southern white non-meritocracy as a convenient and legal extension of slavery. Did she intend any irony in this or was this just another way of doing (music) business? I really have no idea).

Stylistically more of the same difference is **Lula Reed**'s **I'll Drown in My Own Tears (1951)**. There's that voice again, like beaded sweat - we hear the same tonal characteristic in Dinah Washington's singing, in LaVerne Baker's and Ivy Anderson's and Little Esther's. It's a tight Southern vibrato of the type heard from certain country blues singers and, yes, once again, from our old friend Elvis. Reed's work is considered by pop historians to stand for a new stage in black pop, and I concur. This kind of balladry - the song was later recorded by Ray Charles - with its maudlin aura of self-pity-on-display, was perfect for the new, sentimental world of rhythm and blues balladry, which differed from blues balladry mostly by name, but also in it's consolidated simplification of the harmonies that populated jazz standards. The song was written by Henry Glover, who needs to be recognized as one of the early black trailblazers of the independent record business (he worked for King Records among others). Yes, he toiled for a white man, but he quickly opened up his own musical territory. For Syd Nathan, who owned King, the only measure of success was success, which was measured in sales; and Glover was successful, as producer, composer, arranger, and, most significantly, as a label executive.

It didn't last forever. By 1958 Glover was fed up and, to complete his tour of Jewish-owned goniff-associated labels, he went over to Morris Levy at Roulette, for whom he had additional successes (and I mention the connection to Jews and the record business as a pre-emptive strike against anti-Semites out there; I have discussed this earlier in the book. Though Jews do have a complex relationship with black music and black musicians, there were plenty of non-Jewish thieves in the pop night in those days). Later on Glover went on to work with The Band, and was inducted into the blues hall of fame (and we won't even ask why he is not in the rock and roll version of same).

But still the old timers refused to lay down and go away. There was more than medicine in that medicine show model, and older veterans were still more than ready to go at it. **Pink Anderson**, who had been touring with medicine shows since the second decade of the 20th century, recorded **I've Got Mine on 5/29/50**, and it registers as yet another stimulus to the folkie imagination of the future. As we go through this study we realize that just about everything we hear in the 1960s folk revival has easily identifiable sources; musicians like Pink had the kind of attitude that stuck, historically-speaking, an old-time dose of shrewd professionalism, a theatrical sense of convincing and even dismissive artifice. There is a concept in theater of "the illusion of the first time," whereby multiple performances of the same material, as done by the same performer, must all be made to appear new, as though being revealed for the first time. So it was with performers like Pink Anderson, but even more so. There was a major lesson to be learned from this by the young folks who would start to learn the music in the next 10 years or so - keeping it real meant appearing to *not care* about keeping it real, feigning social indifference through a socially subversive neglect of community standards. *I've Got Mine,* about a crap game, is a narrative, a commentary on not just life but on the commentary itself, with ragtime swing and pithy musical gestures like the string pull/glissandos at .22 and .41, which are like humorous commentary on commentary.

More ambivalent about the old time sound is **Johnny Beck** on **You Gotta Lay Down Mama (1950)**. This is a good song to listen to if you want to get a sense of how things change even when they don't seem to. It's acoustic with electric intent - it has the new drive, the new bluntness of the post-electric, of modern attitudes about sex and relationships. Love is now a mechanical thing and so is a lot of the music written about it. Which is not to say that the old blues wasn't equally blunt; this is just a little more off-handedly demanding, a casual approach to love based, apparently, on certain presumed male prerogatives (none of which would meet the *Me Too* standard). I hear it as tied to the old school, in the way it seems to vent about casual encounters. But it is also tied to the new school in the way it wreaks of casual entertainments, of songs knocked off to make a point and keep things flowing. But Johnny

Beck, historically speaking, seems, unlike a dedicated country hound like Howlin' Wolf, to be losing ground. As compelling and solid a performer as Beck is, he hasn't found a way to circumvent the demands of the new blues by circumventing the old. Wolf, on the other hand, in his prime is like a country mammoth, a new blueser refusing to be contained by old-time constraints; Beck is a visitor to the present, more a tourist than a man in his own skin.

He might have looked at Tampa Red for a few hints at how to remain in the here-and-now without losing a sense of the there-and-then. Tampa Red was a mainstay of the post-War, Bluebird Chicago scene (meaning those who recorded for the Victor records subsidiary Bluebird, which housed some peripheral if still-profitable blues, country, and Western Swing acts). Tampa Red was a good guy, by all accounts, who ran a blues salon and was always welcoming to the Southern newbies. He was a good slide guitarist with a talent for colloquially-phrased blues composition, and he masterfully caught the zeitgeist in all of its variable and changing commercial moods. Listen back a few volumes to Texas Ruby's recording of Tampa Red's song *Don't You Lie To Me* (Vol. 23), which is a perfect expression of the temper of the times, a blunt-force blues with a user-friendly lyric that spoke to a new, urban audience (and was a favorite, I should add, of Mike Bloomfield).

**Tampa Red's 7/3/50** recording of **Love Her With a Feeling** has the exact same kind of blue-market currency. It is casual, good-natured, and just plain warmly sincere. I can see why '60s blues-rockers like Bloomfield liked Tampa Red's writing so much. The spirit of 1950's new blues as it carried itself into the next decade had many of the things that made certain types of 1960s rock/blues so tempting and accessible: it is casually personable, easy on the ears, and just a little bit ironic, even sarcastic - or, maybe, more accurately, in its casual approach to meaning and love, perfectly adaptable to the ironic, sarcastic temper of the new (1960s) times. Certainly Bloomfield had all of those particular characteristics, adding to the mix, in his unique way, a heimische, friendly smugness.

In his autobiography the trombonist Clyde Bernhardt describes life on the road with the blues shouter **Wynonie Harris**. It's not a pretty picture, but one of pettiness, nasty performer's ego, and hostile unpredictability. Harris was nothing if not a raging alcoholic, and his accompanists bore the brunt of his alcohol-fueled egotism and tirades. On the other hand he was a major figure in the post-War blues, who drew big crowds on the circuit as a blues bellower with plenty of depraved feeling.

Harris first made his star with Lucky Millinder's late-Swing orchestra, as part of the post-War transition from jazz-accented shuffles to the neo-rhythm and blues rituals of blues and stomp. Bebop had interrupted the commercial flow of the music, and so the trend in black pop in these years was in the other direction, toward vocal formula, with dance as a way of breaking down the audience barriers erected, of necessity, by bebop. Just as Laverne Baker's singing stood for a new kind of social emancipation so did Harris,' as a manly art meant to flex the sonic muscles of a new generation.

Harris' **Baby Shame on You (10/19/49)** is pretty typical of the type, for both song and singer. In front of a growling trumpet Harris growls the standard warning to his girl to observe social decorum and not embarrass him in front of the world (well, it's more a threat than a warning). He sings loud, he sings coarsely, and he sings like it's an announcement of how things, at least in the blues, are, moving forward, going to be. Or is it? In some ways Wynonie Harris was just Wynonie Harris, master of his own mean-spirited domain.

**Amos Milburn** was another vessel of what seems, on a personal level, to be a trend towards blues-self destruct. But the disasters that made up this thing we call American life left, in their wake, the world littered with odd, sub-categories of music. It all varied, if often in small but niche-like stylistic ways; there were corners in the corners. As in Milburn's **In the Middle of the Night (1950)**, which owes its distillation of blue-like melody to the kind of simplified, bluesy pop song that was all around in those years. Black vocal groups were starting to break the quartet format into smaller solo pieces, with lead vocalists branching out and becoming stars. The best of this pop reformulation was in songs like Henry Glover's *I Guess I'll Hang My Tears Out to Dry,* and the sheer amount of product flooding the market was a sign that a commercial explosion of one kind or another was coming (was this a youth market like the one that later shifted to rock and roll? Although some theories posit that rock was a conspiratorial attempt to restore white commercial dominance and rob black artists of commercial success, I don't agree, for complex reasons; let me just say that young white Americans didn't need a cynical reason to favor other young white Americans making music. Rock and roll was a kind of independent, revisionist social movement, inadvertently and even historically necessary as an aesthetic kick-in-the-ass to pop complacency of all racial derivations).

The formula was clear - and formula, always important in pop music, will come increasingly to cover most of the bases of repertoire: it meant simple melodies with little or no chromatic harmony (almost everything, with the exception of the occasional blue note, was diatonic), smooth, reassuring voices singing about love, love, and then more love; jazz-like accompaniment with the occasional guitar solo in a very basic, blues/jazz manner; and a simple bridge of melody just to break the monotony. Milburn was especially good at all of the above, as the smooth crooning of Nat Cole's and Charles Brown's disciples fused with the languid mid-gospel of jazzy vocal groups, and then matched up with the lighter side of rhythm and blues.

The idea of blue balladry extended to some unlikely places, and I have to admit I was somewhat shocked to discover a **John Lee Hooker** version of the Cecil Gant (see Vol.22) hit **I Wonder** (which was also recorded by Louis Armstrong; see my blues collection once again). Hooker, who was as deep as the blue sea, decided to take a stab at this pop ballad in **1949**, and he carries it off with spooning delight and not a bit of ironist's taint. Hooker even inserts a few would-be jazz riffs at the beginning on guitar, and as the performance develops it begins to sound like the drunken result of a lost bet. Hooker never hesitates, never does anything but sing with determination and conviction in a deep and rich voice which shows the bluesman-as-consumer - think Tommy Johnson's version of *I Want Someone to Love Me* in Volume 13. And then think about the amount of flack that Elvis Presley caught in his post-rockabilly years as he fought to claim his place on the hit parade between Bing Crosby and Dean Martin. Maybe now we can see that Elvis' idea of the pop mainstream wasn't such heresy after all, but just the natural result of an artist's natural curiosity and even boredom. Sometimes change for its own sake is not a necessity so much as it is a process of elimination; try this, try that, and see what, if anything, sticks.

But whatever his reasons, Hooker shows, in this performance, how accustomed to life in the mainstream of the margins the average bluesman could be. Northern migration created a (relative) normalcy, and there is nothing so jarringly normal as hearing John Lee Hooker, dedicated blues singer and guitarist with a cavernous sense of blues reality, a master of the rational rage inherent in blues consciousness and consummate showman-of-the-people, sing *I Wonder*.

In the rock and roll critical wars, consistency is not exactly a hobgoblin, but it *is* a risky and difficult thing. What wars am I talking about? you ask. Well, it's really *a* war, fought mostly in my head though occasionally in print. In the most public way I have wrestled my way through more than a few related battles on Facebook, where I remain in residence through thick and thin, insult and intellectual battery. Let us just say that I tend to rebel against the conventional wisdom in all of its guises, not just because it's conventional but usually, well, not so much wrong as wrongly emphasized. In American musical history we best construct the truth one small piece at a time, remaining mindful that other pieces, at some later date, will need to be inserted between those pieces. Though when it comes to rock and roll and its determinate origins, it all goes to pieces, to quote the old song. And the exception rules.

What makes a good and noteworthy and interesting musician? Many things but most fundamentally, I might suggest, the sound, not of surprise (circumventing Whitney Balliet's all-to-glib descriptor for jazz) but of life. Well, maybe that's even more bland than Balliet's idea, at least potentially, but we should accept no substitute, bearing in mind that my definition of life is more expansive than the average (maybe). To me life is also death, but also dream and the para-rationality of the unconsciousness, but, finally, even more important, the talent for imitation - the ability to mimic that which doesn't come naturally but which begs for the imagination to restore it to its natural state of mindful disorder. We picture realistically the things we can picture realistically, and we add to the mix, in subtle and unsubtle ways, the things we cannot picture except through re-creation, and then we order them all with all of the discordant logic we can muster. The result is art; not always good art, but art just the same.

Rock and roll, to my way of thinking, is just that: the discordant logic of white life, discordant aesthetically, racially, socially, and politically (and there is that supposed and contradictory insertion of music as political, once again). If rock and roll, as I sincerely believe, is a white re-imagining of black music and life, then white life is a constant search for sources of inspiration in pursuit of that re-imagining (or is it re-imaging?) (and let me insert here that in various ways I find that almost all white expressions of black musical forms reflect the same basic desire. Jazz musicians, blues players, certain kinds of folkies, are almost all, in one way or another, in search of methods with which not to bury the African American impulse but to use it in personal ways, to rebuild it, reimagine it, to their own specifications).

In feeling our way through life, searching for ways to do such a thing, we white folks need to look in all the presumably wrong places, at least as defined by the Jeff Sessions of the world. We start with black music at its lowest frequencies and we go wherever the search leads us, even, yes, if it takes us on some crazy tangents. And if we are lucky we find things like the opening cadences of **Every Day Will Be Sunday Bye and Bye**, especially as sung by **Dorothy Love Coates and the Original Gospel Harmonettes (7/5/51)**. This is everything that white folks look for and need in their pursuit of cultural happiness, of emotional templates, forms, and sounds that makes sense

But enough of whites; look at this music on its own terms. It is not only intense, it is slick and incessant. At this point in history, gospel music, having found its emotional center, is finding an audience of those who work to both remember and forget - to remember the old Jim Crow ways (because they were what they were and because you can run but you cannot hide from their effects; the South is still the South and the North, or wherever else you might be living, is part of the same country) and then to forget them in ways that allow individuals to be individuals again (as Ellison sought to be not just recognized as a *black* writer but as a *writer*). Of course such things are easier said then done; as any Jew will tell you no one ever, especially in subtle ways, lets you forget you are a Jew, and as Dizzy Gillespie said to me once, no one ever lets you forget you are black. And though the two conditions are much different in terms of historical impact in the USA, the trials they speak of, of fear and paranoia, have a lot in common at the source. *Every Day Will be Sunday Bye and Bye* is more than a prediction or prophecy, it is a plea for existential-justice-in-rhythm.

And though I have often defended the white prerogative of rock and roll, there is no question that this (gospel) music rocks, rocks steadily, and rocks incessantly. **Prophet Powers' The Tree of Life is Waiting for Me** (1950) is a case in point. Once more the common denominator is the ring shout rhythm, the battling hand claps which, though seeming to emphasize 2 and 4, really re-enforce the equal power of 1 and 3. It also helps to have a voice that rides over all of this like an emotionally-guiding hand. *The Tree of Life is Waiting for Me* has a momentum, anyway, that is foreign to the essentials of white roll, leaving this kind of gospel music to rock in a much different way. As I have pointed out before the very idea of rock and rockin' has cross-religious/secular meaning, of ecstasy and pleasure of more than one kind. The particular thing about black gospel music is that, though we might assume it refers mainly to pleasures that are not of the body, we are likely wrong.

And herein lies one particular black/white divide: black gospel is a release from the flesh at the same time that it is a celebration of same; white gospel tends to pretend that the flesh does not exist. So rock and roll, in social defiance, takes up the subject once more, and the (adult, official) white world, from all eras, looks down at it with fear and horror. Which is not to say that the black religious world is not also offended at the bodily emphasis of black popular music, but that it is often in a kind of denial about its own habits and emphasis (which of course doesn't take into account that African American religious practices are not monolithic and reflect, themselves, divisions and differences across religious and class lines). So what is my ultimate point here? Especially since there is an entire and separate school of white Sanctified religion which closely mimics the black model of aisle-rolling and speaking in tongues? Well, as the song doesn't tell us, the circle is constantly being broken. Rock and roll borrows from many kinds of expressions of religious and near-religious ecstasy and imposes its own ideas, drawn from hidden worlds of both white and black.

Another refugee from the turf battles of rock (and blues, sort of) was Joe Turner (see Vol. 23), who we have already discussed. Turner could do everything, hard blues K.C. style, jazz blues K.C. style, and rockin' blues K.C. style. His music from this period, made as a lot of the black and blues world flailed around in an effort to find market space, is a decent if finally unconvincing (to me, at least) argument for the proposition that rock and roll was just another word for black. From whence does that argument arise? Well, I would say, first of all, from that heavy backbeat, sometime so self conscious as to sound almost like a parody of jump music (the general term sometimes used to described this type of bouncing blues). Listening to **Joe Turner** and band on **Jumpin' at the Jubilee (ca. 1949)** you can almost see an invisible conductor, standing out front and jumping and landing with heavy boots on the 2 and 4 of each measure, gesticulating like Lionel Hampton used to in front of audiences to build fake excitement - well, maybe not fake, but definitely synthetic. *Jumpin' at the Jubilee* has all the right moving parts - a good vocal (sounding, at least to me, like Turner, an expert at things like this, is just going through the motions), a moaning saxophone, a riffing guitar (distorted), and a boogie-type piano solo. I love 'em all, but these guys are working just a little too hard to be really convincing. The search for a path to a new youth market would have to go on.

Still, if we want to continue the search for the very first rock and roll record we might want to consider looking in a different direction, one which I have already suggested in various ways in this study. Country music of one form or another, in my opinion, is the key, not the blues or rhythm and blues, as much as they all fed from and into common musical sources. I have defined country in a way which may seem to constantly vary, and I apologize for the inconsistency. As the saying goes, I know it when I hear it, implying as it does that common beat of passive sophistication, and a sense of open personal, physical, and musical space that the heavier thud of rhythm and blues lacks. Not to mention the musical/scale aspects, the way the blues and country fuse themselves together by the use of certain intervals. Whatever *your* orientation, *I* get excited and feel a sense of such pre-rock discovery when I hear performances like **Walter Brown's Lou, Cindy Lou (10/31/49)**, which instantly signals a different kind of black musical orientation, one which is so much closer to the rock and roll impulse by way of what I would call the rocking country - or rockabilly - portal. Rockabilly was the post-honky tonk, blues-tinged, post-boogie sound of white countrymen, augmented with subtly Latinate rhythms (as with Elvis on the *real* first rock tune from a commercial standpoint, *That's All Right Mama*), lending themselves to that classic Caribbean subdivision of 3,3,2 in the guise of a classic, country two-beat rhythm. It was lighter than rhythm and blues, not necessarily racially-speaking, but in terms of musical exposition, in its vocal and instrumental backing. With all that in mind, listen to *Lou, Cindy Lou*: first, the voice. Brown was a big-band bluesmen whose instrument was small, like a miniaturized version of Joe Turner's. It's a whine rather than a yell, so right away we are in country territory; everything is reduced. The field-of-sound, instead of wielding that rhythm and blues steamroller, is basic and in miniature, intimate and personable. The rhythm is, yes, a two-beat thing, the subject is a girl and just a girl, and there is a separation of musical functions in that rockabilly and then rock and roll way. The elements have a feeling of being separate but equal, and they are more audible in separation because there is more aural space in the arrangement. This is something I firmly believe became part of the actual rock and roll method, with exceptions, of course, but with exceptions that fed a very white aesthetic, with a lightness of being that was generally, if not always (hence *Lou, Cindy Lou*) foreign to black musicians and black music.

And then there is the country duo of **Johnny and Jack (For Old Times Sake, 1949)**. It was Dick Spottswood who pointed them out to me, many years ago, as an essential modern country singing team. Since that time, as much faith as I have in everything for which Dick advocates, I never quite "got" Johnny and Jack. I liked the music, but it never sank in, even in an historical sense. But as I prepared this study and chose this particular performance I decided it was finally time to dig in, to figure out what I was missing. So I searched Youtube for some Johnny and Jack and - almost instantly it hit me like a brick. Missing from the recordings but so clear on some old country music show broadcasts, and very well preserved on Youtube, was a sense of their sheer audacity, a kind of (to borrow one of those cliches I normally run away from with a sense of utter critical panic) rock and roll attitude that was not, really, rock and roll but rather a strange hybrid of honky tonk brashness and corny-country humoresque. On television their smiling sense of the silliness of it all just compounded the uniqueness of each performance, with their odd repertoire of near-novelty tunes, honky tonk charades, and the kind of story songs which give country music its populist pull. They smiled and smirked and mowed their way through tunes that were driven by a vocal force-of-personality, and it worked. In one sense they were a completely unique force in modern country, and yet in another they were typical of the old hillbilly sound before it got ensnared in the tentacles of Nashville and the world of the professional, assembly line country song. So my suggestion is, listen to the records, but run to Youtube.

Such kinds of country, commercial but real, were still around if you knew where to look for them. **Link Davis**, singer and instrumentalist, was still something of an oddity in that country music world, unafraid and even daring, if such a thing was still possible. Stylistically he was everywhere, from Cajun music to honky tonk, mainstream country to Western Swing. I have heard a recording of a saxophone solo he made that puts him squarely in the realm of Herschel Evans-tenor (Evans was in the Basie band at the same time as Lester Young and his style was an interesting contrast to Young's, throaty and moaning, less mobile and more from the sound of the older tenor school of neo-Coleman Hawkins). **Joe Turner (1949)** is an old time blues that Davis executes in a somewhat classic white, late-country way, with open vowels, baritone-voiced soul, and nice sense of the blues as a pop technique, cleanly and clearly articulated with just enough emphasis on certain bluesy inflections and vocal bends. This recording opens and closes with a saxophone solo, relaxed and swing-oriented, that may be Davis himself; the group backing him has a Western Swing instrumentation, with piano, fiddle, and pedal steel guitar. The whole thing is something of a relief in the context of all that country music was slowly becoming, homogenous and slick and heavy with production. The only strings here are of the kind you might have heard in the old days. Everybody was now lean and hungry, looking for a different kind of hit record than in early country times, when regional sales were enough to satisfy record companies. Happily, with singers like Link Davis around, as unsettled and varied as their work might be, there was still a quality that was above and beyond that of competent professionalism.

I have a mixed sense of and mixed feelings about what has commonly been called alt.country, going back to the outlaw recordings of Waylon Jennings et al in the 1980s. A lot of what I hear just seems to be the same-old-same-old dressed up in new clothes - and yet I do find, from time to time, some alt.country that, whether depraved or just indifferent to the repulsive trend of hat-acts which populate country today, seems to have the hunger, the desire, the will to take the country template and throw it into the fire. In our current day this has produced some intense redistricting in the land of country music; 70 years or so ago, alt. meant something a bit less rebellious but still a challenge to the country status quo. Though those with alternate approaches often ended up back in the country mainstream, at some point some of the ones with real country street cred made an effort at dipping into tradition as they knew it, like the blues, hillbilly flatulence, and those plain-spoken elements of sincerity which were slowly, in the big country picture, becoming synthetic remnants of the old-time, down-home world of their fathers. Like **Webb Pierce**, soon to be of Decca Records, who recorded the Jimmie Rodgers (see Vols. 14, 15) standard **In the Jailhouse Now** in **1950**.

There is nothing revolutionary about this recording, but it has a certain reflective and unsentimental strength to it, a way of looking back without nostalgia at that relatively recent if aesthetically ancient period when country music was starting to feel its power, to grab audiences on a national level. Pierce has a voice that doubles as a form of musical conscience, so well does he seem to be guarding the gates of tradition. Listen to the way he vocalizes "but I found out last Sunday," at about .043, the way he rises on the last syllable with a knowing blue-country emphasis. It is all *real*, to use a word with indefinite meaning yet clear signification of something produced from the heart. And yet - and yet, the commercial arm of the law was never far away from popular music in those years, and who knows what was really going on in the minds of performers like Pierce. It's probably enough that what he did sounds authentic because it is faithful to what we imagine to be his inner country being - a needlessly obscure way of saying that from the sound of this he had to satisfy himself in order to produce something good enough to satisfy audiences who had an intuitive sense of who was trying to fool them and who was not.

And yet, for all its fakery, we call commercial country music in the coming decade synthetic at our own risk. I might ask myself, how can something which is already an invention derived from out of thin air - since all forms of writing and composing are, at least in theory, creative inventions - be attacked as false or fake? I can't really answer that, but I do think that country's increasing standardization in these years still led to true moments of light and revelation. You can't blame men and women for trying to break one mold - the funky, drunken, blue template of country in the 1920s and 1930s - while trying to create another, for new-time's sake and professional survival. Country composition has all kinds of virtues in these years, from revivalist-type dance hall music that is really anything but (infused as it is with Western Swing and honky-tonk by-way-of-the-blues-and-pop song) to new kinds of balladry that have more than their share of common-man charm. Take the song **Release Me**, later done memorably by Ray Charles, but recorded in **1950** by its composer **Eddie Miller**. Miller doesn't really have much of a voice, but he has written something that is essentially a linkage of three eras of country song, one a bit older, one current, one still-to-come. "To live together is a sin" he tells us, with moralistic attitude (well, sort of; by just by acknowledging it he has established himself as an Enlightened and Modern Man who has considering doing such a thing), and the record itself sounds like a demo done among friends. Listen to the hollow sound of the recording, done, in the old way, by a group of musicians just standing around a microphone in a room, and so, like all recordings in those days, subject to room acoustics. The steel guitar, the fiddle, the guitar, are all in constant motion, like a Dixieland version of country, or really as Western Swing reincarnate. In this way it's a thing-of-old at the same time that it is is a prophecy, of the kind of pop stylization that will tear through the music in its coming Nashville incarnation. Voice or no voice, Eddie Miller has set a stage for something of which he may or may not have been aware. It all led, in its way, to Ray Charles, who heard in this song those elements of new country - it's now-oblique relationship to the blues, its long-lined vocal possibilities - that probably only a few people noticed in 1950. So, while nobody was looking, Eddie Miller changed the (country) world.

And still the specter of rockabilly/rock and roll hung over that world. Rockabilly, as we have indicated, was that early form of country rock which, derived from shards of honky-tonk music (the sound of the post-war white roustabout working class) as mixed with the blue dream of young, shit-kicking country boys, raised the musical center of gravity of it all. Some of it was rock lite, as in the **Delmore Brothers' Pan American Boogie (1950).** The Delmores had been recording since the 1930s (see also Vol. 16) and their sound was quintessential *Country Brother*: emotionally sympathetic, with transparent harmonies in the service of tradition-bound country song, with an added emphasis on the "old" values of acoustic instruments and string-band orientation. Even their blues-and - boogie, which is often cited in basic country music histories as a precursor of rock and roll (and which I think is basically an accurate characterization) was a bit pale and malnourished (and less energetic than the work of someone like Wayne Raney, see Vol. 24), but that was part of their whole m.o. and charm. As country stumbled into a new world of modern recording techniques and musical spectacle, they were place-holders of the tradition.

It may - or may not - be little bit misleading for me to use **Lefty Frizzell**'s version of a Jimmie Rodgers tune, **Travelin' Blues (1950)**, as an example of Frizzell's country performance style.. Frizzell is a central figure in the new school of post-modern country singing, of a white soul school which varied, in its

Southern ties, from run-of-the-mill country balladeer (and there were some very good run-of-the-mill country balladeers who might have been more than that with the right material) to deep singers of honky-tonk narratives. Lefty was certainly not averse to the idea of commercial appeal, and he had lots of it. It was his singing voice that did it for him - and us - professionally, and that was passed on in country succession, through later singers like George Jones (see Vol. 27) and especially Merle Haggard. This was a whole new school of country croon, and Lefty was at the head of it, especially after Hank Williams' death in 1953. Honky tonker that he was, Frizzell is generally thought of as the guy who smoothed out the rough edges of the style. He had a way with syllables, of caressing and stretching them to their limits, with that ur-country cry that was a below-the-staff alternative to the high yodel. As I implied above, *Travelin' Blues* is not typical of his material, which usually leaned toward country ballad, calm and pacifying if at times borderline bland (in a way very much like some of Merle Travis' studio output).

This was country firmly in the mainstream, though to their credit, Frizzell and Merle Travis (another of this school) never sounded like they were phoning it in. But they were at their best in less formal situations, like the LP Frizzell made of Jimmie Rodgers tunes for Columbia, from which *Travelin' Blues* has been taken. *Travelin' Blues* might be thought of as Lefty-after-hours, left to sing for his own pleasure and amusement. It certainly, to my ears, is not just more authentic than his usual work but more indelibly soulful, a beautiful patch of country performance as it might have been, away from the constant and demanding spotlight. It has a clarity that calls attention to all the things that country still was when it wanted to be.

As do two other performances from the beginning of this decade by two different singers: **Trouble in Mind (Jerry Irby, 1951)** and **Walkin' on Top of the World (Peck Touchton, 1951)**. Touchton has, from what I can determine, become something of a country legend by reason of obscurity (I can find no biographical details) and an impossible-to-pronounce last name. In the 1950s he was part of a stable of hard-honky tonk stylists who recorded for a Texan by the name of Charles Fitch for Sarge Records. In this way were the white-minded independents, like the independents in blues and rhythm and blues, reaching out for niche audiences. Touchton was in and out of the studio and left us this pirated version of *Sittin' on Top of the World*, a tune written by the black group the Mississippi Sheiks and recorded by a lot of folks, including the country/Western Swingster Bob Wills. My guess is that the title here was changed under the influence of Fitch to avoid paying royalties, larcenous as many in his line of business were. Touchton sings with conviction and sincerity, and there is a lot to like about this performance. It emanated, I would say, from that corner of the country music biz which was simply trying to match itself to those regional listeners who heard the music as both a needed distraction from life and a closer reflection of their own lives than, say, Frank Sinatra or Benny Goodman. Internet lore seems to tie singers like Touchton directly to rockabilly. Though I believe there is a lot of common ancestry between the two forms, I hear this as not just honky tonk but as spinoff, as honky-tonk lite..

*Trouble in Mind*'s Irby is better known as a honky tonker with a multi-decade career that ended in Evangelism (*Trouble in Mind* was written by the black Richard M. Jones, a pioneer composer and producer of early race records). The introduction to Irby's version is all Hank Williams, down to the steel guitar, and Irby's voice has, once again, the kind of crowd appeal we hear from the more sedate side of honk tonk (and *sedate* may be the operative word in a lot of honky tonk once it was corralled by the major record labels; is it any wonder that the newer generation of white kids saw Elvis and rock and roll as a pressure valve? When even the alt.country music of those days had become part of the mainstream it must have seemed there was nothing to do but hit the rock and roll trail). Irby has a talent for it, in the way he phrases in long-syllables, stretching lyrics over the time in a way that would have made Lefty Frizzell proud; or should I say, Frank Sinatra? There was certainly a connection in this to the pop-ballad broadside. Once again, this was basically a very conservative style of country croon, tailored to fit the needs and mood of an audience which may have welcomed it as a soothing alternative to the slowly-disintegrating social contract.

As I have said in the past, my complaint about much work that is labeled *avant garde* - referencing a term which seems vague but is not, meaning as it does those on the frontlines of any artistic movement - is that it is often more interesting and even necessary in theory than in practice. I celebrate the many such movements in the 20th century because each aspect - musical, theatrical, literary - signified a new step of artistic liberation, the freeing of artists from arbitrary technical and philosophical requirements, from the coercive association of art with "meaning," tradition, and linear development. The truth is that when it comes to expression, anyone should be allowed to do what they want - and before you ask 'what or who is stopping anyone from doing anything?' I should add that I think there is an authoritarian streak present in certain kinds of criticism, which seem, in their *categorical* condemnation of certain kinds of work, to advocate repression as much as criticism. When Albert Murray, in one of his old essays, attacks Jean Genet as just another trendy artistic radical he is, to my mind, advocating for a kind of aesthetic criminalization of such challenging forms by labeling them as decadent in the same way the old Soviet system - and the Nazis, let us not forget - condemned and then banned certain kinds of non-representational art. Certainly Murray had no such intention, but I find the effect to be much the same, just as Wynton Marsalis' vehement anti-pop and anti-free jazz screeds have contained the bitter seed of the desire to see all such things purged from the public sphere.

And yet here *I* am, strongly critical of avant garde works which I find guilty of *formalism*. I think certain artists suffer from the conviction that once an artist reaches an epiphany of form - as in "I can now liberate myself to play music which freely associates with nothing but itself," or "I can now compose literature which is critic-proof because of its lack of connection to conventional poles of representational meaning" - then their work is, from a standpoint of substance, essentially done, and that anything accomplished afterwards in the name of formal liberation has, by it very nature, solved the overall artistic problem: form and content are now artistically fused, and so cannot be criticized by conventional critics who are too tied intellectually to old forms to be open minded enough about the new. My own sense of this is much more complicated: I think all of the above, the abandonment of narrative scheme, the stretching and/or elimination of harmonic tonality, the suggestion of time as a fluid and ever-changing element (and not just in music), are all essential artistic steps. The importance of the whole liberationist movement of free-form music and literature and theater was in the way it pointed the way to even newer means of liberation, in the doors it opened to allow creative oxygen to flow and circulate throughout the art form. But I find that there are too many artists of every discipline who, as I see it, are very good at theorizing but mediocre at doing the work itself. This is the result, I think, of formalism, a tendency to mistake new formal techniques for solutions to what are, at the root, artistic problems.

And yet it doesn't have to be this way. One can take radical steps in directions that require discipline, formal cohesion, linear and narrative non-linearity, and even an understanding, in a deep and even dismissive way, of tradition. And though those are all statements that make me nervous for the way they may be co-opted by critical conservatives, they serve as a way to introduce some of my ambivalence toward **Harry Partch (The Letter, 1950)**. Partch was an early re-shaper of musical sounds into a unique yet peculiarly American shape. I am no Partch authority, but a good deal of his appeal seems to have been in his invention of new instruments, and the way they allowed for reorganization of scales and hence melodies, as adjusted by interval and rejection of older habits. I have listened and listened and, much as I appreciate his work, I rarely revisit it. He seems to have made his musical point and then carried on. More power to him, and long may his music live; but nothing I have heard of his excites and energizes me, as both listener and composer, as much as *The Letter*. If I had to explain why I would probably conclude that it is unique in his *ouevre* in the way it admits the outside world, if only briefly, into the private realm of his musical and literary consciousness. [32]

*The Letter* is, I think, a perfect realization of all of the above. I love *The Letter* because of the singular way in which it combines the convention of narrative - through the written epistle, as his friend (who is hoboing across America) tells Harry that he is cold and worried about being arrested because, in his own words, he is not handsome enough to survive on his looks - with a sonic background that, in its musical shifts of fancy and formal informality, takes us on a hard-reality trip. And it ends with a signatory declaration that it is jarringly effective because it retreats into "realistic" territory (shades of William Burroughs' early work):

"I'll say good night and good luck...
hoping to hear from you at once and tell me all the news...
your....pal.....Pablo"

---

[32] Note that I do not say *unconscious*, because I think the key to exceptional work is in activating the *conscious* mind. Anyone can tell you their dreams or the irrational associations they make in unhinged moments or as they improvise. The deeper challenge is to translate material reality into something that makes more of it than what amount to still-life photos, images that are no more than what any tourist would see. Anyone can do that. What are more interesting are what I would call existential snapshots, pictures taken when no one else is looking of objects no one else can see.

## Chapter 26: Born-Again Blues

Not long ago I had a minor conflict with a minor writer/critic on Facebook. I know that sounds mean, but sometimes it cannot be helped, in this case because this person has, of late, been shadowing me with snark after snark. So although I will not give a name for you to attach to the complaint, I will tell you that this particular snark was over my praise for the old medicine show performer **Harmonica Frank**, whom I regard as one of the most significant American musicians of the 20th century.

The first person to pull our collective coats to Harmonica Frank was Greil Marcus in his landmark book *Mystery Train*. Greil had it exactly right - I strongly suggest you read his whole book - so what can I tell about Harmonica Frank that you cannot gather in a much more efficient way by reading Greil's chapter? Not much. I do remember feeling somewhat skeptical as I approached recordings like Frank's **She Done Moved** and **Goin' Away Walking** (both from **1951**). Was he really that great? Well, yes. This stuff hit me where I wasn't expecting it.

Who is this masked man? you might ask, as his voice comes out of the speaker like the Sybil of folk/country, with multiple personalities, changing stories, a surface lightness of being, and a series of profoundly telling musical gestures. First of all, what can you say about a performer who, in a three minute space (*She Done Moved*) predicts both Elvis Presley and Bob Dylan? Harmonica Frank is a bluesman of sorts at his core, but a bluesman who comes from that part of the white American soul that feels the blues in weird and out-of-body ways, as an offshoot of medicine show minstrelsy, as a synthetic form synthesized from other synthetic forms. From the white musical mind these were entertainments that made light of deep personal feelings while birthing even more profound moments of (aesthetic) enlightenment out of supposedly simple musical formations. Listen, on *She Done Moved*, to those Elvis-like and near-parodic minstrel black-isms that sound, in a newly whitened way, like nothing so much as Amos' (of Amos and Andy) greeting of "helllooo Sapphire" (and I mean the black, television Amos). These, in this song, go down deep into the bass-bottom of the voice with weird distortions, like the strange and bottom-heavy vocals of contemporary white gospel quartets, exaggerated yet surprisingly musical. Did Elvis learn them from Harmonica Frank?

I have heard no other singer, pre-Elvis, who sang like this (and yes it is possible it represented a medicine show thing that was making the rounds). The way Harmonica Frank (and, later, Elvis) does it turns it into just another aspect of style, subtly-enough related to its (likely) source to stand on its own, to sound bizarrely interpretive rather than offensive. Add that harmonica and the way, on *Goin' Away Walkin,'* Harmonica Frank puts the blues in an entirely different context, stretching it out like a free-form form of entertainment, and you hear a side of what became Bob Dylan. Dylan, as a white outsider approaching the music of other outsiders, kept his respectful distance while looking for - and finding, as Harmonica Frank does - a direct way in. Which closes a circle of white-black blues fusion, showing the ways in which the circle had enough gaps in it to allow for the strangeness of those who were, in that odd Southern subculture, other to the other.

All of which is not to ignore Harmonica Frank's uniquely universal musicality. He was a vernacular everyman, using American song forms as vehicles for a sensibility that was intensely personable yet weirdly alienating, in the same way that minstrelsy was. This was a white mask, and one which was passed on to some other white men like Elvis and Dylan; it was reality as seen from a whole other plane of existence, through the eyes of someone who was, from the sound of it, only an occasional visitor to this one.

Almost anything we listen to, in Harmonica Frank's wake, seems hopelessly conventional. But we would be doing a performer like **Jimmy Murphy** a grave injustice to look at his work from this perspective, especially as his recording of **Big Mama Blues (1951)** is not that far off from the spirit of Harmonica Frank.

At one point Murphy, signed by Columbia Records, tried to be a *cat*, to take his place in the new generation of post-Elvis rockabillies, but, unsurprisingly, as Wikipedia notes, every single he made in this style failed to sell. To get an idea of why, mozy on over to Youtube and check out a thing he recorded called *Grandpaw's a Cat*. I'm not altogether sure about Grandpaw himself, but with lines in the song like…..

"dancing up and down the street
doing the rock and roll to a
brand new bebop beat"

...it is highly unlikely that anyone was cattin' out in the vicinity of this record (and for the record a *cat*, from the old days, was a hipster on the psychological outskirts of town, later a hillbilly cat a la Elvis. Though even before Elvis the term as in *country* was thrown around in a number of odd ways, as in Harry Choates' tune *Cat'n Around*, a more feral reference to the alley-cattin' practice of chasing females. But in its essence a cat was a cool, aware, guy, with apologies to all the women who were, in that day, thereby excluded). By the time Murphy gave it a try it had a currency that was instantly negated by the silliness of the song and the way he sang it with Elvis-directed hiccoughs and novelty sarcasm. It was clear that his heart really wasn't in it.

It is interesting to read notations around the internet that claim Murphy's earliest influences were Leadbelly and Blind Boy Fuller. While this is not unlikely, it would be useful to see citations about this, of interviews where he admitted as such. I don't doubt anything about Murphy, who was something of a jack of all country trades, but still a master of some. *Big Mama Blues* is from a kind of stylistic-no man's land (something which he *does* have in common with Harmonica Frank), a sprint through the blues similar in intent and execution to Bill Carlisle's *Bell Clappin' Mama* (see Vol. 19). This was musically transitional, in flight from the old hillbilly impulse, an instrumental virtuosity of its own kind, riding on bluegrass coattails and avoiding, like the plague, Nashville's long-armed idea of commercial compliance.

It's easy to dismiss, in these years, the often awkward attempts of that older generation of country gentleman to ease themselves into the youthful mainstream. Life was changing, and the science of demographics, if still imprecise (in those days the only algorithm was the one in your head), was slowly, by capitalist osmosis, becoming as important to the music industry as junkets and swag would be only a few years later. Elvis was born in 1935, Carl Perkins in 1932, Jimmy Murphy in 1925, and **Tillman Franks (Hi Tone Poppa, 1952)** in 1920 - so you can see where I am going. Age isn't a barrier until it is a barrier, and there are interesting exceptions to this non-rule. One thing claimed by singers like Carl Perkins is that Elvis' sudden cloudburst of local rock and roll was just a continuation of things that had been happening for some time on the honky-tonk and white juke scene, and though this is, I would say, only somewhat accurate, recordings like *Hi Tone Poppa* do indeed tell us that something was happening, even if a lot of people didn't recognize it, well hidden as it was in plain sight.

Franks, who has been inducted into the Rockabilly Hall of Fame, falls, as a performer, and like just about everybody else in the realm of honky tonk music of those days, into the category of Hank Williams wannabe. That's not an insult but a statement of reality and essence, so pervasive was Hank's influence, like Charlie Parker in the bebop era. But still, Franks was a good songwriter, a good occupier of that Hank-space where swallowed vowels took their place next to a blue-and-boogie formula of steel guitar, jazz-like lead guitar, and the occasional fiddle. And maybe things like *Hi Tone Poppa* show that I have been just a little too quick, in the past, to dismiss the old claim that "blues had a baby and they named it rock and roll" (per Muddy Waters). Let me clarify: maybe certain parts of the blues, once birthed, were baptized and then *raised* by white people as rock and roll, as children of a mixed marriage of Sanctified gospel singing and Sanctified guitar playing, with Ring Shout relatives who rarely visited, though when they did they frightened the children and anyway it was too dangerous to allow them to stay for any length of time due to Jim Crow and the continued denial of common black/white ancestry. And though this may be a lot to lay on Tillman Franks, he was more a cog in that Southern race machine than a mover and shaker in it. *Hi Tone Poppa*, which lays down on the beat with just a little bit more, rockin' emphasis (listen to that drum in and around 1:35) then usual, is, musically, less rock than it is a passive acceptance of the fact that something needs to give in this musically-evolving cracker world. That reality-in-waiting is rock and roll, and its aesthetic necessity is audible - the music has become too passive and predictable for its own good and is in need of a re-awakening; which will come, we can be sure, in just a few years, as the born-again blues meets the afterlife spirit of old-time tent-Revivalism, and conceives, in the after hours and behind studio doors, that strange and alienated baby which we will have no choice but to call rock and roll.

Remember Gig Young, in the movie *Lovers and Others Strangers*, repeating, with hilarious and clueless self-confidence, "no gap here"? He was referring to the Generation Gap, a phrase invented in the 1968 to show the chasm between youthful rebels (the freaks and hippies of Frank Zappa's description) and their parents. Well, I wrote a few paragraphs earlier about the apparent futility of an older generation of country singers who, trying to navigate the winds of change between honky tonk music and whatever else was brewing in the early 1950s, were working with sweaty persistence to find a niche that the "youngsters" (to quite Ed Sullivan) would find appealing. Invariably they failed but there are a few tantalizing glimpses in the country world of just what might have or could have been if the earth's axis had been tilted enough to send Elvis and Scotty back in time just a few years, to show these older men of country just how to do it (and though Elvis was only 3 years away from full bloom this was a lifetime in the music business, if only a time-lapse-in-the-bucket in the time-travel business). One of the best singers, pre-Elvis, conceptually speaking, was **Jimmy Logsdon** who, six years **(1951)** before he made the record that turned out to be his one and only hit (*I Got a Rocket in My Pocket*) recorded something that was prescient in a rock and roll way: **I Wanna Be Mama'd**.

To be sure, *I Got a Rocket in My Pocket* was full-blown old-fogey rock and billy (Logsdon was 35 when he made it), not a great song, but noteworthy for the phallic imagery in the title and lyric and Logsdon's fully-committed vocal. Logsdon, evolving from his early Hank Williams incarnation with a mannered but effective vocal sneer, recorded *Rocket* for the Mob-connected, vertically integrated Moe Levy at Roulette Records; unlike so many other aging rockabillies, he had an actual hit with it. The song hasn't really aged well (and we should also note that he recorded it under the name Jimmy Lloyd so his country fans wouldn't be offended), but it does have a period charm, a "this is what the kids want" naivete which almost works. *But I Wanna Be Mama'd* (the first record he made for Decca) is really the recording that gives us a sense of what, in a sane country music world, Logsdon could have been. It has, once again, that odd, new-grass feel of Bill Carlisle and Jimmy Murphy, a rapid, acoustically-driven old-time-new-time drive, and Logsdon sounds like he actually means it. Once again, it's a blues, another sign of the times, of rock in gestation through the midwifery of that essential song form, if in a much different way than Muddy Waters pictured it. And the voice - what a terrifically pure country voice, in the days before Logsdon twisted his jaw to emit just leftover Hank-isms. The world didn't need another Hank Williams, but it sure could have used a real Jimmy Logsdon.

Women's place in country music has tended, as far as I can hear, to be liberated in song more by intent and desire than action.

There were not a lot of them in those days, but there is something about the Southern assertiveness of female country vocalists in the years just before and after World War II that gives them a strength greater than their numbers. It's not that we hear from them any obvious sense of protest against the male-dominated business of country music; what we do hear, however, are songs that seem to be pushing upwards against the glass professional and social ceiling, and outwards against sexual restrictions (in all senses of the phrase). Even when they sing from a position of relative subservience, the way they sing and the subtextual message within (and the hell with Sam Goldwyn) is clear and obvious.

A case in point is **Jean Sheperd**'s recording of **Twice The Lovin' (In Half The Time) (1952)**, which she co-wrote. The title is, if course, suggestive in and of itself, but the song as it goes is not exactly a liberational anthem. In most ways it is a conventional "I'm done wasting my time on you" declaration. But what a declaration it is. The twang in her voice (like that of another great free-women-of-non-color singer of later years, Dolly Parton) sounds like a form of disarmament; maybe it makes her a little less threatening to her audience and less alienating all around. The message is clear, but what makes it real is the way she delivers it, letting the medium (per: Marshall Mcluhan) send it like a late-delivered but urgent epistle to American women who might, if they have the nerve in these conformist '50s, do the same (and interestingly enough in one her late appearances as featured on Youtube she seems to have lost the twangiest parts of the twang: www.youtubewatch.com/watch?v=nLgpaWv7P_U).

Interestingly, as well, Shepard's career has a first and second act, in her initial stardom and then a later series of hits in the 1960s and 1970s. By the time she appears in a series of heritage country shows (like the one on Youtube, above) she's a much different singer and it's a much different world. Or is it? In 1952 Hank Thompson, with the biblical urge for condemnation, sang:

> "I didn't know God made Honky Tonk angels
> I might have known you'd never make a wife
> You gave up the only one that ever loved you
> And went back to the wild side of life"
> (from the song The Wild Side of Life)

To a lot of women this must have sounded hollow, as a kind of moral pre-emptive strike at sin or, really, a projection of male unfaithfulness onto a vulnerable target. So maybe country music was growing up, out of the humorous battle of the sexes that preoccupied the hillbilly portion of our show and into the serious business of cheating and sex. Was the subject of Thompson's gently regretful song real, or a straw-women built as a distraction, to throw audiences off the heavier scent of men who continued, to quote Floyd Tillman's honky-tonk hit, "slippin' around"? To their credit there were a few ladies who refused to take this sitting down, and that same year **Kitty Wells** recorded **It Wasn't God Who Made Honky Tonk Angels**, which, though written by a man, answered the above with:

> "It wasn't God who made honky tonk angels
> As you said in the words of your song
> Too many times married men think they're still single
> And that's caused many a good girl to go wrong"

….and tried to place the blame where it was obviously due. This was a daring thing for any woman to be singing in that day and age, and Wells' version captured her great and morally-transcendent dignity. **Rosalie Allen's** version of same, made in **1952**, is almost equally compelling. There were limits in those days to feminist outrage and to certain kinds of female sexual declarations of independence. But Allen, an Eastern cowgirl (born in Pennsylvania, she worked in country television in New York City) was a good and upstanding roll model. Not to mention that her career teaches us quite a bit about the growing and multi-regional popularity of country music. Her appearance on several New York local-yokel television shows (using hillbilly/cowboy music references in their titles like *Swingbillies* and *Prairie Stars*) made her into, according to one poll, the most famous country music singer in New York, where she remained during much of her professional career. Who was her audience? Damned if I know, but it is interesting to note that her Eastern popularity coincides with the first, progressive folk surge of groups like the Almanac Singers and figures like Woody Guthrie, Pete Seeger, and Leadbelly. There is no sign that she worked with or near any of them (something tells me that radical politics would not have been her thing) but she did, in those years, open up something called Rosalie Allen's Hillbilly Music Center, on West 54th Street, which may have been the first specialty music store to cover country music.

By the time country gospel arrives in the 1950s it has a whole new sound, weighted with electric guitar and swollen with echo. So it goes with **Satisfied** by the **Blue Ridge Quartet (1952)**. This is, as we have indicated, Good-News music. Gone is the whole early-warning system of the sanctified school which, joyous as it occasionally was, still gave off dark hints about the consequences of violating god's rules and practices. The Blue Ridge Quartet tells with a big, gaping smile that it's "that old time religion" which has done the trick of rescuing them from permanent death, and that fat echo on the lead vocal is a signal to audiences that this is no longer your little old church on the lane. Can the classic rockabilly slap delay be far behind? Though even as these late white gospel quartets go this is still a bit over-ripe, harmonically speaking. The Blue Ridge Quartet was essentially a franchise with shifting personnel over the years, and the strange, cookie cutter quality of this may be a result of excessive professionalism. At times (and especially at the end as they go into something that practically screams out "finale") they sound like the Four Freshmen or one of those other pop vocal groups that began to sprout on variety shows in the 1950s like televised escorts: "This way to god's mansion ladies and gentleman…..". And while you're at it, don't forget to tip the pool boy……

When it comes to describing the relative commercial appeal of 1950s country music I am a bit out of my depth. I tend to approach studies like this one as I would approach a literary history. I worry less about sales and demographics than I do about musical acuity and historical succession - and in some ways less about historical succession than aesthetic progression and regression, the little dance of time that music performs for us as it dances in our heads. By the time **Frank Hunter and his Black Mountain Boys** record **Long Time No See** in **1952** bluegrass is a seething presence in country music, if something of a sidetrack from all the country roads leading to Nashville and other commercial destinations. Though I might have some relatively negative things to say about what bluegrass has become - like bebop, but in even a much more predictable way, it has become a victim of formula and technique - it is still, in the 1950s, a thing of hearty, virtuoso sweat and tears. The best of the old/new sound is neither worshipful nor rejecting of old-time music. The old-time sound is just *present* in what the new-grass players are doing, in their revivalist energy and forward-motion dedication to the ghosts of country-music past. There is nothing antiquarian about this, about the seething fiddle of *Long Time No See,* the sublime instrumental chaos, the surging vocal harmonies, even the occasional recorded distortion as these groups, unregulated and set free in recording studios by small independent record labels, let loose as though they were standing in front of an audience. Once again there is a lot to be said for the analog glories of these early days, in the way old tech captured group delirium.

There was a surge in those years of bluegrass creativity and intensity, getting higher and more lonesome by the day. A wonder peculiarity is **Holsten Valley Breakdown** by **Ronnie Knittel and the Holsten Valley Ramblers**, recorded, as far as we can tell, in **early 1950**. I would call it an anachronism, except by now in this study I don't think anything in old music is an anachronism. It all just comes and goes and then reappears in strange places and ways. This record, from a private pressing (and latter reissued by Rounder), is basically a ragtime piece, especially in the recurring interlude with its rag-timed chord progression of 6-2-5-1 (A7-D7-G7-C7 in the key of C, for those of you keeping score). And maybe this tells us about something I have never seen discussed in country music chronicles, or really asks a relevant question about the style - was bluegrass in its essence a reformulation of ragtime, a white-ish revival of ragtime's double-timed rhythms, a renewal of rag's display-piece virtuosity as rescued from hillbilly decadence?

Knittel's strangely progressive musical career is like a canary in the mine shaft of country music's weird musical evolution, a microcosmic study, to press our mixed metaphorical advantage, of the diverse winds blowing across those in-bred Southern mountains. Thanks to the heroic research of Eugene Chadbourne as documented on the AllMusic web site Knittel's life is blood and flesh instead of just a series of 45 rpm recordings: his family was from Tennessee and he sang with them, in his younger years, in a vocal quartet (showing us how that format, as old as the hills and as black as the white folks in them, was still a musical connector of Southern sound); he turned to rockabilly when the world began to change (there are some good examples of his excellent rock work on Youtube); and then moved into and through a nether world of black/white pop and rock, adjusting his audience, he later claimed, from white to black through the medium of Ray Charles covers; and then ended up in the poultry business.

One of the things that makes pop and vernacular music so interesting and so much fun throughout the 1950s and 1960s (and I should mention that I include jazz in this odd mix) is how actively all of its forms seem to be in search of themselves (and apologies to Larry Kart, the great jazz critic, whose collection of pieces is called *Jazz in Search of Itself*). But that's what change and progress amount to in any art form worthy of the name, a constant search for communal forms of self. And though I continue to emphasize African American music as being at the root of all domestic musical progress, I think it is important not to qualify such progress, when it occurs at the hands of white folks, with faint praise. The more things change the more they do remain the same, and it's possible, if somewhat improbable, to make the argument that musical "evolution" in the 20th century is actually a form of continuous *devolution* and evolution, a strange and repeating dialectic of racial conflict and consensus. White people can be black people without knowing it, and so black people may be white, even without self awareness, in cultural and existential ways. So while I have often complained about sociological expectations in the service of racial conformity - as when people tell someone black, in particular, that he or she needs to behave in certain specific ways in order to really *be* black - maybe it's ok to recognize the racial strangeness of someone who acts, sociologically, so outside of expectations. But maybe it's not ok to comment on it.

But I digress; for some of the next citations let us walk step-by-step through that strange night of the American musical hunter:

### Black Gal Walter Horton 6/51

Some people prefer Walter Horton - sometimes called Big Walter - to Little Walter, who I have described in these pages as the emergent master of modern harmonica playing. Little Walter swung and he was funky as all hell, and he was the center of the modern blues-harmonica movement. But Big Walter had something a little bit different, a little more country in his soul and his sound. He was a deep-Southern player who early on was performing with acoustic Delta bluesters, though his first recognition came for recordings he made of old-style yet modern blues for Sam Phillips of Sun Records. That whole Memphis black blues scene, smartly documented by Phillips before he realized that the solution to his financial woes was Elvis Presley, was, in ways both obvious and subtle, a rock and roll incubator. Though I risk contradicting my own conclusions about whiteness and rock and roll as I say this, the Memphis blues of these years had a kick and a buzz that dragged it away, kicking and screaming (literally) from the swing-derived sound of rhythm and blues. So it is probably no accident that Elvis (and Carl Perkins and a few others), living in proximity to Memphis and its environs, to juke joints and a new kind of flat-out musical hysteria fueled by the blues and country and god-knows-what-else, started doing their own white things in, if not direct response, then in cultural parallel. Black music always had this effect, even at something of a legal distance. *Black Gal* is sort of in-between, very much in the style of the transitional black country blues of those days, from the 6th (guitar) chord, a la jazz, at the opening to the powerfully distorted guitar comping that follows. Add some surging piano, and then Walter's un-amplified harmonica, which seems to be begging for a volume boost. The guitar, though, by the late, great Calvin Newborn (and this was recorded by Phillips but not issued by Sun) is the thing that kicks this into the new age. A terrific jazz player, he knew, unlike a lot of jazz guitarists, how to kick things along in a real, down and dirty, blues way. So although this is a bit less ensemble-rich and "modern" than a lot of the Memphis blues of those years, it's still a musical outlier.

**By and By Sister Jessie Mae Renfro 1951**

I sure am glad there is an internet, where I habitually find things which, true or not, are certainly fascinating tidbits of Americana lore (and I realize that that sounds like a classic Trumpie response to questionable historical assertions; I have had more than one tell me, upon being corrected, that "well, it's interesting anyway;" no it's not and never is, you fucking idiot). What I mean and what I should have said is that sometimes misinformation, in the cultural sphere, is full of some grains of truth that have gotten, through the years, mixed with myth. But still, as I tell people, you have to use your own judgement. And by my own judgment the following, retrieved from Facebook and posted by the Church Of God In Christ International Mass Choir, about Sister Jessie Mae, has more than just the ring of truth (and note that they add Sapp, which was her married name):

"She was the first female artist to be signed with Peacock Records during the spring of 1951 and remained Peacock's only female soloist up until early 1963. She performed professionally for over 52 years, and became an influential voice in the development of Gospel music, both in recordings and music ministry.

Evangelist Jessie Mae Renfro Sapp was born to Nesiah and Jessie Hayes, October 3, 1921 in Waxahachie, Texas, where she was brought up in the Church Of God In Christ and into a musical family, where she was immersed in gospel music – playing and singing from an early age.

Although tempted to sing secular music, she made her mind up to sing Gospel, and traveled with the Sallie Martin singers during the mid-1940s. While with Martin, Sister Renfro picked up kudos from Rosetta Tharpe, Clara Ward and Emily Bram whom she much admired. Although she began recording in 1946, it was not until the early 1950's that she found success with songs and a singing style that attracted public attention.

An early May 1951 Billboard Magazine announced that Sister Jessie Mae Renfro was auditioned by the great Marion Anderson who picked her as possessing one of the greatest voices in the spiritual field. In 1951, she signed with Houston-based Peacock Records and had such hits as 1952's "I Must Tell Jesus", "God Is So Wonderful", and "You've Got to Move" among many others. Her album "He's So Wonderful" remained on Billboard's Gospel charts for nearly three years and earned her a place as a soloist alongside such greats as Mahalia Jackson.

Evangelist Sapp passed away on January 15, 1996 in Oklahoma City.

Though I rarely copy and paste such things verbatim, I accept, without reservation, that she "was one of the last great traditional Gospel Singers to pass in the 20th century" and I am thrilled to see such a well-worded declaration in Facebook, rescuing another black performer from obscurity. Renfro/Sapp is in the great tradition of gospel evangelist, going back to Bessie Johnson and Sister Rosetta Tharpe. Gospel music of the 1950s is all things racial, from cracker-smooth quartet vocalizing to roll and rock (my terms for the non-rock and roll rocking of black groups and singers) to, with some finality (as we will see a couple of volumes hence) a new white revival with, finally, some true moments of feeling. Which may finally tell us modern gospel music's true place in the American musical picture, as a shock to an emotional system torn apart by war (WW II and then Korea) and politics (HUAC, the Cold War, and the rise of Joseph McCarthy). And even if none of these stylists knew about the other, gospel was the great emotional leveler, a kind of control for the music of old and new, for rockers and old-time religionists of all colors.

**Don't Jive Me Smiley Lewis 4/51**

Ah, New Orleans. Though I have rebelled in the past against the simplistic labeling of New Orleans as all things to all styles of jazz, we do have to recognize how central that city is to

American music, how, as a "Caribbean port of call" (Dick Spottswood's description), its codification of certain aspects of American musical left a heavy cultural imprint (though maybe less and less of one as the 20th century fades from memory and autotune takes over, replacing the African Diaspora with an electronic diaspora of indeterminate lineage). There's that rhythm, the ever-present clave in all of its ways, but primarily there is the casual intermingling of musical styles and shapes. New Orleans rhythm and blues, whatever form it took, was a true precursor of rock and roll, whatever form that took. But most of all I hear that African triplet (a further subdivision of the three of the clave) as surging through all of New Orleans music, to the point of cliche and distraction, but surging just the same. And New Orleans music had room for just about everyone, including the charming Smiley Lewis.

*Don't Jive Me,* by Lewis, is the epitome of New Orleans strut, part of that tradition of slow-black tempo that I have defined as combined racial technique/cultural signification and we-do-it-because-we-can-motherfucker declaration of cultural independence and indifference to white frailty. The deep two-beat, which white countrymen and women adapted to much different ends, the behind-the-beat vocal, and Smiley's fearless crooning (unfazed as he was by any potential charges of corniness) give balladry of this kind a whole new meaning. This is a sort-of blues; harmonically speaking it is written to form but it follows a free-verse approach with rhyme and contains no couplets of the traditional blues kind. And listen to the effortless way Smiley hits those ninths at key points of the melody, a jazz indicator that feels appropriate in light of the tail-gate trombone that follows throughout. This is real black balladry, timeless, devoid of sentimentality in that nice, non-ironic way of black style and lyric poetry. No matter how much the music changed, there was always room for this kind of effortless soul.

**Juiced Billy Love 6/51**

Want more pre-rock? *Juiced* is exactly the kind of thing I was referring to, above. Listen first to that half-assed piano-jazz intro (very possibly by Phineas Newborn, who did a fair amount of studio work in those days). This is soon abandoned for some real blues posturing, a few hard, distorted guitar chords, and a great yelp by Billy Love; we are off to whatever races this represented stylistically. It sounds at first sort of like the *au courant* jump blues (which was a variation on, or really acceleration of, the hyper-shuffle of swing), but it soon becomes clear that this is a new kind of depravity. And then that guitar solo, which sounds at first like someone surprised the guitarist by pointing at him and commanding a solo, though he soon recovers (sort of) and is either playing in the wrong key or forgot to tune his instrument. But it doesn't matter, because something tells me this whole bashing/jumping thing was particular to Memphis, whose black musical citizens were clearly undergoing some kind of musical renaissance; all the more reason to hate American racism, because it is no market-accident that Sam Phillips, who was a good guy, couldn't make a living with this sound and these records (though I do wonder if there were ways around this kind of market segregation as the Chess brothers, who were wizards of promotion and circulation, found out so profitably). So although this raises all kinds of other questions that I cannot answer, we are left with this incredibly spirited blues-in-the-body experience, a celebration of all that getting juiced meant, and a tribute to the the stoner high, a model for upcoming stoners of every musical generation (though something black musicians and their followers already knew well; hence Charlie Parker and the supremely stoned Bebop Generation).

**Lone Town Blues Junior Brooks 1951**

So you want to hear some black rockabilly? Rockabilly is the word used to describe the primarily white style that crossed over from honky tonk's drunken, lovelorn territory into a new place where boogie was in vogue, country twang transformed itself into guttural hiccups, the two-beat was (occasional) king, and the beer-bottle-throwing trajectory of honky tonk's drunken tossers was replaced by amphetamine-fueled road trips. It was the blues and it was the slightly hysterical sound of sanctified gospel, at first glance whitened-out but not really; the holy rollers who founded the white sanctified church were, if largely musically undocumented from the earliest days, just as cravenly hysterical as the black Church of God in Christ and its offshoots, and therein lay the emotional center of rock and roll's white, clouded, origins (for a taste, see Brother Claude Ely, Vol. 28, and peruse Youtube for some amazing clips of modern-day white sanctified churches shaking, rolling, and doing the James Brown sag-and-collapse).

But what does all of this have to do with Junior Brooks? Well, listen to that recurring guitar riff. It's sounds like a more animated and soulful Chuck Berry (who happily admitted his debt to country and hillbilly music). It's all up and down the scale, but it's a country scale, if there is such a thing, by way of the use of the major third and sixth intervals, two tonal points that immediately, in the modern era, distinguish (usually white) country guitarists from black bluesers. In this case, as in some of the early work of Earl Hooker, we have a guitar player who is walking the line; well, really, crossing over it into country music; check out his solo at 1:22. Overdub a little bit of Ernest Tubb-like vocal and you might think you were on a record date for Decca, but there's no mistaking Junior Brooks for anything but a musician loyal to whatever his roots happened to be. And listen not just to that two-beat, but to the way in which, presaging Elvis and *That's All Right Mama*, it becomes a wall of rhythm, outflanking the 4-beat blues and boogie. It is like a hurricane of rhythmic sound, which is another way of saying that black musicians beat the hell out of rhythm even without especially trying. It was just the thing they heard in their heads.

This is the beginning of the era of crossover, and once again I have to wonder if white 'billies like not just Elvis but also Carl Perkins and Billy Lee Riley were listening to this kind of thing, which was showing the way to common musical ground. It might have been interesting if the new young, white audience had been exposed to sounds like this; it's not that there weren't black rockers in these early days, but that we've been looking for them in a lot of the wrong places.

**You Go To My Head Bob Graettinger Stan Kenton 9/15/52**

Stan Kenton gets a bad rap these days. Some of the fault is Stan's (he was a Goldwater Republican who had some odd things to say about race and jazz), but some of it is the curse of The West Coast, especially as evaluated by East Coast critics. Most criticism of Kenton has been directed at the Wagnerian excess in his music, and he was certainly guilty of some of that, but he also allowed his arrangers and musicians free reign, or was it Free Range? There are so many different sides to the Kenton Orchestra that to describe it as all one thing or another is to give a false sense of its overall impact. Most interestingly it was a popular orchestra, even for some of its more adventurous work. And who but Stan Kenton would have hired and recorded entire albums by the likes of Bob Graettinger, an eccentric-genius modernist who was one of the first to actually realize the post-bebop avant gardist's dream of devising a harmonic and melodic language to go along with the ambition, expressed by certain modernists, of getting beyond the predictability of bebop's intervals and harmonies?

He wasn't the only one - George Russell, William Russo and George Handy come to mind as composer contemporaries who were striving to apply the lessons learned in contemporary "serious" music to jazz pedagogy of the practical kind. But Graettinger was probably the greatest and most radical of them all, an eccentric, oddball outsider who lived in what was essentially a garret, spoke little, and befriended almost no one. Impressions of him from some of the old Kentonites ranged from awe to bewilderment to even a little nervousness at his distance and general oddball character. But Kenton, to his eternal credit, used his work and gave him an entire album, something for which we should be extremely grateful. Graettinger, who died shockingly young (at 34 of lung cancer) was an original. *You Go To My Head* is a good example of his brilliantly-devised compositional/harmonic method, which from the beginning of the song is compelling, symmetrical, and dissonant, yet perfectly organized. Those opening chords seem to be leading us to any place *but* a pop song, but it is indeed a standard tune that he is reinventing. With its mellow dissonance and the free-flowing parts (which seem to be coming apart and then piecing themselves back together), the arrangement is like a series of sketches written separately and then pasted together with spectacular unity. It seems to be pulling itself together - and then there is the sudden release of the original melody at 2:05, an easing of the chaos of its moving musical parts, a slightly more conventional merging of sections, and a reiteration of the internal, repeating riff, a recurring motif throughout. And then it ends.

Somewhat amusingly, one of the few Kenton musicians who got to know Graettinger at all was the saxophonist Art Pepper, who said they hung and smoked pot together and got along just fine. This was the perfect relationship, and I don't intend the slightest bit of sarcasm in that statement; maybe it took a perpetual outsider/junkie like Pepper to recognize that alienation is a matter of not just social isolation but also of the self-imposed limitation on how much of yourself you choose to expose to the world. And about the only part of himself that Graettinger chose to show in his limited time on earth was his music.

**Strange Things Henry Green 3/52**

Indeed there are; the Bible tells us so and our senses confirm. Who was Henry Green? Just another musical prophet who was pretty much here and then gone, in the professional if not existential sense (he made only two recordings). His song is executed with a kind of country precision but also with an updated musical and even social attitude. The lyrics of the whole thing are poetic and practical at the same time:

Well, ships are sinkin' in the ocean, planes are havin' collision in the air
Well people, you may not believe it, there is something wrong somewhere
Well, no matter where you go, you hear about things you never heard before
Strange things are happenin' every day

Some folk, they go to church, and they say they are livin' right
We have some so-called Christian, always ready to fuss and fight
And they say they with the Lord, you better trust in my God
Strange things are happenin' every day

Some fool wish that they were dead, some are glad to be alive
We have some who are killing each other, some are committin' suicide
Well, there is a better way, if you just fall on your knees and pray
Strange things are happenin' every day

My God is ridin' on the water, and he ridin' through the storm and land
Well, Church, you better get ready, do as my God command, he said,
"As you see Me go today, I'll be back the same old way."
Strange things are happenin' every day

You don't have to believe in god or the church to go along with this premonition of disaster. Most interesting of course is the close relationship of this to the old Delta sound, though the electric/vocal unison and the thumping minor key puts it squarely in the realm of urban blues a la Chicago and Detroit (think John Lee Hooker, who had a similar country/city identity). No other group of Americans has had their faith tested like African Americans. What distinguishes the tone of their warnings and spiritual suggestions from that of white gospelers and other assorted white religious advocates is a matter of alliance. White folks have faith in both God and Government, whom they consider to be allies. Black folks know that for them religious institutions are in many ways substitutes for the political. They had, particularly in those days, no one to turn to but a god of alleged and sketchy existence and questionable advocacy.

The opening of **Boyd Gilmore's Take a Little Walk with Me** (1/23/52) sounds surprisingly like the opening of some of Utah Smith's recording (see Vol. 22), setting me, as with some other recordings in this collection, to wondering what other connections I may have missed over the years in examining that great oddity of sound called American music. Of course the blues has its own conventions, and it's possible that Utah Smith caught this idea from somewhere else, but I have never heard that strange, free-form kind of riff in any place but Smith's work. I do suspect that the guitar on this, including the slightly odd but very good solo starting at 1:17 (it has an unconventional asymmetry of phrasing) is played by Earl Hooker, and as such it is illuminating in an entirely different way. Earl Hooker, John Lee's brother, is a bit of a mystery; B.B. King said that Earl was the best blues guitarist he ever heard, though there is precious little on record to support that claim. Hooker's own recorded history is rife with halfhearted attempts at rock and blue gimmicks, rushed performances that sound frustrated and indifferent. This, however, is something else. Was he more likely to play well when his name wasn't on the marquee, so to speak, when there was no pressure to produce except as a sideman? Well, listen to this solo, with it's slide-articulation (Hooker was an expert at the slide guitar), and then it's flailing near-triplets and non-articulated (in a very musical way) pull offs, the way it all seems to generate from a slightly abstract, blue-guitar sensibility. This is the sign of an extraordinary talent, though unhappily one that never really found a consistent path in the new blues (and one thing said to have held Hooker back was that he was not a good singer. Fortunately Gilmore is). The overall performance sounds to me like a fascinating shadow act, post-Robert Johnson, pulled together from common stanzas and a lot of post-war bits and blues pieces. Gilmore, the fusionist, is himself a very fine singer, with the knack for taking a pedestrian title and lyric and making it is own personal, pedestrian title and lyric. Put it all together, Gilmore/Hooker, and a post-War blues that sometimes was little more than electric country/down-home music, and you have a passive style waiting for active musicians, as here, to convert it into something more progressive.

An even better example of the coming confluence of the blues and rock and roll is **Walked All Night** by **Charlie Booker (1952)**. In this we head into what I think of as the last great stage of the first great stage of post-war electric blues. Was this the Greatest Generation of the blues? Meaning: Elmore James, Ike

Turner, Sonny Boy Williamson (Rice Williams), Willie Love, Little Milton, et al, all of whom, cumulatively speaking, came at the blues with a newly liberated sensibility? Just as returning black war veterans might have assumed that the black blood left behind in the ruins of Europe would lead to a new life back home, so might these blues players have assumed that their own cultural sacrifices combined with new music and new media would create the cultural space necessary to allow them some meaningful access to the growing American musical marketplace (and they were right, though mostly in the long term).

Booker was a deep Southerner (born in Mississippi) who didn't so much transplant himself as re-plant himself, as part of the sub-migration of the Great Migration. He was one of the new masters of electro-acoustic music, of music which used the newly-minted electric guitar as not so much a substitute for the acoustic but as a new and loud badge of cultural and personal independence. There is a defiance in all of this, always musical and always personal, that may even be heard as a *substitute* for the political.

And what music it was. Just listen to momentum these players build from the beginning, that immediate shot of rhythm and guitar, the 2-3-4 accents that establish a new means of syncopation, of the kind that more of the deeper rockers, black and white, took up in a few years. This is, as I am so fond of saying, the loping, leaning 4-beat time stamp that was carrying the blues into a new age. It is head-nodding music, a rhythm of smooth all-beat emphasis (well, of second, third, and fourth beat emphasis) with moments of old-time syncopation that are less a nod to the past than a fusion of country and city sound and movement (and I can hear in this the angularity of black dance, that post-Diasporan, angled physical posture that, yes, has been traced back to Africa).[33] This represents a final break (for this school, at least) from the swing-jazz shuffle of jump blues and rhythm and blues, though of course that particular style (as with Joe Turner, et al) was not going away. And talk about drive - this particular rhythmic method was not based on speed but on sustaining the same steady feeling and pulse and building time from the bottom up. The whole instrumental feeling - dense but full of

---

[33] For the best accounting and explanation of this kind of Diasporan movement read Jacqui Malone's history of black dance, *Steppin' on the Blues: The Visible Rhythms of American Dance*.

open spaces - was the very thing white rockers, in due time, grabbed and put to their own use, raising the sonic center of gravity, replacing bass-bottomed sonic emphasis with a lighter tread. And there is nothing more satisfying then the sound of a guitar pushing the tubes of a low powered amp into overdrive. Though not a new technique, it is now a central part of the music, a bold and independent voice.

More on the wild side but less on the rock and roll side was **Monkey Motion (Houston Boines (1952))**. Boines was one of a number of bluesman recruited in the early 1950s by Ike Turner for Modern Records (another was Charlie Booker, see just above). The wonder of it all is, as with the field trips made by the major labels in the 1920s to find and record acoustic country blues players, how much raw talent was out there, in the South, where immigration patterns were fluid and every guitar player and his brother was looking for a way to somewhere else.

(In-text footnote: of course the same thing happened when record companies went in search of white hillbilly songsters; which proves a number of things, at least to me: that 1) there was an incredible amount of talent both black and white in the South, nurtured by this early Cultural Revolution and first Black Arts Movement, and by what was becoming apparent was a white country-boy genius at grasping the cultural strands of black life and culture and using them in smart ways; 2) that claims (see footnote below) recently made that the establishment of country music as a white form were the result of white supremacist outlook are patently false; that such a musical division was mostly, in my very humble opinion, based on observations by record scouts of indigenous habits and of contrasting white and black means of making sound, which were obviously different, sometimes radically so, though, yes, stratified and re-enforced by statute and by race and class; but that such separation, enforced by post-reconstruction structural racism, didn't prevent musicians, in an indigenous way, from copying each other, working together, and collaborating, even if all of that was done unofficially, since we now know that the history of Southern race relations, up-close and personal, was more complex and interdependently defined than we might have previously assumed. Though once again this doesn't mitigate Jim Crow and native anti-black terrorism, but it does tell us that there were, to quote Henry Green, strange things happening, yes, all around in venues where black-white relations and relationships were less subject to (white) public scrutiny and official terror.

Though to get back to my original point, the sheer numbers and variety of musicians, black and white, who were recorded throughout the first half of the 20th century tells us that there are representative racial samplings out there in a lot of old records, in everything from 78s to 45s to 33 rpm LPs of both black and white musicians, and that the responsibility to do what the major record labels didn't do, to sample and categorize more accurately, and *explain*, is now ours. To me this is a form of multi-racial reparation with an emphasis on the least enfranchised, who were definitely black musicians, though we tread carefully so as not to distort history any more than it has already been distorted).

But back to *Monkey Motion*, which is essentially a visitation to the old-style blues and boogie. Interesting as well is how much, like some things we have previously heard, it seems to reference Robert Johnson (in this case *Dust My Broom*), which tells us even more about some latter-day claims that Johnson's place in the blues hierarchy of the time has been overstated. But it's 1952 and there is no mass media engaging with the myth of Robert Johnson, just a new musical aggressiveness overrunning the acoustic blues, which RJ not only predicted musically but of which he was a living, breathing, and then dying, example.

Were there people (other than myself about 30 years ago) who, upon first hearing **Elmore James**, felt much as Fats Waller did when introducing Art Tatum ("I play piano but tonight god is in the house," Waller famously said one night when Tatum walked in to hear him play)? A few years back when I checked out the Rock and Roll Museum in Cleveland I had fun but was generally underwhelmed, until I came to an exhibit that included Elmore's guitar, at which point I had no choice but to sit and stare. It was like looking at a weapon of some old Norse god and feeling not just in awe of its very existence but also somewhat surprised at how plain and ordinary a tool it appeared to be. But that's probably the point; as we examine black ways of making music and listen throughout to the conditioned efforts of black *blues* musicians in particular (but also jug band and other street players) we begin to understand that the the whole concept of improvisation involved not just the music that was made but the *way* in which it was made, on old and sub-par instruments adapted in some very practical ways. Want to play electric guitar with an acoustic guitar? Then strap it on with electric guitar pickups that are essentially just small microphones designed to send an electrical signal to small, low-powered guitar amps (often ungrounded electrical shock hazards), and let it blast. Decorum be damned, this is music, and the brilliance of Elmore James, like the brilliance of Jimi Hendrix, was based on the realization that sound and ideas, in the electric sphere, were inseparable. What you play is not just what you play but how you play it (and saxophonists had known this for a long time; the guitar was still, technologically-speaking, evolving).

So let James' **1/52** recording of **Please Find My Baby** wash over you in all of its "distorted" glory (because there is nothing so clear and expressive as true electric guitar distortion). This is the first and foremost electric slide (well, there was Earl Hooker, see above, but I am uncertain as to who initially put this electrical technique into action). Note Elmore's voice, with its occasional Elvis-y sub tone (which, for those of you who criticize Elvis relentlessly, is worth citing; you call it copying but I think it's notable to show just how much music Elvis really *knew*, from the inside out. But damned if he did, damned if he didn't....). And listen to the way James modulates the distortion and the noise, controls it manually (meaning he probably just uses his hands and fingers) in the same way that years later Hendrix stood in front of those giant amplifiers and digitally (with his hands and fingers, I mean) manipulated his guitar's volume control while jockeying for position and feedback. And note once more that this has an electrical current that flows back more than ten years to the unplugged efforts of Robert Johnson, and forward another ten to the astounding blues adaptations of Johnny Winter; all from a cheap guitar that now hangs on a wall in Cleveland.

On occasion I have gotten into some trouble for expressing a dislike for some of the sacred and semi-sacred musical cows of the music industry. A partial list of those who I have dissed and for which I have faced varying forms of public intellectual flogging would include: Ahmad Jamal, Oscar Peterson, Charles Rouse, Chuck Berry, Dave Brubeck, and **Fats Domino**. Call me a glutton for punishment, but I do sometimes feel like the little boy who notices, while everyone else is ordering hot dogs and beer, that the Emperor is exposing himself. Often I understand the popularity and reputation, even as I shake my head at what seem to me to be mediocre talents accompanied by, on occasion, a knack for composition. Which is what takes us to Fats Domino, who is a bad singer and mediocre pianist with a real talent for the catch-paraphrasing of popular composition and who has an undoubted place in the early history of rock and roll - or what I would call pre-rock and roll, that stylistic area between the first heavy, bass-laden sounds of hard rhythm and blues (late '40s, early '50s), hard urban blues (Muddy Waters in Chicago et al) and the skyburst that was Elvis Presley. Among other things New Orleans was a warm bed of the kind of blues and rhythm that certainly predicted and effected early rock - the Latin rhythmic underpinnings, the lighter swing, the blues-based lyrics and lightly-accented vocals that often went from deep blues intonation to pop-breezy in the space of a three minute single. **Reeling and a Rocking**, which Domino recorded on **1/52**, was made in the domain of the great producer and recording engineer Cosimo Matassa, whose whole method of monophonic sound imaging had a revolutionary effect on the new sound of near-rock and roll (or roll and rock, perhaps a better term for this no-man's-land music of blues and rhythm). *Reeling and Rocking*, in spite of Domino's obvious limitations as a singer, makes a very strong musical point. From it's jazzy alto saxophone solo to the very basic-blues 6th chords played by the guitarist, to the exceptionally original way in which Domino resolves the melody (in a very non-blues way), it has that great pop-hook feel, the familiar appeal of a song you think you have heard before. This is a non-blues with blues reference yes, and a memorable composition. Add the equivalent of a very distinct, recording *mis en scene* (with Matassa very much the auteur, putting his personal stamp on everything that came out of his studio), the way in which the whole aura of studio seems to augment Domino's very meager vocal technique, and you have, years before studio automation was invented, some of the earliest human form of popular song's mechanization.

The black arts movement, of sorts, continues to play out in some non-surprising, surprising ways. It's no longer news that black pop was unafraid of dealing with sentiment, of bouncing it around like a cat knocking a ball across the room. But sentiment can take many forms, sometimes as heart-on-sleeve display, other times like a diary that only subtly exposes deeper feelings. And I am always hesitant, anyway, to make generalizations about black (well, American) music for fear of being contradicted by the next song that comes along. So we take black pop as it comes - sometimes as something tough and gritty, sometimes as something unisexual, sometimes as something biblically intense, sometimes as something ridiculous, and sometimes as just a thing that floats through our consciousness and settles on a clear narrative and finite story line.

Certainly the black balladeer **Percy Mayfield** was a great middle man of black song and black pop, a wounded veteran of the emotional wars whose casual yet pithy blue pop songs were easily adaptable by singers as particular as Ray Charles (*Hit the Road Jack*) and Dinah Washington (*Please Send me Someone to Love*). Mayfield's performance of **River's Invitation (1/22/52)**, a portrait of down-and-out suicidal ideation, is typical of his musical attitude: "I spoke to the river/and the river spoke back to me/you look so lonely/and full of misery." We know now that thematically works like this were, for Mayfield, semi-autobiographical, and though it doesn't change the quality of the music it does give a whole other dimension to Mayfield's musical output (one of his first hits was *Two Years of Torture*; as my wife would say, this man sounds depressed). He was also nearly killed in a car accident while on the road (he was pronounced dead at the scene but survived), and in a unique way his pervasive personal sense of doom-and-gloom serves up a glib yet poetic pop perspective on death. *River's Invitation*, as something that was, again, "in-between" back and white pop and blue-ballad styles, fit right in, as something that didn't quite fit right in.

No black bluesman was as relentlessly up-to-date as **B.B. King** who, though he flailed around a bit in his early years, had a flair in those days for a harder-brand of the blues than that which ultimately made him popular and then Caucasian-rich.[34] **Fine Looking Woman**, which he recorded in 1952, might surprising you. The opening guitar solo, apparently made before Lucille tried to domesticate B.B.'s sound, is a distorted wash, as are the rock-solid blue-guitar interjections. B.B. was working in the same Memphis hothouse as some of those other bluesman whose work we have previously described as foreshadowing the confluence of the hard electric blues with pre-rock. This was all the result of, I would say, the big bang of: the new hard-blues, country-music exile (those lone musicians working outside the mainstream of the

---

[34] I am going to tread carefully by explaining here that in my early years I encountered two wonderful men and fine musicians, Eddie Durham and Professor Snead, both of whom at one point in their lives made some real pop-related money; Durham on the disco version of the song *In the Mood*, and Snead on the Lovin' Spoonful version of a song he co-wrote with Piano Red, *Bald Headed Lena*. Both men, in describing to me how these songs had brought them second-tier riches, used the exact same term - as Professor Snead said to me one day, "that song made me Ni**** rich." Durham, around the same time, said to me the exact same thing.

mainstream), two-beat blues and country, four-beat blues, post-ring shout gospel hysteria, guitar-playing preachers and fellow travelers; and, finally, the fusion by Southern white-boy rockabillies of high-lonesome with low-down to make rock and roll.

In the post-Reconstruction South, when separate-but-equal masqueraded as a doctrine, in that conservative, "constitutionalist" way rather than what it really was, a cover for racism, a system of schools-for-the-blind went into operation. Part philanthropy and part dumping ground, these schools were a model of American social ingenuity and denial; for the purpose of sweeping certain social problems under the rug, well-intended and increasingly detached forms of noblesse oblige served well as white cover.

Still, out of this system came some ringers - blind citizens, like **The Five Blind Boys of Mississippi** who, in fulfilling what must have, by then, seemed a traditional Gospel role, created some of the deepest and most achingly soulful modern, hard gospel (hard gospel being the descriptor used for groups in the modern era for whom lead singing was either a matter of improvised, melismatic roving through the hills and valleys of gospel harmony, or something passed around from voice to voice in a tag-team style of exhortation, godly pleading, and just plain hysterical vocal preaching). The Five Blind Boys, whose lead singer Archie Brownlee had probably the greatest voice ever to commandeer a small gospel group, and who was an influence on Ray Charles, recorded **I Was Praying** in **1952**. This was the epitome, culmination, height, or whatever you wanted to call it, of the new gospel movement. The rocking harmonies, the deep wall of sound, were one thing, but Brownlee's voice, as either a prediction of or influence on soul music, was a pining, yearning, brooding - pick your word again - thing of raging beauty. As with so many others, this group was its own rhythm section, building with a sense of righteousness and a craving for salvation - until, at 1:55, Brownlee lets go with a great whoop and spiritually-dissonant cry. This is an internalized form of distortion, exposed in sound, and represents the ultimate fusion of musical purposes in the vernacular/pop/religious continuum; it is the sound of the music turning spirit into body as fanaticism in human form, a way, metaphorically speaking, of restoring eyesight to the blind.

A few years back I got some incredulous response when I mentioned, somewhere (probably Facebook) that **Doris Day** was one of my favorite singers. There was a reason I encountered so many non-believers, many of whom grew up on those 1960s *Doris Day Movies* (yes they were so popular they had their own nomenclature, like *Jerry Lewis Movies*) in which her wholesomeness overwhelmed her talent. She was really a very good actress (check her out in two musical movies: *Love Me or Leave Me* and *Young Man With Horn*) and more than a good singer. But her vocal style, sultry and silky throughout the 1940s and through most of the 1950s, changed as she became a movie star. On those later soundtracks she changed from sexy to girlish, in effect from alcohol chaser to malted milk. Her phrasing changed, her rhythm changed and, I assume as cause rather than effect, her repertoire went from deep standards to fluffy pop. This may have been an image thing, a way of selling the vocal personality of the 1960s actress, who was now all demure modesty and family values. It's a pity because a performance like **I'm in the Mood for Love** shows her at her best: voice soft but always *present*, phrasing right on the melody. This was a particular way of great white female 1950s balladry in particular, through Chris Conner, June Christie, Julie London, and, most centrally, Anita O'Day. Though O'Day was an unapologetic jazzer, the others moved between adoration of the melody and jazzy paraphrase, though Doris Day, even at her best, was the most conservative of all. She had a great purity of tone and paid close dramatic attention to the lyrics. Her time was pure as well - very deliberative, on the beat, off the beat, always calm and composed. All of which had to change if, as Oscar Levant noticed, she wanted to reclaim her virginity in the New Hollywood. [35]

When it comes to rock and roll and its origins, the more I change my mind the more it stays the same. In constructing this book and assembling the music for it I have found, with frightening ease, more and more 1950s black blues that falls, sonically and stylistic, directly in rock and roll's line of procession. So, although my basic impression of what rock and roll *is* has not changed (as I call it, a white way of thinking about black music), my understanding of its antecedents has altered somewhat. There were clearly some major blues changes in the air prior to Elvis' world-shaking Sun-burst in 1954. Some of it I have cited in this chapter, and some of it revolves around the recycling of the

---

[35] Oscar Levant, talking about Doris Day, was famously quoted as saying "I knew her before she was a virgin."

Latinate clave subdivision of the American beat, possibly as filtered through from New Orleans, possibly not (because I don't know how much, if at all, these Chicago and Memphis blues players were listening to New Orleans rhythm and blues). But there's something almost startling about the Chicagoan **Robert Nighthawk**'s recording of **Maggie Campbell (10/25/52)**, with it's upper-frequency rhythm and drumming (strangely reminiscent of some of the ways Buddy Holly recorded at his peak of popularity), and that rapid clave beat.

Now of course a little checking shows that Nighthawk, on his way to Chicago, spent some real time in Memphis and recorded for Ike Turner, who had become a blue/rock recruitment center for labels like Modern, which were trying to navigate through the commercial fog of the post-War blues. There was a lot of product coming around, and Turner seems to have had a talent for focusing past both the typical blues and the usual rhythm and blues, pushing a more dynamic rhythmic and sonic style. This music is relentlessly intense and time-driven, with a complete understanding of local blues conditions. *Maggie Campbell* even has an oddly prescient rockabilly sensibility; listen to the bass, which seems to emulate (well, really, predict) what will become the famous and characteristic rockabilly bass-slap delay (though this player is doing it manually instead of electronically). The tune is open and spacious, has very little on the bottom end to muddy it up (shades, yes, of Elvis' *That's All Right Mama* and the overall country prerogative of certain early rock and rollers) and is altogether a very *musical* predictor of things to come.

Though as with all blues and gospel, the hysteria of spirit possession was never far behind. **Me and the Devil (Rev. Chambers, 1952)** is a return to congregation-style music. The modern gospel movement was institutionally tied to the churches of its singers and stars, and sometimes this meant re-creating in the studio the sound and relationship and pious desperation of religious gatherings. On the accountants' sales sheets there was no such thing as separation of Church and State.

*Me and the Devil* is fairly standards gospel fair, a cookie-cutter performance with that staple of sanctified singing, a growling lead - and with one little musical surprise - that surging, distorted guitar, which stays hidden at first and then emerges at about 1:25 for a solo that makes apparent reference to the old country/blues standard *Guitar Rag*, of all things. This Sylvester Weaver tune (see Vol. 3) seems to have had an interesting survival, maybe because it stood so calmly astride the world of country (as in White) and the blues. Whoever this guitarist is he plays with solid authority and comes only briefly out of the shadows, but, in that hidden and compelling way of certain kinds of deep musicians, he shows he still *remembers*.

Billy Ward owned the Dominoes - the name of the group and all future rights to the name of the group. He ran it like its members were tenant farmers, placing them on small salaries, and depriving them of anything even approaching the idea of profit sharing. And like a lot of entrepreneurs he had an inflated sense of self entitlement because the concept of the product (the band) was his, even if its success was driven by talents far greater than his own. One of his early lead singers, Clyde McPhatter, who was really the voice of the band and who really made the Dominoes, in its early years, so much of what it was, started with nothing and ended with very little, dying young of alcoholism, as "a legend but hardly a success," in the words of one writer.

McPhatter was a gospel-trained singer with a liquid voice and tightly-wound vibrato, a combination of soul-singing pop virtuoso and slightly-corny love balladeer. This is the side of black pop singing which sometimes gets buried in the historical mix, part of that whole tradition of vocal (and other kinds of) cross-dressing, as filtered through a unisex, falsetto aesthetic. McPhatter sang in his natural register, it is true, but the high-pitched and sometimes heavy-handed way with which he delivered the musical goods was part of secular music's search for the godhead of gospel music, especially as it transferred its visceral essence to the secular deity of pop and roll. In other words, pop/secular musicians wanted the feeling without necessarily being saddled with the message and all of the obligations that it implied. McPhatter was a master at doing this, and his vocal techniques and those of other singers in his stylistic orbit leached their way into musical spinoffs like doo wop. This is another of those very self-conscious cultural retentions of black song, showing how the old gospel quartets, so essential to black form and style (and also to white form and style) made their way into the modern era. **Have Mercy Baby (Billy Ward & His Dominoes (McPhatter) (1952)** is a perfect piece of soulful, black-group Muzak, with the Dominoes backup sounding like (well, predicting) Nashville Elvis (anybody remember his backing vocal group The Jordanaires?), lots of plate reverb (a mechanical way of producing room resonance), and a McPhatter vocal that makes a very interesting novelty set piece out of the blues.

Cajun musicians, who we may recall as a mix of folkloric legacy and modern musical flailing, were listening to a lot more than just Cajun. And so was born Cajun Honky Tonk, a curiously anachronistic form of music. I honestly have little idea what kind of venues these musicians performed in, but I can guess that they had jukes of their own, dance halls and other informal places where like-minded people gathered. The internet - and the literature - is not a lot of help on the social (or even the musical) focus of post-war Cajun music, content to describe it as "modern" (this from Wikipedia, which lumps too much of it together and seems a bit clueless on the the subject) or "smooth" in a honky-tonk way (from a web site called *64 Parishes*, which is guilty of over-generalization). Certainly the **Texas Melody Boys** recording of **Ain't No More (early 1950s)** is anything but smooth, and gives us a sense of what has been lost in the slickification of Cajun music in the last 40 years of so. It's not that the aim of pleasing an audience has changed, but that the musicians have, in the spirit of the anti-Walter Benjamin (who said with authority that there was no such thing as *an audience*, but rather endless segments and variations therein), gone for the money. Personally I prefer the style and sound of Cajun unspoiled, and here it is with the Melody Boys, even with the strange, overlaid artifice of party-like cries and minstrel whoops (a la Bob Wills and Rose Maddox and Her Brothers). Harder and harder as it has become to realize the ideal, it is still possible for a good time to be had by all.

# Chapter 27 Church in the Back Seat: If I Could Sing Better I would

Whenever we can, we like to go against type. But sometimes there's so much music that goes against type that it actually becomes type. Is this one of those cases where the exception becomes the rule? In a world where up is down it sometimes feels like there are no more rules; in black music the typical becomes atypical when we compare it to others of its kind that are supposed to be typical.

The most difficult aspect of writing this book is in trying to put something into historical context without letting that context overwhelm the music. And yet sometimes it has to overwhelm the music in order to help us get to where the music is, aesthetically speaking. Am I making any sense? Well, let me simplify: in my early days of writing about American music I resisted using any form of evaluation other than aesthetic (largely under the influence of the the late, great Richard Gilman's critical attitude, which to this day effects my every critical move). But then I realized that there were some things, some forms and sounds, that I was having a great deal of difficulty relating to and so evaluating and writing about. And that often, after learning something about their historical and social *reason de etre*, I was able to unlock their aesthetic secrets. Which violated my previously inviolable belief that everything creative can and should be evaluated strictly on its own terms without historical or social intervention (as in "he is important because he was a Jewish cross-dresser from Kieve who, though he couldn't sing or play an instrument or compose, still tried to do all of that while dealing with the burden of his unresolved sexuality; at the same time as he fled the Nazis and lived the next 5 years in the forests of Poland where he killed and ate squirrels and rabbits and self-bar mitzvahed").

Ultimately I resolved my sense of contradiction. Sometimes a musician's creativity and importance is a result of certain external stimuli, which act on him or her in a socially complex way and even compress his or her world historically so that everything interacts in an inevitably aesthetic way; meaning that the history of his/her life and the social dialectic of his/her daily existence weave themselves into his/her art and craft in compelling ways that are completely integrated with the life as lived. So it is useless to resist the idea that everything can be divorced from material reality in favor of pure invention. Sometimes life is invention (and re-invention).

So here I am dealing with white and black music, hearing it as a struggle between black and white and yet as an isolated phenomenon of the mind and body. Having that knowledge, what do I do with it? Well, I listen closely to things like **Dream Girl** by the singer **Jesse Belvin (1952)**, another of those musicians for whom the tragic arc of a short existence (he was killed in a car accident at age 28) is both a conveniently tragic hook and a strangely relevant irrelevancy: his death occurred after he ran into some problems with racists on a Southern tour, after which the tires on his car, which may have been sabotaged, failed, leading to a head-on collision (which happened apparently right after he had played what was the first integrated musical concert in the history of Little Rock, Arkansas). So she was truly a victim of American life, which gives an added poignancy to his soulful balladry, which in this context feels, because of his death in these absurdly typical circumstances, like a lyric admission of the futility of it all.

Musically-speaking Belvin, with his smoothly textured, but still textured, voice (unlike some white balladeers in particular whose technique seemed to be to remove the human bumps and curves) was an important influence on Sam Cook, who took the image and practice of black pop to the middle - not of the road, but of the market. Belvin's slow and patient vibrato seems to massage the bluer of his phrases, even as the lushness of his vibrato speaks, once again, to the manner of softly-moaning lead that characterized doo wop and other black ballad singing of the day (related, of course, to Clyde McPhatter's work, see Volume 26). So we see a clear if broken (yes, historical and social) line through all of this, knowing as we do that a short productive life, in instances like these, is like a black badge of courage.

**Billy Wright**'s **Goin' Down Slow (10/8/52)** is an altogether different kind of blues, whining and lisping, with a gospel attitude. Though just about everyone is fond of telling us that the blues is everything in American and black music, that it gave us gospel music, for one example, I say not quite. We don't even know if the blues gave us the blues, based on historical precedent (though I tend to doubt it, it is entirely possible, based on actual evidence, that *pop music* gave us the blues, whose harmonic innovation, all raw simplicity and coupled with pointed lyrics, was represented in old sheet music before any place else).

Billy Wright was a something of a mentor to Little Richard, with the tongue-between-the-teeth voice, and the hair, yes, the hair, which Wright was said to have suggested to Little Richard after his own. High and processed, it seems to have been (though I hesitate to say this, echoing as I am certain academic approaches) a coded signal of gayness, and so a uniform of solidarity. Certainly much less was said about such things, at least publicly, in those years. But Wright had a way of singing that was similar to Little Richard's, a preaching quality that was part soul music and part party-time screecher, mixed with the wholesome musical values of religion and observed without irony, though with the occasional wink. 'Pass the plate and shake in tongues like it's Saturday night and church is in the back seat of a car,' it seemed to be telling us, with a universal sexual appeal that suddenly made the new teen audience, black and white and partial to rock and roll and its blues and swing offshoots, seem like the enlightened souls of a post-Jim Crow world. But let's not jump the gun. Americans have always been able to separate their racism and their homophobia from their tastes in music, usually with only short-term effect.

One thing we hear in some country musicians of these years is an exploratory cautiousness. Everyone is testing the waters, jockeying for commercial position. **Roy Hogsed** was among the new breed of country singer, working his way out from the Nashville-tinted mainstream, but still keeping a foot on the formula out of necessity. He made his recording name out on the West Coast; Capitol Records established its beachhead in Nashville in 1950, but it was far from the only place the country music industry was establishing itself. There had been a steady migration West of white folks for quite some time, who planted themselves in different spots where they established their own local country beachheads (eg, Bakersfield, whose red-hot scene spawned Buck Owens among many others and, and Modesta where the Maddox family settled (see Vols. 23. 29 ).

Performers like Hogsed and the Maddoxes, unlike, say, Tex Ritter (see Vol. 23), were truly indigenous in their musical attitudes and socio-aesthetic orientation. The Maddoxes fled Alabama and the caste system of sharecropping and barely made it cross-country as they moved from one migratory trap to another before being liberated by a West Coast homestead and their father's new job. They had always had a family band (a very Southern thing) and it was only a matter of formalizing it for professional work. Buck

Owens migrated with his family to Arizona (out of Texas and a farm) and, to escape schoolwork, turned to music, though it was a job as a truck driver that took him fully West. Ritter, in contrast, was a Southwesterner who aimed a little bit above his raising, going to law school and then ending up doing country music on New York City radio, where he cultivated an image as an erudite yet folksy teller of musical tales of life. But no matter how many times he came back to the land, he was now fully and finally a transplant.

Hogsed, from Arkansas, was, like the Maddoxes and Buck Owens, a core-Southerner. He was also a member of a family band, a working class unit that taught him how to play. He toured in a limited way before he went West, hooked up with various types of post-honky tonk music, and signed first with a West Coast record label called Crystal. One of his biggest hits was a frantic drug anthem called *Cocaine Blues*, a surprising piece of early country outlaw-ism, indicating that he had, along with many others, found a new creative freedom on the West Coast (was this a prediction of country outlaw-ism like that of Waylon Jennings and Willie Nelson, or was it closer to the evolving country fascism of Southern skinhead/Aryan nation, drug-addled nonconformity? I leave that to you to decide).

It has been claimed that Hogsed and his band were an early manifestation of rockabilly, and while that may be a bit overstated, they did have a new honky-tonk (or was it honky?) intensity that was unlike most of what was coming from the country-horse's mouth, if still shy of rockabilly-boogie's intense blue drive. **Ain't a Bump in the Road (11/17/52)** is a truck-driving anthem (with, yes, something of a background chorus, which may just be his group vocalizing). It is driven by a smooth pedal steel guitar, a nice country fiddle, and an incessant backbeat that almost seems inserted for commercial purposes (predicting the drum-machine steadiness that fueled 1980s music, with the similar intent of providing dancers with a rhythm they could rely on). Hogsed's vocal is cheerful and clear (diction-wise). This was radio music, audience-ready and cleanly executed in that wiseass, homegrown way.

More conservatively placed along the country music spectrum were the **Church Brothers**, whose **Darling Brown Eyes (ca. 1950)** is straight bluegrass without much variation. This is still tradition, and hardly even dressed up in modern cloth. In a funny way this recording is very much in the new American image of backwoods country amiability - like the kind of Mayberry jam sessions you used to see on the Andy Griffith Show. Which isn't a way of damning with faint praise, because that show was probably one of the few to ever get any form of American vernacular music right (there was one memorable show with the band The Kentucky Gentleman in which the legendary Clarence White appeared; and Griffith himself was a good guitarist and singer). *Darling Brown Eyes* is secular-pious, a non-new form of country song in which love and death become occasions for affirmation of faith. For country music this was old reliable, a theme with variations that it would turn to over and over again.

But speaking of frantic (see my Roy Hogsed entry, above), bluegrass, perhaps most acutely when out of the spotlight, was still ready and willing to throw caution to the wind, in the spirit of not just virtuosity but of country bragging rights. This was apparently the music of a growing cult of dedicated pickers, like Buster Pack, a Virginia boy who, it has been said, very early on defeated Ralph Stanley (of the Stanley Brothers bluegrass duo) in an instrumental contest. **Buster Pack and his Lonesome Pine Boys** recorded for a Southie independent label called Rich-R-Tone which, as far as a I can determine, leaned toward new-grass and other forms of free-range country music that were thriving far from the so-called centers of country music's activity.

(And as I was doing a little online research for this section I found a wonderful Rich-R-Tone recording by someone named Earl Peterson, *The Sky is Falling Down,* which now makes me want to self-flagellate at having missed it for inclusion in this study. *The Sky is Falling Down* would fit perfectly into something we might call "Underground Country," as a study of the kind of unselfconscious and unpretentious, lyric, sincere, really deep performances that are not only currently virtually non-existent - even in the so-called realm of alt.country, good but hyper-slick and self conscious as it occasionally is - but that are what keep me caring about country music in the face of an almost complete loss of its soul; and which is the whole reason I spend so much time listening and collating these kinds of songs into collections like this).

**Better Late Than Never**, which Buster and his boys recorded in **1952**, is like a late-early flowering of bluegrass. The music had already spawned a lot of satellite disciples who nurtured it in their own sincere, preservationist, if somewhat irreverent and wacky way. Those aspects of bluegrass that were already becoming somewhat ossified - the sheer speed of execution, the passing of the musical baton internally from instrument-to-instrument - are plainly and even sometimes painfully obvious in performances like this, but more relevant is the un-jaded spirit of musical adventure present in each re-worked phrase of the music. There is a frat-boy solidarity to this, a keenness of purpose in the tight harmonies and instrumental acuity - listen to the way the banjo, at 1:41 onward, switches octaves for effect, pushing this, like a wild horse race, toward the formulaic ending that had become, for these country boys, the musical equivalent of Charlie Parker's insertion, at the end of certain bebop romps, of a quote from Percy Grainger's *Country Gardens*.

There is a sameness to the new-grass virtuosity of these years (even more so later on), but it is possible that hearing it as such is the equivalent to the way some people hear bebop, as just a giant splotch of speed and noise. Maybe the ears have to grow accustomed to the way in which all of this flows together, less like a smooth-flowing stream than as choppy rapids. Or maybe not; technically speaking, unlike bebop, Bluegrass uses, over and over, the same chord progressions and the same, pentatonic-like country patterns for soloing (which begs a few questions of bebop's own repetitions, but I won't get bogged down with that question except to note that what many people hear as repetition and sameness in "modern" jazz reflects their lack of technical grasp. Even Louis Armstrong, baffled by bebop, referred to it as "Chinese music," clearly indicating that it was, even to him, just a mass of noise).

**Old Grey Goose**, by **Red Belcher and the Kentucky Ridgerunners (Early 1950s)** is a case in point. What I like most about recordings like this is how the old analog way of recording, with all the musicians in the same room around a few microphones, permitted a natural-born chaos that no recording engineer in our current-day would allow. All the better for us to hear and understand the power and energy that this music exuded. From the git-go it is like a Ramones performance, fast and furious, a rave from A to Z. These guys meant it, and it translates directly into music, preserved on recordings like this one as an extension of, to coin a cliche, life. Once again this was the day of the deep-country Indie, of record labels who scoured the woods looking for hillbillies who were no longer hillbillies but rather 20th century men and women with 20th century ideas. Some of them (like Buster Pack, above) flailed around commercially (Buster tried his hand, with some good effect but little lasting value, at rockabilly before receding into the life of nine-to-five), and most of them ended up with day jobs (though one might make the argument that in this particular world *music* was a day job; talk about the creative economy). Still, this is much more than a time capsule. It is a real thing, a frame of reference that frames an entire culture, and a musical belief system that persists to this day.

Speaking of sheer virtuosity, look out for **Arkansas Traveler** by **Jimmy Bryant and Speed West 12/8/53**. Both of these men were true country jazzers, and they and their fellow travelers (like Homer and Jethro and Hank Garland) codified, in the Nashville studio world of these years, a new kind of country virtuosity. They had actual jazz chops and were educated musically but able to make it all sound, at country sessions, like down-home slick. They knew the changes and, unlike most of the bluegrass players, they had the true jazz touch of chromaticism and flex-time.

Though *Arkansas Traveler* is done mostly as a display/set piece, we can hear throughout that Bryant in particular has a jazz education - listen to the line he starts playing at 1:33, which is an uncanny variation on *Arkansas Traveler's* traditional melody, fused with a classic country scale and a twist of jazz harmony. Bryant, like West, was a new-country studio man in these years, of the kind who, called upon to interpret virtually any kind of country tune, showed up, tuned up, and kept it real.

And if the new country was going to fuse itself with jazz, what better model, for the country gospel quartet, than the Mills Brothers? The Mills Brothers were a black vocal quartet who had long presented themselves as a pop/jazz machine of knowing sophistication and smart versatility. Their best work was done in their early years, when they took the rhythms of the Swing Era and converted them to vocal instrumentation, imitating brass and saxophone sections and integrating voice and instrumental accompaniment like a band-in-a-box. They were broadly popular, so it is no surprise that their work bled across racial lines. We certainly hear that whole Mills-Brothers-by-way-of-black-vocal group sound on the **Bob Angliano Quartet** version of **Bye and Bye (1953)**. We might think, at first hearing, that these guys are black, but it soon becomes clear that this is just a bit more vanilla. There is a bit less movement in the harmonies, and, most particularly, a higher musical center of gravity, something which (with apologies, and to repeat myself) is coming, more and more, to separate white and black popular music. Still, this is a convincing piece of old-time religion, and, yes, it swings. The harmony is very much a function of the rhythm, and it skirts the question of whether using the devil's music (basically, anything of black derivation) to circumvent the devil is appropriate. Personally I think this is a good thing, and I also doubt that anyone in their congregation and/or audience had a clue as to the real and deeper musical lineage of *Bye and Bye*. This was the South, after all, where the whole act of of white cultural appropriation was as natural as the natural selection of segregated life and racial discrimination, and where official and publicly-acknowledged cultural *integration* was still just a twinkle in Group Captain Parker's eye.[36]

If you are having company and they just happen to be a bunch of white liberals and you want to drive them to distraction put on **There is Only One** by the **Four Leaf Clover Quartet (1953)** and watch how things develop. I am partial to a particular kind of white religious singing, though it's the kind of thing that a lot of Northern progressives feel superior to: first of all it is non-reflective to a fault, with a kind of amateur, we-are-all-at-home around the stove ethos (or on the porch or in the living room); it is deathly sincere, which does not, even when it is also unpretentious, mean it is worthwhile or listenable, unless it is coupled with a particular brand of white, heartfelt expression of either actual or accurately-synthesized faith. It doesn't matter if we cynical liberals, based on out knowledge of historical events and the latter-day sins of evangelicals and other cults, feel that such honesty is really a form of dishonesty. Or that these people are all unsophisticated, cornball fakes. To my way of thinking this is where the soul of man and woman not only dies with some regularity, but where that soul also transcends political beliefs and events, where the great leveler is an artful ability to voice meaning-as-belief, even if that belief is based on elements of what we might label hypocrisy, and rationalized with dead systems of conviction and ideals. This whole method of performance, dignified yet still capable of emotional meaning and even explosion, is transparently and audibly naive. Paradoxically there is no authentic innocence in any of this, only one that is rebuilt self-consciously out of faith. These Christians are capable of creating their own artificial universe built on despair as praise. It is as though the need to constantly affirm and reaffirm

---

[36] Yes I mean that venerable old con man and musical grifter, Elvis' manager Colonel Parker, whose title I have adapted to the more appropriate German reference of rank (yes, I know he wasn't German) and also to make reference to Dr. Strangelove.

their own righteousness has left a rawness in their souls, a wound that reopens whenever they return to the source of their troubles and their supposedly godly resolution - meaning that the belief system upon which all of this is based is built on a religious house of cards that has already, for over 400 years, tumbled and crumbled so many times over and been reconstructed so many times over as to make the revisiting of all the old sins a deliberate waste of time; it is still commercially and religiously profitable. So, having negated itself by the power of its own hypocrisy and by its own sense of the falseness of the system by which it lives, religion of this sort is left with nothing but a *sound*, with lyrics that really mean nothing to anyone anymore as *lyrics*. The only thing in this that has meaning is that *sound*, of the rising lead, of the convergence of quartet harmony with a transparent belief system. And yet, having lost all connection to reality or true human virtue, this music persists, for the sake of the *sound*, and nothing else. Proving once more that music, at its essence, is not only a-political, but that religious music, at its essence, is non-religious.

Cajun music of these years succeeds by refusing to relinquish its own unique view of musical history, even as it moves into the modern era - mostly by doing what it always did before but with a more youthful way of doing it, though with old attitude. Hence, **Grande Nuit Especial** by **Iry LeJeune (1953)**, which is a dancing, tradition-ladened (but not burdened) trip down a lane with some, if rapidly fading, memories. Cajun, first a commercial phenomena in the 1920s, had been swayed, in the interim years, by the string bands sound of country, and had forged ahead with its own Western-Swing hybrid of lead fiddle and hoarse-voiced vocals. By the 1950s the venues in which it - and much of country music - made a living had coarsened somewhat, from outdoor stages and dances under the sky to roadhouse and roughhouse dance halls. But suddenly the music of Cajun did a bit of a turnabout, bringing the accordion back up front and into the lead. LeJeune, killed at the side of a road while changing a flat tire (at age 26), was an unlikely, accordion-playing revolutionary who struggled early on against the dominance of the fiddle in contemporary Cajun song. It was only through some persistence that he and band broke through, to an audience that was apparently quite happy to relive old times. This was an energy music, perfect for dance, and refocused by the strength of that incessant, double-timing accordion. It was like a return, as well, to the more emotionally-direct ways of old; listen to that deeply affecting "oh" in the vocal at .31, which we might, glibly and incorrectly, call out in its relationship to the blues cry of old. No, this was the Cajun cry of yore, and if it bore any relationship to the blues this was in its actively passive acceptance of fate.

1953 was the year before Elvis' great breakthrough and, as in the years just before the revolution that was bebop, musical change was in the air, as country looked at and reassessed its own set ideas of formula and necessity. Note that in **1953** the song **Rock Me** was billed as by **Lucky Joe Almond**; by August 1954, after Elvis had checked in, the band (which I should mention was white) was called Lucky Joe Almond and his Hillbilly Rockers (Elvis had released the shockingly new *That's All Right Mama* just two months earlier). *Rock Me* was made the year before, and it's clear, from the sound, the terminology, and the whole musical stance, that there was something new happening, or just about to happen.

The song was written by Willie Perryman, and there is nothing subtle about where it stands in relation to the meaning of "rock me," which, as we have seen, had both sexual and religious implication (which, out of the black tradition from which it came, may have seemed scandalous to some but was, even so, pretty much accepted as a way of taking the emotional temperature of the song; sometimes passion meant rolling in the aisles, sometimes it meant rolling in bed). Perryman was Piano Red, brother of the great pianist/singer Speckled Red (see Vols. 15, 20, 29). Not as overtly talented as his brother, he had a sound and style that was the definition of home-cooked music. He didn't have much in the way of what we might call piano technique, and he didn't have much in the way of a singing voice, but in combination it was like listening to the great earth-mother of the blues rising out of the underground (an underground, by the way, that Jelly Roll Morton, in his Library of Congress Recordings, clearly recognizes as one, very disreputable, antecedent of jazz). Perryman's composing was like a great distillation of all that the black vernacular had left behind in terms of play-song lyrics, melodic repetition, and the back-room pleasures of bawdy simplicity. Almond, of whom I know very little (and who, interestingly enough, recorded for Trumpet Records, which was largely a blues label) takes it all in stride, with country-music delight. He knows where and when to twang it, and he knows where and when to lean on it with a blues-white, sexual taunt.[37]

In these days it feels like the *idea* of rock and roll is a gasoline-soaked pile of tinder just waiting for Elvis to commence ignition. How else to account for singers like not just Joe Almond but also **Charlene Arthur (I Heard About You, 1953)**? Arthur predicts and reflects country sass and brash, sometimes non-sexual, female aggressiveness, from Texas Ruby to Wanda Jackson (see Vols. 23, 30), Loretta Lynn and even Dolly Parton. It probably took rock and roll, as a form and attitude, to fully liberate women singers in this vein; even country feminists like Kitty Wells (see Vol. 29), great as they were, seemed committed to monogamy as a women's-way-of-life, and were largely tethered to male expectations of their ultimate role in that life. What they rebelled against was not domesticity but its absence, the way in which men had a freedom of movement which they not only were denied, but didn't really want. They just wanted those men, at the end of the day, to come home and stay home. By 1953 Arthur, who was known for her absolute professional independence, had gotten - and was giving out - the message of country sexual equality. It wasn't just in what she was singing but in the way she was singing it. Her tone was pissed off, dismissive, and way beyond the resigned disappointment of Wells, whose persona was more like that of someone who expected little more than she got, unfaithfulness and an empty bed.

Extremely interesting is the fact that Arthur was discovered by Colonel Parker (soon to become Elvis' managerial auteur) and brought to RCA, where she recorded in 1952. She was also reportedly an influence on Elvis; her defiance, anti-sentimentality, and blunt-force application of lyric were new ways of singing that Elvis also explored, though her career, unlike his, faded from a lack of sales and, probably, the realization that a woman could knock her head against that glass-rocker's ceiling as much as she liked, and even with great effect, but could never ever really expect to break through it.

In spite of all of this country-flailing, successful and not, at the rock and roll dream, and despite the circe-like lure of

---

[37] Which is something of an answer to those who worry about black stereotypes in old song, of sexual insatiability. It is just as prevalent in white song of country variation, back to hillbilly ditties of single and obvious entendre.

Nashville, there were still lines of the music that expressed a real sense of, at least, the idea of independence. Singers like **George Jones (You Gotta Be My Baby, 1954)** were more in line with the Hank Williams wing of the music than with the smooth-as-a-baby's-butt production values of country balladeers; but though they continued to sing for the Grand Ol' Opry and tour with the Louisiana Hayride (which was as down-home as it gets) they were still, in many ways, trapped by the Nashville song machine. Sometimes that machine turned out good material, though it seemed that certain singers, like Jones, either had poor taste or bad professional advice. I realize that this is a minority opinion, but having listened to a lot of Jones' work and having scoured Youtube and viewed a lot of his television appearances, it sounds to me like either he or his management had decided to try and tame the wild streak that made his personal life so chaotic, by picking songs that were in some imagined mainstream, from ballads to predictable honky-tonkers. In other words he was a better singer than the songs he sang, with that curling voice (a la Lefty Frizell, see Vol. 25) and deceptively casual country soul, which seemed to hold back a lot of blues and passion. *You Gotta Be My Baby* is perfectly nice, sung well and paced like the mainstream style it now represents. But Hank Williams it ain't, though it does follow the honky tonk pattern musically and rhythmically. As a song it just seems to sit on the shelf, avoiding what someone may have seen as the pitfalls, in the new modern country era, post-Hank, of revealing one's true and actual self.

Black lines of music in this era continues to defy some of our ideas of black-and-blues continuity. Even as the idea of sales and mass appeal started to clamp itself more and more tightly around the body of popular and vernacular music, a lot of it still stayed loosely outside of the (perceived) mainstream, wriggling free with a little help from independent record labels. As I mentioned earlier, in the years before Elvis, Sam Phillips of Sun Records explored the Memphis blues underground. This gave us **Junior Parker**, whose work from those years remains, for me at least, as some of the most prescient and creative, giving Elvis a pre-run for his money. In later years Parker, a terrific singer with a deep, liquid voice, moved more toward the blue center, with a classic blues and rhythm and blues approach based on the common, post-shuffle ideas of the day. In **1953**, however, he gives us what amounts to a full-fledged blues taste of rockabilly, yes, rockabilly. Performances like his **Love My Baby** are early rock and roll, in a way that is not, at first, easy to grasp, but which soon becomes obvious. Memphis must have been a fluid and fertile musical scene in those days; this is full of new ideas and rocking implication.

Listen to the opening guitar phrase of *Love My Baby*. What is that and where did it come from? No, it's not a blues derivative, much as we have been conditioned to place everything that comes from black musicians into that blues framework (this reminds me of what the writer Paul Beatty said in an old interview when asked if, as a writer, he was "signifying." "Isn't that," he responded with annoyance, "what they say about any black man who does anything?" Well, the blues has come to serve the same function, as a way of characterizing just about anything a black musician plays).

But back to that opening; it is like a blues paraphrase of some old hillbilly idea, in the time, the notes, and the intervals. Sure, the flat third grabs you at first, but then the little run at about .05 delivers a classic, country, descending line that starts from the sixth and bends the flat third into a major third - this is anything but the blues. Was Scotty Moore (Elvis' guitarist) listening? Well, something tells me that this was part of some shared musical world. And even if it came from white sources - which it very well may have, given its pentatonic connection to possibly even old-white fiddle music - who else was synthesizing it in this (literally) electric way in 1953? The only equivalent that I have heard was Utah Smith (see Vol. 22), who was fusing old black sources with old white sources and running with it in a way that no one else of his day was. And the whole rhythmic thrust of *Love My Baby* - well, turn your time machine forward to Elvis' Vegas years, because this was the rhythm with which they brought him onstage, riff-based, of the kind that players like Parker soon abandoned for more mainstream blues sounds. But did they lose as much as they gained when they recalibrated their music for the blues mainstream? And does the abandonment of this whole approach tell us that the re-focus by Phillips and others on white rock and roll was not simply based on racialist formula, but as much on a clear racial/musical dividing point, and one that only a few people at the time divined?

Parker also explored this new and fascinating musical territory, as a kind of chugging, free-form blues with twanging country guitar, in **Feelin' Bad**, recorded the same year **(1953)** for Phillips once again. This has more of a typical blues motion, but with a crucial and style-defying difference: remember how I have cited, in various places throughout this study, what I call a rise in the center of musical gravity as a sign of rock and roll's largely white, new musical emphasis? Well, here it is in embryo; although this follows a fairly typical blues route (there's that riff-like rhythm again), the new musical/lead emphasis is on the treble-drenched sound of the lead guitar, which carries this performance all of the way through and gives it, for want of a better word, its *meaning*, as a driven, new, black-country music, leaning toward "white" by means of its sonic *clarity* - and I use that word (clarity) carefully, because it is racially-charged in this context. I am speaking in relative terms, about the separation of musical elements in this, the division of instruments, and the layering of instruments, rhythm and voice. This is something we haven't heard much of before, at least on record (though I am assuming, correctly or not, that it reflected things that were happening outside of Sun Records' studio as well). So while this whole performance stays within certain blues limitations, it stretches those limitations to the limit, telling us that something much more complicated, stylistically and racially, was happening in Memphis.

In Chapter 26 I described **Charlie Booker** as being part of "the last great stage of the first great stage of post-war electric blues." Certainly **Baby I'm Coming Home (1952)** fits this description, as another of the powerful, riff-based blues things that sounded between country and the city. There was a new energy to these kinds of performers and these kinds of performances, no doubt fueled by the (relatively) new electrified guitar and the now common sense that every blues band needed a drummer (even Muddy Waters, who arrived musically, in Chicago, drummer-less, had to be convinced by the Chess brothers that this was the way to go).

*Baby I'm Coming Home* is basically blues with a boogaloo-boogie beat (not the right wing idiots, but the Latin rhythm), which relates it as well to that emergent clave, rhythm and blues thing, to New Orleans, and hence, yes, to rock and roll.

Also stylistically to the point in the new music was **Little Walter**'s startling and stark, electrified harp recording of **Blue Midnight (1952)**. I have read with amusement a lot of the critical attempts to explain Walter's novelty and appeal; he has been called the Charlie Parker of the blues harp because of his slick way of getting around the instrument. Yes, there was a rhythmic mobility to Walter's playing that distanced it from old-style country harmonica; but what made Walter unique was the way he drew from post-*Swing* rhythm and blues saxophonists, who growled and squealed and riffed. Little Walter applied this approach directly to the mouth harp. Just as important was the way he amplified the instrument, creating a cavernous, dramatic sense of pause and sustain - it took electrification to do this, just as guitarists used the new sustain effect inherent in tube compression to let single notes ring out and breathe. Walter had soul to spare, and he expressed it by way of the harmonica's paradoxically thin-but-rich sonic texture, the way in which its notes rose and faded with harsh overtones that implied all kinds of tonal possibilities. What he was doing was helping, in the modern blues, to re-establish the polytonality that was central to nearly all post-Diasporan black music (though expressed in varied ways; jazz musicians in the modern era implied tonal ambiguity by the way in which they leap-frogged through chords and related scales; blues players like Little Walter got a similar effect by letting the individual notes speak, behind and in front of the beat, with vibrato and variation and odd, atonal resonance - though of course jazz players did this too at times, if generally in less exaggerated ways). Through it all Little Water was a core bluesman - listen to that emotional shake he makes at 1:45 and just afterward.

Another amazing little oddity is **Blue Smitty and his String Men,** whose blue dirge (**Crying, 7/11/52**) is a prime example of how to take what at first sounds like a gimmick - that trilling guitar solo heard from beginning to end - and turn it into new color, a background that sounds obtrusive but then becomes a part of the natural mix (foreground as both foreground and background? This may have been a very black form of sound-stage). Let me explain what I am thinking here: in the early years of multi-track, once engineers realized that they had the power to control every level of every instrument in relative terms - meaning the sonic balance in both micro and macro terms, the ability to move any instrument from a position of ensemble dominance to one of background - then we all were, in terms of balance and clarity of sound, in some trouble. Many mixing engineers in the new age took this new sonic flexibility as meaning that every instrument could now be brought to the fore simultaneously, to sound in your face as part of the front line, while supposedly preserving the mix; in the process a lot of engineers turned ensemble sound into a big sonic mess. Sure, those drums and that bass could be reduced, level wise, as a corrective, but now everything was right in front of us, the sonic image unnaturally "alive" and annoyingly direct and unrelentingly bright. Everything felt (not in all recordings, of course, but frequently enough) like a cold splash of water.

The contrast between this and the old-school way of recording - live to one or two tracks, the group in the room arranged so as to produce a natural mix, matching much more closely what we hear in real-world experience - was made clear in the technological rush to multi-track convenience. This new method of multiple-track saturation was much easier for recording engineers to control and manipulate, especially as re-enforced by isolation techniques that made it sound like each individual musician had phoned in their performance (a problem that persists to this day). In the old days (meaning, with all of the recordings in this collection) sonic balance was created in the studio in real time, and though this often created its own problems, it is why, for certain kinds of music - jazz, blues, folk - many of those old, post-War (and even many pre-War) recordings sound better and more natural, easier on the ear than music recorded many years later - like musicians are actually playing together in the same acoustic space with sympathy and a sense of mutual support and response.

Which brings me back to *Crying,* a simple but effective slow blues in which that moveable guitar lead, gimmicky but a good fit for this small, acoustically perfect performance, turns it into a poignantly-musical plea bargain. What we hear in this recording that makes every element so clear is the *room*, the natural acoustics of a space, and the way in which these players, so obviously used to each other's way of playing, adjust to the space. We can hear how, instead of relying on an engineer in post-production, they self-calibrate, moving in and out of the sonic image, never really completely out of it but rather sometimes in the background, waiting patiently, with musical purpose, for their chance to return. The result is an audible, humane sense of musical empathy, a genuinely cooperative effort (and we could, but won't, go into the whole communal meaning of Diasporan music from which this feeling derives). The point is that this performance, this song, this singer, all have a reality that is too often denied us in the present-day world, in which recorded sound has regularly become just another symbol (though, yes, an often necessary one)[38] of mechanical, cultural distance.

I took several of these performances from a collection of what were considered to be anachronistic and late country blues performances, recorded by some small but determined record labels. These labels, who wandered off the beaten path looking for music and hoped, usually in vain, for a commercial breakthrough, still managed to preserve some essential ways of musical being. A lot of the old ways hadn't so much died as gone into cultural exile; as with **Country Jim Bledsoe**, who managed to get a perfect piece of country-blue pleading called **Dial 110 Blues** on record in **1952**. Bledsoe, about whom little is known except, perhaps, that he was born in 1925 and was from Shreveport, Louisiana, gives us another odd, out-of-time snapshot of local culture. This performance seems to exist in some other musical dimension, where the date of recording is less relevant than how well the music seems to match the interior life of the performer. Even if it sounds out of its time, it isn't; it is not a form of revivalism. When it is done right and done well, in whatever format, from blues to jazz, it is simply the music of that performer at that particular moment and in that particular place. It's neither new nor old; it just *is*.

*Dial 110 Blues,* in which Bledsoe seems to be accompanied by a very discreet drummer, is, like so many of these types of performances, done in a way that gives it a very life-like musical presence. It has what James Joyce described as the sense of something witnessed while already-in-progress, of events stumbled upon as they happen, in continuous fragments. Listen to the sudden riff that ends the tune, the way in which the song stops as abruptly as it started, likely after a signal from the recording engineer that the limit to the record's length had been reached. Like the life it reflects it's not an ending but a pause.

That same year **(7/52)** someone named **Bobo Thomas** went into a studio with **Sonny Boy Williams** (the second, real name Rice Miller) to record a new version of **Catfish Blues** (originally written and recorded by Robert Petway, see Vol. 21). *Catfish Blues* is

---

[38] What I mean here is complicated, as sometimes the alienation effect of certain kinds of music is also culturally central and necessary. I don't just mean electronic music, though that is one kind, but also music that is creatively pieced together by means of cut-and-paste, or that reflects an acoustic rejection of the so-called "real world," or that is an extension of a creative mind and process that rejects objective and representational sonics as expressed in linear form.

one of those tunes that reflects the Delta blues genius for subtle but trenchant variation, even within a form and tradition that encouraged repetition. The way Petway plays the chorded, constant riff of *Catfish Blues* is very effective, but what really makes the song are the verbal repeats at the end of each stanza, representing a significant formal departure from the usual blues-verse orthodoxy. Petway was "covered" by musicians like Muddy Waters and, in later years, Jimi Hendrix and Gary Clark. Unfortunately Clark, usually a very effective performer, misses the whole point of the composition in his version and turns it into just another riff-based electric blues. Clark's version seems based on Hendrix's which also, sad to say, misses the musical/textual point, avoiding those repeats (possibly because, like Clark, he has never heard the original), though Hendrix is such a powerful musical force that it seems to matter less. Thomas/Williamson's version is still deeply ensconced in the country blues stylistically, though there is something about the shared guitar/harmonica riff and its co-dominance that makes this something a bit different, not to mention Williamson's powerfully inserted harmonica. Together they are more faithful to Petway's original, and the juxtaposition of old/new is as a result much more effective, in its evocation of blues memory, than in either Clark's or Hendrix's version (and there is also a Johnny Winter performance which, to my surprise, also leaves out the repeats. Though happily, as I was finishing this section I discovered an acoustic Muddy Waters version recorded at one of the American Folk Festival tours of Europe in the 1960s. This not only remains faithful to Petway's formal innovation but is a perfect example of how musicians like Muddy, with unselfconscious access to the tradition, were able, with much more depth and a greater sense of personal discovery, to get at it from the inside).

Of course any kind of transformation, technological and otherwise, in the blues of the 1950s was welcomed by some musicians, resisted by others. As with all musical forms technology acted on it in sometimes unpredictable ways, though these were never divorced from more practical, living considerations.

A lot of this change was migratory in nature, as in the lives of the musicians who struggled with it. New venues and new audiences called for new techniques and also new ways to differentiate one's self from the musical crowd. The incredible guitarist **Guitar Slim,** an almost-literally electric performer, amped up his guitar like a Sanctified preacher, and along the way started using longer and longer guitar cords, which allowed him to roam among club audiences and even out into the street. Slim, from New Orleans, was a revolutionary performer not just because he played the electric guitar, but because of *how* he played it: loud, distorted to a the point of cognitive interference, and with an intensity that was disruptive to the old established blues moods of husky contemplation or contented boogie. This was not the way of busking, of street musicians or even of new city bands as they plugged in and wailed away in small, smoky clubs. This was a new form of blues aggression, and Slim played it for all it was worth, with emotional highs and lows worthy of that Sanctified Church (reminding me of that New Orleans connection, of that city where indigenous musicians like Sammy Price and Pleasant Joe both, in their autobiographies, cited the Holy Rollers - a particularly virulent sect of sanctified religionists - as being a root-cause of jazz and other down-home New Orleans music).

All of this is apparent, with some limitations imposed by the studio, on Slim's pile-driving recording of **The Story of My Life (10/26/53)**. Listen, first, to the way his guitar-lead responds to his own near-maudlin vocal, as a kind of anti-sentimental counterpoint, with piercing, spiky, staccato riffs. And then there is that stunning guitar solo at 1:45. I might even guess that this is where Hendrix got his heaviest sonic ideas, from guitarists like Slim, whose sonic innovations were all based on using the tools at hand. We don't know everything that Hendrix listened to, though we do know he was voracious in his musical appetites and unafraid to beg, steal, and borrow from every blues and pop direction (and to publicly acknowledge same). Slim, along with Elmore James (see Vol. 26) was the commander of a new Guitar Army, marching to the sound of newer and more powerful amplifiers, better guitar pickups, and a recording technology that was, day by day, become more and more accommodating to pure *sound*, to things previously unheard in the developing world of white - and even a lot of black - aesthetic consciousness.[39]

A book was published years ago called *Poets in Their Youth,* about a generation of brilliant writers whose lives were much less orderly than their work. The interesting thing about it all, aside from the mess some of them made of their families and relationships, was how freshly they looked at life in these early years, how much good poetry they made out of events and lives that were anything but poetic. To read about all of this was to identify with the relative innocence of early creativity. It's a time when there seems to be little if anything standing between one's self and imaginative re-invention; early work, good and bad, seems to come together with a relative ease. There is less conscious resistance to ideas as they flow freely, though it doesn't always last, as life presents new and persistent ways to block or stunt creativity.

A similar book might be written about Musicians in their Youth, about the early and amazing blooming of work by certain musicians, of the kind that seems not just mature in outlook but almost innocently revelatory. This means everyone from Charlie Parker, who burst onto the jazz scene seemingly fully developed, to Louis Armstrong (whose first music was not just spectacularly original, but synthesized from what can only be assumed were personal, internalized forces of a classic, everyman's, radical vision), to bluesmen like Charley Patton (a ghostly, haunting force of sepulchral strangeness and splendor), Robert Johnson (a moody genius whose moods were recorded), to **Muddy Waters**. Waters (see also Vol. 22), "discovered" by Alan Lomax living in a small cabin on a plantation, seems ready to roll, professionally speaking, on his first plantation recordings from 1942, though as we now know there was a lot more to come. By **9/24/53**, when he records **She's**

---

[39] I mention this in spite of my general aversion to political correctness, because it was white people who controlled a great deal of that world of recording and distribution. And it also made me think of George Martin's recollections of when he started work at British EMI; the technicians who were employed there all wore lab coats and made sure everything was properly balanced and recorded according to an unofficial, internalized Rule Book. Any idea of distortion and re-tracking, reverse dubbing, etc, was a Limey no no, which was something that his new clients the Beatles struggled against in instinctive and musical ways. To our incalculable benefit their popularity bought them a freedom which had long-term artistic and industry effects.

**All Right**, he is well into the second act of an amazing and varied career.

Muddy was a force of some kind of nature, but not one that had necessarily been previously identified as present in the world of American popular music. He was a *presence*, on record and in clubs - though the professional integration of regional label with local stardom was still something new in those days, very much an urban black thing, of hometown fame mixed with a dream of national fortune. By this time Muddy had a real band (something he resisted at first but which the Chess brothers insisted on) and it really brought out so much more of everything in his music. The ensemble feels like a blues collective, and Muddy responds with a new kind of blues power. This is the modern and essential blues personified, harmonica/guitar riffs (Little Walter is on harp) shadowing ever gesture, the lead voice rising like a vision of some kind of old/new music, the overwhelming sound of rhythm-as-inevitability. It is part reality show, part shaman ceremony, like a modern painting unveiled to sudden and mind-altering effect, technically overwhelming yet a clear sum of familiar parts.

The maudlin methods of black vocal music evolved in somewhat mysterious but stealth ways. There was a sound, newly popularized, of black lead singing that was less blues shouter than blue whisperer, as with Billy Wright (see Vol. 27). There were also, in the 1940s, black pop, quartet-based vocal groups, out of jazz but then into pop balladry. They were part of the pre-history of doo wop - a group vocal sound that owed its feeling to older, Jubilee gospel styles, with liquid harmonies and gently flowing leads. Out of all of this came the black pop crooner, applying that gentle and oh-so-slightly effeminate sound to both earlier jazz balladry (the black band singer Pha Terrell) and, later, proto-soul material. One of the most distinct of these was **Johnny Ace**, whose recordings (like **Saving My Love For You (12/53)** are usually cited, correctly, as an early sign of a new thing called Soul Music (a category of song which developed more completely in the 1960s, and which combined gospel-emotionality with some blue tonality but a more expansive, ballad-like approach; done in the service of what were basically black pop tunes constructed from late, neo-song-form harmonies and simplified lyrics, and recorded, with a lot of exceptions, with lush, full instrumentation surrounding hard-blues-like rhythm sections). Ace had a gentle voice with feeling, and his sessions were produced, significantly, by Johnny Otis, a bandleader who had a real feel for jazz-tinged rhythm and blues, which made him a star in those in-between years (in-between, that is, the end of World War II, the commercial fading of conventional, jazz-based swing bands, and the start of rock and roll). Otis saw the gold that was to be made from the sudden and deep-selling stratification of new black musical styles, with everything from big-band-backed blues shouting to treacly, soul/maudlin balladry to jazz-like horn-shouters walking an imaginary bar in the space of a three-minute single. Johnny Ace was one of his proteges (as was Esther Phillips, see Vol. 30). Ace sang with great poise yet was appealingly immature, teen-like to the bone. Such was the new identity politics of American pop.

I don't know who or what **Louis Armstrong**'s demographics were, as he set himself up to enter his fifth decade of life. Everyone? He certainly (like Elvis in his supposedly declining years) thought of himself as a musical everyman. His producers threw a lot of music at Armstrong in those days, some good and some bad, but to his credit he treated everything like it was a Harold Arlen tune. **The Gypsy**, a pop ballad written in 1945 and recorded by Armstrong on **10/22/53**, was something in-between, an extremely good song that seemed to have been written with down-scale ambition for a less discerning pop audience. The song itself had a strong melody and good chord changes - Charlie Parker recorded it for Dial in the year it was written - and it was a very good vehicle for Decca Records-era Armstrong. It allowed for a bit more vocal restraint than in some of his earlier and wilder pop departures (after all this was the 1950s, when the strains of his earlier pop radicalism where somewhat under wraps, in the service of a new and more sage-like sound of wizened observer). *The Gypsy* coats him with a very nice and very "contemporary" arrangement (floating brass and the chunk-chunk-chunk of a rhythm guitar), launching a beautifully paced and satisfyingly long trumpet solo that shows the genius and revolutionary soloist of yore had been, contrary to myth, wide awake and listening through the intervening years; this is about as majestic a thing as he ever played, with a beautiful, fat tone. There was still an art to his art.

As **Miles Davis** said, even as he was picking away at and discarding the most intimate connections between his and Armstrong's music (the populist symmetry of phrasing, the knack for perfect melodic paraphrase, and the sonic talent each had for showing how the notes themselves were often less important than the way in which they were expressed), "You can't play anything on a horn that *Louis* hasn't played." Maybe he was right, maybe not, because truthfully, much as I revere Louis Armstrong, I have never heard him play anything that sounds remotely like **Tempus Fugit,** which Miles recorded in **1953.**

Miles was many things, a cutting and unsentimental cultural commentator yet sometimes an incurable romantic and sentimental sap, if in new, razor-cut-like ways. The jazz world had never before seen his brand of well-paced sexual sarcasm, and most took it, understandably, as sheer romanticism. What else could you say about a musician whose private life was as violently (and I mean this literally) chaotic and dismissive as his musical life was orderly and calculated, with vision and pace and a sense of an artistic business plan that kept an image of audience - or some idea of it - in sharp focus? Of course, things like *Tempus Fugit* show a side of Miles that was less concerned with getting ahead than with a kind of impulsive, consciously disorganized (because it kept everyone else off balance), musical behavior. From the top, this piece (composed by Bud Powell) is like a distraction - from bebop as it had become a bit too organized, from lovelorn balladry, from a cool aesthetic that was beginning to be espoused to the point (as I have a feeling Miles knew) of deranged journalistic and critical cliche. This performance is the sound of planned near-desperation, of an anxiousness to let go of the more obvious things Miles had learned in the rush of his brief but intense bebop apprenticeship. The opening phrase of his solo is a clear expression of anti-bebop, one of those things that Miles seemingly invented, like a jazz scale to nowhere, a reaching up toward harmonic areas closed off once the tune, with its multiple and accelerating chord changes, is launched. Though even in the midst of a very good, bop-based series of lines he finds ways to escape the obvious, with elongated phrases of mid-air-like pause and grace, emphasized with that cool bite of emotionless heat he was so good at projecting.

Some people called the jazz pianist **Lennie Tristano** (see also Vol. 22) cool, cold even, but as Lenny probably would have been the first to say, that was exactly the point, whether they got it or not. Jazz had been through one revolution already when Tristano arrived like a seer, surrounded, cult-like, by followers who eagerly accepted his theories on the dangers of ego and emotion. Though I am sure that Lenny, were he alive, would tell me I was completely full of shit (because he was the kind of guy, and I have known many of this type, who could never allow someone else to put words in their mouths, even if they were their *exact* words), he believed that systems of intellectual analysis, smartly applied, could save art from itself, from the propensity of forms (and especially jazz) to repeat themselves and rely upon ideas that had already been absorbed into the mainstream through predictability and repetition. His belief, whether I agree or not as to specifics, was not that emotion was bad, but that certain kinds of it were just the ego in disguise.

He certainly proved the possibilities inherent in this system and approach. His recorded work and that of his disciples, from 1946 on, shows that jazz did, indeed, even after bebop, need someone like him to come and goose it along in the direction of greater harmonic and rhythmic flexibility. His solos were inspired by bebop, with some of its typical intervals and phrasing, but with a lot of twists and odd turns in the direction of unusual resolution and stuttering, outer-directed rhythms. The music was very tonal at the same time that it allowed for polytonality, though, as with Charlie Parker, Tristano et al (like the saxophonists Warne Marsh and Lee Konitz) it showed how some of the furthest of intervals could be resolved in both non-consonant and consonant ways (and the results still discomfited many listeners). It is also interesting to note that in spite of Tristano's predilection for relatively straight-on ways of playing the piano he was still able to come up with a recording, in **1953**, that was as radical a departure from jazz orthodoxy as **Descent Into the Maelstrom** (the title of which was taken from a short story written by Edgar Allan Poe) was. *Descent* is a ruminating abstraction of line and cluster, radically revolutionary in its fearless commitment to sound and noise (and no one in the jazz world was doing anything remotely like this in 1953, though in a few years Cecil Taylor, who I don't believe heard this, started to evolve toward his own and similar theories of melodic rhythm).

We might think of this type of thing as experimental, but I have grown to hate that word when used in relation to art. There is no sense in this that Lenny was experimenting in any way. He was simply playing from a different side of his id (he might have told us if asked), a side where the supposedly "natural" tendencies of jazz improvisation were overcome by certain conscious and unconscious forces of internalized chaos, derived from the natural world but also corralled and made into something of non-formal beauty.

And then there's **Big Bill Broonzy**, a powerful and benevolent force in the post-War blues world (as Muddy Waters told it Broonzy was a kind man who helped anyone who needed it in those years of professional struggle and adjustment). Though Broonzy was still a few years off from his great commercial success in the 1950s version of the folk revival, his recorded worked showed how open he was to new ideas and how formally clever he remained. **Diggin' My Potatoes**, which he recorded with his cousin **Washboard Sam** in **1953**, is a remarkable piece of musical prophecy. Once more I note that the evolution toward called rock and roll involved a higher sense tonal gravity, an emphasis away from the bass-heavy sound of rhythm and blues, a near-acoustic lightness of being, and the use of those upper-frequencies as a kind of rhythmic accelerant (all of which was probably powerfully effected by the Southern acoustic blues). *Diggin' My Potatoes* is rockabilly by any other name, a city/country mesh of two-beat time (kept on the washboard, though there does appear to be a bass in this as well), and countrified guitar (there is a de-emphasis in this on blues intervals). Broonzy is an amazing musical conceptualist; listen to the guitar double stops at .52 and you feel like you are on an episode of Hee Haw, in the middle of one of those relaxed, good-ol'-boys, behind-the-(cardboard)-barn jam sessions. Was this a way a lot of black musicians were playing in these years (if so I would like to hear more than the very few recordings which reflect it)? Was Broonzy, like Chuck Berry (see Vol. 30) listening to a lot of white hillbilly music (I have a feeling he was, since this is the most obvious explanation)? This a rare and unusual sound and, I say with some pride, I remain deeply puzzled as to why, in the succeeding years, no one but me has ever noticed or cited it.

The singer **Eddie Jefferson**, in an old interview, was asked about how he came up with the idea of "vocalese," which is the name that has been given to a method by which jazz singers took the melodies of improvised horn solos and fitted lyrics to them. He told of having a conversation with the singer/jiver Leo Watson (see Vol. 22), who had made something of a career out of fitting nonsense, hipster syllables to pop/jazz melodies. Watson, he remembered, believed "he had taken scat about as far as it could go…he advised me to sing lyrics. You know, like you could still improvise but do it with lyrics." Jefferson, as far as we can determine, was the first to do this in this particular way, and others (like King Pleasure) were quick to lift from his inspiration and sometimes his lyrics. The result was a strangely powerful, novelty approach, a ghosting of jazz musicians both living and dead (the most famous of which are probably Annie Ross' lyrics to Wardell Gray's tenor sax solo on *Twisted*, which hit the big time via Joni Mitchell's rendition).

Jefferson didn't have a good singing voice, per se, but he had a nice musical way with that whole lyric approach, as on his recording of **Body and Soul (7/11/52)**. Based on Coleman Hawkins' famous solo on the same tune (which to a lot of people's surprise, because of a complex yet linear harmonic development that virtually ignored the original Johnny Green melody, became an actual hit), Jefferson's version is built around a set of chord changes which remain fresh to this day, shaped as they are in a slightly unconventional way. Compositionally this was art music; Jefferson half-enunciates, half mumbles his way through it. He has a genuine warmth in his voice, limited as his range and as questionable as his intonation sometimes is. It all has an un-trained appeal as he swallows his syllables, never losing sight of solo/lyrics but sometimes sounding as though he needs to pull them out of his throat. It works well because he has a weird sense of cautious dynamics, as though he is thinking, or really saying, by way of his whole manner, "hey folks, if I could sing better I would."

# Chapter 28
# Dark Nights of the White Soul

I love categories, particularly musical. They make me feel good, they comfort me in times of great uncertainty. They make my life easier, and they make it a bit simpler to organized a collection as large and unwieldy as this.

First, in this volume, Country Music:

### Have I Waited Too Long Faron Young 1953
What's that old saying about living life to its fullest in the most reckless way possible? Oh yeah: live fast, die young, and leave a good looking corpse. The problem is, if in the process of living to excess you don't die young you end up going slower and slower, dying in middle age, and leaving a corpse that only a mother could love or grieve for. Country music is full of such men and women (well, really, mostly men), especially a few who I always picture, as I listen to, as rough guys who are working class no more, and whose hardest decision is whether to get up in the morning. So it was with Hank Williams (who actually did die young, but as a drunken, physical wreck) and then, for our purposes here, Faron Young, who shot himself at age 51 after experiencing some of the normal career ups and downs and killing his health with large doses of alcohol (and scaring a few people, including his wife, away by flashing and occasionally shooting off a gun). But whatever he did, to himself and others, he is, in those Nashville recordings, the exception who proves nothing except that Capitol Records, for whom he was recording, was smart enough to leave record producing to the country music professionals who, if they tolerated a certain amount of shlock, didn't send the real thing packing when they saw it.

*Have I Waited Too Long* is formulaic in that 1950s, Nashville way, but it's saved by Young's artistry. He has a powerful and resonant, plangent, post-Hank voice. The arrangement is not so cushy that we cannot hear what a fine sense of country pacing that he has, and how dramatically solid his understanding of country-song dynamics is. The story is typical, about the kind of honky-tonk lost-love that must have been a particular problem in those years; was there a bar somewhere where all the girls who dumped all the guys hung out and compared notes and break-their-hearts techniques? I don't know, but I do hear the way in which Faron Young refuses to coast on the memory of lovesick songs past, and the way his final phrase, pausing just before "too long" has the unmistakeable sound of, yes, truth.

### It Don't Hurt Anymore Hank Snow 12/16/53

In 1954 Hank Snow convinced the Grand Ol' Opry (a weekly country radio show with national waves) to book Elvis Presley, and for that alone we should be grateful, that some people in the country music industry still had their ears to the ground. Elvis opened for Snow, and at the same time was introduced to Tom Parker who, at first together with Snow, took over Elvis' management. Before long Snow was on the outs, Parker became Elvis' sole manager, and the rest is...well, the rest is an RCA contract, Elvis in the army, long-term drug addiction, Dr. Nick, more drugs, Los Vegas, and early death. Oh well.

But back to Snow: it's no secret that the so-called Nashville Sound (Snow moved there from Canada in 1949) was just another phrase for a cookie-cutter approach to songwriting and record production. Though by current-day standards those old and beautifully recorded songs (particularly by the Nashville majors, Capitol and RCA) are under-produced (these were the days of live recording in good rooms, and these recordings, many reissued in the CD age, still sound good), there was still a certain sameness to it all. On the other hand, after suffering through today's army of country hunks, line-dance twerkers, and hat acts, listening to 1950s Nashville song stylings can be something of a relief (yes, a lot of it sounds minimalist by comparison). In spite (or because?) of the new standardization of song there were more than a few singers who had a new-found warmth and consistency. Some of the songs were not that bad, with what felt like accurate emotional centers and serviceable melodies.

Songwriting in these days was basically assembly line and controlled by copyright-engorged song publishing companies, though the industry was more than tolerant of a few independent performers and composers (like Harlan Howard, Boudleaux and Felice Bryant, Johnny Cash). Some singers, like the aforementioned Faron Young and also Hank Snow, were able to not just overcome substandard material but also to convert it into something of lasting value. Not to mention that Snow had an early hit with a song he wrote, *I'm Movin' On*, that was a prophecy of changing times in country-world, and which is actually cited in some studies as an early "rock and roll" tune. I would tend to agree, as it is a country oddity in its time, full of musical and lyrical bombast, with rock and roll implications. Also excellent was Snow's recording of I*t Don't Hurt Anymore* which, once again, was inhabited by the usual instrumental suspects but was distinguished by that excellent lyric hook (wrongly reported initially as *I Don't Hurt Anymore*, and repeated this way through the years) and Snow's oddly-accurate Canadian-country drawl (which was really, in his voice, a slow, soulful, nasal projection, once again out of the dominant school of Hank Williams).

### Honky Tonk Gal Carl Perkins 1954

There were some performers out of Memphis in those years who suffered in more than one way from living professionally in the shadow of both Elvis Presley and Jerry Lee Lewis. One problem was how overwhelming both Presley and Lewis were in terms of popularity, by sales numbers. The second problem was related to the first. Sun Records, under Sam Phillips, a man of mammoth ego, had relatively few resources, financially and in terms of distribution, and either had to narrow the label's sights and focus on what it could focus on, or barter talent away (as when Phillips sold Presley's contract to RCA). Billy Lee Riley, a great, great singer of country, rock, and blues (I was lucky enough to work one gig with him in 2001) complained to the end of his life that his own career and chance at stardom had been sacrificed at the alter of Jerry Lee Lewis, who, after Elvis left the Sun Records building, had Sam Phillips' near-complete focus.

Carl Perkins' situation was a little more complicated. He was a classic country music journeyman musician, an excellent singer and accomplished guitarist who worked his way up and sideways through the juke-like circuit of white musicians of the late 1940s and early 1950s. He later described the music that he and his brother played in their early band as sounding very much like what Elvis did from about 1954, with souped-up, country-fried versions of honky tonk and old-school hillbilly. Certainly the way that he emerged musically, with excellent songs and a loose but effective grasp of the new rocking-billy idiom, showed, at the least, the likely truth of his statements. Unlike a lot of old-line country singers whose attempts to jump on the rock and roll bandwagon were marred by the laughable ways they jumped the tempos, hiccuping and muttering their way through faux rock and roll tunes (which tended to sound like unintended parody), Perkins was in it from (almost) the beginning, though clearly it took the stimulus that was Elvis Presley for him to completely adapt to the style. The problem he had, commercially, was that he wasn't Elvis, though it is likely he would have had more of a direct ascendance, career-wise, but for a bad car accident and an increasing alliance with the bottle.

Perkins is a perennial favorite, and he was lucky in the post-1960s rock world in that remained (unlike Elvis, who was quickly, by way of Los Vegas, placed on the big-haired pedestal that he sat on until he died) as one of the boys, keeping up the road-grind and sense of alcoholic immediacy. It helped him fit right in with the new rocker-hippy White Boys. He was also a fine guitarist and a solid singer. His 1952 recording of *Honky Tonk Gal* shows that he wasn't doing exactly as Elvis did two years later; he was still partially clad in post-Hank Williams' stylistic drag (listen to the little Hank-ish phraseology he turns out at .16). But - and remember, this is two years before Elvis' debut - there is a beat and drive to this that is prophetic, a four-on-the-floor kick that is significantly beyond what most honky tonkers could or would do at this time. And listen to the guitar solo he plays at .033! This really is an early world of near-rock, more succinct and soulful than even Scotty Moore's (Elvis' guitarist) more laid-back, country-nee-rock fret work. All done by Perkins on the treble pickup, it lays out what sounds like a template for the eternal values of rock and roll guitar. This is followed by some more Hank-ish vocal inflection, another perfect guitar solo, and a shout-like out chorus that, to my surprise when I first heard it, includes a replication of Arthur Crudup's "dee dee dee" scat-like vocal insertion, of the kind that Elvis included in some of his recordings (see Crudup, Vol. 25). What had we here? Well, more proof that Crudup was probably playing on a lot more radios and turntables in those days than we might previously have guessed, and more indication that the overused word *continuum* needs to be revised for country, cross-racial purposes.

**I'm So Lonesome Hobo Jack 1954**

I tried to get a line on Hobo Jack with some internet research and was all excited to find a namesake, but I soon realized that this was a different Hobo Jack. Or, really, a lot of different Hobo Jacks, and they all seemed to be involved in inter-state bumming. There seems to be a Hobo Jack industry, though none of them are related to the Hobo Jack of bluegrass "fame" ( I use quotation marks because, even though he seems to be known, there is little information available about him, which is a pity, as he may be the most individual bluegrass personality who ever recorded).

I was lucky enough, however, to stumble upon the following, from the County Sales web site (County Sales deals in country music releases old and new):

"Here's an interesting re-issue that will be of appeal mainly to those who appreciate the early examples of Bluegrass music that started appearing on 78s and 45s in the late 1950s and the 1960s. Hobo Jack, from eastern Kentucky, had enough odd-ball recordings (both 78s and 45s) to fill up a 25 song CD, which is what this British does. Taken from very rare 78s on such labels as Acme, Ace, Big A and Lucky, and then on Starday 45s, these recordings include topical songs of tragedy like KENTUCKY SCHOOL BUS and OUR LADY OF ANGELS, as well as a handful that were recorded by other artists including the Stanley Brothers --ANOTHER NIGHT and BIG SANDY RIVER for example. The music verges on primitive, but it does have soul."

Along with the above there's a picture of a CD with a guy on the cover leaning against a car and holding a guitar, looking very sporty in a tidy, well-pressed set of clothes and a cap. And that's really it, though the description, above, is really perfect (letter-caps and all, which I leave because they seem appropriate). You can come to this music expecting bluegrass and you will get it, but it quickly becomes obvious that this is really grass of a slightly different color. The instrumentation and the routine fit, but something isn't "right." Or maybe something *is* right, the whole tone of the proceedings which, dynamically, indicate a very unique emotional skittishness and harsh overall outlook on life. Of course, instead of being put off by this whole dynamic of desperation I am attracted to it; these are the very things that make Hobo Jack's music so magnetic, of the kind that, if and when I find them, keep me listening to country music. Just as country music in general - and even a lot of Bluegrass - has started to sound to me like a cure for insomnia, along comes Hobo Jack. Just when I thought I didn't want to hear another mandolin/banjo/whatever else introduction there arrives Jack and his band, too loud, it seems, for the original studio where they recorded. The group's levels here are into the red, and then in comes Jack, croaking the lyrics like he's fed up with life in general and with country music specifically. It sounds like he's in hurry to push through the lousy three minutes he's been allotted, get in, get out, and then get to the next gig. And that's exactly what makes this the kind of country music I live for. After I've waded though smooth-sailing ballads, watered-down honky tonk (from hundreds of Hank Williams' castoffs), and tired novelties, Hobo Jacks reminds me that there are actually human beings at the other end of the recording chain. Listen to him at .015: "I guess I t-ryyyyyy," he sings, and you have the picture of country slur, the emotional twang that launched a thousand honest honky tonk singers, here half-transplanted into bluegrass, chased through the country music weeds by actual and unadulterated feeling for a change. By this time Nashville has sacrificed its virginity for a lot of pieces of silver and Bluegrass is headed over a stylistic cliff without looking back; suddenly there is Hobo Jack, like a great splash of cold water on the face of the whole profession. He swallows those words like the good backwoods boy he probably is, with the soul of someone who never really left home and has the emotional scars to show for it.

And then there's Old Time Southern White Religion:

**I'm Crying Holy Unto the Lord Brother Claude Ely 10/53**

There's a book out on the life of Brother Claude Ely which, though it is too long and sprawling, poorly focused, and a bit of an organizational mess, is worth getting. It casts its eye with some specificity and depth on White Sanctified religion, which, I swear to you, really does exist (quick digression; a few years back a scholar on black sanctified music came to speak at Yale. In a Q and A I mentioned to her that there was also a substantial white tradition of same, and that the two - black and white sanctified religious practice - had started out as an integrated movement during something called the Azusa Street Revival. She not only shot me down without any intellectual formalities, she told me that such a thing as white sanctified singing did not exist and had never existed. I thought, but did not say at the time, that she only had to head over to youtube to discover the modern-day white sanctified performance movement. Oh well, what did I expect? It was Yale...).

I have Dick Spottswood to thank for introducing me to the reckless pleasures of Brother Claude Ely's music and, through the Brother, to other forms of white emotional verity (this is only one of many things I have to thank Dick for, but it is one of the most important). To listen to this kind of music is to discover a whole new white universe of sound and feeling, even if one is already familiar with the sanctified recordings of groups (see Vols. 9,10,11) like the Phipps Family. This is deeper and blacker (well, maybe not; I will have to consider that as it seems to deny white sanctified singing its own and well-deserved space; on the other hand, clips on youtube of white sanctified religious services really mimic, very closely, black sanctified religious services), though it is not something we have never, in its intimation of those dark nights of the white soul, seen before. We can find previews of that soul in certain gothic Southern novels, in Faulkner's interior/anterior mind-scapes, in filmic snapshots from *Midnight Cowboy* or *Night of the Hunter*. Musically it is clearly laid out in the music of the Old Regular Baptists and in the Holy-Roller remnants of Brother Claude Ely and his somewhat-rabid musical followers.

That book about Brother Claude Ely points out clearly why the Holy-Rollers (white in this case, though there were black disciples as well; as I have mentioned, the pianist Sammy Price and the singer Pleasant Joseph both cite, in their autobiographies, the holy rollers as being central to the origin of jazz and other New Orleans music) were so emotionally unique. They were religiously inspired to great outbursts of faith-based insanity and other forms of berserk. They rolled in the aisles, spoke in tongues, and otherwise seemed to be physically inhabited by morally ambivalent demons. In Brother Claude Ely's case they were directed by a guitar-playing preacher who put it all down like a musical sermon with vocal exhortation. It is from this direct line of descent, in my only somewhat humble opinion, that rock and roll received it's most powerful points of inspiration.

*I'm Crying Holy Unto the Lord* is the music in a nut (literally) shell. As destructive as this kind of religious fanaticism has been to our world, the music that has been left to us, in its rise from the ashes of religionist, scorched-earth political insanity, has been nothing short of sensational. Brother Claude introduces the song like a coarse warning and then tears through it with blind-conviction and hoarse-voiced, blunt force. Add a little mandolin (bluegrass anyone? 'fraid not), ring-shout clapping, a chorus of inside-outsiders (by his flock) and you have, with what I hear as some mild inhibition (this would have been even more intense in person), what can only be called, with, yes, some Southern-based irony intended, actual and authentic White Power.

**Ain't No Grave Gonna Hold My Body Down**
**Caudill Family 1954**

This song has had multiple lives, with some slight but minor variation. Most famously sung by a black man named Bozie

Sturdivant and recorded for the Library of Congress (Sturdivant was a quartet singer who worked menial labor all his life) it was later copy-written and claimed, falsely, by Brother Claude Ely (see above). Sturdivant's version, technically solo (but apparently with his group in the background) was powerful and as deep, and sounded as though between several different styles of black gospel. The more current, still emerging when Sturdivant recorded *Ain't No Grave* (1942), was known as hard gospel, in which the elements of gospel style - harmony, group voices, and lead - were variable and mobile and shared, with a great degree of vocal movement and even improvisation. This song, despite Brother Claude's claim that he wrote it in the midst of a physical and then religious fever, is probably traditional and probably black in origin. But no matter where it originated it has inspired a lot of emotionally supple, fervent religious expression.

The Caudill Family's 1954 version is no less compelling, falling, once again, within that heavenly kingdom of white religious persistence. It sounds, as usual, like the near-desperate plea of a sect trying to stake its own particular claim to salvation, for a plot of heavenly land. What makes it most effecting, starting with the opening, swelling phrase, is its harmonizing of Southern white dialect; it sounds like a fusion of various, not-quite-compatible twangs. It has the kind of amateur ethos which proudly informs a lot of vernacular music, the odd and stunted formality of talented hobbyists. The way in which the lead interludes are passed around gives it the feeling of a fluid, democratic process. And I just can't stop hearing, in my head, those blocked-out voices as they repeatedly hit the word "grave," sounding like a drunken bluegrass band. And the female lead at 1:31 forward - it feels odd to hear this kind of unashamedly black, blues-like phraseology coming out of the mouth of a white lady with mountain twang. But it works, as more than just a moment of true feeling.

### Hide Me Rock of Ages Speer Family 1955

The Speer Family is something of an inter-married religious franchise, passed on and exchanged through death, marriage, and childbirth (though they seem as a species to finally have become extinct in the early 1990s). Their sound is, I should note, something of an acquired taste, a taste I acquired maybe twenty five years ago (though I should mention that when I ran a clip from this group on Facebook, in the response you could almost hear the sound of Northern Liberals trampling each other in their hurry to disperse). Aside from containing that low-class twang (or what liberals and other snobs *think* is a low class twang for what it signifies about region and race and supposed levels of intelligence and education), musically it is like a glass of warm milk, with thin instrumental textures that scream *Sunday mass*, plus some quaint, tinkling, old-maid piano and some strange, bar mitvah-rock gestures like bouncy drums and white-man-and-lady lead voices. Plus some very pale but nicely-balanced voices, with that obligatory and strange, wandering white bass voice, and a near-overdose of wholesome harmony. But that's what I like about it. It is an unembarrassed baring of white, white bread, soul, in full view of generations of congregants and other assorted (mostly white) spectators. Beneath that white exterior is - well, a white interior, and beneath that white interior is - well, more white: pious virginity, buried passion, and a worldly sincerity that masquerades as innocence, a disguise donned for protection in this sinful world.

Try this recording on and see if it fits. It is, on some levels, religion made safe for democracy, from a strangely-disguised part of the South that seems in denial of its ties to hillbilly hedonism; less ashamed of its roots and where they came from, I would say, than wanting to look at where they are now. It's the way of an entire genre of White Gospel, of the kind that wears coats and ties and skirts and dresses for breakfast.

**Do Lord Deep South Quartet 1955**

These people don't live, musically, far from the Speers, and they are well trained. This is another piece of organized religious harmony, an old-time religionist anthem that sounds suspiciously like *It Takes a Worried Man*. It is instructive to listen to this and the Speers and compare it to the the harder edges of Brother Claude Ely and his congregants. Is the distinction to be made between the different styles one of class or sect? I suspect that it is both, though I must admit I don't know enough about Southern religion to explain it, except in the context of certain religious expressions as I have heard them on record. But they clearly represent different sounds and approaches - maybe we should think of the more radically inclined Sanctified/Holy Rollers as the Method Actors of Southern religion, as those who put every aspect of religious practice through the prism of their own experience - with, I should add, a great deal of imaginative damnation thrown in.

But back to this, a white gospel quartet that has even more of that quaint, Speer-like, over-ripe sense of harmony, a rhythmic bounce and a tonally high-and-neighborly attitude seemingly meant to replace the apocalyptic visions of the Holy Rollers. This is, once again, like the Speers, on the cusp of a new commercial niche for White Gospel, studio-spotless, musically hygienic, and yet black-quartet-like in its broad harmonies, though those harmonies are scrubbed clean in a way that shows a particular, commercial world view. But even those over-arching tenor voices and that weird precision don't completely mask their sources - listen at about 1:19. The pianist, a la Arizona Dranes (the first great black gospel pianist, see Vo. 5, whose four-wheel drive rhythms were an early prediction of rock and roll time), uses the keyboard like an accelerant, stepping out, for just a moment, like the memory of some old country church. For a few seconds we hear the passion, not necessarily of Christ, but of human beings.

I managed to piss off more than a few people some time ago by suggesting that although Aretha Franklin was great there was something lacking, for me, in her singing, that there were others, out of that tradition and new-soul/gospel feel, that I preferred. As that style of song and sound moved, Post-War, before larger and more loyal audiences it, unsurprisingly, expanded, musically, dramatically, and vocally. For black gospel this was a new world in which the secular and the religious, which had long conflicted, now actively crossed paths in ways that no longer necessarily acted at cross-purposes. The methods behind the great gospel post-War divas were not much different than the methods of the 1950s women who sang rhythm and blues and then Soul Music. The most effective of these sang loud and with borderline hysteria, though it was a line they only sometimes crossed. I hear in the best of these singers, like **Bessie Griffin (Too Close to Heaven 1954)**, something which I was about to call emotional intelligence, but as I write I think it was more than that. It was an acute instinct for emotional kill that receded almost as soon as the moment of truth arrived, an artistic/aesthetic instinct for withdrawal and detachment that seemed to remove the singer from the room at the point of highest emotional saturation, creating a distance that equated to power and control. And it was an instinct that I think Aretha Franklin lacked.

Bessie Griffin was one of the stars of the new gospel movement, and we can hear her playing to the crowd in this recording, in more ways than one. Her slow and steady buildup to whatever emotional denouement awaits, the subtle and not-so-subtle manipulation of the audience, and the way she alternates between baring it all and then holding something in reserve, are all time-tested emotional techniques. She is in complete command, using the technique of the preacher, who proselytizes for the sake of the spiritual but settles for the instant gratification of the material.

Compare the deep harmony of the (black) **Gospel Songbirds**, on **God's Creation (ca. 1955)**, to the way those white folks mix it up on *Do Lord* (see above). There is, in the Songbird's method, an extremeness of what is essentially spiritual patience, a willingness to tread that baptismal water, such as it is, rhythmically, in anticipation of the musical climax - or, really, series of climaxes. The extraordinary way in which the blend of voices, at the very beginning, seems to eliminate individuals while implying a communal delirium, and in which the the performance opens up to reveal the lead (it feels a bit like god, or somebody, is shining a spiritual spotlight on him) is about all we need to distinguish this from what appears to be the dominant *white* mode of gospel.

Whiteness in this era, in the mainstream of religious singing, was generally cordial and perfunctory. It invited you in the door, but only to show you around the house. There was no feeding and little nurturing. Black gospel, in this golden era of quartet singing, was like a mass rejection of the jubilee style, a newly liberated (in this pre-Civil Rights era of growing black-cultural nationalist feeling) sound that was finally getting beyond religious and political symbolism. It had a passionate warmth that was inviting to sympathetic white folks and yet a warning, in its implied depth of complex feeling, for them to keep their distance.

If early (black) spiritual singing of the antebellum-era was often enmeshed in finding ways to say things without actually saying them - engaging itself in increasingly obvious metaphors for physical as well as spiritual liberation - and if early 20th century black quartets were a mix of show-business pragmatism, minstrel co-option, and religious affirmation - the black hard-gospel quartets of the post-War era were free and freer even before they were truly and totally legally free. Just as some jazz players in the 1960s saw Free Jazz as a tone parallel to their own attempts at autonomy, so did early and late hard gospel groups, in the 1950s and as their audiences and venues expanded, start to articulate, in rhythm and texture, their own determination to discard the tyranny of white expectation.

*******************************

...and though in later years Miles Davis, in one of his more racially "generous" moments, ceded the blues to white people ("they got 'em, they need 'em, they can keep them" he said), the blues of the 1950s was of a kind rarely seen, to cite Martin Duberman, In White America.

Some diligent internet researcher has discovered that **D.A. Hunt**, who recorded **Lonesome Old Jail** in **5/53**, was fully named Daniel Augusta Hunt and lived from 1929-1962. *Lonesome Old Jail*, on Sam Phillips' Sun Records, comes from that time when Sam had something of a professional revolving-door policy. He was searching and searching in Memphis' black blues community for the key to record sales and economic security, and though he soon learned that that key was white, his openness to all kinds of performers served him - and history - well. This song and performance is a nod to the old style of country blues, though Hunt interjects, with some regularity, a cry-like twang that sounds as part black field-style plea and part white honky-tonk regret; and he is a country guitarist who freely interjects more than a few old-school gestures. And then there is that voice - it has a smoothed-out soul that evokes, though with a lot more feeling, Josh White's, and it seems to call for a style of accompaniment other than his own stark playing, as though begging for a Bobby Bland-type background, not smooth blues but blues with a few less pointed edges. It's not jazz, though certain jazz singers from out-of-town (like Jimmy Rushing) come to mind.

**Pat Hare** is perhaps best known for killing his girlfriend and the policeman who came to investigate. But he was also a pioneering electric blues guitarist whose recording of **Bonus Pay (5/14/54)**, recorded for Sun, shows what all the talk was about. Sam Phillips has recounted that Hare had an early, low-powered, tweed Fender amp called a Champ. The Champ was of the new generation of tube amplifiers that allowed guitarists just a little more head room (meaning volume before distortion), though it was perhaps just a bit too low-powered to allow for as much *room* volume before the single power tube which it used allowed for what guitarists call tube breakup. Still, this was a very new sound; other guitar amplifiers had served similar purposes, but Leo Fender was now designing things which had just a little more strength and clarity (for which the ultimate blues machine was a bigger and sweeter amp called the Tweed Deluxe). Still, the Champ got the job done (and the tweed series, we should mention, differentiated itself from the later blackface series of Fender amps by its emphasis on mid-range frequencies, which gave it a little bit more soul and which also distorted more quickly than upper frequencies).

Hare uses that available wave of distortion as a front-line sonic tool, in a way which became more and more common, particularly in the rock and toll years (and which was re-worked for punk and metal music, both of which generally relied instead upon what is called *pre-amp* tube distortion. The distinction, in short, is that pre-amp tube distortion - derived from pre-amp tubes instead of the power tubes that gave early electric blues its sound - is more top-heavy sonically, "breathes" less and, at least in my opinion, is a lot less soulful).

Of course, as I am fond of saying, you could take the blues out of the country but not necessarily the country out of the blues; as in **Eva Lee** by **James Walton** (ca. 1954). Just what is this? Does it represent some Luddite resistance to all that was changing, technically, geographically and thematically, in the blues of the 1950s? I don't really think so, and ultimately I think the question is of little relevance. What is relevant is that there were still performers like Walton, alive and well and in need of the blues. And for all the surface sense that this was Old School, there is something very new about it, a new sense of musical urgency transposed onto an old(er) format (of course something else to realize is that the golden age of acoustic country blues occurred only some twenty five years previous to this, meaning that this was separated from Charley Patton et al by less than a generation. It was to these guys like 1995 is to us as I write this in the year 2020).

Of course some things - like misery and loneliness - are not only universal but timeless, and Walton seems to posses both in abundance. There is no scent of old-timey reconstruction here, not even a whiff of revivalism; as a matter of fact the very insistent, background accompaniment - electric guitar and steady piano - places this very decisively in the blues new age even as the music seems to be lagging, in a stubborn way, just a little bit behind. Personally I find recordings like this to be amazingly revealing time capsules of sound, recorded in an era of analog innovation. This is the sound of tape, with its generous sonic depth-of-field, and nothing in our braver new world of digital can replicate its roomy reality and you-are-there presence.

And you *are* there in **Billy Emerson's Hey Little Girl**, from **1/11/54**. This is another of those Memphis, Sam Phillips recordings that I keep citing, as telling us that, in those pre-rock and roll years, there was something of major significance going on in that city. Was this the stuff of the working musician for whom the recording studio was something of a lab, a way of formalizing things invented on the fly and on the bandstand? This is a boogie-thing (listen to that constant and steady boogie riff, buried in the mix) of rock-like intensity, but boogie woogie with a difference. Notice that the rhythm is a hard, even four with a backbeat - something which I have long maintained is part of the essence of the new rock and roll, and a relative of the ring shout. Though Phillips in the rush to whiter pastures soon abandoned this kind of music, it had its own parallel life as neither blues nor rock but something I call, as before, rhythm and rock. It was for other black musicians - like Bo Diddley and Chuck Berry - to develop sonic and song techniques closer to what the white kids wanted, but that's a different history with a different meaning and a different, if still racially charged, conclusion.

And a strange fusion, indeed, of all of this was **Jolie Tee Caitin** by **Clarence Garlow (1954)**. This recording has a natural and danceable quality and sounds like a cultural fusion of various inevitable musical moments. It has the beat of a natural-man performance, a strange percussive beauty (a kind of oom-pah drum figure), a perfect room-sound in its riff-based guitar solo, a bi-lingual charm, a honking, out-of-tune saxophone, and a voice so buried in the mix as to sound like someone playing music while staring down at his feet. And what about the endgame cries and yells? This was an era of planned music that was not too well planned, with an unwitting spontaneity born out of a cultural instinct which barely exists today (hip hop in its purest state may be the last bastion).

**J.B. Hutto's Lovin' You (1954)** comes at us like a flashlight in the dark. It's a hard blues with a loud guitar, a washboard, and a crying harmonica. By a black singer, it is a basic statement of manly persuasion, of the kind that white singers were only starting to understand in the new era of rock and roll assertiveness. We have talked in this study about the way white folks shadowed black music and culture for hundreds of years, but have tended to think mostly in terms of sonics; in the rock and roll era this turned into a method of theme and attitude and social posturing. The new white musical aggressiveness of rock, out of the mouths of Elvis et al, was an affront to white, church-going folk, but in the long run it was something they learned to not only love but to do (as they had been, for a very long time, in church).

**Clifton Chenier** is a black Cajun singer/accordionist whose **Just a Lonely Boy (1955)** is accordion blues-as-tragedy. This is a scene from life, in the language of the rawest of blues, and has that tell-tale cry which unites entire vernacular schools of music. Chenier, who died in 1987 and who received numerous national honors, both in his lifetime and posthumously, was a leading figure in the *Zydeco* movement, which Wikipedia defines as "a music genre that evolved in southwest Louisiana by French Creole speakers which blends blues, rhythm and blues, and music indigenous to the Louisiana Creoles and the Native American people of Louisiana." So be it; like all such definitions it is both too broad and too narrow, though I hear the category, as represented here, as signifying a repopulating of Cajun music with blues style and pop ambition.

Chenier also comes under the relatively new category of musician-as-folklorist. It is not that the function of the music or the player as changed, but that the external focus of arts institutions has. Probably his best work was done in *this* era, in the 1950s, when he was poor and unrecognized and before he started receiving arts awards. It's not just that this early work has a poverty-driven dignity, but that inevitably, in vernacular music, something gets lost in the translation from commercial recognition to institutional visibility. *I Am Just a Lonely Boy* is so brilliantly unselfconscious, the blues as meditation on the consequences of existence, that it supersedes NEA proclamations. Listen to the natural musical balance, the way in which each player in the group holds the sonic line, never violating the leader's protocol. Chenier's accordion, trapped in a blues loop, does its job, but most central is his voice, hoarse and pleading, begging for attention.

A different kind of a thing was **No Nights By Myself** by **Sonny Boy Williamson 12/12/54**. Sonny Boy, real name Rice Miller, and who we assume took his name from the original Sonny Boy

Williamson (of *Good Morning Little School Girl*, see my blues history), recorded for Trumpet and then Chess records, two white-owned but relatively benevolent record labels who let their contractees (both black and white) have a great deal of musical and artistic leeway. *No Nights by Myself* is a slow, tortured blues built around those dark nights of the soul when nothing - sleep, dream, rest of any kind - is a palliative. How does Sonny Boy do it? With a shivering harmonica and a self-contained call-and-response. This is what we (should) mean when we refer to the good old days, to certain essential musical and spiritual values that have been lost in the digitally-layered, 256-track world, in the trend toward the synthesizing of acoustic spaces (which have also come to represent, poorly, *emotional* spaces). And yet this is very much a creature of the recording studio, of the way in which recording technology in these years eliminated the middle man; who needs a large band when you've got this kind of intimacy? There is a closeness here not unheard of in a live situation but which was still likely difficult to replicate in the professional world of the blues musician of that era. And listen to the wordless duo of voice and harmonica from 2:06 until the end; you may never again get this close to feeling of any kind.

And then there's **Chuck Berry**, who has gotten me in trouble over and over again on internet discussion boards and Facebook. I just don't find him particularly interesting as a performer, though he wrote a number of very good songs. His singing voice is only so-so, he has a nice, if limited, feeling on guitar (built on a finite range of riffs), and the songs, yes, are catchy but not really that lasting in value. Before you slam this book closed, accept my real regret that I just do not appreciate his work, though I do appreciate the historic importance of his legacy, relative to the early black contribution to the practice and repertoire of rock and roll. Berry was a pro, he sold a lot of records, and, I suppose, he occupies a certain center of the 1950s teen imagination (this is the legend, of his adeptness at seizing the thematic day of teen concerns. And it is a legend, as I have no way of confirming that it is accurate in any sense of the 1950s' zeitgeist). **(Downbound Train, 1955).**

A lot has been written about **Thelonious Monk** by throngs of critics trying to make themselves heard above all the noise about his musical and cultural significance. And a lot of it, for once, is true; the conventional cultural wisdom finally, at some point in American (and Monk's) life, caught up with reality, though as usual I tend to look for what everyone else has missed. With Monk this is easy.

I recall a panel at Jazz at Lincoln Center in which a group of distinguished scholars and musicians struggled to explain why Monk was so unique in jazz and American music, or why his artistic example stood out. I moved restlessly in my chair (I wasn't on the panel) and said, only in my head:

A big part of Monk's significance is that he is unique but not unique. The tradition from which he comes is classic relative to the wave of black vernacular musicians who emerged in the 20th century. Their musical methods involved what I call a virtuosity of style, a means of sound production and of creating ideas out of what are essentially personal, homemade techniques, as applied in the most eccentric and original ways; it's not that no one ever instructed them on how to play, but that the way they applied that instruction involved techniques that were outside the (white) sonic and cultural norm. In these years a specifically blackened texture, of sound, timbre, rhythm of sound and tonality, became part of the new American vernacular in everything from hillbilly music to blues to jazz. It all grew from the African American tradition of self-instruction and self-application, of personally assimilated style, even if based on other assimilated styles. Once again, it is not that these musicians were uneducated in the ways of music or that they were primitives in any sense (though yes, some were). What was important was that one thousand (black) individuals played in one thousand different ways, because the way they were taught and the way they applied that teaching allowed for a growing distance between the cause (study) and the effect (performance). This distance was largely the distance between American life as lived in the minds of white folks and American life as lived in *reality*, on the assorted margins of African America. In between these two points lay a whole other reality that was often denied but usually intuitively recognized by audiences and artists. It was in this space that musicians like Thelonious Monk lived and worked.

**Smoke Gets in Your Eyes (6/7/54)** is a perfect example of Monk's art and craft. Listen to the series of sixteenth-note phrases he lays down starting at about .018. It's like a bebop abstraction, an application of double-time in an unconventional way, and Monk lands on intervals that even Lennie Tristano (who was not a Monk admirer) should have appreciated. In many ways it is most instructive to hear Monk as he is on this, as a solo pianist, because it makes his methods so clear. He is a master at planned-spontaneity, of ideas mapped out well in advance through what I imagine was an intense method of trial and error (Dick Katz told me of going back and forth between Monk's apartment and a rehearsal studio when they were working on the music for Monk's Town Hall concert. Over the many hours Dick shuttled between the two places he heard Monk, in his apartment, always working on the same, solitary piano piece). *Smoke Gets in Your Eyes* is from the American standard repertoire, which Monk, as usual, handles with respect and a few traces of irony, but never with a sense of ridicule or any hint that the material is in any way beneath him. That wasn't in his nature. His love of American song was based on his appreciation of the way in which melody circled harmony in this repertoire, and of the additional rhythmic possibilities suggested by vernacular speech-as-lyric (and I have an unprovable theory that this kind of direct, Tin Pan Alley spoken-word poetry, as fused with black speech rhythms, was one key to Monk's amazing and personalized sense of vernacular time). His playing, to my ears, was based on the conviction that he, Thelonious Monk, knew exactly where each of those essential song elements belonged, and in what musical and rhythmic relationship to each other.

The jazz singer **Helen Merrill** shows, on her recording of **Don't Explain (12/54)** how this balance - between sound and time, open space and musical resolution - can be used to somewhat different, if equally jazz-compatible, purposes. Merrill (still active as I write this) had the purest of voices. One of her most startling techniques was the way she held a note for much longer than expected before sliding into vibrato (which is the moving of the pitch to a point just above and below the stated note; holding the note without doing so is a challenge to any singer to stay in tune, and Merrill was uncannily precise in this respect).

Merrill, I should mention, further begs the question of "What is a jazz singer?" As I discussed earlier relative to Frank Sinatra (who I do not think is a jazz singer), such a distinction is to a large extent based on time and phrasing, which require a certain knack for displacement of the beat; but another distinction is, I think, in emotional tone. Sinatra at his peak was personable and self-involved to a point that approached but did not cross the line between self-expression and self obsession. Great jazz singers - like Merrill - maintain their distance from the emotional core of songs like *Don't Explain*, even as they use the technique of self-obsession as, paradoxically, a means of alienation and separation. This is, yes, a fine line (between self-expression and self-obsession), and one which can be crossed - or, really, even approached - only at great artistic risk. But the musical effectiveness of any jazz musician requires, I think, an understanding of how to ring even greater feeling or more detailed emotion out of (non-ironic) distancing, out the self separating itself from the self. In this respect Merrill's singing is like a 20th century primer, showing how emotional accuracy is a matter of neither irony nor emotional saturation, but rather of movement between those two near-incompatible planes of personal reality, and in such a way that ultimately evades both.

*Don't Explain* is a Billie Holiday composition which some critics, in a political miscarriage of justice, might condemn as an anthem of, at best, low self esteem, at worst, self-hate. Personally I feel Holiday, in this sense, is beyond our criticism. The current politically-correct way of holding her out as symbol and victim is condescending and even arguably racist. As I feel certain Holiday would complain, she was only herself and not to be used as anyone else's model for racial and social justice denied. Which is not to say that she was not acutely aware of race and her status as a black woman in America, but that she would not be made into a martyr or victim; she was too confident and self possessed an artist for all of that, and too independent to function as a part of any political movement that had more interest in her as a symbol than as an individual (as you can imagine, I say all of the above because of what I have seen as the simplistic internet - and Facebook - portrayal of Holiday as a neglected artist who was little more than just another un-loved victim of American racism. The reality is that, for all her difficulties, she was popular, successful, and critically praised).

But to Holiday's singing - **Prelude to a Kiss (1954)** comes from a late session she did with her close musical companion, the great and lyrically-quirky pianist Jimmy Rowles. This is from the last phase of her difficult life, and her singing has a fragility that sets it apart from her early work. The sound of it is filled with a sense of unmerciful self knowledge, a fatalism based perhaps on what had to be her recognition that she was living on borrowed time; she seems determined to use her remaining spark and technical ability to make some final and finite statements. And it helped, a lot, that she was doing it with the assistance of someone as personally and musically sympathetic as Rowles.

Now, anyone who knows anything about Holiday and Rowles knows that their repartee in this (their conversations from this recording session have been preserved) was really a friends/intimate form of affectionate back-and-forth. Not for one Holiday biographer, however, who insisted on making a great leap of racial faith from this conversation, describing it in terms of Rowles the white outsider being held at arms length by an innately and racially distrustful Holiday. Nothing could be further from the truth. While I don't doubt that Holiday had little faith in white people as a whole, Rowles (to quote Charles Mingus in a different context) was an artistic devotee of the same church that she attended. The life and faith of a jazz musician was of paramount importance to her, and as one can hear in her and Rowles' recorded conversations and in this poignant performance, they had, between them, nothing but a great, spiritual love and affinity.[40]

**Don't Cry Baby Little Jimmy Scott 4/22/55**
**Don't Worry About Me Julie London 1955**

Little Jimmy Scott is an acquired taste that I have not quite acquired. *Don't Cry Baby* is really, however, a lovely performance absent some of his more maudlin excesses, though I have to allow for the possibility that I am missing the point in a particularly white way. Is this part of that whole school which I have cited before, of androgynous black singing, walking the line between high-note range and falsetto? Or is it a Monty Pythonesque musical drag, blurring the line between artistic strangeness and just plain musical oddity?

I have to say, first of all, that I prefer Scott's early work, as here. Aging may later have covered his pliant, desperate-sound-of-a-voice with stretch marks and finally pushed him across the line, out of the bounds of good taste. In 1955 he still makes the notes with a definition that keeps things in check, somewhat. The first weeping phrase of *Don't Cry Baby* leads, with relative restraint, to unrestraint, to the way in which the the word "cry" hits like an emotional hammer. Things simmer for a few seconds until he hits "you know" with another sledge, before calming down to suggest to his paramour to "dry your eyes." This is all a very temperamental form of realism. "You know I didn't mean…to treat you so mean" he tells his lover near the end, hitting each note so necessarily on

---

[40] The bio in question is Farah Jasmine Griffin's *If You Can't Be Free, Be a Mystery: In Search of Billie Holiday*. She needs to keep looking.

pitch, with just a touch of typical miasmatic bend.There is more than a hint here of the school of post-gospel singing which, only a few years later, broke through into black pop as *soul*, but the voice is less the brick wall of the soul singer than it is the brought-down-by-life confessional of the reformed gospeler. This particular non-blues singer had what might conventionally have been *called* the blues, except for our recognition that the deep spirituality of certain black ways of singing and repertoire made an end-run around the blues' strict formalist boundaries, to evoke a misery which was, by then, encoded into their DNA.

Julie London had her own sense-memory way of making herself miserable enough to sing ever so slowly and ever so sadly, as though life was cloudy with about a 90 percent chance of teardrops. I was told a story, years ago, by the late bassist John Daley, about the day London recorded *Cry Me A River*, probably her biggest hit and best-known tune. Daley advised that she recorded *Cry Me a River* after having just broken up with the actor Jack Webb (of Dragnet fame), and that in the recording studio - at which Daley was present - she was constantly on the verge of tears. And I believe it - *Cry Me a River* is ripe with throbbing, you-are-there misery.

Fortunately London wasn't a one-trick emotional wreck but rather a very good singer with good time and an appropriate way around a lyric. Even her more blatant performances work because she exhibits a very artistic emotionalism, of the kind that forces me to clarify some of what I recently wrote about jazz and emotional detachment, especially in contrast to that of a singer like Frank Sinatra. Jazz singers to me always have a kind of double consciousness; Sinatra's is very much a uniform one, of condition and presence. He is always *there,* emotionally available. Julie London on the other hand, in that jazz way, appears to be right in front of you, but reach out for her and it is like grabbing for a ghost. She sings like she is trapped in an emotional bubble from which she cannot escape, but pop that bubble and the apparition is gone, disappeared. There is nothing left but mist.

What we do have is a compelling recording she made of the Rube Bloom composition Don't Worry About Me (1955) (check out online, if you can find it, a very late and effecting Billie Holiday, live, performance of same). The song is a beauty, with repeated sections and no bridge, so well composed melodically that it just bulls its way through with compositional logic. This is, once again, out of a particular white school of female singing, a la Doris Day and June Christie, Anita O'Day and Chris Connor. It is one of my favorite schools of jazz-jaded pop singing, pure of tone and of purpose, possessed of a way with lyrics prone only on occasion to sullen excess. These girls (pardon the term, once again, but I am trying to be period-correct) were non-shrinking violets and even socially significant, with artistic status as listen-but-don't-touch models of independent sexuality.

Once in a while in my listening travels I come across a recording that is so crazy and distorted that I have to use it in a project, any project. This includes anything from crazy-white minstrel pop to nutty, eccentric jazz, to cave-painted blues to, well, things like **Papa Lightfoot**'s version of **When the Saints Go Marching In (4/17/54)**. As a friend once said to me while listening to something which didn't really fit into any prior and known musical category, "what is the social construct?" In other words, what the hell does this mean, where and what does it come from and, really, what the hell is it?

Unlike the song Papa Lightfoot was a Mississippian, not from New Orleans but from Natchez, which is just across the way, and he is generally considered a bluesman, though this song tells us, maybe, something different. It was Steve LaVere, a bad-samaritan of blues ownership, who (almost) rescued Lightfoot from obscurity by recording him in 1969 and getting him a place in line at the folk revival (sadly Lightfoot died soon afterward). But Lightfoot's early recordings established him as an original, or at the least showed him to be a bit of a rhythm-nut, a very good harmonica player and only a so-so singer whose sheer sheerness, whose force-of-personality, put him on the blues map, or really the entire map. Was this some of the first Outsider Music? I don't know, but it certainly qualifies as music with a point of sonic view, and one that doesn't let you alone. *When the Saints Go Marching In* is phantasmagorical, a recording of manic obsession. This is music unfiltered and unhinged, flailing at itself and lighting up the room like a seance among the living (as are more than a few of Lightfoot's early recordings). He growls and howls his way through. And check out that harmonica; his real solo starts at 1:07 - in the upper - is it register or reeds? - part of the instrument, and he soon shows that, though there is a drummer, Lightfoot himself is in charge of the rhythm section. The last harmonica solo (starting at about 1:56) is the kicker - a variation on everything in not just the song but probably Lightfoot's head, high notes, low notes, with screaming double (or is it triple?) stops, rhythm thrusts, time twists, and then an ending that is like Lightfoot telling us, in a practical rather than philosophical sense, that he is out of time.

**Elvis Presley** probably died for his own sins, and I feel badly about it, as you should, too. He was the lone professional charge of Colonel Tom Parker, a somewhat mysterious figure of questionable citizenship (one reason, it is said, that Elvis never went to Europe to perform was that Parker was afraid to cross any borders) who may have had a sordid past (or not) but who guided Presley's career like a professional den mother. After the unholy and early rock and years the Colonel tried, in his way, to Brian-Epstein Elvis, to clean up his act and make him safe for democracy (and Southern theocracy). The result was a spit-shine Elvis who could still do what he had to do to make the girls moan but who mixed, in an uncanny way, self-effacement and middle-class moralizing with a me-also, seductive assault on the senses; still, at least in the public image, he kept little Elvis zipped up and out of sight.

And yet, beneath that mom-and-pop exterior, as we well know, was a restless and drug-addicted, permanent adolescent yearning for release. And that inner teen was released with regularity, if usually behind the scenes, in most cases settling for quiet dates or for movie theaters rented for private screenings for himself and his friends. And yet, again, beneath the drugged up but image-conscious facade was another facade, of deeper disturbance, a yearning (and this is only a theory) to truly escape the shackles of not just polite society but also Colonel Parker's book of etiquette. This Elvis was not just addicted but addled and crazed, and had the need to consume mind-altering substances, shoot off guns, and picture the world as if it lay prostrate at his feet. To achieve the latter he shuttled off to Los Vegas, where he could be all of the above, loved and drugged and free to indulge in excesses that were, whether the Colonel knew or understood it or not, Elvis' way of defiance. This was just after the Woodstock years, after all, and Elvis went from free love to freer love, and though he hated hippies and even offered his services to the US government to spy on longhairs and other assorted subversives, he was, in reality, like a hump-backed child of the 1960s. Though an outsider by appearance and temperament, he worked his way back in by seizing upon and using the new freedoms for his own personal brand of self destruction.

Whatever happened to Elvis and why, he was a great singer and, I will always insist, the true *auteur*, the real author and inventor of rock and roll. It was he who put it, all of it - country bounce, blues repetition, rhythm and blues sneer, honky tonk irreverence, radical evangelical religious passion - together, who put the rock together with the roll, though he rarely, to this credit (and it was one of the things which made him so beloved in the South) got above his raisin.' From all accounts he never thought he was better than anyone else or entitled to anything more than the right to perform. He just knew he had a certain talent and drive, and he used it like a motherfucker. As on this stunning version of **Blue Moon of Kentucky**, recorded live on the Louisiana Hayride radio show in **1954**. From the first hiccuped "Blue Moon of Kentucky," to the thrilling, tight-vibratoed, wailing way he drives a wedge through the song (a Bill Monroe composition), using it like a roadmap to previously unexplored musical territory, Elvis has complete control. It is now *his* song. Add a tidy interlude by guitarist Scotty Moore (the perfect accompanist for the country-fried - in more ways than one - Elvis), a slapped, subtle, finessed bass (no drums yet) and you have more than a musical revolution, you have a compete American musical change of life.

There are many interesting things about **Charles Mingus** as a person and musician. At certain moments of "weakness" he seems to have let his guard down and faced certain realities, even as race interfered. Back in the 1960s, for example, he went public to defend Dave Brubeck from some critical remarks made about him by Miles Davis. Brubeck was an extremely imperfect modernist, and his music has not aged well; though he was clearly sincere, and though it must be admitted that he never played anything but what he wanted to play, to me Brubeck's music was a sad case of under-qualified experimentalism. He just did not have the chops or, more particularly, the imagination, to successfully take the kind of liberties with jazz harmony and linearity that he wanted to take. He was, however, early in trying to establish a way of taking the music outside of its normal normal, and it must be said that he worked very hard at it. Sadly, his performances come off as cut-and-paste polytonality, with amateur polyrhythms and long, ponderous solos of no apparent destination.

However....Brubeck had great personal musical integrity, and Mingus knew this. And Brubeck, right or wrong, was trying to re-shape jazz, trying to show that, as a modern form, the music could do things other than bebop. Failed as he did, at least he tried. Mingus, I have a feeling, admired him for simply making the effort, because Mingus too, in the last decade, had been working at some of the same philosophical/musical ideas. Witness **Thrice Upon a Theme**, which Mingus recorded **12/54** with the clarinetist **John LaPorta** and the tenor saxophonist (and later producer of Miles Davis and Thelonious Monk) **Teo Macero**. Now there are a lot of things I can say about this piece, but first I should point out that at this point in his musical life Mingus had yet to devise the expressionist, hard-bop-funk dynamic that (later) made him and his recordings great and famous. At this point, in a way which he would later either deny or disavow (or ignore) he was clearly under the sway of certain white, post-Tristano concepts of New Music, with contrapuntal daring, tonal yet explorative harmonies and lines, and a meandering kind of post-bop, multi-tonal approach, a means of distance-focus that worked to avoid bebop bursts of sound, that instead tried to alter the sonic depth-of-field in favor of wandering harmonic resolutions and vague yet deep sonorities. Not to mention that much of this material, as John Laporta points out in his autobiography and which I discussed with him on a few occasions, was written, arranged, and conceptualized by LaPorta. You wouldn't know this if you read the reviews of this material, which are often historically challenged and victims of the old-school race wars, by which it had to be assumed that Mingus would never do anything in which he deferred to white musicians.[41] Well, he did so here, and the music is lyrically adventurous and profound. I think we may assume that Mingus' later shrugging off of this period in his career was, at the least, based on some kind of embarrassment at being associated as a follower, rather than a leader, of white players. But it shouldn't really matter, because there was very little wrong and a lot right with these very fine collaborations. All of these musicians were making the effort to stretch things beyond the bebop comfort zone; both LaPorta and Macero were brilliant instrumentalists and important composers who had long and brilliant careers, and it does the music and its history no good to make them into invisible men.

---

[41] Here's one such dumb-shit of a reviewer, who obviously has no clue that there were other important musicians on the recordings who were actually making an effort and a contribution: https://www.allaboutjazz.com/thrice-upon-a-theme-charles-mingus-aim-records-review-by-matthew-miller.php

# Chapter 29: The Song is Him

If you are in showbiz, do you have to die before they make a movie made about your life? Maybe; think: Hank Williams, Billie Holiday, Charlie Parker, Hank Garland, Ray Charles (well, he was close; they started making it while he was alive), Ruth Etting, Bix Beiderbecke, Lenny Bruce, Johnny Cash, and, for our purposes here, **Patsy Cline** (of course there was also one made about Eddie Foy while he was still alive, and George M. Cohan as well; plus another I refuse to see called *Jimmy Carter: Rock and Roll President*. Sorry, but Jimmy, who is not a rock and roller except in his sweaty, Iranian-hostage dreams, is like a bad nickel that keeps popping out of a political slot machine).

Cline, considered one of the major crossover figures in country music, emerged when the time was exactly right. Country's MOR sound was fully developed by **6/1/55** when she recorded **Hidin' Out**, and she was certainly a credit to the style. Sometimes the good crosses over with the bad and the mediocre (because the industry doesn't always send their best people), and I would classify this as one of the good. There was a large and talented school of women singers in this era that were the country equivalent of jazz's golden era of pop-song stylists. We have: Patsy Cline, Kitty Wells, Loretta Lynn, Jean Shepard, et al, who set the (literal) stage for Tammy Wynette, Loretta Lynn, and Dolly Parton. These were like the commandeers of the country standard, of the pop-ballad style tinged with country themes (well, maybe country-songwriter themes, of the good, the bad, and the cloying). Even the method of composition mimicked that of the old Tin Pan Alley-type of song, as written and approved by committee. This didn't mean the songs were necessarily bad, just somewhat standardized. Cline, who had a deep, throaty voice, not unlike that of Texas Ruby, had a real affection for the lower register, a way of grabbing at a song's hook and twisting it; "here we are again hidin' out" she sings, and we have another quaint, if equal-access, country look at adultery, a favorite honky tonk pastime. Add some slick fiddle, a country-tinkling piano, and a few words of regret, and you have the ideal country song, as sung by the ideal country singer.

Country music, like its black partners in culture, had a way of spinning itself off in directions other than those which seemed industrially dominant in the 1950s. I don't mean rock and roll, which I consider to be less a country spinoff than a country cousin. I am thinking of the way certain smaller communities of country musician, whether or not out of dissatisfaction with the dominant means of country production, seemed to take it upon themselves to to go in different musical directions.

Hence the Bakersfield Sound (named after the city of Bakersfield, California), a country offshoot usually seen as a musical reaction to Nashville's rising and blanketing clouds of over-production. One web site describes the Bakersfield Sound, with a publicist's respect for inaccuracy, as a "sub genre of country music – described as a mix of twangy guitars, drums, fiddle, and steel guitar – (that) was a defiant reaction to the string orchestras and the polished sound of albums being recorded in Nashville during the 1950's and 60's."

Well, ok. Listening to lot of Nashville music of the 1950s and 1960s I hear plenty of twangy guitars, drums, fiddle, and steel guitar, so maybe that wasn't exactly it. A more sensible explanation is that Bakersfield took some of its cues from rock and roll, with sideview glances at rock's de-sentimentalization (both lyrically and, musically) of the music in general. In some ways, yes, this was an aesthetic also lifted from the blues, but in n truth I would very much like to see something that I haven't seen, a good oral history of the Bakersfield era, to find our what those musicians were actually listening to and why. As of this writing I remain skeptical of a lot of what has been written about this period, though I can see how this musical enclave, also largely a product of Southern white Western migration, worked its way though honky-tonk assertiveness to rock-like aggression, by way of a working-man and woman's grit and persistence.

One of Bakersfield's leading men was, of course, **Buck Owens**, some of whose earliest work, like **You're Fer Me (1955)**, supposedly shows the effects of rockabilly. But to my way of hearing *You're Fer Me* is very traditional, or at least traditional in relation to what has been happening in country music for the prior ten years - and certainly more conservative than the sound of Hank Williams or Lefty Frizzell. It's sentimental, basic, respectful, and reliably, emotionally consonant; nothing about it challenges the country establishment, which is probably the way a young upstart like Owens, still trying to talk his way into that world, wanted it.

Further along that country highway, and maybe headed for a different exit (yeah, I know, the only thing worse than cliches and metaphors, are cliched metaphors) was the singer **Kitty Wells**, who set all kinds of new standards for fame and sales for country singers in general and country women in particular. I am told she was named the top county female vocalist for 14 straight years, was named to the Country Music Hall of Fame, and, according to Joel Whitburn (whose statistical work I would take with many grains of salt)[42] she was the sixth-highest selling country singer of her time. She was also married to Johnny Wright of the country duo Johnny and Jack, (see Vol. 25), a strangely innovative combo whose approach to country music-making was a mesh of country corn and self-conscious violation.

Whatever we believe about her statistical accomplishments, Wells was a very important singer in country music, as a soloist and as a women. Her most famous song, *I Didn't Know God Made Honky Tonk Angels*, expressed a woman's inchoate outrage at being cheated on, and questioned the whole country sexual double standard on matters of love and lust. It was a huge success and made her reverse her professional course; she had been singing with Johnny and Jack and doing some recording but without much success, and was ready to quit. Suddenly she was, not so much a feminist icon (there were no such things in those days in country music), but a lady who simply stood up for herself against double-dealing men. This was no mean feat; and though there was significant industry resistance to *I Didn't Know God Made Honky Tonk Angels* the song had a life of its own and just kept selling, putting her - and this new country attitude - front and center on a lot of otherwise predominantly male stages. For this she earned the gratitude of several generations of women singers, as well as a substantial and long-term career as a singer. It helped that that her persona was modestly assertive and never hostile, and that she never seemed to

---

[42] Why don't I trust Whitburn? Because his statistical methods re: early music are so bogus as to make me disregard just about everything else he claims. Here's Tim Brooks on Whitburn's Pop Memories:

"It must be said, the entire book is a colossal fraud. But wait, you say, you didn't know there were any popular charts in 1890? You are right. Whitburn simply made them up. The great danger is that Whitburn's apparently precise data, with its impressive looking sources, will be reprinted and enshrined as historical fact by others. This has already begun to happen…Whitburn has certainly been misleading in not making it clear that his "charts" are entirely speculative, and, as we have seen, none too accurate."

For more go to: https://songbook1.wordpress.com/fx/joel-whitburn-criticism-chart-fabrication-misrepresentation-of-sources-cherry-picking/

be challenging the status quo, professional or otherwise. But, in that Nashville way, she sang song after song with that compelling but accommodating twang, like a musical form of feminist home-delivery. Here, finally, was a sad story that women could not only listen to, but also, in the privacy of their own domestic worlds, identify with **(Making Believe 1955)**.

And yet country music's relevance - socially, musically, commercially - was clearly being challenged by the rise of rock and roll. Though in economic terms country was never in any real danger of losing its market share, in vernacular terms it was quickly and easily outpaced by a new generation of rockers. In a previous life these kids would probably have become a generation of drunk and disorderly hillbilly singers; in the current day, the path of least resistance to sex and drugs (lots of speed) and hopefully money, was though the eye of the rocker hurricane. There was a sudden explosion of talent along with a burst of mediocrity. The era of the one-hit wonder had begun; take **Dale Hawkins** who, try as he might for the rest of his life really left us only one thing of significance, though it was quite a thing; his version of **Suzie Q**, recorded **1956**, was a rock and roll masterpiece of riff-making and sheer sonic inevitability, very much ahead of its time and yet an exact piece of it. We will say that no other recording of that day better captured the essence of what rock and roll - especially apart from Elvis - was trying to be, as it sought out a way of singing, playing guitar, and of otherwise avoiding the trap of boogie-woogie and blues cliche.

This was a new world of deep, white funk, as extracted from the blues, from the darker side of white country's honky tonk visions, and from the caveman yield of Southern macho. It really was something new, though we cannot ignore its direct relationship to things like Howlin' Wolf's (see Vol. 25) *Smokestack Lighting*, with its incantatory electric riff. *Suzie Q* was similar but different, in a new and hard-to-define, but easy-to-hear, rock and roll way. The guitar was louder and more treble based, built for more (wooden) sonic resistance and less acoustic resonance (for example, Scotty Moore played a Gibson hollow-body which, due to feedback issues, had limited volume; the solid-body, louder Telecaster lead on this was played by James Burton, a legendary studio player who later spent time in Los Vegas working with Elvis during The King's strangely exuberant declining years). Burton's guitar solo - at 1:36 - is like a rock and roll declaration of war against country manners, especially of the Nashville kind, like the launching of generational hostilities.

*Suzie Q* succeeds for many reasons, not least of which is that it is a real song recorded in real time, live and in a studio with no overdubbing (or tracking as they like to call it these days). Rock and roll was an important thing because it was so *authentic,* as in being true to the the lives of those who played, lived, and listened to it. It was like being witness to a new form of portable religion. If you want to put it into a 1950s perspective, in Cold War terms, and think of it as real life under the sterile shadow of McCarthy-ite conformity, be my guest. I think it would have happened no matter what the political backdrop. The blues had done and said its thing, jazz ran on a distant track, and pop music was denatured and happy about it; so these hillbilly defilers stepped in to fill the clear and obvious void.

Certainly the Burnette Brothers - Johnny and Dorsey - were defilers extraordinaire, though the most frequent target of conflict was each other. Like the battling Dorseys (Jimmy and Tommy), the Burnettes simply did not get along, but they did negotiate a sibling peace long enough to form **The Rock and Roll Trio** with the guitarist Paul Burlison. They had (what I assume to be hostile) energy to spare, and it came across on records like a house already burned to the ground. **Lonesome Train on a Lonesome Track (7/2/56)** is among their best, rhythmically lithe, with an Elvis-friendly vocal and Burlison's reliably blue country-fusion guitar, filling in the rhythm spaces with a steady stream of country-rock lines, done to a rock and roll backdrop. Listen particularly to what he does behind the vocal at the beginning and end of this; here was the kind of interactive electro-acoustic vocal/instrumental exchange that showed how rock and roll could pull away and separate itself, with radical finality, from mainstream country music's overly-mannered division of musical labor. These rock-and-rollers-in-the-wood were treating *sound* and song as something to be divided and conquered; the country business establishment could look at this kind of music all they wanted, could laugh at it and imitate it and, failing all of that, try to isolate it. Nothing could or would succeed at removing it from the life of the market because the *sound* of the new music was just too damned user-friendly and orgasmically attractive. At root it was really just another artistic bastard child of Southern life, produced from the friction of white and black, a cultural overtone with white side effects.

Country music, even when made outside of Nashville, had a tendency in those days to walk the line between the old and reliable hooks of honky-tonk and the simpler pleasures of white blues and boogie, with only hints at what rock and roll might mean to the music in the long professional run. Still, once in a while there was a strange yet satisfying violation of musical norms. Some of this was clearly the sound of a new kind of music, pushing in the direction of rock and roll, defying country propriety, more than a little bit on the wild side, and yet not exactly what Elvis had in mind. Nothing shows this better than the early sound of Eddie Cochran and his brother Hank. **The Cochran Brothers** were what some people liked to call hillbilly cats, and songs like **Slow Down (1956)** were fantastic little hillbilly-boogie vignettes, a country New Thing that was part hipster zeal, part rock and roll, and part kiss-of-country-death. Country music could not long withstand a sustained musical attack of the likes of *Slow Down,* and its answer was not counter-attack but imitation with pallid results.

Musically, at least, the Cochran Brothers (and we should remember that Eddie, who became a rock star, soon moved in other musical directions more in line with what, ironically or not, became the rock and roll mainstream) showed why it was time for country music to get out of the way and give up on emulation. This is a new king of musical steamroller - jangling guitar with a country twang, only twice as trebly; country-brother voices that are no longer part, per that particular tradition of sympathetic sibling harmonies, of old-time Southern scenery, but instead up close and in your face - or, really, in the face of the country music industry; a hard-rock piano that plays every blues cliche like it's the last note it'll ever play; a smart-alecky exchange of lead-vocals; some more country-defiling lead guitar (played by Eddie Cochran); white-blues growls, and an overall happy-time chaos as strange as it is familiar.

I have been challenged in the past when I asserted, in public forums, that I didn't feel that **Jerry Lee Lewis** (yes, the Killer, of at least, just maybe, two wives) was much of a rock and roller. Instead I think of him as maybe the greatest country singer who ever lived, the guy who showed there was a valid new-school approach to be made to old-school country ballad-ing, a rock and roll way to rip the pious sentimentality out of the death-grip of country crooners and sentimental Nashville poseurs. Lewis' country technique was such as to make, at least in the moment, all previous country-white singers of the post-War era (even the good and the great ones) seem somehow insufficient. Such, at least to me, was the power of his recasting of the emotional shape of traditional country singing. One doesn't even have to know his personal history - thuggish, violent, and just plain insane - to hear the tear-jerking threat in his voice, the way in which he seems to be laying down the sentimental law in song. It may be a stupid thing to say, but maybe this was the side of him that, in theory at least, redeemed all of his horrible personal traits, the artistic angel even as it was throttled by the devil of his personality. I am not qualified to make the clinical case, but I do know that recordings like the one he made of the then-current country hit **Crazy Arms (1956)** are country-music revelation-in-sound. This was equal to the way Billie Holiday transformed some early, by-the-numbers, pop songs, by finding their essences and then liberating those essences by locating, in a musical space, their subterranean meaning; by finding a deeper relationship between melody and lyric, and by divining the truth and personal poetry hidden in those lyrics (by in effect turning them into personal diaries). Were Lewis and Holiday making more out of common material then was really there? I don't know, but if so, that makes their accomplishments even more miraculous.

Even Lewis' opening piano in this sounds, for once, like something more than recycled gospel. His melodious drone of a voice, the little repetitions ("not mine, not mine, not mine" brings to mind Louis Armstrong's repeated "oh memory" in his 1929 recording of Stardust), the ease with which he rolls through this with a cheerful anti-sentimentality, show what "modern" country music can and should be. Even more so than the so-called rebels of later country (like Waylon Jennings or Willie Nelson), Jerry Lee Lewis has found a way to superimpose, in a counterintuitive but ingenious way, old-modern meaning on new-modern material.

Country is as country does, to paraphrase a phrase from a mediocre movie that was, nevertheless, very popular. But that's how I see **Jimmy Reed**, a dedicated bluesman of the most dedicated kind.

Reed was a few different things - first of all a solid singer with the kind of voice that we might think only a mother could love, but which in his case made a lot of people (including myself) want to listen. There is something simple yet hypnotic about the sound of it. In some respects, like Melania Trump, he doesn't seem to care, but in other respects (unlike with the woman who I hope, by the time you read this, is the ex-first lady) he has some kind of mysterious (musical) sex appeal. Listening to Jimmy Reed is like eating a good, no-frills sandwich, with plenty of meat and a little garnish, on fresh bread. It isn't terribly exciting, but as soon as you are done with it you want - no, *need* - another. He was also a really good songwriter, who turned out perfect, matter-of-fact songs, recorded so effortlessly that he was the song and the song was him. He strummed away on that old guitar, with no fancy blues footwork but a right-rhythm, and he just always seemed to be pleading for one thing or another. This was and is my definition of country; Reed was a passive receptor of a mysterious and hidden genius for vernacular summary.

And that rhythm, again. It was like tranquilizer boogie, built for a drum-machine-like backbeat and maybe a slow-dance or two. And, he was a really big influence on certain early rockers, especially blues-driven ones like Johnny Winter. There was just something in Reed's time feel and emotionally tactile approach to the blues, a basic basic-ness, that gave it a new kind of white-boy rocker appeal, touched with just the right amount of commercial edge, working almost against type. On songs like **Baby Don't Say that No More (1956)** Reed casts a weird spell, like a form of country hypnosis. It was in the manner of a floating aura, of the kind that might be found at a different kind of crossroads, one where the light folks came to try and meet the dark folks but found, instead, a strange and far-off echo of the blues and decided to follow *that* sound instead. Jimmy Reed's brand of club-boogie was off-the-beaten-path, a simple thing in a complicated world, and its corrupting innocence probably made it appealing to white outsiders like Winter (and other pale outcasts), who found, in its blackened sound, a way to their own confused souls. There was a special kind of country mystery involved in this whole search for white reality in black sound, as a life line for some of these white kids, who not only wanted to play music but who also sought to avoid the Southern death wish of racial self-denial. There was reconciliation and even reparation in this sound.

Was **Little Richard** a rock and roller? He certainly had the street cred of a gospel background and, in his earliest recordings, a guts-and-glory approach to song that put him in some unspecified center of some unspecified circle: this was no longer the shallow shuffle of rhythm and blues. It was way past the country-time beat of certain post-country bluesmen, and it had neither the flavor of black pop or the spiritual certainty of black gospel music. Certainly, in 1955, songs like **I'm Just a Lonely Guy** had large bits of the church in them, but their triplet beat bore more than a little resemblance to the burgeoning rock, rhythm and roll of New Orleans, as spread out among the faithful. And Richard had once been among the faithful, singing first in church and then even opening for Sister Rosetta Tharpe, who offered needed encouragement. Through one way and another he got a taste of, and so picked from, the poison fruit of popular music, and ended up traveling with a medicine show.

This might have been where he expanded his reputation and discovered the joys of sinning. Being gay and black in the 1940s and 1950s South was more dangerous than being just one or the other; and though Little Richard both denied and confirmed his gayness repeatedly for the rest of his life (which had episodes of religious dedication followed by renunciations of homosexuality followed by traditional marriage followed by periods of sexual merger and musical disavowal and then re-dedication), it was clearly part of his act, something necessary expressly for the purpose of public denial, acceptance, and confession. His singing was the same; what gave him power was his manner of near-desperation, as though each performance was an act of confession and contrition, followed by public declarations of sexual and spiritual ambivalence. As for whether he was an actual rock and roller (he is regularly described as the "architect of rock and roll") I have my doubts, though it doesn't really matter to anyone but me. I just hear his act as having universal application - on early works like *I'm Just a Lonely Guy* there is, in particular, an aching need-to-please that applies gospel music teachings directly to something which sounds as a new form of black pop, and one that exists, historically, in parallel to white rock. He certainly fed off of rock and roll music and rock and roll music certainly fed off of him, off of his sexual ambivalence, his sense of moral displacement, and the desire to replace any such uncertainty with an attitude and a beat.

In that regard there are those of us who think that **Nappy Brown (I'm in the Mood, 1955)**, even more so than Ray Charles, connected, decisively, the musical dots between gospel music and the popular staging of black-based feeling in song. I have always admired Ray Charles more than I liked his music - meaning, I liked his music but didn't listen to it much. To me - and this is not, I repeat NOT to be interpreted as a criticism of Ray - his voice and musical manner was more, contrary to my tastes, to the middle-of-the-road, not in any spirit of artistic compromise but because that was where Charles' musical preferences lay, somewhere in the gap between night-club blues, jazz, funky jazz, and the church. His brilliance was in his ability to bridge that gap, without concession to anything but his own taste and ideas, and the results showed he had located the musical nerve endings of a certain kind of American musical preference, one that craved deep and spiritual satisfaction at the same time that it demanded at least a veneer of social and artistic sophistication. Was this both cause and effect of the emergence of a new black middle class division of taste? Damned it I know, but it sounds like a reasonable theory.

Nappy Brown was a different thing altogether, as far as I can hear (and for those of us who still remember the era of the *good* Bill Cosby, Nappy Brown was the composer of *Nighttime is the Right Time*, which became (extra) famous by way of a very funny lip-synced version as performed by the faux Cosby family on the *Bill Cosby Show* - though that version, interestingly enough, was taken from a Ray Charles performance). Recording for Savoy, which had an extraordinary 1950s catalog of black blues, rhythm and blues, and pre-soul singers (the category of *soul music* had not yet been invented) Nappy was, in some ways, the un-Ray Charles, a singer of unreconstructed soul, whose emotionally-shipwrecked corner of the market was an oasis, for those who liked it rougher and tougher, of unadulterated anguish, despair, and begrudging joy. If Ray Charles' music was a place of sanctuary cleansed by directness of manner and a deep-black spirit of cultural, communal consensus, Nappy Brown's was located in that space where the spoils of material success were no longer enough, where, in the heat of spiritual battle, all social bets were off. More, as I am so fond of saying, of the old world in the new.

In the middle of all of this, of '50s neo-soul, shit-kicking hillbillies-in-rock, strange new blues, strange old blues, jazz tone-sampling, and other forms of semi-hostile cultural merger/takeover, there are the occasional eccentric musical oddities that occupy hard-to-define musical spaces. **Bobby Short** is a case in point, as a distinguished singer of a distinguished repertoire, a very good pianist who chose consciously, the way I hear it, to sing in such a way that it sounds like he is singing about singing. Short, a black man, had a very special kind of cultural independence. Stylistically he really did fit in, but not with the categorical ease of your average black pop or jazz singer. His was a new kind of performance art whose focus was on process, on the public artist as a private person, who reveals himself at will and with cultivated calculation. Bobby Short made an art out of the proper and carefully-enunciated phrasing of the American standard-song lyric, building his style from, I would guess, the idea of vaudeville vocal projection (gotta reach the cheap seats), a respect for the words and what they meant about the composer's true intent, and even, just possibly, from a minstrel sense of exaggerated but ultimately (in black hands and as a result of the reclamation of the style by black-minstrels) respectful if sometimes exaggerated distance. [43]

    **Hottentot Potentate (1955)** was originally performed by Ethel Waters in a show called *At Home Abroad*. It was presented on Broadway in 1935 as directed by Vincent Minelli, and was composed by the white song team of Arthur Schwartz and Howard Dietz, (of standards like *Along Together,* Y*ou and the Night and the Music,* and *Dancing in the Dark).* Those last cited were like musical crystal and characteristic of their work, elegant and carefully crafted. *At Home Abroad* was different, a musical travelog, with songs reflecting the various locales encountered on a cruise around the world; Ethel Waters was given the African stop, of course. The song is strange and very much of it's strange time, and the lyrics bear repeating here:

"All the crowned heads of Europe
Have troubles with their thrones,
But I've got a kingdom in the hollow of my hand,
Cos' I'm the Emperor Jones!
I came from Harlem, settled here,
Knocked the Congo flat on its ear.
I came and I saw and I conquered a nation
With my trickeration!
My witchcraft made them build a crown for me,

---

[43] This one, this concept of exaggerated minstrel respectability, is complicated. It originates in the portrayal, by white people, on the minstrel stage, of black people as fops, dressed with shabby yet pretentious formality and so ridiculed for their supposedly futile ambitions of respectability. I have a feeling that black minstrel troupes took this degrading stereotype and ran with it in the interest of reclaiming their own dignity, so that it could no longer be denied them through impersonation and ridicule.

The natives do a lot of bowin' down for me,
And anyone of them would go to town for me,
The Hottentot Potentate!
I brought my bottle of Chanel with me,
I brought along the script of Lulu Bell with me,
I let them on, but oh, it raises hell with me
The Hottentot Potentate!
I wooed them, wooed them from the start,
And I ghouled them! I ghouled them!
I played a part.
But I fooled them, fooled them,
Gave them my art.
I gave all them movement,
Modern improvement.
The new name of the jungle stampin' ground
Is Emperor Jones' Afrikaner vampin' ground
I don't allow no trampin' on my campin' ground
I'm hot and potent!
Potent and hot!
Hottentot Potentate!
The jungle now has got some chic to it,
A touch of cloisonné and de Lalique to it,
And who brought all this drawin' room technique to it?
(Growl it out, baby doll!)
The Hottentot Potentate!
It was wild and it was savage open airy land,
With lions and with tigres was a scary land,
Until I made of it a savoire-fairy land.
The Hottentot Potentate!
I swayed them from the start,
I played them, I took part.
I made them copy my art,
I gave them that hotcha
Je ne sais quoi-cha.
The jungle's more than one supposes now,
They're even sleeping on a bed of roses now,
And got earrings they're wearing in their noses now.
For the hot and potent!
Potent and hot!
Hot! Potent!
Hottentot Potentate!

So: the singer came to the African jungle and tamed the native savages, but in a very charming way and, I will venture to say, in a manner that was no more racist than in Bert Williams and George Walker's *My Little Zulu Babe* (see Vol. 1). Short's method is different, however. Williams and Walker savaged the idea of those stereotypical savages; Short uses a classic Broadway-show, proscenium-like presentation, declaiming like a narrator, varying his delivery to sectionalize the song, to give different meaning to different parts of the narrative, which is written and sung with tongue-in-cheek, perhaps, but with only a veiled, satirical self consciousness. This is not, as with Williams and Walker, broad comedy, but instead an ultra-sophisticated parody of Western attitudes, of the popular sense, even in those pre-Trumpian days, that anything non-American or European was a shit-hole awaiting the civilizing influence of enlightened explorers (the Hottentots, we should note, were some of the first natives located by early Europeans in the region of Southern Africa). But what made it ultra hip was that it was also a social self-critique. As a song sung by a black man or woman it begged the question of middle-class detachment from those Diasporan roots, and gently mocked the singer's own overconfidence.

Even so, the song was undoubtedly written (and hence sung) from a "black" point of view, even if white-manufactured, and so had an aura, in its lyric range, of self-possession and entitled irony. Waters' version, recorded in 1935, was less demonstrative than Short's but had the same sense of material control, was possessed of a confidence that she could, indeed, sing these white words in a white show without apology. To the credit of Schwartz and Dietz it was that good a song, melodically and lyrically, and to the credit of Bobby Short it was a perfect vehicle for the singer-as-self-dramatist. By performing songs like this Short continually left himself open to inevitable challenges of racial (in)authenticity. The rolled r's, the set-piece formality, and the whole way he held himself up to a respectable (white?) light made him vulnerable to such charges; though, as we have learned, to be an American musician of any color is and has always been a matter of realizing that the final arbiter of racial authenticity is and will always be the performer.

Sometime in **1955** the singer **Bobby Blue Bland (I Woke Up Screaming)** had, as he tells us herein, a really bad dream. Once again this particular performance, in the years of blues drift, in a time when the music was adjusting itself to audiences and vice versa, gives us an unfiltered picture of the growing, expanding, black vernacular. Singers like Bland, whose raw power is apparent even in the service of this old(er) recording technology, were somewhat between rock and a segregated place, even as the music, on all fronts, presented, in its own wild and crazy way, more and more of a challenge to Jim Crow marketing. Bland recorded for a black Jew (the unpredictably crooked Don Robey) and a black label (Duke Peacock), which was Texas based and clearly had its hand on some part of the region's (and hence, maybe, the nation's) musical pulse. Though to backtrack I will reiterated once more my conviction that this "old technology" was in many ways more accurate and faithful, in its analog splendor, than more recent technologies to the sound and spirit of music like this. Find me a digital equivalent of this kind of raw, room-fed power, of the kind that makes you feel you are in the very same room as a bunch of hungry and down-home, inspired musicians, black or white. Bland understood the process, and his singing is unfettered in the way it would not have been, fifty years later, singing from the inappropriate comfort of an isolation booth to a track of a distant rhythm section, horns and effects to be added later.

This is, yes folks, the real thing, or, maybe, as close to the real thing as you will get if you were born in the last thirty or forty years. Listen to the action, of Bland vs Guitar (the legendary Wayne Bennett), the way they listen to and react to each other. And then listen to the guitar solo, the way Bennett sums everything up musically with a lot of the right notes and a tone driven by, yes, guitar amps and the soul of tube technology. It's done in a studio but the audience is in their head and the music is in the room. And consider yourself lucky that Robey, the Wandering Hebrew, had the wherewithal and sense of greed to know that it was something that had to be done, for whatever reasons, and that he actually did it.

Who was **One String Sam** and why does he sound like the last of the New World Africans on the recordings he made in the 1950s, **Need a Hundred Dollars (1955) and My Babe (1956)**? Well, let us check what the internet has to say:

> "In 1956, an unknown street musician named "One String" Sam Wilson walked into Joe's Record Shop on Hastings Street in Detroit, carrying a plank of wood containing a single string. The shop also had a recording studio in the back, and Sam proceeded to record two songs on his diddley bow, 'I Need a Hundred Dollars' and 'My Babe.' One String Sam used an empty baby food jar as a slide."[44]

---

[44] https://www.guitarworld.com/news/diy-musician-one-string-sam-backstory-jack-white-s-diddley-bow

The Diddley bow was an old Southern instrumental concoction, one string stretched across a piece of wood, and the inconsistent, non-musical tension it achieved was actually very musical, evoking, it its vibrating overtones, a series of harmonic overlaps. It allegedly had ties to African music making (likely true) and it was a poor-man's - well, a poor man's instrument. What was so fantastic about Sam's recording, and the way the instrument resonated, was the way in which it showed how, as with jug bands and Thelonious Monk, the homemade musical methods of African Americans were not only very much a Diasporan extension (a call to the homeland, so to speak, though I doubt very much that Monk would have agreed) but also built on a concept of false simplicity. As Monk seemed to be pairing down the jazz tradition, reducing pianism to a few choice notes that, in their spaced-out (in more ways than one) voicing sounded thin and dense at the same time (thin as in transparent, as each note in a harmonic spread seemed visible and isolated; dense in their implied dissonance, both cultural and sonic), the single, twanging notes that One String Sam laid down seemed fraught with harmonic possibility, nervous with harmonic meaning. One note meant two in the right places, or three or four, all of them, like Monk's, visibly matched with each other yet so wide-apart harmonically as to sound equally clear as both single notes and in their relationship as intervals. One String Sam, who was rediscovered in the 1970s and hit the blues circuit briefly, was in that long and hallowed tradition, of musicians who seemed to make it up as they went along, who trusted their instincts (and yes, this is Monk, too) to lead them, digression after digression, back to where they had started.

I have written of **Bo Diddley** as one of the true rockers of early music, one of the few stylistically accurate *black* rockers of early music, and I not only stand by that statement, I will try to explain it here.

What distinguishes rock and roll from the blues and rhythm and blues that came before it? Well, many things. First of all the rhythm of its 4-beat stream separates it from rhythm and blues, though this time-feel (four beats solid, emphasis on all 4, with drops on 2 and 4 that are less like backbeats than rhythmic interruptions) connects it to blues of the hard variety as heard in the post-War, electrified music that came out of cities like Detroit and Chicago. Not to mention the occasional but extremely significant insertion of the Afro-Latin based clave, which may be described, in basic terms, as using a 3-3-2 subdivision (and which, I am told by knowledgeable folks, originated in Africa). Sonically rock and roll (and I apologize for repeating myself) had a higher center of gravity than either blues or r&b, less mud in its bottom, less bass and more sonic space in the rhythm section. Lyrically rock and roll was a secularization of the secularization of the blues in many respects (particularly pre-Bob Dylan, at a time when rock and roll writers lacked what we might, for want of a better description, call poetic ambition), a simplification, in blues and vernacular terms, of the sprawling poetry of the blues in favor of universally-understood symbolism and back-to-basics, leering, lovelorn, emotionally-glib, broadside-like declarations (hence my own citing of the original Sonny Boy Williamson's *Good Morning Little Schoolgirl*, with its cheerful-pedo outlook and abandonment of blues-couplet principles, as maybe, in terms of subject/vision, the first rock and roll tune).

Bo Diddley is all of the above, and then some. He is also a sonic pioneer whose transliteration of the down-home sound of old-world Southern blues (he was from Mississippi) into contemporary rock and roll terms puts him at the center of the music's flurry of 1950s creativity, its mad scramble, musically, to define itself, in those years, sonically and commercially. Listen to the insinuating guitar tremolo of **She's Fine She's Mine** from **1956**. Check out the clave-based maracas, the distance between top and bottom (there is almost no bass on this), the mild distortion inherent in the the way this drives itself, with a natural acoustic balance and with an up-front vocal (by Diddley) that fearlessly overloads those old analog meters. Not to mention the title, which is very pop and rock, and which immediately separates this from not just the country blues but also rhythm and blues, (whose musicians would never have used such a fey lead in).

We might call this, in its early innocence, the passion of rock and roll. The origins of same is easily recognizable in just about everything the **Gospel Songbirds** (see also Vol. 28) did. **When They Ring Those Golden Bells (1955)** is like an air-pump of emotion, emanating, as the strength of this performance does, from the lead, who propels the performance from his opening cue with startling power. There is nothing fey about this (actually there is nothing fey about Bo Diddley's performance, just, maybe, the title). It avoids either musical or spiritual abstraction, and has the concrete world view of classic black gospel music, the optimistic yet also fatalistic sense that life is essentially an endless, apocalyptic battle, of the world versus Heaven, or, really, the world versus itself. Though competently accompanied, the Gospel Songbirds are their own rhythm section, relentless and humanly insistent. This is like the free-thinking version of the old-style black vocal group. The hard-gospel edge in this is a particular source of rock and roll's extra-blues intensity, but also a particularly interesting contrast to rock and roll's regular and constant state of spiritual denial.

That exact kind of gospel-vocal introduction, a solo way of setting the mood, is mimicked in **Earl King**'s wild-eyed **You Can Fly High (12/56)**. This is another post-origin prototype of early rock and roll, the rhythm section built on the principles of New Orleans rock and rhythm (and King, a black man, was from New Orleans). Not only have King's compositions been performed by everyone from Professor Longhair to Stevie Ray Vaughan to Jimmie Hendrix, his whole method of lyric objectivity was another early and significant contravention of the lyric conventions of the straight blues. As I note above, in relation to Bo Diddley, the transition from the poetically constricted (but, yes, profound) world of early country blues to the modern, objective, dramatically reduced (I was going to say dumbed-down, but that's really not quite the term) *mis en scene* of pop music was a serious thing. There is no easy way to characterize the quality of writing of working musicians in these years in contrast to those who wrote most of their songs in the privacy of business offices (think Leiber and Stoller, for starters, two pros with supposedly deep vernacular connections), though I do think there is an urgency in the work of Earl King that is absent in the songs of the proficient, white, Brill Building-like teams of composers who began to dominate the rock/rhythm/pop field in the 1950s and 1960s. This whole recording is a powerful case-in-point. King's opening solo-vocal cry and the way in which this performance roars and rumbles its way through, as a vernacular counterpoint to the gospel desperation of groups like the Gospel Songbirds, is no (sanctified) accident. Black music of different styles in the 1950s was still able to tap into that deep well of religious sound in order to execute a transference of feeling. And note that the slightly depraved backbeat of *You Can Fly High*, King's gnarly voice (substituting throughout for the gospel moan), and the whole arrangement, loud and with a single dynamic level, makes this a part of the classic New Orleans rock template.

One of the sonic inventors, if not the inventor, of that template was a man named Cosimo Matassa, a New Orleans-based entrepreneur who, like Sun Records' Sam Phillips, opened his own local recording studio with little planning other than to market his services to local musicians, and ended up with a musical empire and membership in the Rock and Roll Hall of Fame (for what that's worth, and there are many people who think "not much"). Matassa, an excellent recording engineer, made records with a specific sound, and it's the sound of Earl King, though I am unable to confirm that *You Can Fly High* was made in Matassa's studio. I do know that **Ooh-Wow** by **Roy Montrell (8/18/56)** was made there, and in certain respects it sounds like they took Earl King's backing tracks and just overdubbed another guy - which, of course, did not happen, since the technology to do so did not exist in those days. But *Ooh-Wow* fits the pattern. Montrell, who worked as a session musician with people like Fats Domino, has a great growling voice (also like King - was this a New Orleans thing?), and the backing players here, whoever they are, chug their way through another New Orleans-type, backbeat-heavy rocker, which includes a cookie-cutter saxophone solo, party lyrics, and not much bottom to the sound (confirming, again, one of my pet theories about rock and roll and the sonic musical change it represented). Matassa, like Phillips, had figured out how to get a natural room balance, and the result is like a documentary of what some musicians, and the men who were trying to make money off of them, were thinking.

Blues-wise, note that the rhythm of **Louie Myers' Just Wailing (1956)** is a sped-up version of the pre-rock and roll, loping beat I have cited in sources as far and wide as Romeo Nelson (see Vol. 12) and Charlie Booker (see Vols, 26, 27). It was inevitable that someone would take this catchy, shuffle-plus rhythm and dress it up in blues-and-boogie terms. I know I have said this ad-nauseum but it bears repeating: this was one major piece of the rhythmic revolution that was rock and roll: the four-beat rush of this and the way it accents as in a kind of rhythmic push-pull was a new thing relative to this musical world. If you count in 4, as in one-and-two-and-thee-and-four-and, each *and* (all of which are up beats) is like its own form of back beat, a prompt for the immediately-following down beat to sharply mark it's own rhythmic territory. So instead of having an emphasis on every beat this makes an accent on every half-beat, a maddeningly busy way of keeping time. This was not, as I said, unlike what Nelson and Booker had done, but the rapid way Myers and group execute it was new and different. Myers (who regularly teamed up with his brother Dave) was a main player on the Chicago blues scene of those years, regularly serving as backup for local headliners, and even spent some time as a replacement for harpist Little Walter in Muddy's band. It's easy to take journeymen musicians like the Myers brothers for granted, but instructive to hear how distinctive they can be when let loose to do their own thing, as on *Just Wailing*. This has its own peculiar blues-swing, and Myers (who plays harp on this) has some of Little Walter's jazz-and-boogie push, though the powerful momentum of this - the strong harp riffing and the unrelenting, interactive near-chaos - is unique in the whole canon of Chicago blues.

What and who were **The Drifters**? Well, I refer you to Wikipedia for a sense of their unwieldy history, which I won't try to summarize here for fear of confusing dates, lead singers, ownership, and death notices. They seem to have had shifting personnel (their most famous lead singer being the constantly exploited Clyde McPhatter, see Vol. 26, who was for a time entrapped and underpaid in the Dominoes as well), a lot of hits, and a few different record labels. We might call them a doo-wop band, as Wiki does, except for the fact that they didn't sing doo-wop. So instead we can substitute the generic "black vocal group" because, historically, they do fit the black quartet mold with variation in size and personnel. And they seem to have repeatedly fallen victim to the business, which is no great surprise in those mob-controlled years. There were various lawsuits over the rights to use the name, though I would refer you, once again, to the internet if you want to research and try to understand just who did what to whom. Suffice to say that they came under some good musical supervision; they had Jerry Leiber and Mike Stoller, of Leiber and Stoller fame, who wrote **Ruby Baby**, which the Drifters made on **9/19/55**, and also Jessie Stone, the former Kansas City bandleader turned Midas-touch pop composer, who wrote *Money Honey*, another of their hits, but they were knocked around and cheated, not just on paper but also in life. They were even for a time owned - yes, owned - by George Treadwell, the husband of the jazz singer Sarah Vaughan, who kept them on salaries while he made the bigger bucks from professional affiliations and concerts (and no, he was not Jewish). In the end a lot of people got rich off their music, but not the Drifters.

By the time they made *Ruby Baby* McPhatter was gone, though this song was typical of their material. There was a veneer of rhythm and blues in their accompaniment and in their vocal sound, more than a touch of gospel give-and-take in the group dynamic and floating lead, and a good sense of vernacular novelty in the way this took a catchy lyric and hooked it memorably onto a blues or blues-based melody. And they had soul, something without which Lieber and Stoller and Price, money-makers all who never, as far as I know, stood up for anyone other than themselves in the business, would have been unemployed and broke.

Listening to that opening, spanking guitar solo, at the beginning of **Johnny Guitar Watson's Three Hours Past Midnight (1956)**. What was one to do with the electric blues in these still-technically challenged days, and where to go with the music? Well, you are listening to it. Watson (one of those perpetually contemporary musicians who in later years embraced, successfully, everything from soul to funk and disco and whose biggest pop hit came in 1977 when he was 42 years old) was from Houston, and the way he made these bluesy, musical catch-phrases, the kind of basic but rangy melodic shapes he formed out of very narrow source material, was typical of the electric Texas blues (think: T. Bone Walker, Johnny Winter, Gatemouth Brown, Freddie King, Albert Collins, and Pee Wee Crayton, not to mention Blind Lemon Jefferson and Lightning Hopkins). Watson's way of manipulating sound, reportedly with delay and echo and other electronics, was legendary, and can be heard to some extent on *Three Hours Past Midnight*. That clipped, treble-plus tone was noted by a lot of other musicians, and Jimi Hendrix was reported to have said that this recording inspired him to pick up the guitar. So much, as with nearly all blues guitar, of the impact of Watson's playing comes from his sense of time. One can hear in it some strongly-rooted ideas of the kind that had a great impact, both rhythmically and sonically, on some emerging white guitar interpretations of rock and roll. Listen further to his brief instrumental interlude, beginning at about 1:20, and then to his full solo at 1:42; this as complex, rhythmically, as anything a jazz musician has ever done, in its odd note groupings and time-twisting rhythm. And like almost every important new thing played by any musician at any time and in any place, this whole thing sounds completely strange yet enticingly familiar at the same time.

Some musicians self destruct in grand and grandiose ways. They go out like a Fourth of July celebration, with bright flashes of light and great streaks across the sky, and their deaths are celebrated like those of the Pharaohs, as though they will have eternal life (though none, to my knowledge, was ever, like the Pharaohs, entombed with a virgin). And then there are figures like **Big Maybelle**, an enormous presence on record and yet a modest and un-sensational presence in history, a nice lady who just went about her musical business but who unfortunately had some bad habits, which killed her. She also happened to be one of the great black pop 'n jazz singers of all time. She started off recording for that great Goniff-in-the-Sky, Savoy Record's Herman Lubinsky, a man who made Ebenezer Scrooge seem like a spendthrift. Later Maybelle recorded for Okeh, and these, along with the Savoys, are the records she is best known for, though it should be noted that on every label for which she made music until her death at age 48 (in 1972) she made music that heroically played to her strengths and passions, even as she was physically fading from both those bad habits and diabetes. The Savoys and the Okehs, like her version of **There I've Said it Again (7/20/56)**, are fantastic collaborations between Maybelle and some of the best studio players of that era, jazz musicians who augmented their creative lives with pop and rock side-jobs. Their sympathetic and deep accompaniment, to a singer whose presence must have offered some relief from the work-a-day monotony of rock and roll and rhythm and blues sessions (and I know this because I was told by more than a few older jazz musicians that they found that other music boring and repetitive to play), is audible.

Big Maybelle was the real thing and one of the lucky ones (sort of) who, coming out of the big band era, had the chops to not just adapt to the newer forms of black commercial music but to crossover in a way that predicted soul music, that sounded a lot like jazz from the Bessie Smith tradition on, and which combined many of the best features of gospel pop and rock as heard from Rosetta Tharpe, Ray Charles, and Nappy Brown. Maybelle really did have it all; listen to her razor-sharp phrasing on *There I've Said It Again*, a once-treacly ballad introduced in 1945 by Vaughn Monroe. The occasional growls are Big Maybelle marking her territory, letting us know that his is *her* song now. She sings big and she sings small, and there is great detail in her cunning reimagining of this pop song in what can only be called black terms, ringing the "truth" out of material which was not necessarily intended for that purpose.

And this she continued to do, in one way or other, until her death. In the 1960s she made an incredible version of Hank Williams' *Cold Cold Heart*, as she howled and spit her way through in a manner with which I think Hank would have approved. She probably recognized that she and Hank were kindred souls, as wounded comrades forced against their will to smile for the public no matter how sick and miserable they felt.

The great guitar tremolo that opens **Uncloudy Day** by the **Staple Singers (9/11/56)** is like an announcement that this is something a lot different, at least on the surface, from the gospel world from which they came.

Not to change the subject, but do you consider my definition of country music, as music of "passive sophistication," or, in the post-War world, as music that played like it was from out of town, to be too general? Well, then think about this: some years ago Pops Staples, who led this family band, described in an interview how they had at first been rejected in Chicago (where they moved from Mississippi) by the new urban class of African Americans, as "too country." This was a problem relative to certain kinds of black music and post-War black audiences (who had settled North and West in the Great Migration). Certain sounds hit them too close to (down) home, were reminders of things that they wanted to forget, of the old days, the Old South, segregation and racial threat. This included not only guitar-centric things like *Uncloudy Day* but also a lot of neo-country blues, all heard as greenhorn leftovers, played by people who, they thought, didn't know any better, who were spending too much time living in the past. It took a while for the Staples Family to be accepted on the new gospel scene, though I hear them as anything but country-simple. *Uncloudy Day* is about as as hip and current as any gospel performance ever recorded. The guitar introduces the Staples' signature, deep-spectrum harmonies, ripe with thick undertones and brilliantly-dense unison shifts of mood and timbre. The family makes those harmonies with confidence and emotional certainty; this is a real predictor of the 1960s folk revival, respectful yet radically transformative. Sure, this is/was a playback of older moods, but then, so was/is any piece of music that is worth listening to more than once; black music is black autobiography *and* memoir when done right.

I have already written in great detail about the amazing pianist **Speckled Red** (see Vols, 15, 20) and his ties to that great in between - the music and history in between the black vernacular (blues, Songsterism, minstrel practice and revision) and black art music (also known as jazz). But I may not have spent enough time pointing out that his amazingly broad repertoire showed how indiscriminately black vernacular artists borrowed from and showed respect to certain middle-of-the-road sources of song. Music really was a moveable feast in the great smorgasbord days of the 1920s. Though some contemporary critics have complained that our sense of old-time repertoire has been distorted by the way in which white record company producers of those years segregated the market into black and white (meaning: blues and pop song, jazz and country), thereby causing historical confusion as to who, in a professional sense, played what, the truth is that all we need to know, in terms of repertoire and vernacular music, is hiding, in that world of recorded music, in plain sight. Instead of complaining about how the recording industry was structured in those early days we should be celebrating the incredible diversity of sound that was documented. Separate but equal? Well, artistically-speaking, yes, in economic terms, no. But purely in artistic and aesthetic terms the amount of ingeniously conceptualized and executed black music that we have from those years tells us that any unequal tilt, critically and historically, was to the black side.

But back to Speckled Red. He was still performing into the 1950s, 1960s, and 1970s, and it's easy to forget that by **1956**, when he recorded **All on Account of You** he was not a young man (64 at the time) but still obviously in his artistic prime, an artist made for the folk-generational revival of the 1960s. As song, *All on Account of You* is hard to pinpoint, not because of the tune itself but because of Speckled Red's way of performing it. I can find no information on its authorship or year of composition, but it sounds suspiciously like a 1920s pop song of possible Tin Pan Alley (or its environs) origin.

Once again I point to the fascinating ways with which this performance, typically (of Red) skirts certain ideas about jazz and improvisation (the only pianist I can think of immediately who approaches the piano like this, but with considerably less art, is Fess Manetta of New Orleans; see my jazz history). What sets this apart from the musical world of most old-time pianists is Red's barrelhouse finesse, the way in which his drum-like pounding makes a very fine mess of some very neatly composed music. Listen to that odd moment of departure at .018; it's like Art Tatum on an off day, but not really. Maybe it's more like an inversion, well, no, really an overturning, of conventional, schooled, jazz flights of virtuosity. It's as though Speckled Red is saying, "that's what *you* know, so now listen to what *I* know." Compare it to Monk's versions of relatively basic and even simple pop tunes, like, for example, *There's Danger In Your Eyes Cherie* (which Monk recorded solo for Riverside in the 1950s). As with Monk and *Cherie,* Red's version of this is not a political statement about race or repertoire but really a declaration of absolute and unequivocal social, artistic, and musical independence (which, yes, for a black man *is* a political statement). And also as with Monk there is nothing condescending in Speckled Red's approach to old material. He accepts it on its own musical terms, and I would venture to guess that this is where, if indirectly (because Monk may have listened to any number of other players) Monk learned his respect for old and out-of-the-way music of suspicious and (for some musical ideologues, because of its absolute whiteness) disreputable origin.

Speckled Red's gritty and charming vocal is a brilliant counterpoint to his increasingly dense and complicated accompaniment. And then there's his solo - from 1:03 on he plays what can only be called an ingenious synthesis of pounding, barrelhouse swing and off-stride, inserting brief and not-quite realized chromatic sections, interrupting the "flow" with sudden exclamation-points of sound. It's all like a demented pop song. And you want free improvisation? Listen at 2:07 to his mad insertion of upper-register beats, like a summing up of these odd musical proceedings. It's all wild and mysteriously old, like a piano roll come to life

And though this is not a study of jazz, it is a study of a lot of music that either would not exist if not for jazz, or, possibly, vice versa. I have written an entire book on jazz of the 1950s (which may see the light of day in my lifetime); the changes it was both experiencing and advocating had a lasting impact on all of American music into the modern era. To wit:

### Social Call Betty Carter 5/55

Lionel Hampton, with whose band she sang, called Carter "Betty Bebop" because, I have a feeling, of the way in which she not only felt herself to be a part of that artistic movement but also because of how she sang with a subtle displacement of rhythm and intervals, reflecting the new consciousness that was (and we love labels) Bebop. *Social Call* is a lyricized version of an instrumental piece written by the saxophonist/arranger Gigi Gryce, himself a fascinating jazz figure who, by insisting on professional independence and the right to his own music, got himself exiled from the music business (but that's another sad story).

In later years Betty Carter became an avant gardist of jazz vocals, in the way in which she re-shaped her repertoire to fit a radical idea of song-form restructuring. It was very effective if a bit of a bore, like watching a great singer take lyrics and melody, write them on paper, snip them into fragments, thrown them up into the air, and sing them in whatever order they landed. Some people loved her for it. I didn't, and I prefer her 1950s work, the way in which she handled the bebop chromaticism of songs like *Social Call*, incorporating bop's subtle but telling shifts of harmony as they impacted inevitably on melody. Most compelling, in that new, modernist way, was how she alternated between an expressionist approach to sound (clear diction and a conventional way of riding the melody) with subtle shifts of emphasis, separating her voice from the melodic line as though withholding some part of herself, emotional and otherwise. This reflects a modernist sensibility, the way in which *the new* tends to attack *the old*, as being too invested in prior techniques. As artfully as those old standards were constructed and harmonized, some artists (like Carter) still felt the negative constraints, when performing them, of audience expectation. They struggled to resist by subverting those expectations from within, by attacking formulaic ways of shaping lyric and melody (hence, I assume, Carter's later, revolutionary rejection of linear song construction and the way this forced her to change her whole way of singing).

### What Happened Last Night Alec Wilder Mundell Lowe 1956

Alec Wilder was something of a professional non-conformist, though talented and smart just the same. He wasn't really a jazz musician, but he *was* a brilliant guy whose book on American popular music (written with another brilliant but much less-known historian named James Maher) is essential. And, just to mention, Wilder was a very good songwriter. But his most peculiar talent was in writing for small-big groups, for sextets and octets in particular. The sound of Wilder's compositions was completely unique, compact and sound-shifting; smooth yet unorthodox voicings alternated with unique spurts of melody. The jazz guitarist Mundell Lowe recorded an entire album of Wilder songs in 1956 for Riverside, and we note that, although this isn't really jazz per se, it took jazz musicians to phrase it in that deep-sourced American way, with an appropriate lightness and just the right amount of swing. Wilder was in that American tradition - well, some American tradition - of ruggedly individual artist, with the kind of mien, of slightly off-centered, cheerfully disdainful mocking, that only the upper-crust can get away with while still maintaining their place in the social hierarchy.

Don't get me wrong - I love Wilder's band work. *What Happened Last Night* is a solemn and decidedly non-farcical look at how "serious" music can remain serious without pomposity. Wilder, for all his foibles, had a keen sense of artistic perspective and a deep understanding of a certain kind of (and seemingly elevated) vernacular. This attitude and way of musical being is, I think, very American. American composers are suspicious of nostalgia while conscious of how audiences demand it, even in disguise. Wilder understood this; his melodies, fresh and familiarly conservative yet still challenging, are like pressed leaves preserved in a trashed musical Book of Days.

### You'd Be So Nice to Come Home To Cecil Taylor 1956

Though I feel certain that, were he still alive, Cecil Taylor would scorn me for saying so, his desire and ability to stick to musical principal in his early professional years, in the face of repeated rejection and some downright nastiness, took great courage. To say he was ahead of his time is to put it way too mildly. He was just one of those artists who *understood*, who constructed a personal musical methodology out of an unorthodox sensibility and intense - maybe too intense - self awareness. This was, I would guess, his method - and reason for - tapping into the labyrinth of his own mind for the sake of spontaneous translation and transference of some little-known (at least in the jazz world) musical truths. I do have a feeling that, like Thelonious Monk, he had no real personal choice but to do so, and was in some ways trapped by the kind of stubborn individuality that sometimes masquerades as principle. Still, Taylor's life is an example to us all, a portrait of the artist who does as he does simply because he knows of no other way to do it.

At the time Taylor recorded the Cole Porter's *You'd Be So Nice to Come Home To* we might say he was in his ur-harmonic period, still concerned with explaining, in artistic terms, the fragmentary way the mind approaches the whole of certain visible yet pliant forms, from painting to language - though in Taylor's case what he was confronting were songs and song form, the piano, and linear ideas of jazz soloing. James Joyce once argued that the way he wrote, the way he drew out the essence of experience and consciousness and reordered them, was much more "realistic" than than the ways of more socially "accurate" writers, much truer to the flow of life as actually lived. Taylor might have argued, in the same spirit, that the way in which he exposed song elements - their fragments of harmony and melody as re-sorted into  abstract but recognizable outline - was much more faithful than more "ordered" ways of jazz performance, much more akin to lived, artistic experience, to the deepest ideals of (jazz) improvisation. No one in jazz, except, perhaps for Lennie Tristano and Bud Powell, had, in 1956, any equivalent sense of freely-associative, intuitive artistry, especially in the abstract. Playing standards that year with "standard" harmony, Taylor seemed to be starting and finishing at the same time. He was visiting "the tradition" at the same time that he was rejecting it, not exploring it so much as trying to see how much of it might still be of musical use to him. In the long term - though here he shows a surprisingly keen grasp of the possibilities of improvised line - the answer was "not much." He never seems bored, but instead appears restless on the edge of disdainful, for all that such songs required of him. In the year before Ornette Coleman completely revealed himself to the jazz world Cecil Taylor chose to take the first steps toward exiting that world, preparing to go so far inside himself that succeeding performances and recordings seemed less like self-introduction than professional withdrawal (assuming, of course, in a way that Taylor would not, that the profession we are referring to was Jazz Musician). And yes, that was a brave thing for him to do in that place and at that time. No one in jazz, in 1956, on any side of the artistic fence, was near-ready for that kind of nakedly revealing and uncompromising self-exposure.

**No More Abbey Lincoln 1956**
Abbey Lincoln's singing in the later 1950s was a complete game changer for jazz vocals - she was tough, and, in contemporary terms, one-of-the-boys (and I realize that this might seem to miss the point, that as an early musical feminist she was issuing an aggressive and principled challenge to the boys-only idea of jazz musicianship; but I am trying to put it into terms which give a sense of how that challenge appeared in her day), a group member of equal - and sometimes greater - standing. Singers until that time tended to find themselves on the outside looking in, and even Billie Holiday, musically equal to anyone who ever played an

instrument, still was subject to certain professional limitations. Holiday did, however, lead the way by taken over the material and starting a revolt against certain kinds of musical propriety; she was lady-like only on the surface. Abbey Lincoln took things a big step further. In her work there was no longer any real distance between singer, song and band. Learning from Holiday's example, Lincoln led the revolution against "feminine" expectations and the critical condescension that coined terms like "girl singer."

*No More*, an exceptional tune that actually pre-dates her more formal liberation (she soon married Max Roach and developed a much deeper racial consciousness, recording programs of feminist independence and Civil Rights advocacy), is really something of an attitudinal prelude. Recorded for Mercury Records in the time-period when Lincoln was still being groomed for lady-like success, it sounds as a giant "fuck you" to both the object of the song and the recording industry in general. Her voice is dense with emotional determination, and she is clearly a jazz singer - though once again (as before in this study) I struggle to cobble together a definition of *jazz singer* that not only covers this recording but which fits others of its kind. Lincoln is emotionally direct, unsentimental, seizes the melody and alters it only as needed, and rides the beat without coquettish remaking of the song's phrases. Like any real artist in relation to their medium she is *willing* the the raw material of objective reality into imaginative, yet non-subjective, form, making this song, in her preferred artistic way, into *jazz*. She sings jazz, we might say, so therefore she *is* (yes, a jazz singer).

# Chapter 30: This is the End (of Part 2)

I once wrote something to the effect that sometimes a decade begins before it begins; meaning that the trends of one ten year period are often visible at some point in the prior ten year period. We tend to characterize decades in glib, sociologically-stunted terminology. And it is true that, as we come to the end of this study, we can hear that the 1950s, in cultural and political terms, had a distinct intellectual and sonic signature. The problems inherent in interpreting things in this way, in ten-year grabs, however, are many. I have read too many books on music that fail miserably by creating themes which they then have to justify with a lot of intellectual hit and run, that stretch the bounds of readability and critical credibility by devising a thesis that they then sweat over and struggle with in order to justify. The problem they have is the existence of material that either stretches central and guiding principles beyond credibility or that contradicts them altogether.

I am reminded of the line from the play and film *Little Murders* (written by Jules Feiffer) in which the detective, investigating a string of killings, tells us: "What these have in common is that they have nothing in common." Fitting square pegs into round holes can be a useful exercise, but only if we also understand how obscure the results of doing so may be. We learn not so much by our mistakes but by recognizing the strangeness and irrationality of our actions, by understanding that not everything has quantifiable meaning. Because, artistically speaking, sometimes such things, like random chords played on a piano, combined with random but related intervals, tell us something not just radically different from our expectations, but also something which sends us in an unexpected direction. It is the same with collating a collection like this, in which recordings can be shuffled and reshuffled in random ways, rearranged (and even discarded) until their relationship with each other is not so much clearer as it is different.

From the country/rock and roll singer **Wanda Jackson (Half as Good a Girl, 1956)** we learn the limitations of Big Hair as as a statement of cultural intent. Was she a rock and roller or a country singer, or some combination of the two? I tend to think she was a rocker who held something in reserve for the protection of those segments of her audience who would otherwise have looked disapprovingly at some of her more explicit musical hints of an active sex life. I don't think she *had* an active sex life (from what I have read about her early days of touring with her parents in tow) but certainly her songs had one, even if their orgiastic implications were only acted upon in the minds of her less puritanical, or more closeted, fans.

*Half as Good a Girl* tells us so, even if it is not as volcanic as her bigger hit, *Fujiyama Mama (*which crossed a lot of stylistic lines). *Fujiyama Mama* was a post-atomic anthem of questionable taste, with lines like:

> I've been to Nagasaki,
> Hiroshima too
> The things I did to them baby, I can do to you
> 'Cause I'm a Fujiyama Mama

And yes, it was a huge hit in Japan, a surprise only if it did not somehow lose something in translation. But so goes the market. More importantly, Jackson was a new kind of lady country singer, an inadvertent feminist (given her own conservative upbringing) but inadvertent with a vengeance. Her voice was anti-sentimental, more than a little bit hostile, and seemed to declare absolute independence. She sometimes hedged her bets, occasionally issuing an A-side of tainted rockabilly, a B-side of respectable country; *Half as Good A Girl* walks the line in this respect, but it's a finer line then usual. It follows the format of contemporary country ballad, delivered by Jackson with her customary twanged-sneer of a voice, her delivery like a country power-walk. The lyrics tell us that she is about half as good a girl as her mother thinks she is, implying that she is no country virgin, but the music tells us that she is still save-able. Still, there is that voice, which gives off the unmistakeable scent of rockabilly sin and temptation.

In her later years she and her husband slunk back into the church, as did so many country singers, but soon the call of the rockabilly revival was too strong to resist (I heard her on radio maybe 10 or 15 years years ago singing at a roots fest and it was strange - at 70 plus years old she still had a powerful voice but it sounded a bit unhinged technically, like she had spent time trying to re-learn her youthful ways but lacked a strong enough connection to what she had done when she was in her 20s. The body was willing, as the saying goes, but the spirit was lost). As a singer (country or otherwise) she certainly belongs on the same stages as Dolly Parton or Loretta Lynn, though everything she sang in her later years seemed haunted by some lost rockabilly ghost.

As you may have gathered, when picking material for these books I have tended to gravitate toward things that reflect my own tastes and musical inclinations. The result is a series of performances writ both large and small, some reflective only of a short-lived, recording-studio impulse, others with odd folkloric connections. One of the reasons I like rockabilly, which was the early explosion of country rock and roll inspired by Elvis, is that a lot of its practitioners had what sounds like only a casual relationship to the tradition from which they came; it was, however, the casualness of this connection that gave their music so much depth. Unlike modern-day revivalists of all musical types, they had so internalized this music that they had no need to show it off, to exhibit it like a badge of cultural nationalism. For a lot of rockabillies the music of their ancestors just *was*, present and all around, in the air that they breathed and the hootch that they drank (and the speed they ingested). As assimilated as it was in real terms, so were their related-performances real in every sense of the word, from the musical to the vocal to the entire way in which each performance lacked a sense of self-conscious emulation.

So, in particular, was **Warren Smith**'s record of **Black Jack David (1956)**, which not only had an historical resonance to which even rockabilly was unaccustomed, but also a strange dignity (to which the whole hillbilly school of throw-it-against-the-wall-and-see-what-sticks derangement was definitely unaccustomed). It helped, though I am not exactly sure why, that *Black Jack David*, an 18th century British tune, was reputed to be the oldest song ever recorded by a rock and roller (yes, according to Wikipedia). It does have something different about it, especially in Smith's restrained but intense delivery and in the song's overall arrangement, which half reminds me of Johnny Cash (especially from his slightly-more-edgy, pill popping days; there's nothing like speed to put the rock in roll), and half reminds me of something that might have come off of a film soundtrack like *The Man Who Shot Liberty Valance*. Smith, I should mention, was of that early generation of Memphis rockers who Sam Phillips recorded in the wake of Elvis, and there is no question but that his recordings got around.

Interestingly enough Cash approached Smith, in later years, to be his opening act, and Smith, who thought of himself as a headliner, declined. For once in the music business self-estimation did not amount to self-delusion; a few years later, when Smith went to Europe, he was astounded at the massive crowds he attracted. As often with vernacular music, Europeans proved to have a much keener sense of history than Americans did (though sadly, in the midst of organizing another Euro tour Smith dropped dead of a heart attack).

In the light of day **Charlie Feathers** sounds more like an alt.country-rocker than a rockabilly, and he was, as a rock and roll cult figure, a pioneer in the subjective way he composed and sang. Musically he had a long shelf life, and made extremely good records even in his later years. But he was also crazy-paranoid and thought the record/music business had conspired against him; what he didn't realize is that the record/music business conspires against everyone, even its successes. In those days in particular it conspired to steal copyrights, royalties, and performance fees, though it was more successful in its evil plan with some musicians than with others. It is doubtful that Feathers was treated any worse than a slew of other failed rockers (in other words he was treated very badly), but it is important to note that he was not just any-old rock and roll journeyman, but rather one with an unusual amount of talent, charisma, and musical presence. And he knew it, and had a high estimation of his own professional worth. And though, as with what seems like every rockabilly, Feathers started professionally in Memphis with Sam Phillips and Sun Records, he did most of his important 1950s work for Syd Nathan at King Records.

Feathers was a compelling performer, the kind who grows on you, slowly but inevitably. He performed a lot of strange vocal gymnastics, of the kind that put him just a little bit north of Elvis - with hiccups that were like weird exclamation points - or was it question marks? - a powerful rhythm in his playing, and songs, most of which he wrote, that were self-arranged little dramas with an electrical-acoustical force that was completely unique on that rockabilly scene. In **Can't Hardly Stand it (1956)** we can hear how he created, by sheer artistic will, with the intensity of what later came to be called outsider music, a cult of one; and an early, true idea of alt.country.

But you can't have alt.country without mainstream.country, and there would be nothing to rebel against without certain kinds of visible, conventional role models, like **Ray Price (Crazy Arms,**

3/1/56). Price's life, as far as I can tell, was scandal free. He was married to one woman for many years, he was a mensch and an honest man, and he had a very strong and individual voice, so more power to him. Maybe the Nashville era wasn't all bad and maybe there is a proportionate truth to a lot of music that came out of that city. We have to remember that it really was the beginning of the country music industry, providing the kind of institutional backup and support that allowed musicians like Price and many others to make an actual living, to depend less on the brutal and sometimes-dangerous whims of the road. And yes, I am studiously avoiding the race issue, the segregated truth of country music and all that it implied and enforced, through collaboration with the Southern legal system and the professional institutionalization of Jim Crow. Where were the black studio musicians and producers and engineers, not to mention performers? I am not historically qualified to separate the white from the black in Nashville of the 1950s and 1960, but I would assume that the country industry's racism was built into nearly everything it did in those years.

But I like Ray Price, who started out as a honky-tonker and evolved, with great success, into a convincing Nashville balladeer. What was the difference? Well, probably about several hundred thousand dollars; plus the benefits that Nashville offered promotionally, plus, musically speaking, new-country's musical security blanket, the web of studio sound which cushioned the blows of unfaithful spouses and forbidden love. Maybe that was what the alt. and Outlaw crowd was rebelling against, all the sonic barriers that were placed between audience and performer. Price was great, but *Crazy Arms* was shielded by strings and soft-steel guitars, by muffled drums and the newly expanded dynamic range of the tape medium. Yes, the song had a more "modern" attitude, a hook-driven title, and the plain-spoken emotionalism of the new country, but it took Jerry Lee Lewis (see Vol. 29) to bring out its full potential. As a matter of fact, Lewis' version may have exposed things about the song that even the composer didn't realize were there; is this a new auteur theory of country music? There is nothing novel about the suggestion that great singers bring out elements of their material that are otherwise hidden. Still, Ray Price did his best, and his best was quite good; which might be a fitting epitaph, if one ever needs to be written, for Country Music.

There was some recent discussion of minimalism on Facebook, initiated by yours truly, in which I attacked the compositional work of Steve Reich and others from that school. In historical terms I have to admit I was a bit out of my depth, as I don't really have a full grasp of how that movement emerged and evolved. Where I do trust myself is in my evaluation of the music, most of which I find wanting in crucial ways. I hear two essential problems: composers (and other musicians) who cannot tell the difference between an idea and a gimmick, gesture and mannerism; and the sin of formalism: certain artists seem to feel that once they have solved the problem of form - of how to escape the trap of older, worn out artistic designs, of linearity and narrative, continuity and "realism" - that they have solved other, long-term artistic problems. In other words they seem to be saying "discard those elements in favor of freer and more pliable and flexible forms and art inevitably results." I think this is not just delusional but leads to formalism, a false sense that, by directly confronting the dilemma of form and the way in it can inhibit an artist, they have solved all other aesthetic problems; they have not. In Reichian terms the results equal gimmicky forms of repetition, a cut-and-paste simplicity disguised as an intellectually complex form of fragmental composition (such kinds of assembled composition are frighteningly simple to accomplish, I can tell you from experience), and a glib and false sense of social and psychological commentary.

I did realize, in the process of arguing about Reich, that there was at least one figure in this realm whose work I love, who has taken the outlines of the minimalist approach - pieces of melody, designs of language and composition - and assembled them in truly compelling and artistic ways. He was the artist known as **Moondog** (Louis Hardin), formerly a deep presence on the streets of New York (from the 1940s until he moved to Germany in the 1980s), a real poet of a musician who seemed to just know that musical composition - well, art - was a balancing act. Whereas with artificial composers like Steve Reich everything toppled over onto the side of process (because the method of *the doing* was now more important than the result), with Moondog, as on pieces like **Death When You Come To Me (1956)** the formal aspects of composition - the sounds, the notes, the rhythms, the spoken word - unfolded and develop in their own guarded and eccentric ways, with a steady sense of creative design and variation. Though certain of Moondog's recordings succumb to the kind of mind-numbing and uninteresting repetition that composers like Reich - ironically, I would say - seemed to have drawn the most from - *Death When You Come to Me* succeeds by the sum if its finely-wrought details. The result is something of intense structure (yes, form as emotion) and substance. Its little pieces of Asian-like melody, inserted like world-music fragments, the timid recitation (in Japanese, by this then-wife), all give it an aura of solved mystery. Moondog, unthreatening and ever the respectable non-conformist (or, really, gentle revolutionary) was admired by Bennie Goodma, Toscanini, Charles Mingus and Charlie Parker, some of whom we may assume admired, at least on some level, his dedication to the the un-middle class, his pioneering slacker-ism. As Moondog responded when asked about begging in the street, "it's not degrading. Homer begged, and so did Jesus Christ. It was only the Calvinists who ordained that no man shall eat who does not work."

If you live long enough eventually all honors will come to you (or at least that's what I tell myself). Ralph Stanley of the **Stanley Brothers**, born in 1925, lived until 2016 and was, finally, honored left and right, by the NEA, the NEH, and the CIA, for all I know. Regionally and nationally he received deserved recognition for a lifetime of Bluegrass servitude (along, sort of, with his brother Carter who unfortunately died 50 years earlier), for outlasting Bill Monroe and Earl Scruggs and practically everybody else from that first generation of Bluegrassers. But it was the movie *Brother Where Art Thou*, a strangely ineffective[45] rendering of black and white country life, that made him a star in more conventional terms. That movie's soundtrack opened up, in a market sense, a whole new avenue of American roots music, and the Stanleys were made to order for a new audience of admirers of spanking-clean Americana. Their vocal lines were clear and melodious, though I would say their real era was the 1950s, when **East Virginia Blues (1956)** was recorded. *East Virginia Blues* was a commonly performed and recorded variation on the so-called mountain/modal/blues (the Carter Family recorded it as did Clarence Ashley, and B.F. Shelton - and hell, even I recorded it, back around 2010). It's an easily assimilable melody and, like all of these minor-key mountain things, perfectly adaptable to both guitar and banjo. In the 1950s the Stanleys leaned toward a steady calm of bluegrass lyricism; we tend to hear, in the newer bluegrass groups of that era, a lean and

---

[45]I thought the film was too clever for its own sake. I found its attempt at rendering the universe which produced both black and white hillbillies to be strangely clueless in a Liberal - large L - way. By trying to subvert stereotype - through re-enforcing the satirical side of that stereotype - the filmmakers managed to miss the innate historical drama unfolding right in front of them.

hungry kind of virtuosity, the pelting speed of notes and rhythms spread across traditional lines. The Stanleys, maybe because they were already seasoned veterans, were more temperate in their approach, with a vocal blending that was a lot like that of the Blue Sky Boys: harmonies locked in the details of thirds and fourths, surrounded by Bluegrass fiddle and guitar, all playing what were already the received, counter-melodies of the style.

Soul Music was not exactly a thing yet in **1956** when **Solomon Burke** recorded **I'm in Love**. But the style, the sound, was already in the air, even it did not really flower until the 1960s. By 1956 the music had already heard James Brown, Clyde McPhatter, Sam Cook, Jackie Wilson - all key figures in what I generally tend to call Black pop, for want of a better term, but which I name in the hopes of separating what they do, stylistically, from the blues and rhythm and blues. In the short and long term Soul Music (which, we might say, was the merging of black pop and vocal-group music with a gospel sensibility and certain kinds of (sorta) blues tonality) still had a lot of variation. Personally I think the way of male soul singers was tonally more like a solid block of sound than the slightly watery pop of singers like McPhatter or Jackie Wilson and some doo-wop groups; soul singers seemed to take gospel melisma and not eliminate it but combine it in subtle ways with slow or tight(er) vibrato and (in the gospel way as well) shouts of emotion. Women soul singers are a bit harder to generalize about, though to my ears they seem closer to the gospel template, a little more preachy and screechy and a little less emotionally guarded. But all of the above rules were, indeed, made to be broken.

Solomon Burke recorded for Atlantic Records in the years when the label was still riding the crest of rhythm and blues. *I'm In Love* seems to be carrying water for the slightly-older school of black balladry, a la the sound of doo-wop and rhythm and blues; listen to the way he repeats "I'm in love" starting at 1:23, with the slightly corny, heart-on-sleeve sound of older pop. Soul music, arriving soon, was all set to strip such sentimental, pining, vocal emotion from its sound and replace it with emotional protest. By 1962, when Burke recorded *Cry to Me* (one of his early hits) he had replaced beseeching with demand. And so, reflecting the times, had Soul Music.

And then - James Brown. What do we make of a man who wrote in his autobiography that, if given a choice, he'd rather listen to Bing Crosby than the blues? And what do we say about a man who, the personification of back liberation, black independence, and black capitalism (to cite one of Richard Nixon's pet plans) sang *Happy Birthday* to the ol' racist, segregationist, rapist[46] Strom Thurmond (in 1993 at Strom's 91st)? Well, there's nothing to compare James Brown to in American music, no point of reference pat and consistent enough to explain the phenomenon of a so-called uneducated musician who became, just maybe, the greatest arranger of American vernacular music in the 20th century, Duke Ellington, probably, excepted. To get a grip on it all we might start with the proletarian poetry of those one, two and three-word phrases, of the kind, like *Please Please Please* (one of Brown's earliest hits), that had the budding alta cocker Syd Nathan shaking his head and wondering at the strange nerve of this *schwartze*.[47] What was with the pleading voice, the sudden way he collapsed on stage, only to be revived as though from the near-dead, with a cape flung over his shoulders, by his bandsmen and then walked off stage to recover from his withering, if only temporary, grief? This last part, of course, was straight out of the sanctified church, where the apocalyptic ecstasy of irrational religious visions so inflamed the brain stem as to sometimes cause an actual loss of consciousness, as though the body and mind were unable to handle the spiritual overload. But what did Syd Nathan know of such things?

*Please Please Please* and **I Don't Know (1956)** were James Brown's way of speaking, musically, in tongues. The sheer lyric repetition was a dizzying way of spinning language into a frenzy of church-like ecstasy. And, yes, maybe it was all even a specific and knowing rejection of the blues, a form which may have been heard by a new generation as hopelessly old school. Even if Brown didn't describe it this way, his method of composing, singing, and arranging (he assigned parts to every musician in the band) seemed

---

[46] It was revealed in his later years that Thurmond had fathered a black child with a black mistress.

[47] *Schwartze* is the Yiddish word for black, and arguably a substitute for the "N" word, and I use it here because for an older generation of Jews it was like an open question about 'those people' and their strange cultural habits and weird ways. And yes, it is a racist term which I use because I have no doubt that Syd Nathan, who I have defended for the racial diversity of his work force, had, like many of his generation (Jewish or otherwise), severe limitations in his understanding of "the other" when that "other" was black and prone to strange cultural outbursts. And even though Jews had once been the "other" themselves, as they assimilated in a social and business sense they started to take on the attitudes of the goyish majority, with many of the same prejudices and at least some of the same provincial social outlook.

to have come to him as a new-age, ecstatic osmosis of black song. And though we reach for an explanation of genius such as his, it is likely, in the big picture, that he was simply a musician who, like Charlie Parker, emerged in a way that was not so much a sum of various parts as it was a conquering and transcendence of those parts. This was soul music, not yet completely formed in 1956 but still *there*, as an idea and an ideal. Brown was like a crazed if lone prophet who had come down the mountain, certain that his followers would get the message before too long. And he was right.

Though of course if **You Can Bet Your Life (I Do)** by **Esther Phillips (5/2/56)** isn't soul singing, then I really don't know what is. The searing guitar that enters right after Esther comes in sounds like a classic blues accompaniment, but there's something different about this, something less refined than some of the more orderly black pop of the day. There is a sense, even as this fits into the general black repertoire of the day (ie, blues and rhythm and blues) that something else is happening. And it's not coincidental that it's happening at the same time as rock and roll.

This just sounds like one of those times in commercial music history when certain new and common ideas were floating around and through the music, when certain kinds of technology were allowing for more intensity, particularly, in this era, of the tube, analog kind (as with that guitar, which chews its way through this performance like a thing on fire, not unlike what was happening on the other side of the musical/racial fence with players like James Burton and Roy Buchanan). The idea in this new world was to stick the guitar up front and ride that treble pickup as loud as reasonably allowed, bringing recorded sound a little closer to the in-person experience. Esther Phillips is close in spirit to Dinah Washington, but as a rhythm-and-ballad singer with less jazz in her soul, and a lot more of the personalized, soul-searching, preaching habit of what is about to become, as you may have guessed, Soul Music. Phillips rides the beat with an intense and immoveable drive and boasts a strangely out-of-tune melisma, singing with a nasal-intensity that seems to signal a new day, of ladies-who-no-longer-sing-only-the-blues.

Further along this line is **Betty Everett**, whose **I'll Weep No More** was recorded for Cobra Records **(1957)**. This fits the emerging idea of soul music like a flexible glove. Listen to those fluttery triplets on the snare; this is in-between, in-between gospel and pop, on the verge of Soul music, which did, as is commonly said, harness the emotional side of gospel music in the interest of secular, commercial crossover. Everett's voice is incendiary and there is not a lot of space in the way she sings. Everyone seems to be running (well, playing) in circles, and the way in which this is arranged distances it, I would say, a bit from Soul, which had a certain formal separation of musical roles; whereas this, like a lot of rhythm and blues of the day, was just plain joyously chaotic.

Cobra Records, owned by Eli Toscano, was a short-lived label that, in its A&R, perfectly captured the spirit of those (black) times. In these years just prior to what we call the Civil Rights Era one can hear, even without social hindsight, a new musical aggressiveness and assertiveness in black music-making on the blues, pop, and rhythm side. I have no idea if Toscano was consciously aware of this, but he was smart enough to take advantage of these cultural changes, recording people like Magic Sam (a great bluesman who died too young, but whose output in the next 10 years put him right at the intersection of blues and soul), Ike Turner (another interconnecting figure whose hard-blue-rock approach to guitar and to recording was original and kinetic in a way that prophetically paralleled rock and roll), Buddy Guy (a great screaming, whining vocalist who played great screaming, whining guitar) and the more unreconstructed bluesman Otis Rush.

**Otis Rush**'s **Groaning the Blues (1957)**, from the time when Rush did, I think, his best work, was definitely the blues, wholly the blues, and nothing but the blues. Is he really groaning here or is he yelling and pleading in a way that places this only a step or two away from soul music? I think this fits in with the newer, post-Muddy and Howlin' Wolf, Chicago-based electric blues, in outline and intensity, and I mean *electric* in every possible way. But listen to that little moan at 1:40 and you will hear one clear sign of soul singing, closer to the blues than I might have previously noticed or mentioned.

This was made in the midst of a crucial year in American popular music as it leaned on the vernacular: Elvis was at RCA, the beginning, for him, of life as theater-in-the-round. He was both the center and the periphery of American music, everything to some people and nothing to others. Recording technology was better, guitar technology was better, sound was better; electric blues and rock and roll were circling each other, in the market sense, like wrestlers preparing to go into battle. But in many ways it all complemented each other - listen to that treble-guitar-lead that

Rush plays along with himself, the gospel-like creaks and groans in his voice, the harp that plays behind him like a church organ. Something new is here in almost all of this: the communal sense of hope and desperation, the rocker-white way of protesting in sonic terms and the black way of doing so with emotionally over-the-top tales of personal tragedy, all of which only partially mask racial anger and hostility: *this* was the new music, of social protest as personal, dramatic exposition.

And so was **Everything Gonna Be All Right** by **Magic Sam (1958)** really the blues, but more. This recording, another Cobra, comes from early in Magic Sam's career and so has the more formal, Chicago-derived blues design. But even this shows how Sam was going in a new direction, and were it not for a sudden and early death (he died at at age 32 in 1969, just as he was starting to hit) he would likely have made a mark with the all those white kids who were starting to listen, in those crazy but creative times, to anything and everything (and yes, it was these white kids who rescued Jimi Hendrix's career, and who even George Clinton credited with life-changing open minds and ears,[48] who hugely expanded the audience sense of marketable and sustainable music, black and white. So give them some credit). The swelling, electric volume of this, the hot tremolo, and, once more, that pelting treble lead, points not just to parallel developments in rock and roll (and it would be very interesting to know exactly to whom Magic Sam was listening in that day) but to, once more, certain crossover aspects of Soul Music (think Otis Redding, for a start, and also check out Sam's solo from 1:37 on, with tremolo superimposed on a classic lead and treble-drenched line; this, in its blues/rock fusion, was something new). Magic Sam also had the singing voice for it and the musical inclination, which is made particularly clear on his 1960s recordings for the Delmark label. The younger generation of Chicago bluesers was not to be held captive by older blues attitudes, and Magic Sam's exploratory attitude fit right in with the rising treble tide of rock and roll.

---

[48] I have caught a lot of crap over the years for claiming it was possible for white people to influence, in a good way, black musicians. Aside from Hendrix, here is an illuminating quote from George Clinton on what made him a star: "Probably going to Boston when we had our first hit record and taking acid. Some Harvard kids came to the gig and they were all talking about Timothy Leary's project— blah, blah, blah...tune in, turn on, drop out. So we hung out with them. Everybody was tripping. That changed me from this straight ghetto doo-wop singer to wanting to do a worldwide thing."

Yes, there was something in the air and in the music and in the studios in those days and, credit where credit was due: **Ike Turner** was up front and center in a lot of it, even in the days before he hooked up with Tina and made her an abused star. Can we separate the artist from the brute, the brilliant musician and producer from his worst character traits? Well, we have to, because Turner's work as a pianist, guitarist, producer and all-around talent scout for various independent labels was pioneering. He produced a body of work which was drenched in what the academics like to call "tropes," of hard blues and near-rock, a post blues, pre-Soul mapping of certain new musical ideas and attitudes. There was a whole new youth movement, North and South, black and white, even before the countercultural 1960s, and Ike was keen to join it. He was busy making records as a producer, writer, and player even before he and Tina Turner grabbed soul music by the ears and tweaked it with sex and drive, like the one he made with **Jackie Brenston** singing lead called **You've Got to Lose (1958)**. Listen up - this ain't the blues, or at least the blues as the urban legend it had, by this time, become. Though I wouldn't call it rock roll, mindful as I am of some of the racial issues this raises, it *is* somewhere in between, in the land where categories, much as I love them, make little conceptual difference. Turner understood how important the guitar-centric sound was becoming in the new music, and, to be honest, his work, at its best, was miles ahead, in terms of soul (small *s*), execution, and rhythm, of what the white kids were turning out in those years in the realm of what generally passed for rock and roll (and I would say that, aside from the money to be made as a rocker, he and we should not worry about the comparison, so much better was his hard-blues and post-blues work than contemporary white equivalents). His work was also far in front of what was coming to be known as the Brill Building sound, which was centered around a clan of white composers who were writing for black groups in particular, and black solo singers, in a very smart and pop-oriented way, but one which ultimately succumbed to the Carol King-ing of style and sound. Turner just had something, and it was so solid and real that it stood out. *You've Got to Lose* does have those driving piano sixteenths or eights (depending on how you count this) of 1950s rock and pop legend, of a shuffle backbeat over clave rhythm. This is a New Orleans rock and rhythm beat, with a vocal by Brenston that is an entirely new thing, as blues for a new generation, with Little Richard-type whoops, and a liquid density that was like a generational sign of things to come. Maybe this *was* rock and roll, of a new, black, cosmic and even segregated universe.

As was **Respectable** by the **Isley Brothers (1959)** a fantastically intense piece which predicts the Black Rock Coalition of many years year (the Black Rock Coalition was an alliance of black musicians which was formed in the belief that the dividing lines heretofore erected between black and white popular music had the effect of not just segregating but reducing the artistic and earning possibilities of African American musicians, and in a commercially coercive way (http://blackrockcoalition.org/). The Isley's had an amazing musical history, and were early employers of Jimi Hendrix. This was, definitely, music in stylist flux (not fluxus but pretty damn close). They had an old-school vocal group feel but their time was aggressively contemporary. *Respectable* has a gospel-like momentum, a freight-train rhythm of straight-4 backbeats, but the lead vocal is a ride on the soul part of that train, with borderline falsetto and an intensely 1950s-like chord progression. This was shout music in the age of rock and roll, a black alternative to a *white* musical youth culture that, although it led to an expansion of the overall market, was beginning to close itself up to black musicians in particular ways (and this is a more complex conversation than we can have right now. There is no doubt that the new age of rock and roll was racially skewed, just as there is no doubt that the new age of rock and roll reflected a true flowering of white-youth creativity and a new spirit of white self-determination - all of which was a good thing in racial and political terms, paralleling as it did the whole Civil Rights movement. But on the other hand there were too many other hands, like the continued question of unequal access, the crushing power of the mob-controlled music industry, and the overall sense that rock and roll was a more comfortable thing for white music executives because it, to their minds, consciously or not, restored the racial balance of power in favor of whites. Which is something I throw out there as an unproven thesis for more informed discussion).

In the midst of all of these underground culture wars we have the blues singer/guitarist **Buddy Guy**, who was said to have been forced by Chess Records to tone down, in their studios, his natural inclination toward a new and more reckless blues dynamic. There was for years a legend that Guy had to hold himself in reserve for these early record labels but, as I learned first hand, it was much more than legend. When I saw him in person in New

York City in 1969 or 1970 I was simply astounded; nothing I had heard of his playing on record prepared me for the wild man on stage, stomping out incredible, rhythmically dense blues lines, and singing in what can only be called a top-of-the-lungs, gospel/soul/confessional wail. This was near over-the-top, but in such a musically and soul-satisfying way that almost all blues performances that I have seen in the years since suffer, in memory, by dynamic and emotional comparison. Guy was a player who, we found out later, had powerfully influenced Jimi Hendrix, whose sonic stretches and rhythmic virtuosity mirrored Guy's early experiments. It all raised the question of cause and effect, because I have no doubt that, though Guy had clearly always leaned in this musical direction, he was also obviously liberated in a very public way by the sonic revolution of rock and roll music (which was not just Hendrix but also Jeff Beck, Jimmy Page, et al). But the truth of Guy's early capabilities is revealed in recordings like **This is The End (1958),** another Cobra recording, which is like a crazy-quilt of controlled blues hysteria. This was Guy's way of speaking in blues tongues, and his treble-tilting guitar solos were fantastic insertions of vocalized intensity-on-the-strings. He was a purer blues player then Magic Sam, with a much more traditional perspective on blues phrasing, but this Cobra side captures, in ways Chess never could, the strange and church-like intensity he always held in reserve (and for an even more amazing view of Guy's capabilities check out his playing and singing in the film *Festival Express*, which is nothing short of insanity-on-parade, in front of white audiences who ate it up).

And while we're near the subjects of soul and blues: what king of band were **Hank Ballard and the Midnighters (Let 'em Roll, 1957)**? This particular group sound, with its history and musical connections, was like a thread through all of black music in the 20th century: vocal groups, gospel vocal groups, jazz vocal groups, jazz/pop vocal groups, novelty vocal (with a hint of minstrel mixed in) groups, doo-wop vocal groups - we hear these strains in every era, though by the 1950s they are mixing and matching in a lot of different ways. The Midnighters seem, to me, to be pulling away from the puffery of Atlantic Records-type black rhythm and rock groups like the Coasters or the Drifters, toward a harder, tougher sound (which I associate with Soul Music). *Let 'em Roll* is like a combination of masculine and feminine impulses in the new music, muscularity alternating with androgynous falsetto preening, soul music in its formative years.

I have tried to look a little bit less, as I write this book, at connections between music far and wide. What I mean is that although yes, I take great pleasure in hearing things as they interconnect musically and culturally, I try to avoid some of the gamesmanship involved in doing so (like, for example, as I have mentioned, the old "what was the first rock and record?" sweepstakes). It's not that I don't enjoy doing this, it is that I don't want anyone to *know* I enjoy doing it, as I don't want to be trapped doing what too many critics too, which is to always put things in comparative terms: this sounds like that, that sounds like this, and *that* sounds like something else altogether. But sometimes I get a thrill when I find small but significantly related things, nuanced points of music that I don't think anyone else has ever noticed. As on **Lord I Come to Thee** by **Deacon Leroy Shinault** (and, apparently, congregation), from **1956**.

Let me explain. In Volume 1 I discussed a white Sanctified sect called The Old Regular Baptists, and the mysterious way in which they seemed to reflect deep black influence. The problem was (is) that we have no Old Regular Baptist recordings made before the 1950s. The later recordings that we do have are meaningful because they show the ties that have bound black and white sanctified aesthetics over the last century, how the emotive ways of deep, deep religious singing spread and animated the singing of both black and white religious patrons and their sometimes-fanatical followers. The blackness of the Old Regular Baptists' flowing hum, of the leader's groaning, moaning vocal beseeching, tied these groups together in more obvious ways than that of the white country Sanctified groups that we have on record from the 1920s (like that of Ernest Phipps, see Vols. 9,10,11). Instead of finding early white recorded equivalents, which don't seem to exist, I have had to search out black groups that sounded like they likely, from the sound of it, had powerful effects on whatever led to the music of the Old Regular Baptists. For one example, listen, in Vol. 6 to *Come Let Us Eat Together* by Rev. ED Campbell and Congregation. Here is a type of soul that was somehow more accessible to white ways; the resemblance to white singing is *not* in the paleness of the music but in the way it manipulates emotions. Deacon Shinault and group have that sound, too, and it's also a rock and roll sound, in the way the beat glides through the ensemble with a light-heavy 4-beat roll. The crazed unisons here bring to mind the Old Regular Baptists, and those whole notes are beat nearly to the death by the distorting volume of the congregation, rising and sinking and sinking and rising. This is religious fervor at the edge of hallucination, where, finally, it is not just the blind who can see.

 I was lucky enough to catch **Elizabeth Cotten** in person when I was in college, some time in the middle 1970s. She was on tour with a folk festival of like-minded folks - not folkies - and I wish I had more information on the groups who played, a program or listing of some kind. The reason I say this is that this was not a gathering of young singers bent on replicating the music they loved but rather, as I recall, the real thing, singers from Appalachia and other points South, from regional hot spots of actual Southern music, both black and white. I would guess, at this late date, that they were on loan from the NEA, which in those years was conducting folk and folklore festivals in which, to their credit, they employed indigenous musicians who were important not merely for their indigenousness but for the way they *played*. They looked like every-day people, they dressed like every-day people, but they sang and played like artists, as though from a prior day when everybody did this and no one was self-conscious about it. These were people who were so connected to the music, so connected to their instruments, so in touch with their voices, that one immediately, in their presence, understood not just the appeal of this music but its meaning - and here I define meaning in the broadest possible sense, not as some set of rules and outlines, but as something that felt like a profound parallel to life. I now understand why the Lomaxes did as they did, searching for musicians who had escaped the attention of mass-distributed media and so had, yes, remain unspoiled by certain kinds of attention or financial re-enforcement. We might duke it out here over the term, but these people really were authentic, though I emphasize, as I have elsewhere, that contrary to stereotypes about young white kids and Americana, we thought they were authentic because we liked them - we didn't like them because we thought they were authentic. There is a very big difference.

 Cotten was all of that and more, a not-so-great singer who was still a *presence* because she was such a powerful, distinctive musical personality. Listen to her on two songs in this collection: **Going Down the Road Feeling Bad** and **Wilson Rag (1957)**. If you want to hear the difference between black and white musicians of the folk kind, press your ear to the speaker; her time and swing is so completely effortless as to make the listener almost miss the effort it takes to produce music like this, with so much detail and internalized rhythmic movement. Her guitar playing is, perhaps, out of that Piedmont school we have discussed, picked with varying bass notes and a lot of passing variation. But to me it is her *time* which sets her apart.

This music has some of the most gentle yet intense swing you will ever hear, and I have to say that I have never heard a white folk musician of any kind come close to the way Cotten so subtly rides the beat or swings so effortlessly. Check out, on *Going Down the Road*, the transitional bass notes she plays at .40 leading into a new section, the way she plays those upper-register double stops at .50, and the way she manages to build in subtle intensity by means of subtle variation, even as the music remains on low heat.[49] I remember, 45 years ago, watching her as she sat on the floor, right in front of us, and played to a small circle of college students like myself. She seemed as interested in us as we were in her, her artistry just an extension of her basic humanity.

Once in a while (well, really, much more than that) I like to let my own personal tastes interfere with the music I am writing about. Until someone invents an Objectivity Pill you, dear reader, are captive, if you haven't stopped reading by now, of my own musical orientation (I would say preference, but I don't want to get into that bottomless controversy). And there are certain musical figures who, though needing no introduction, will still get them, like the saxophonist **Sonny Rollins**. For me, at least, a first hearing of his recording of **There's No Business Like Show Business (6/22/56)** (which I first encountered in 1968) led me to the the enjoyable obsession that was jazz (which became, really, a gateway musical drug for everything else I have been writing about here). This recording, made during Sonny's first flush of uber-musical greatness (meaning, it was the signal that a new and major cultural force had not just arrived in American music but had become an

---

[49] There is a story of some folk tour where Gary Davis kept telling Cotten that she should let him give her some guitar lessons, since he felt her playing was too weak. Well...I prefer her playing to his, I have to say, because she never sweats and she swings like no other folk guitarist I have ever heard. It's a pity that Gary Davis didn't hear this in her playing, though it does at least partly explain his own limitations.

instant icon, as both reality and symbol, of jazz as an even newer and more universal avant garde-ist force). I will dare say that, for all the work that Charlie Parker, Dizzy Gillespie, Bud Powell and Max Roach had done to develop a method for jazz's acceleration into the modern era, it took Sonny's extra-musical push to consolidate all that *they* meant to the music, to really summarize bebop's possibilities as a poly-rhythmic, polytonal, abstracting artistic force and signifier of a new modern mindset, and give it not just new meaning but a new reason to live on, as and beyond bebop. In other words: the 1950s in jazz is packed with modernist wannabes who are still, at their core, bebop-centric in their orientation, all holding out the promise of new forms of musical awareness. But there are also in that day some brilliantly sharp advocates lobbying, in effect, for a restructuring of bebop in terms of tonality and even feeling. People like Lennie Tristano, Paul Bley, Teo Macero, Charles Mingus, George Russell, Johnny Carisi, John LaPorta, Hall Overton, even Cecil Taylor (in a different way) were trying to take advantage of bebop's radically liberating spirit while reorienting it in terms of line and harmony. To some extent they all eventually succeeded, but it took, maybe, Sonny to show how jazz, in its historic and stylistic ambivalence, could impart a sense of backward reference while still engaging in radically forward stylistic motion (though he was soon joined in this by John Coltrane and Ornette Coleman). *There's No Business Like Show Business* is a life-altering look at old Broadway, at old Irving Berlin, and new Sonny, who was entering, perhaps, the first stage of the continuous series of creative crises that made his music his music; Charlie Parker, as always a shrews observer of life and its hazards, said, "from the oyster comes the pearl." Creativity, as Bird knew well, was a constant irritant.

I wrote, in my history of 1950s jazz, about how prophetic **Sun Ra and His Arkestra** were, how so much of what became the jazz avant garde of the 1960s was described and predicted by Sun Ra's 1950s band.

Before I go on, however, let me explain my own musical predilections in regards to changing concepts of jazz. Free jazz was free jazz; it opened a lot of new musical doors and liberated more than one generation of jazz musician from the potentially coercive effects of harmony and song form, particularly as shaped by the style of music called bebop. The concept of open improvisation was clearly something that had to happen in order to shake jazz out of stylistic and ideological doldrums, to force musicians of all generations to look closely at what they were doing and why. Though I am fascinated by the first generation of "free" players and the amazing creative spirit of their earliest musical declarations of freedom (spurred of course, by Ornette Coleman and John Coltrane in particular), the "new thing" of jazz, within about 10 to 20 years of its inception, had created it own set of cliches and suffered from its own tendencies for repetition and self-reference. To me the most interesting of early musicians effected by this school were the ones who were able to use the new freedom in near-literary ways, as a method by which to reconcile freestyle narrative with linear exposition; like Jaki Byard, Roswell Rudd, Marshall Allen, Paul Bley, Miles Davis (the mid-1960s band band) Don Ellis, John Coltrane, and, orchestrally, Gunther Schuller, George Russell, Gil Evans, et al. Their music had a richness and depth, drawn from the cultural experience and continuity represented by not just the blues and its offshoots, but also by certain ways of using time and space, with flexible approaches to tonal centers and intonation. To me the work of these quirky followers of modern jazz fashion is the most interesting of that done in the first wake of Free Jazz.

Sun Ra at his best was an amazing example of all that. As a pianist some of his later solo recordings are brilliant and canny mappings of song form as it was deflected by the new freedom; the soul of a lot of jazz (but not all; I repeat, not all) was in the odd twists Sun Ra made in the direction of the so-called "tradition." For once a jazz musician with avant-garde leanings understood the old music and paid, not homage so much as *attention,* to it, grasping all of the ways in which it was still so useable, and realizing all that was implied in its harmonically astute formatting of song. And so did he direct his 1950s Arkestra, as on things like **Images (1958)**. Back in those days he and the Arkestra were dealing, in their own early way, with modality, repetition, and dissonance, even as they toyed with some of the common phrasing and rhythms of bebop. Sun Ra knew how to divide and conquer bebop by implying new directions in the midst of putting the Arkestra through some typical bebop motions - listen to the way the melody in *Images* reclaims itself in an unpredictable way at .054, as Sun Ra inserts a new line that seems to ride over the old, imposing a slightly jarring melody over a very bebop-worn series of orchestral voicings - all as the ensemble begins to resolve in a conventional, classically-voiced but fresh bebop way. Shades of

Tadd Dameron, whose arrangements had a similar sense of open-ended melody and expansive, yawning, harmonic signature.

Sun Ra was, in his way, preparing the band for the 1960s, when their music became a combination of free-zone head arrangements, the leader's pithy piano, sharp soloists, and mystical head trips; at the time *this* was made, the mothership still needed some prepping.

In those years I don't really know who, in jazz, was listening to whom, though the music, as we hear it on records and CDs, has an in-bred quality, a kind of fraternity which seems, for better or for worse, gone from today's jazz scene. Certainly the 1950s were an experimental stage for jazz improvisation and composition - though maybe not really. Take **John Coltrane**; even though his most creatively dissonant and explorative work lay ahead, it is impossible to listen to his 1950s playing and think it was merely transitional. It was transcendent in every way, from his profoundly human, piercing tone to the incredible technical manner with which he was beginning to navigate intervals, scales, and rhythms. Even more so than Sonny Rollins, 1950s Coltrane spawned generations of saxophonists who wanted to, *had* to, replicate his feeling. On **Black Pearls**, recorded by Coltrane in **1958**, we can hear that nothing, within the context of his own musical desires, was missing, technically or spiritually. From the outset he is like a short-distance sprinter gone rogue, working to sustain, against what might have seemed like all logic, longer and longer lines of harmonic continuity, executed with the rapid and inevitable logic of genius. Miles Davis told him, famously, to "just take the horn out of your mouth" when Coltrane worried that he didn't know how to stop playing some of these labyrinthine solos, but this was one of those rare occasions when Miles missed the musical point. Coltrane's whole method was more Joycean than that of anyone previously in jazz, more, in its eruption, like the continuing of one long sentence, and stopping would have just delayed the inevitable (which was more notes, more playing, more sound).

Coltrane, at this stage, was relatively easy for critics to grasp musically. Most had heard him as he moved through the musical ranks, from Miles Davis' mid-1950s bands to later appearances at Newport and, of course, to his appearance on the record *Kind of Blue*. **Ornette Coleman**, who came seemingly out of nowhere, was much more of a shock to the jazz system. He appeared suddenly on the West Coast (from his native Texas) and popped in on one of **Paul Bley**'s gigs at a black country club called the Hillcrest, where Bley insisted he join the band for the length of the gig. "I knew we would probably get fired," Paul told me years later and, sure enough, with Ornette's constant musical companion the trumpeter **Don Cherry** in tow, that's exactly what happened. Fortunately Bley had the foresight to record the great event (with **Charlie Haden** and **Billy Higgins** on bass and drums) and one of the results was **Crossroads**, made at the Hillcrest in 1958. And what a thing it was (is), from the opening shock-riff of sudden melody, executed by Ornette like the first flush of virtuoso genius, which it was. Though people like Bley immediately recognized what a non-tenuous connection this music had with jazz and its traditions, few at the time were completely prepared to match this kind of brilliant creative overflow with anything they had heard before. Some, however, quickly got the point; there was something decidedly Bird-esque in Ornette's wail, something very liberating in the music's discrete yet clear connection to jazz's rapid, even frantic, historical evolution; and of course it had an obvious attachment to the blues. Trumpeter Cherry was only slightly the lesser among equals, with his startlingly, Clifford Brown-like width of tone, and the sense he gave of being able to breathe as one with Ornette on these rangy themes.

    I have tried, throughout this two-volume study, to approach each and every performance on its own terms, to avoid what they call "received wisdom," the repeating of prior knowledge, or of what passes for prior knowledge. Much of what we tend to say about the deeper sources of American music (called in some places Americana) is based on what we have been told as opposed to what we hear. So as I go through I try to listen to each recording with fresh ears, or new ears, or virgin ears, as though it was all coming at me for the first time - which, I should add, is virtually impossible to do after more than fifty years of listening and performing and writing about listening and performing.
    So what shall I say about **Cowboy Roy Brown**, traveling street singer and itinerant musical prophet, who was in his 80s by the time he recorded **Under the Double Eagle** in what was probably **1958**? Well, we think he was born in 1875, which means he passed through a number of musical generations, and saw more than one modern age pass into what amounted to another modern age and then into yet another modern age. He does, I have to say, represent,

in real terms (not just as an idea), everything that I like about the music of the American vernacular. He has a repertoire that encompasses whatever he likes to sing, and which reads and sounds like a road-trip through the American vernacular musical mind. He sings, even at this advanced age, with a spirit and grit that just *is* American music, as annoying and cliched as that may sound. He has the same contagious musical spirit as my much-missed old acquaintance, the jazz pianist Jaki Byard: he loves what he is doing and he loves songs, no matter where they come from or in what form they have arrived - ragtime, blues, Tin Pan Alley, the minstrel stage, Broadway shows, black and white ditties; he clearly understands, as a performer, the art and the craft of it all. In certain ways he reminds me of Gary Davis at his most eclectic, though I say, once more at the risk of raising the Wrath of Folkies, that I prefer his work to that of Davis. Brown has a joyous flow, a swing and verve that sometimes overcomes his technique - on this there are a few technical slip-ups on guitar, though that may be because of age - and a lightness of touch and technique that makes it all sound like a musical form of action painting. He sings, he croons, he marches, he one-steps and two-steps, he comments, he barrels his way through the song - he is like that one-man band, in that grand black tradition, the African American equivalent of a crazed musical stage show in-the-round. *Under the Double Eagle* is performance and intermission, kazoo and guitar, vocal and string-band interlude, both in and out of time; this is American song from every possible side, multiple voices saying the same basic thing if in slightly different languages.

**Link Wray** lives, in every punk who ever picked up an electric guitar, wondering "how hard can it be?" Wray didn't like his own singing voice very much, but there is no other rock/blues singer I like better, none who captured better than Wray the tortured, soul-drenched white rocker zeitgeist of the 1950s and (early) 1960s. Wray's mother was a wandering street preacher, full of the kind of religious, god-fearing dread that makes your typical, college-philosophy existential angst seem like a walk in an Existential Theme Park. What is it about these hillbilly cats, these hicks who seemed to have been bred in the South in ways that filled their life with such intense feeling? Yes, I know Wray's mother was a Native American, and I know their are theories about the relationship of Native American music to the American vernacular, but, though I will allow for the possibility, I have yet to see much solid proof. I hear Wray, who recorded a lot and in a lot of different ways (including a very good late '60s hippie phase) as part of that casual musical defamation movement of hardcore rockers who stood up against nothing that they they could really articulate except in loud, pissed off, pre-metallic sound, tinted with the blues and done like the resident artists in the school of LOUD that they were. Loud music, loud guitar, casual distortion. These guys just stood up and spilled their guts, like Link Wray on his recording of **Ain't That Lovin' You Baby (1958)**. Wray, who only had one lung, used it like a billows, sneering his way through this Jimmy Reed tune like the un-Elvis he was (sorta; there are actually some odd Elvis vocal references in this). In spite of Wray's major-label ties this was essentially a rejection of the civilizing effect of corporate rock, a la Elvis and RCA. His guitar solo is not so much down-to-earth as under-earth, his guitar tone like sold rocks, his whole demeanor punk and reckless. Do I hear a hint of Howlin' Wolf in this? Maybe; but this is white-rocker blues heaven, a hint at all the hell that these guys had seen and been through.

The first time I heard the recording of **Poor Pilgrim of Sorrow** as sung by the **Congregation of the Mt. Olive Reg. Baptist Church (1959)** I had one of those "a ha!" moments that I have now and then while listening to old American music. This is the music of The Old Regular Baptists, something of a missing link in the gospel chain - missing because there are just no equivalent recordings of white groups singing with this neo-blue - or is it neo-black? - congregational sound made before this one. In the absence of such, as I have commented already, I have sought out black recordings from the 1920s and later, with the thought that this was the only way to trace the gospel lineage of The Old Regular Baptists. I did find a few, as I have noted in the text and on the accompanying CD set. There is no way except aurally to prove my assumption, of African American gospel antecedent, but one listen to *Poor Pilgrim of Sorrow* and I think you will agree with me that this quite directly reflects the black ways of white singers. Though this particular recording lacks some of the typical, swelling, congregational unisons of the style, the solo lead is clearly of what we might now called a blues persuasion (by way of phrasing and interval) but which I suspect confuses cause and effect - meaning that I have a sense that this type of what we might call blue phrasing likely pre-dates the blues and is more likely to have fed into the solo field singing (African American) styles that prepared the way for blues form than the other way around. Whatever the cause and effect, this performance is a primer on soul of the legendary blue-eyed kind.

Who is **Robert Zimmerman** and what is he doing at the end of this study? Well, you know him under a different name, and we will let it go at that. But in **1962** he decided to sing a version of a song first recorded by the New Orleans-born singer Richard Rabbit Brown in 1927, **James Alley Blues**. Brown's original performance is a blues with a twist - meaning that the essential form is blues but that the way he vocalizes is more medicine/minstrel show than blues, with a broad, guttural vibrato, stagey and warm, very different in its sound from what became of the so-called Delta style. Zimmer-man was ahead of his time, and maybe the only one to "cover" (I hate that term) this tune as early as he did; we can assume he learned it from Harry Smith's Anthology of American Folk Music, which was a bible of the in-between folky generation, for those "in between" Leadbelly, Broonzy et al and, say, Mark Spoelstra. Zimmerman was one of the few (if not the only) singers of that generation to understand how to handle the old blues in ways that did not smack of strange, white-boy mimicry (he was a master or phrasing and time, in a way that evoked the old school without sounding like parody), and he takes to this tune as only he could, making it one with his own style in that half-mumbling way, with harmonica on top. It is a sign of the times, or maybe of his times, of the personal struggle he was going through in trying to browse his way through the American vernacular. Everything he sings in this era (pre-1970) sounds perfectly filtered through his own broad frame of musical and aesthetic reference, as though he has the whole world of folk music in, yes, his hands (and he was also more than a serviceable guitarist). Folk tunes, new tunes, originals and knockoffs, all become Zimmer-man songs because Zimmer-man sings them (and to get a sense of how wrong-headed American folk revivalism has become, listen to Wilco's 1998 version of *James Alley Blues*, from Farm Aid, which can be viewed on Youtube; talk about historically clueless. Wilco sings the song to the tune of Zimmerman's *She Belongs to Me* and the result is a weird kind of third-party plagiarism once removed, most notable for the fact that it is such a pale kind of plagiarism that likely nobody will either notice or care about it - except, of course, for me). But to (not) quote another prophet of a different kind of musical movement, it's all right ma, we're only bleeding ourselves dry with Americana of the most vacant kind.

# Index

A Chicken Ain't Nothing but a Bird 145,146
Ace, Johnny 305,306
Across the Sea 179,180
Acuff, Roy 197,198,199
After You've Gone 44
Ain't a Bump in the Road 288
Ain't No Grave Gonna Hold My Body Down 317,318
Ain't No More 284
Ain't That Lovin' You Baby 387
Alabama Boys 76
All on Account of You 358,359
Allen, Rosalie 262
Alley Boys of Abbeville 111,112
Almanac Singers 135,136
Almond, Lucky Joe 294
Anderson, Ivy 180
Anderson, Pink 240
Angliano, Bob 291,292
Anytime 61
Ardoin, Amede 36
Arkansas Traveler 291
Armstrong, Lil Hardin 23
Armstrong, Louis 306
Arthur, Charlene 295
At the End of the Trail 171
Austin Coleman, Joe Washington, & Group 32,33
Babe, Sugar 85
Baby Don't Say that No More 343
Baby Don't You Want to Go 232
Baby I'm Coming Home 298
Baby Please Don't Go 48
Baby Shame on You 242
Baker, Iron Head
Baker, Laverne 238,239
Ballard, Hank 378,379
Barfield, Johnny 124
Basie, Count 92
Beck, Johnny 240,241
Belcher, Red 290,291
Bell Clappin' Mama 77,78
Belvin, Jesse 286
Berry, Chuck 326,327
Better Late Than Never 289,290
Big Joe and His Washboard Band 130
Big Mama Blues 257,258
Big Maybelle 356,357
Big River Blues 16,17
Billy Ward and His Dominoes (McPhater) 283,284
Bivins, Lester Pete 86,87

Black Gal 265,266
Black Jack David 366,367
Black Pearls 384
Blackwell, Scrapper 43
Blackwoods Brothers 170, 171
Bledsoe, Country Jim 301
Bledsoe, Jules 24
Bley, Paul 385
Blind Man Stood on De Road and Cried 117,118
Blind Pete and Partner 27,28
Blue Midnight 298,299
Blue Moon of Kentucky 334
Blue Ridge Quartet 222,223
Blue Ridge Quartet 263
Blue Smitty and his String Men 299,300
Blues in the Bottle 52,53
Blues Trip Me This Morning 141
Bo Diddley 350,351
Bobby Blue Bland 348,349
Body and Soul 310
Boines, Houston 275,276
Bonus Pay 322,323
Booker, Charlie 273,274,275
Booker, Charlie 298
Boots and his Buddies 63,64
Born to Lose 149,150
Boyd, Bill 53,54
Boyd, Bill's Cowboy Ramblers 53,54
Brenston, Jackie 376,377
Bronzeville, Lewis 129,130
Brooks, Junior 269,270
Broonzy, Big Bill 14,309
Brother Claude Ely 316,317
Brown, James 372,373
Brown, Milton 51
Brown, Morris 117,118
Brown, Nappy 344,345
Brown, Othum 189
Brown, Roy 207
Brown, Roy 385
Brown, Walter 247,248
Bruner, Cliff 76
Bryant, Jimmy 291
Burke, Solomon 371,372
Buster Pack and His Lonesome Pine Boys 289
By and By 266,267
Byas, Don 161,162
Bye and Bye, 291,292
Byron Parker and His Mountaineers 103
Cabin in the Caroline 227,228,229
Caitin, Jolie Tee 324

389

Callahan Brothers
Callahan, Homer 34,35
Campbell, Brun 174,175
Campbell, Muryel Zeke 140
Can't Hardly Stand It 367
Carlisle, Bill 77,78
Carlisle, Cliff 100
Carmichael, Hoagy 40
Carolina Cotton Pickers 92
Carr, Leroy 43
Carter Family 126,127
Carter, Betty 359,360
Carter, Buster 5
Carter, Preston 5
Catfish Blues 133,134
Catfish Blues 301,302
Cats and the Fiddle 128
Caudill Family 317,318
Cavalry Quartet 225
Charles, Ray 208,209
Chenier, Clifton 325
Chenier, Clifton 325
Cherokee Rambler 51
Cherry, Don 385
Christie, June 185,186
Church Brothers 288,289
Church of God in Christ 142,143
Clank A Lanka Sleep on Mother 10,11
Cliff Bruner's Texas Wanderers 77
Cline, Patsy 336,337
Coal Creek March 78,79
Cochran Brothers 341
Cold Iron Bed 22
Coleman, Austin 33
Coleman, Ornette 384,385
Coleman, Walker 89
Coltrane, John 384
Congregation of the Mt. Olive Reg. Baptist Church 387,388
Conn, Eva 12,13
Coon Creek Girls 97
Coquette 162,163
Coquette 63,64
Cotten, Elizabeth 380,381
Cowboy Rhythm 84
Cowboy Roy Brown 385,386
Crackling Hen 27,28
Crazy Arms 342
Crazy Arms 368
Cripple Creek 54
Crossroads 385
Crudup, Arthur 234
Cryin' at Daybreak 235
Crying 299,300
Curry, Ben 13,14
Cuttin' Out 211

Daffan, Ted 149,150
Dallas Blues 211,212
Dallas Jamboree Jug Band 57
Darling Brown Eyes 288,289
Davis, Link 248
Davis, Miles 306
Davis, Reverend Gary 62,63
Day, Doris 280,281
Death When You Come to Me 369,370
Deep Elm Blues 16
Deep South Quartet 319,320
Delmore Brothers 16,17
Delmore Brothers 251
Descent into the Maelstrom 308
Dexter, Al 83,84
Dial 110 Blues 301
Did You Ever Try to Cry? 187
Diggin' My Potatoes 309
Dixon Brothers 80
Dixon, Dorsey 80,81
Dixon, Floyd 211,212
Dixon, Howard 80,81
Do Lord 319,320
Domino, Fats 277
Don't Cry Baby 330,331
Don't Explain 328,329
Don't Jive Me 267,268
Don't Worry About Me 330,331
Don't You Lie to Me 177
Dorothy Love Coates and the Original Gospel Harmonettes 245
Down by the Ohio 50
Downbound Train 326,327
Downhearted Blues 173
Dream Girl 286
Drifters 354,355
Dunn, Bob 121,122
Dunn, Bob 74
East of the Sun 157,158
East Texas Drag 86
East Texas Serenaders 85,86
East Virginia Blues 370,371
Edwards, Cliff 38,39
Edwards, David Honeyboy 141,142
Eighth of January 128
Ellington, Duke 144,145
Elm Street Woman Blues 57
Emerson, Billy 324
Empty Bed Blues 181
Eva Lay 323,324
Evans and McClain 6,16
Everett, Betty 373,374
Every Day Will be Sunday Bye and Bye 245
Everybody's Truckin' 75,76
Everything Gonna Be All Right 375,376

Famous Bluejay Singers of Birmingham 10
Farrish Street Jive 59
Farther Along 101
Fast Train Through Arkansas 221,222
Fats Raybo Ramblers 56,57
Feathers, Charlie 367
Feelin' Bad 297
Ferguson, Ben 8
Fiddle and Guitar Running Wild 93,94
Fiddler's Dream 49,50
Field Mouse Stomp 38
Fine Looking Woman 279,280
Five Blind Boys of Mississippi 280
Five Junks 90
Footprints in the Snow 100,101
For Old Times Sake 248
Ford, Tennessee Ernie 203
Forgive Me 201
Foster, Leroy 237,238
Four Leaf Clover Quartet 292,293
Four Picked Peppers 100,101
Four Southern Singers 19,20,21
Frank Hunter and his Black Mountain Boys 263,264
Frankie and Johnny 76
Franks, Tillman 258,259
Frazier, Nathan 128
Freeny Harmonizers 48,49
Frizzell, Lefty 251,252
Fuller, Blind Boy 111
Gaillard, Slim 119,120
Gallows Pole 134
Garlow, Clarence 324
George Ku Trio 21
Georgia Browns 18,19
Gillespie, Dizzy 155,156,157,158
Gillum, Jazz 130
Gilmore, Boyd 273
Glory in the Meeting House 71,72
Go 'long Mule 13
Go Down Old Hannah 25,26
God Didn't Like It 205,206
God's Creation 321
God's Mighty Hand 158,159
Goin' Away Walking 256,257
Goin' Down Slow 286, 287
Goin' to Virginia 214,215
Going Down the Road Feeling Bad 380,381
Golden Gate Gospel Train 89
Golden Gate Quartet 89
Gonna Ride 'til the Sun Goes Down 125
Gonzales, Baba 197
Good Room 117,118
Gospel Songbirds 321

Gospel Songbirds 351
Graettinger, Bob 270
Grand Nuit Especial 293,294
Grant, Cecil 153,154
Green, Henry 272
Green, Lil 147,148
Gribble, Murph 179,180
Grievin' Blues 205
Griffin, Bessie 320,321
Groaning the Blues 374,375
Guess Who's in Town, 53,54
Guy, Buddy 377
Gypsy 306
Haden, Charlie 385
Haig, Al 155,156
Haley, Bill 229,230
Half as Good a Girl 364,365,366
Hall, Adelaide 107,108
Hall, Roy 101,102,103
Hallelujah Side 11
Hallelujah We Shall Rise 222
Hamblen, Stuart 35,36
Hambone Am Sweet 19,20,21
Hank Ballard and the Midnighters 378,379
Happy Hayseeds' Ladies Quadrille 20,21
Hard Times Will Soon be Over 222,223
Hardin, Louis 369,370
Hare, Pat 322,323
Harmonica Frank 256, 257
Harold and Hazel 30,31
Harris, Wynonie 241,242
Have I Waited Too Long 311,312
Have Mercy Baby 283,284
Hawkins, Dale 339,340
Hayes, Roland 117,118
Heading for Texas and Home 98,
Hear de Lambs Plenty 117,118
Hemphill, Sid 165
Hensley, Larry 34
Hey Little Girl 215,216
Hey Little Girl 324
Hi Henry Brown's Preacher Blues 11,12
Hi Tone Poppa 258,259
Hide Me Rock of Ages 318,319
Hidin' Out 336,337
Higgins, Billy 385
Hittin' the Bottle Stomp 61
Hobo Jack 314,315
Hogsed, Roy 287,288
Holliday, Billie 329,330
Holsten Valley Breakdown 264
Honeydripper Part I 152,153
Honky Tonk Gal 313,314
Honky Tonk Train Blues 57,58
Hooker, John Lee 205

Hooker, John Lee 243,244
Horton, Walter 265,266
Hottentot Potentate 346
House of the Rising Sun 136
How You Want Your Rollin' Done 32
Howell, J.H. 96
Howlin' Wolf 235
Hugh and Shug's Radio Pals 85
Hunt, D.A. 322
Hunter, Frank 263
Hunter, Ivory Joe 217,218
Hurdt, Walter 93,94
Hutto, J.B. 324,325
I Ain't Got Nobody 218,219
I Almost Lost my Mind 218
I Be Bound to Write to You 150
I Believe I'll Make a Change 43
I Can't Give You Anything but Love 107,108
I Don't Know 372,373
I Feel Like Dyin' in this Army 32,33
I Got to Cross the River Jordan 212,213
I Heard About You 295
I Just Keep Lovin' Her 189
I Looked Down the Line and Wondered 108
I Never Loved but One 126,127
I Wanna Be Mama'd 260
I Want Two Wings 158,159
I Was Praying 280
I Woke Up Screaming 348,349
I Wonder 243,244
I'd Rather Drink Muddy Water 128
I'll Drown in My Own Tears 239,240
I'll Get Mine Bye and Bye 121,122
I'll Remember You 153,154
I'll Weep No More 373,374
I'm a Soldier in the Army of the Lord 165
I'm Crying Holy Unto the Lord 316,317
I'm Going to Lift Up a Standard for My King 142,143
I'm in Love 371,372
I'm in the Mood 344,345
I'm in the Mood for Love 281
I'm Just a Lonely Guy 344
I'm Moaning All Day for You 90
I'm So Lonesome 314,315
I'm Talking about You 181,182
I'm Through With You 130
I'm Troubled in Mind 42
I'm Walking this Town 42, 43
I'm Wondering and Wondering 208,209
I've Got Mine 240
Images 383,384
In the Jailhouse Now 249,250

In the Middle of the Night 242,243
Indiana 161,162
Irby, Jerry 252
Irby, Jerry 252,253
Iron Head Baker and Others 25
Isley Brothers 377
It Don't Hurt Anymore 312,313
It Never Entered my Mind 191
It's Too Soon to Know 202
J.E. Mainer's Mountaineers 80
J.H. Terrell and Congregation 163,164
J'Ai Fair Tout Le Tour Du Pays 33
Jackson, Wanda 364,365,366
James Alley Blues 388
James, Elmore 276,277
Jefferson, Eddie 309,310
Jenkins, Hezekiah 5
Jimmy Peters and the Ring Dance Singers 33
Jivin' Woman Blues 111
Joe Turner 249
Joe Turner Blues 150,151
John's Idea 92
Johnny and Jack 248
Johnny Moore's Three Blazers 188
Johnson, Elder A. 205,206
Johnson, Robert 66,67
Joliet Blues 235,236
Jones, Buddy 121,122
Jones, Buddy 73,74
Jones, George 296
Jordan, Louis 145,146
Juiced 268,269
Jumpin' at the Jubilee 246,247
Just a Lonely Boy 325
Just a Lonely Boy 325
Just Because 15,16
Just Dream of You 90
Just Wailing 353,354
Katie Dear 94,95
Kelly, Jack 22
Kenton, Stan 270,271
Key to the Highway 130
King Solomon Hill 8,9
King, B.B. 279,280
King, Earl 352
King, Queen, and Jack 40
Knittel, Ronnie 264,265
Knocking on the Hen House Door 86
Koko 144,145
Laffing Rag 13,14
Lanham, Roy 225,226
LaPorta, John 335
Lasky, Louis 32
Last Fair Deal Gone Down 66,67
Laughing at Life 129,130

Laurie, Annie 211
Leadbelly 134
Leadbelly 26,27
Lee, Julia 210,211
Lee, Peggy 218,219
LeJeune, Iry 293,294
Leroy Carr and Scrapper Blackwell 43
Les Bleues De Bosco 56,57
Let 'em Roll 378,379
Lewis Bronzeville Five 129,130
Lewis, Archie 17,18
Lewis, Jerry Lee 341,342
Lewis, Meade Lux 57,58
Lewis, Smiley 267,268
Life is a Problem 200
Liggins, Joe 152,153
Light Crust Doughboys 140
Light Crust Doughboys 85
Lightfoot, Papa 332,333
Lincoln, Abby 362,363
Little David Play on Your Harp 224,225
Little Liza Jane 29
Little Maggie 79
Little Miss Sharecropper 238,239
Little Walter 236,237,238,298,299
Lofton, Clarence 114,115
Logsdon, Jimmy 260
London, Julie 330,331
Lone Star Cowboys 15,16
Lone Town Blues 269,270
Lonesome Old Jail 322
Lonesome Train on a Lonesome Track 340,341
Long Tall Mama 14
Long Time No See 263,264
Looking for a Woman 207
Lord I Come to Thee 379,380
Lord Will Make a Way 206
Lost on the River 223,224
Lou Cindy Lou 247,248
Louie Bluie and Ted Bogan 28,29
Louisiana Lou 12,13
Love Her with a Feeling 241
Love Me or Leave 178,179
Love, Billy 268,269
Love, Dorothy 245
Lovin' You 324,325
Lowe, Mundell 360,361
Lulu Belle and Scotty 31
Lusk, John 179,180
Lutcher, Nellie 207,208
Maceo, Big 138
Macero, Teo 335
Maddox, Rose 191,192
Maggie Campbell 282,283
MagnoliaWaltz 51

Mainer, J.E. 80
Mainer, Wade 79,80,95,96
Making Believe 339
Mama Knows What Papa Wants 136
Mama Let Me Lay it on You 89
Market Street Swamp 23,24
Martin, Carl 46
Matchbook Blues 34
Matthews, Roger 46,47
Matthews, Sister 202,203
Matzoh Balls 119,120
Maybelle, Big 195,196
Mayfield, Percy 279
Mayflower 59
Mays, Slim 70,71
McClennan, Tommy 140,141
McGee, Dennis 37
McGhe, Brownie 174
McGhee, Rev 165
McShann, Jay 144
McTell, Blind Willie 212
Me and the Devil 282,283
Mean Old World 152
Melrose, Frank 23
Memphis Blues 105,106,107
Memphis Minnie 209,210
Merrill, Helen 328,329
Merriweather, Major 138
Milburn, Amos 242,243
Milk 'em in the Morning Blues 203
Milk Cow Blues 77
Miller, Eddie 250
Miller, Emmett 60, 61
Milton Brown and his Brownies 50
Mingus, Charles 334
Minnie Wallace and her Night Hawks 38
Miss Handy Hanks 17,18
Miss Rhapsody 173
Missionary Sermon 163,164
Mississippi Jook Band 61
Mississippi Mud Mashers 63
Mitchell Blues 96
Molly Married a Traveling Man 96
Monk, Thelonious 146,147,326,327
Monkey Motion 275,276
Monroe Brothers 68
Monroe, Bill 68,69,122,123
Monroe, Charlie 68
Montana, Patsy 84
Montgomery, Little Brother 58,59
Montrell, Roy 353
Moon Country 41
Moondog 369
Moonglow 63
Moore, Gatemouth 187
Moore, Johnny 188

Morris Brown Quartet 117,118
Morris, Zeke 79
Morton, Jelly Roll 116,117
Moten Swing 144
Moten Swing 92
Muleskinner Blues 123
Murphy, Jimmy 257,258
Muskadine Blues 236
My Babe 349,350
My Baby Left Me 234
My Good Gal Has Thrown Me Down 34,35
My Soul is a Witness 33
Myers, Louie 353,354
Na Pua O Hawaii 21,22
Need a Hundred Dollars 349, 350
Nettles, Bill 196
New Jelly Roll Blues 83,84
New Mississippi River Blues 192,193
New River Train 68
Nice Work if You Can Get It 147
Nichols, Manny 200,201
Night Owls 105,106,107
Night Watchman Blues 209,210
Nighthawk, Robert 282
No More 362, 363
No Nights by Myself 325,326
Nobody in Mind 193,194
Nobody's Business 123,124
Norfolk Jazz Quartet 90
O'Day, Molly 226
Oh Lord, Don't 'low Me to Beat 'Em 90,91
Old Dad 72,73
Old Grey Goose 290
Old Ship of Zion 143
Old Time Blues 46
One More River 75
One String Sam 349, 350
Ooh-Wow 353
Orange Blossom Special 101,102,103
Orioles 202
Owens, Buck 337
Pack, Buster 289,290
Pan American Boogie 251
Paramount Juniors 143
Parker, Byron 103
Parker, Charlie 143,144,155,156
Parker, Junior 296,297,298
Partch, Harry 255
Patterson, Frank 128
Peetie Wheatstraw and His Blue Blowers 39,40
Perkins, Carl 313,314
Peters, Jimmy 33
Petway, Robert 133,134

Phillips, Esther 373
Piano Red 232,233
Pickett, Dan 232
Pierce, Jack 70,71
Pierce, Webb 249,250
Pigmeat Strut 186,187
Pine Ridge Boys 101
Placetas 195
Plantation Blues 103,104
Platt and Scruggs 227,228,229
Please Find My Baby 277
Po' Laz'us 47
Podunk Toddle 48,49
Poor Ellen Smith 226
Poor Pilgrim of Sorrow 387,388
Powell, Bud 220
Pozo, Chano 194,195
Pray for the Lights to Go Out 104
Prelude to a Kiss 329,330
Presley, Elvis 333,334
Price, Ray 367,368
Professor Longhair 215,216
Prophet Powers 245,246
Puckett, Riley 123,124
Railroad Bill 183
Raney, Wayne 221,222
Raybo, Fats 56,57
Reaching for the Moon 4,5
Rector, John 72,73
Red Belcher and the Kentucky Ridgerunners 290,291
Red, Speckled 112,113
Reed, Jimmy 342,343
Reed, Lulu 239,240
Reeling and a Rocking 278
Release Me 250
Remember Me 169,170
Renfro, Sister Jessie Mae 266,267
Respectable 377
Revard, Jimmy 52,53
Revard, Jimmy and his Oklahoma Playboys 52,53
Rhythm Wreckers' Never No Mo' Blues 81,82
Richard, Little 343,344
Ritter, Texas 184,185
River's Invitation 279
Roche, Betty 167,168
Rock and Roll Trio 340,341
Rock Me 294,295
Rockin' With Red 232,233
Rogers, Roy 97,98
Roll in My Sweet Baby's Arms 5,6
Rollin' and Tumblin' 237,238
Rollins, Sonny 381,382

Ronnie Knittel and the Holsten Valley Ramblers 264,265
Rose Maddox and her Brothers 191,192
Ruby Baby 354,355
Ruby, Texas 176
Rush, Otis 374,375
Sad and Disappointed 195,196
Sally Gooden 7
Sam, Maggie 375
Sapps, Booker T. 46,47
Satisfied 263
Sauceman Brothers 222
Saving My Love for You 305,306
Say it Isn't So 23,24
Scott, Little Jimmy 330,331
Sewing on the Mountain 97
Shaw 'Nuff 155,156
She's All Right 304,305
She's Done Moved 256
She's Fine She's Mine 351
She's Selling What She Used to Give Away 73,74
Shelton Brothers 45
Shepard, Jean 261
Shinault, Deacon Leroy 379,380
Shines, Johnny 235,236
Shoeshine Boy 65,66
Short, Bobby 345,346
Shout You Cats 5
Sinatra, Frank 189,190,191
Sitting on Top of the World 45
Six White Horses 122,123
Skoodle-Dum-Do and Sheffield 172
Slewfoot on the Levee 140
Slim, Guitar 302,303
Slow Down 341
Smeck, Roy 4,5
Smith, Arthur 49,50
Smith, Hobart 182,183
Smith, Utah 158,159
Smith, W.M. 7
Smith, Warren 366,367
Smith's Carolina Crackerjacks 99
Smitty, Blue 299,300
Smoke Gets in Your Eyes 327,328
Snow, Hank 312,313
Soap Box Blues 70,71
Social Call 359, 360
Somebody's Been Using That Thing 52
Son Simms 4 150,151
Sons of the Ozarks, 103,104
Sons of the Pioneers 98
Soon in the Morning 165
South Memphis Jug Band 22
Southern University Quartet 42
Speckled Red 357,358,359

Speer Family 318,319
St. Louis Blues 39
St. Louis Stomp 112,113
Stack-O-Lee Blues 40
Stand by Me 138,139
Stand by Me 202,203
Stanley Brothers 370,371
Staple Singers 357
Starr, Kay 178,179
Stay Out of the South 85
Steele, Pete 78,79
Stewart, Slim 161,162
Stormy Weather 167
Strange Things 272
Streamline Train Cripple 114,115
Stripling Brothers 59
Strong, Luther 71,72
Strothers, Jimmy 54
Sugar Babe 31
Sun Ra 382,383,384
Sun Ra and His Arkestra 382, 383,384
Sunset 37
Sunshine Alley 35,36
Suzie Q 339,340
Sweet Georgia Brown 220
Swing Low Sweet Chariot 24
Take a Little Walk with Me 273
Take a Look at that Baby 6
Take Out Some Time 238,239
Tall Skinny Poppa 175
Tampa Red 241
Tampa Strut 18,19
Tatum, Art 43,44
Taylor, Cecil 361,362
Ted's Stomp 28,29
Tempus Fugit 307
Tent Show Rag 174,175
Terrell, J.H. 163,164
Terrell, Sister Ola Mae 199,200
Terry, Sonny 174
Texas Melody Boys 284
Tharpe, Sister Rosetta 108,109,110,138,139,175
That's the Stuff 174
The Blue Sky Boys 94,95
The Gone Dead Train 8
The Letter 255
The Sons of the Pioneers 74,75
The Spirits of Rhythm 42, 43
The Story of My Life 303,304
The Tree of Life is Waiting for Me 245,246
There I've Said it Again 356,357
There is Only One 292,293
There's Another Mule in Your Stall 207,208

There's No Business Like Show Business 381,382
This is the End 378
Thomas, Bobo 301,302
Three Hours Past Midnight 355
Thrice Upon a Theme 335
Throw Me in the Alley 39,40
Tiger Rag 116,117
Tindley Quaker City Gospel Singers 11
Too Close to Heaven 320,321
Too Many Blues 196
Touchton, Peck 252,253
Travelin' Blues 251,252
Travis, Merle 186,187
Travis, Merle 224,225
Tristano, Lennie 159,160,161
Tristano, Lennie 307
Trixie, 213,214
Trouble in Mind 184,185
Trouble in Mind 252,253
Trouble Trouble 167,168
Try and Treat Her Right 8
Tu Peus Pas Me Fair Ca 111,112
Tubb, Ernest 156,157
Turner, Big Joe 193,194
Turner, Ike 376,377
Turner, Joe 246,247
Twice the Lovin' (In Half the Time) 261
Two Poor Boys 6
Tyler, T. Texas 169,170
Uncloudy Day 357
Under the Double Edge 385,386
Unloved and Unclaimed 198,199
Up Jumped the Devil 103
Vaughn, Sarah 157,158
Wait for Me 30,31
Walked all Night 273,274,275
Walker, Lawrence 56
Walker, T. Bone 152
Walking the Floor Over You 156,157
Wallace, Minnie 38
Waller, Fats 107,108
Walter, Little 189
Walton, Jay 323,324
Ward, Billy 283,284
Washboard Slim 309
Washington, Joe 33
Wasn't God Who Made Honky Tonk Angels 262
Waters, Ethel 165,166,167
Waters, Ethel 346,347
Waters, Muddy 131,150,151,237,238,304,305
Watson, Johnny Guitar 355
Watson, Leo 162,163
We Will Know 225,226

Weave Room Blues 81
Weaver, Curley 213,214
Weird Lullaby 197
Wells, Kitty 262
Wells, Kitty 337,338
Wells, Viola 173
West McKinney Street Blues 172
West, Speed 291
Western Cowboy 26
What Happened Last Night 360, 361
What is This Thing Called Love? 159,160,161
What You Gonna Do? 225
What's New 185,186
What's the Matter Now? 56
Wheatstraw, Peetie 39,40
When the Saints Go Marching In 332,333
When the Sun is Setting on the Prairie 97,98
When They Ring Those Golden Bells 351
When Your Lover Has Gone 210,211
White, Georgia 136
Why Don't You Do Right 148
Wilder, Alec 360,361
Williams, Big Joe 47,48,130
Williams, Hank 223,224
Williams, Sonny Boy 301,302
Williams, Willie 90,91
Williamson, Sonny Boy 325,326
Willis, Ralph 214,215
Wills, Bob 104
Wills, Bob 181,182
Wilson Rag 380, 381
Wilson Stavin' Chain Jones & Group 29
Wood, Smokey 75,76
Worried Life Blues, 138
Wray, Link 386,387
Wright, Billy 286,287
Yancey, Jimmy 131,132,133
Yancey's Bugle Call, 131, 132, 133
Yodel Your Blues Away 230
York Brothers 192,193
York, Albert 179,180
You Can Bet Your Life 373
You Can Fly High 352
You Go To My Head 270,271
You Gonna be My Baby 296
You Got to Go Down 62,63
You Got to Roll 141,142
You Got to Take Sick and Die Some of These Days 131
You Gotta Lay Down Mama 240,241
You Won't Let Me Go 188

You'd Be So Nice to Come Home To
361, 362
You're Fer Me 337
You've Got to Lose 376,377

Young, Faron 311,312
Young, Lester 64,65,66
Your Soul Never Dies 99
Zimmerman, Robert 388

## About the Author

Allen Lowe is a saxophonist and American music historian, who has recorded as a leader with Julius Hemphill, Don Byron, Marc Ribot, Lewis Porter, Roswell Rudd, Ken Peplowski, Nels Cline, Erin McKeown, Gary Bartz, David Murray, Kalaparusha, DJ Logic, Ursula Oppens, Doc Cheatham, Loren Schoenberg, JD Allen, Noah Preminger, Bob Neloms, and others. He has released over 20 compact discs under his own name; his last project, an 8 CD retrospective of his career, "Disconnected Works, 1980-2018," was released on ESP DISK in 2019.

Books he has written:

American Pop From Minstrel to Mojo: On Record:1893-1956
That Devilin' Tune: A Jazz History 1900-1950
The Lost Generation: Jazz of the 1950s
God Didn't Like It: Electric Hillbillies, Singing Preachers, and the Beginning of Rock and Roll, 1950-1970
Really The Blues ? A Horizontal Chronicle of the Vertical Blues, 1893-1959.

For information on how to acquire CDs of this music and these titles, as well as historical collections of related music,
        contact: allenlowe5@gmail.com
        or visit www.allenlowe.com

Allen Lowe lives in Hamden, Connecticut.